# The Transformation of Man

by  T J  Hegland

Spirituality, Reincarnation & the InterLife, Consciousness, The Matrix, Zero Point Energy, Dark Matter, DNA & Healing Energy, Timelines, Quantum Biocomputer, Greys & Hybrids, and Abduction & the Near Death Experience as Transformation.

**Copyright** © 2014 by T. J.H. v.**22**

**Categories: Metatags**: Anunnaki, ET, UFO, Mankind, origins, Genetic engineering, Greys, abductions, hybrids, DNA, Epigenetics, Archeology, ET influences, soulless, sociopaths, auras, OPs, NPCs, creation, evolution, reptile, Catholic Church, religion, Bible, Bishop John Shelby Spong, Control System, Virtual Reality, Simulation, holograms, Holodeck, Angels, Beings of Light, shapeshifting, souls, brain, heart, Scripts, karma, reincarnation, recycling, Déjà vu, InterLife, soulmates, chi, Bionet, torsion waves, consciousness, Matrix, ZPE, Dark Energy, EFT, Reimprinting, Quantum Biocomputer, Earth Graduate.

**Cover design**:
www.bing.com/images/search?q=spiritual+transformation
index = 427: (585f2b30ab5dcedd7cc7eb0d6a4be399.jpg)

**Images in Book:**
Also see https://images.search.yahoo.com/search/images
Also see: http://www.bing.com/images/searchword

Book text in Garamond 12 font.

**Author may be reached at TJ_cspub14@yahoo.com**

**ISBN – 13: 978-1499130607**

*Other Books by the Author:*

| | | |
|---|---|---|
| Virtual Earth Graduate | (Book 1) | VEG |
| The Earth Warrior | (Book 3) | TEW |
| Quantum Earth Simulation | (Book 4) | QES |
| The Science in Metaphysics | (Book 5) | TSiM |

# Table of Contents

Transformation of Man

# Introduction

This book is a very necessary follow-on to Book 1(VEG) – so-called as a shorthand way to refer to **Virtual Earth Graduate**, also herein called the First Book. There were some issues that needed clarifying and Book 1 was already too big to add them, so it is necessary to write a shorter Book 2 – to clarify, reassess and extend the first one. Begging the reader's pardon, that is also the reason for the heavy references to Book 1 (VEG) – they were one book in the beginning.

## Restated Purpose

This book continues in the same purpose as the First Book – **to show people why they need to get out of here.** Of course it was stated that Earth is not our home and we are not alone, but it is more than that.

Man is going through a Transformation, a process that is changing him week by week, and this is due to the vibrations of the HVR Earth Sphere increasing (largely due to the influx of higher-energy and higher-consciousness beings into the Earth realm – to stabilize the Light, and counteract the PTB's hijacking of this timeline – see Chapter 2). In addition, the Greys are largely responsible for a genetic upgrade in Man that results in a transformational aspect of our world, our society, and amounts to "assisted evolution."

The following chapters are all sharing some aspect of **Transformation**:

> Chapter 1 – offers a reassessment of Book 1's major points, for the benefit of those who didn't read it – Knowledge of what is so is a key aspect of Transformation;
>
> Chapter 2 – relates how **Timelines** either support or hinder Man's growth, and how Man can synch up with a better timeline, and why Man is about to be replaced on the planet;
>
> Chapter 3 – relates how a spiritual walk is better than a religious walk and how some teachings support transformation and others hinder it;
>
> Chapter 4 – examines how **Nutrition** and environmental issues impact Man's ability to metamorphose;
>
> Chapters 5 & 6 – deal with understanding our Path, Karma, Scripts and what significance a soulmate has on one's soul growth and Reincarnation;
>
> Chapter 7 – shows what the LifeScript Process is all about and how we choose Scripts via the **Quantum Computer** to support our transformation from caterpillar to butterfly;

## Anunnaki Recap

Because Man is where he is and the way he is today, thanks to the Anunnaki, a brief review of their influence is in order.

Consider that there was an advanced space-faring race from Nibiru (in Orion) who discovered Earth thousands of years ago and used it as a base and appropriated some of its resources for their use. Man wasn't here then so who was to stop them? As their stay progressed, they decided to **genetically create slave workers** to build their buildings, dig in their mines, and cultivate their food in the field. So they reworked a local hominid (Homo *erectus* would do nicely) and made him just intelligent enough to understand what they wanted, but dumb enough to not consider rebelling.

Time goes on and the space-farers consider Earth their planet. And the slaves have begun worshipping them, and with a few threats here and there, and a few demonstrations of their power, they as Lords keep the slaves in line. As time goes on the slave population grows and the Lords, who aren't always around to control the slaves, decide to upgrade the best of the slaves genetically to a more intelligent model who will operate under the "Divine Right to Rule" dictum, and this starts a separate bloodline going on the Earth.

All of that to say that the new bloodline is smart enough to rule over the sheeple, the slaves, and they become known as the PTB (**Powers That Be**). They like ruling, and assume they are smarter and not only have the right to rule (given them by the gods), but they are becoming the richest people on the planet as well.

To keep the people in line, they institute strict Religion – "Behave or go to Hell where you will burn in eternity!" That was reinforced by the **Inquisition** – "Believe what we tell you, or we'll kill you!" They later initiate Serfdom with Lords and Serfs in Western Europe, and the vicious caste system in India. Earth became an "Us versus Them" world real fast, but that is about to change…

The main party of Lords left Earth in 650-600 BC, and a Remnant of the Lords stayed behind (due to Galactic Law) while Man largely tended to occupy the planet; the Remnant Dissidents and the human 3D PTB run the planet to this day. OK that was Book 1.

Now it needs to be very clear that forms of **racial superiority** still exist on Earth, where the Hybrids and Elite are superior to the PTB who think they are superior to Man in general. Despite 'enlightened' claims to the contrary, we are not all alike with the same potential. And much of mankind is still oppressed, kept in ignorance, and about to be locked down, if the PTB get their way. Great, dumbed down and locked down… is that the future you want to experience? And yet, if you don't know that you have been lied to, or dumbed down (by a controlled Media)…

> The best slave is the one who can say, "I'm no slave, I'm free!"

After World War II and the atomic bombs that were used, and then all the atomic testing in the 50's – we attracted the attention of the "Good Guys" out there. And we got the attention of the **Solar Council** which decreed that the space-faring Lords (Orion Group aka Anunnaki) were not going to subjugate Earth and this solar system as they had done to others. The Council made an agreement with the Good Guys on behalf of the beleaguered earthlings.

## Current-day Situation

The Good Guys stand ready IF ASKED to remove the Bad Guys. They have already put the planet in a **Quarantine** to block further external harassment and interference (Book 1). The space-faring Lords also were blown out of the water, literally, when their marauding **battlestar "planet" Nibiru** came cruising back into the solar system, Spring 2003. (Yes, George Lucas was on to something with his portrayal in *Star Wars* of a huge cruising Death Star. Such <u>was</u> real.) This time the Good Guys were there to meet them. Nibiru is not coming back.

Realizing there would be no reinforcements to simulate an "alien invasion" and assist in locking Earth down, the PTB began to panic and look for more ways to subtly oppress and manipulate mankind. They were met by the Good Guys and asked to stop and leave, but the Bad Guys mounted a valid argument: "We have been here for eons, it is our planet, and we can do what we want. This is a freewill universe, freewill planet, and as their creator, the humans still need us. They are our responsibility and we have to control them or human society will fall apart, and chaos will rule."

The PTB will have to stop and the Remnant can leave (they'd like that) if enough humans stand up, expose and challenge the PTB's manipulations, lies, and abuse. But the PTB argue that "… humans are still slaves, after thousands of years … because they are so pathetically dumb they have bought into our primitive 'entertainment' – sex, violence, drugs, drinking, etc. – we can **entrain** them because they are primitive –They don't have any sense, intuition or discernment that they are being used. They have always been our slaves (because we designed it that way)."

Another brickwall. **Lords who love to rule need slaves to rule** – even if they have to deceive the slaves to get them to agree to that rule. A slave who goes along with a deception is not having his freewill violated… he is so ignorant he is agreeing to what the manipulator wants!

And if you tell people the truth, they just laugh – Humans should ASK for help in removing the Lords… but how to get to that? Humans have been **conditioned to laugh** at things that smack of Sci-Fi: Mermaids, Bigfoot, Nessie, Megalodon, and lately UFOs… the Lords have seen to that – the humans subjugate and oppress themselves with a refusal to seriously check out anything that is not Mom, apple pie and baseball. **Humans have been trained to keep themselves imprisoned** by denial of anything that might liberate them... that was fiendishly clever. Get prisoners to keep themselves in jail.   (also qv: 'Stockholm Syndrome'.)

So here's the bottom line:

The Good Guys decided to contact several humans who could get the story out, be strong enough to withstand ridicule, and begin to chip away at the Fortress of Denial and Ignorance created for Man. That began with Giodano Bruno and Galileo, and lately David Icke, Jim Marrs, Dolores Cannon, and Michael Tellinger, and now

TJ Hegland's two books (VEG & TOM) join a growing circle of truth-tellers out there... Why?

> **When enough people wake up and begin to want to take the planet back and begin to pray and ASK that the Lords, PTB, Remnant, *et al* leave... when that *meme* reaches the "100th Monkey" level and registers as a strong enough coherent energetic vector within the Earth timeline (as explained in Chapter 2), the Good Guys will find the 'demand' quotient is empowered to effect the removal of the Bad Guys and has sufficient voice behind it to justify their action to the Council.**

Failing to sustain a coherent energy to force removal of the Bad Guys, you will want to know how to get out of here... as an Earth Graduate, or how to join the Ascension to 5D. To that end, this book and Book 1 were written.

But it is more than that.

Man cannot take the Earth back, <u>because it was never his</u> (i.e., he was never in control) ... but he can stand up and work with benevolent ETs who are working to set him free, and for the first time in history, kick butt and take the planet over – responsibly. Man's society is being **transformed** by the insertion of hybrids (the next version of Man) which is the focus of Chapters 8 and 9. It is an on-going process that most people are not aware of – Man does not know enough to ASK for ET help, so it is being done for him since the Council has decreed that Earth will not become part of the oppressive Orion Empire.

**History Repeats**

The integration of Hybrids in society replacing current-day humans is actually a repeat of the way Neanderthal was replaced with Cro-Magnon. That creates a **5th Column approach** that uses the same tactics as the PTB and Dissident have used: infiltrate and obstruct – except that the Good Guys are causing so much frustration for the PTB that it is hoped the latter will quit and leave. If not, a Plan B will be brought to bear.

In any event, with the infusion of a **more discerning hybrid form of Man** (including Indigos), the PTB and Dissidents know they cannot manipulate, lie and cheat them... so it is just a matter of time – unless the PTB decide to destroy everything so that no one gets the planet – and that is being carefully watched. It has been already reported that nuclear missile silos have been put offline and nuclear missiles when launched have been interfered with – so it is doubtful that the PTB can start something nuclear and get away with it. Nuclear war on Earth would seriously disrupt the energetics of the solar system and the Galaxy because Man doesn't know yet how all is inter-related through what is called Dark Energy (or Æther) throughout the universe.

The next few years may be tough, but there is Light at the end of the tunnel, and Man is important enough that he will **transform and survive**. This book seeks to encourage people in being aware of what is going on and what they can do to be ready for the Change (discussed in Chapter 8).

## The Problem with Man

As Man grows technologically, he is losing sight of who he is, what he is, and where he is – he is focusing on traditional religion, pursuing material things, believing that Science will solve all his issues, pharmaceuticals are the cure for everything, and he is obsessed with electronic toys. You may ask what the problem is with that…

Simply that Man as a soul is not seeking to be all he can be, researching new ideas and gaining true Knowledge. He doesn't know he is not alone and there is no way he can meet, greet and communicate with **benevolent beings from other worlds who are already here** – until he grows up and loses his Victorian view of the world. It was worse 500 years ago when Man just knew that the Earth was flat and the center of the universe… How could ETs communicate the truth without destroying our civilization – and invalidating the Church which promoted those false ideas? Man has built his world on a concept of God, the origin of the universe, Man's creation by The God, and a belief that we are all the same and everyone has the same potential – and none of that is true…. We are living in the PTB's contrived

## Prophylactic Fantasy

that must collapse if we ever meet ETs who <u>will</u> tell us the truth – otherwise Man will have a collective nervous breakdown, as the Brookings Institute (Chapter 3) said in the 60's! Man is stubborn, yet fragile, and most cannot easily bend with new ideas, and so the deception and ET non-disclosure continue… and Man continues buying into his entrapment, preferring to live in the box that was created for him.

Rocks are hard and water's wet. We need to accept that and stop trying to make Earth out to be something that it isn't. Book 1 accurately described Earth as a School and that was a starting point. It is easier to ride the horse in the direction he's going and it is herein suggested that we stop facing backwards, drinking a Coke, smoking a Marlboro, and trying to get laid all at the same time! When riding a horse, ride the horse… but first you gotta realize there **is** a horse and it's moving…

The Lame Stream Media no longer reports what is really going on in national and international news – everything has a 'spin' nowadays to get the public aligned with what the PTB want the public to think – when they're not sitting on the couch, eating a burrito and watching a zombie thriller. And yet the positive side to that is that full disclosure probably would cause panic and chaos, so keeping the sheeple happy and ignorant <u>for the time being</u> is a proactive thing to do... On the other hand, this book and Book 1 were written <u>for those who want to know</u> where we are, what we are, what's going on, and what can be done about it.

If you knew you were being watched, would you behave differently?
If you respected yourself, would the ETs not see that?
If you knew that the missing children who disappear every year will never be seen again, would you not begin to **respect** other people and animals and stop abusing them, even stop eating them... would the abductions and missing children stop? (The fact that you don't see the connection is why it continues.)

**Alternate Off-Ramp**

If leaving the Earth realm with sufficient Light is not to your liking, as Book 1 suggested, or perhaps some readers find it unworkable, this book offers an alternate way out of here – synching up energetically with a better timeline via intention, focus and visualization. Ascension. That is examined in Chapter 2.

Both books offer much **catalyst** for thought. As Stuart Wilde used to say, "Wakey, wakey!" And, if the books are to do any good, they must confront almost everything you believe... And that is a big reason that Book 1 and this book were written.

At the very least, read them as **"brain candy"** – take a chance that some of it is true for you... It is all **catalyst,** anyway.

You have a choice....

> **Wait** until the Lords win and lock everything down... or
> **Gain** as much Knowledge (Light) as possible to exit Earth when you die... or
> **Synch up** with the timeline of your choice while you're still alive...

and

> **Wake up**, and ASK that the Good Guys are empowered to remove
> the Bad Guys (in our lifetime!)

or

> **Do nothing** and continue to live in mediocrity and fear the unknown.

What will Man choose...?

*       *       *

# Who Voted Me the Messenger?

The wise will question everything they see/hear that is new.

Do not blindly jump to believe new things… it may be disinformation. This author has studied everything presented in this book since 1958 and still does not consider himself an expert, nor has he learned everything – but there are ideas and facts that have withstood the decades of research, contemplation, arguing with others, and passed "inspection" over time **AND are important enough to be shared with others** – hence two books. The reader is free to make his or her own determination of this information.

If one is going to write a book to enlighten others, it should be proactive and contain as much Light as possible. It is a heavy responsibility to present new information designed to benefit the reader – there are penalties in the InterLife for misleading other souls. And I used to lose sleep in the last 5 years worrying about that. Yet, those who are already on a spiritual path should have more discernment than beginners and thus Book 1 and this book should find more acceptance among readers who are already reading, researching and evaluating esoteric information.

After 5 years of careful editing I became comfortable with the contents of Book 1– **because it connected all the dots** – and I put it up on Amazon. I also have confidence in <u>this book which extends Book 1 (VEG)</u>.

Both books are **catalyst** : read and think.

**Genesis of the Books**

This author was visited in 1998 and asked to write a book to help wake Man up. It turned out that I had an agreement to serve made with the Masters during the InterLife (Chapters 5 - 7) prior to incarnating this time. They were waiting for me to either remember my part or ask to do something. I was not told about doing a book during the 1991 Hypnotic Regression and I did nothing for the next 7 years, except continue to question the accumulated years of major data I had found up to 1998. Through it all, I had one **ethical concern** (repeated below from Book 1).

They indirectly got my attention when my doctor announced in December 1997 that I had **a terminal illness with 3 years left to live.** A fervent prayer to serve, asking to do something proactive for mankind before dying was all They needed. (This is a freewill planet and one must ASK – it is part of our training.)

**Interlife Help**

True to Their word, the Masters with whom I had counseled between the last lifetime and this one (in the InterLife), had agreed to help me – as I saw in my 1991 Regression. They showed up in October 1998, following my fervent prayer, to effect some Change in me. I called it **"rewiring"** so I could 'hear' Them and receive Their input. They said They would be there to guide me with **insights** in what They knew I would be doing (writing a book) but <u>the specifics were kept from me until 2008</u>.

Obviously, They weren't in a hurry. But in July 2001 I coincidentally met a healer who actually did heal me (doctor verified it) and I moved forward.

Next, at 3am one morning in January 2008 (when the book was started) I was awakened with the Table of Contents for 15 chapters clearly in mind and I went to the PC and entered it – it is the same one used today in Book 1. During the typing of the book, I'd get stuck and wonder how some of the 50+ years of information I had recorded could be connected, or did it connect? And in **only 7 instances,** did They do a **1-second drop** (see Glossary) – the information comes up from within – as if I had always known it, and it sometimes takes 10-15 minutes to review it all… They are the source of those Insights. They connected the dots for me and with a few new Insights, I transcribed my 50+ years' notes into Book 1.

> *The original book was 868 pages long, and so I broke it into VEG and this book. I made Book 1 as complete as possible in case I would not live to do Book 2. I had a 12-year illness reprieve but now (2014) the illness of 1997 is back.*

Oh, yes, the doctor was right… and They healed me so I could get Book 1 done. Doc reran the tests in 2001-2003, saw the illness was gone, but he kept mumbling 'remission'…. He could not say 'miracle.' Tests in 2014 say it is back.

### Reservations

**Lastly, I had reservations about the finished Book 1** being too confrontational and causing massive **cognitive dissonance and rejection** among the readers… and I didn't want to even appear to be trying to destroy others' faith in Science, Religion or History. So I checked out everything I was given<u>, trying to prove it wrong</u>, thinking that it might still be an interesting book, but **I succeeded in proving Them right**. My 5-year research in 2008-13 produced the footnotes for others to check things out. So I finally capitulated, and then added the Genesis section to the beginning of Book 1 in case people wondered how the book came to be.

### Ethical Concern

My primary concern was to be **not guilty of disseminating disinformation** via the book as that would count against me again in the InterLife. I already had enough to answer for from the previous lifetime (Chapters 5 and 6 this book), which cost me a **karmic payback** in the first 54 years of my life this time (until 1998), and I wanted to do something proactive for mankind before I died. Obviously I needed Their support to put Book 1 together. I remembered after their October 1998 Visit that I had agreed to do a book, but had no idea what it would be about, and so I forgot about it until They reminded me again in 2008… after I had been healed and experienced a few things They orchestrated (events covered in Chapter 5 of Book 1). Book 1 was written in 7 months and it was so complicated that I could not have done that without Their help.

The focus of Book 1 was no longer to expose errors and make people wrong, but to show where we have come from, where we are in Truth, and where we souls must go – back to the 4D Realm where we really belong as **Earth Graduates**. Thus I felt urged to release a more spiritual book with my input in Chapter 15, and the addition of Chapter 16 (that was the only extra thing They let me add to the book). I wanted people to be able to assimilate and opt into a choice of where they go when they die. And because some want to leave Earth while living, that is how and why this book goes into some detail in Chapter 2 and Appendix D.

This book contains a lot of Light and I hope it will be a blessing to those that read it.

# Chapter 1:  Reassessment of *Virtual Earth Graduate*

There are **five major eye-openers in** *Virtual Earth Graduate* (VEG) , that may have been a shock to some people. It was bad enough that several things we all thought were true in Science, History and Religion turned out to be false... but the real issue the book was making was that a lot of what we assume to be our nice, neat world with everything just as we want it to be, wasn't so.

> This is not our planet and we're not here alone.
> Not even the Moon is ours, but that's another story...

Naturally, the above information can cause a lot of **cognitive dissonance** (see Glossary). And people will automatically discount the new information, and ignore it... which is why souls have become trapped on Earth and are forced to recycle or reincarnate – rarely getting out of here because they don't have enough (51%) Light to reach "escape velocity," figuratively speaking.

**Knowledge protects**
**Ignorance enslaves**

Why tell people what Earth really is and what Man is really.... ? Because, and this is the key to the last chapter: if you seek **Transformation**, also called **higher consciousness**, and you are full of disinformation, lies, half-truths, false beliefs... you will <u>not</u> be able to attain enlightenment – and if you die that way, in addition to not knowing what can occur right after dying, you can make the wrong choices and either (1) become a Discarnate, or (2) the gods will send you back (i.e., recycle you). No kidding. That is why I was asked to write the two books. And that is why this book's Chapters 2 and 13 have to share some unpleasant issues.

So five key areas of the Earth paradigm were explored in the first book and yet there may still remain some confusion with them. This chapter will **reassess those major points**, drawing a coherent summary picture, before moving on into Chapter 2 where an alternative way for exiting Earth is given.

## Five Key Points of VEG

**I. Sitchin and the Anunnaki** : my research showed that there were hundreds of thousands of clay tablets, cylinders and stones that related the story of the Sumerians and the Anunnaki – their gods.  Not only were the tablets hidden and discovered by accident when a new highway was being excavated in Iraq, meaning they were not meant to be found, but their very large number meant that the subject matter was very important to the Sumerians. Even Professor Kramer acknowledges their existence but claims it is all a myth – one that the Sumerians recorded in great detail showing their gods to be very mortal and petulant, violent, lying and yet the source of Sumerian civilization. Is this the way one records a myth that does <u>not</u> beatify the gods – but records their ugly appearance, their pettiness, and mortality? I could not prove Sitchin wrong, and so now suggest he was basically correct and the Anunnaki were real visitors who jump-started Man's civilization.

Specifically, the Anunnaki (real name: Draconians from the Orion Group) were on Earth to mine resources. Growing tired of the work, or more likely bored because physical labor is nothing to them, they took an upright hominid and mixed their DNA with it – just enough to make it intelligent enough to understand and follow commands, and they taught these early slave workers how to dig in the mines, cultivate crops in the fields, and how to build their buildings (including pyramids and ziggurats). When it was expedient, they gave the humans weapons and had them fight some of the Anunnaki battles for them, thus teaching Man warfare.

The reason this is plausible is that Man on Earth today is to the point of doing genetic manipulation of species and the only thing stopping Man from doing what the Anunnaki did, is we need the technology to leave Earth and go to another planet where we, too, can design slave workers from the local populace. While *panspermia* is certainly true and a viable means of getting rudimentary lifeforms to Earth, it does not account for the larger lifeforms – largely because whatever the putative evolutionary path was for the bacteria from a comet, it is not still happening, and apes are no longer morphing into humans. Evolution was therefore <u>assisted</u>.

**Clarity #1:** The God of the Universe, the Father of Light, The One created **souls** and the Anunnaki created the **bodies** (or 'containers') into which souls entered for new experiences. Many humanoids played the "Let's create Man" game, by the way, and that is part of the reason for the 5 major races on Earth.

**Clarity #2:** The "Anunnaki" were so-called by the Sumerians and we were never told the visitors' real names or identity. And the Draconians (being the only reptiles in this part of the Galaxy which identifies them as such) were not the only visitors to Earth – the Chinese race was allegedly seeded by visitors from Deneb, and the Aldebarans were the progenitors of the Aryan race... thus the Earth was often called **The Great Experiment**. And by the way, no other planet in our Galaxy has the incredible variety of human forms that Earth does – in all likelihood for the reason we already see: it doesn't work on a planet with young (immature) souls.

**II. Soulless Humans (OPs) on Earth:** This is another controversial issue among moderns – although, as was recorded, the ancients knew all about them: the Greeks would not let them teach their young, nor hold public office, the Mayans called them "figures of wood" in their *Popul Vuh*, and even Valentinism and other Gnostics knew about them... A modern-day researcher, Dr. Mouravieff, wrote several books about them, and I still had trouble accepting it – haven't we all been told that we are all alike? The gods who agreed to help me (InterLife episode during my '91 Regression) helped me out: the *coup de grace* to convince me, was to **let me see auras** for about 3 years. About 60% of the people on any day, wherever I was, did not have auras…

**No aura = no soul = no conscience = potential sociopath**

Whatever the gods did was causing me **eye problems** and I made several trips to the eye doctor who found nothing wrong, but after I had seen enough and made studies – counts and recorded characteristics of those I saw – They eventually removed the ability and my eyes pretty much went back to normal. They had convinced me, and I learned that the soulless (OPs) do exist and have a purpose. But it pays to know about them.

> **The reason for exposing the OPs is that they are a large part of our problems on Earth (in church, business, government and science – they are the agnostics and atheists who promote agendas that lack elements of the soul [which they do not possess]: Love and Light, fair play, Truth, caring about others, and the concept of Creation.)**

Yet, the OPs are a necessary element of the Earth Drama – much as Non-Playable Characters (NPCs) are in a VR Game… you can't control them, but they are there, driving the video script, providing action, challenges, and NPCs are often something to shoot at. In our world, they provide the karmic 'payback' or negative lessons that another ensouled human cannot do for/to you without earning negative Karma themselves. The OP does not have a soul that moves on, so they can do atrocities (if the Greater Script requires it) and when they die, it is dust to dust – they don't pay for anything. **Appendix D** clarifies this.

**Clarity #3**: It will be seen in Chapter 2 that they also serve another purpose, and a significant one. It will also become very clear why there are so many of them. And Chapter 11 and **Appendix D** will clarify some recent exceptions to the 'No Aura' paradigm.

**III. Quantum Physics and Earth Simulation**: This is perhaps the hardest revelation to accept, yet my studies into holograms, vision, quantum mechanics, and simulation/virtual reality were borne out by three things: **(1)** a place where I have lived for 20+ years all of a sudden was lacking trees and buildings that I had always seen whenever I drove down those streets. Suspecting urban renewal at work, I got out of the truck and closely examined the ground where a large building had stood… and a man came over and asked me what I was doing on his property. I asked what happened to the building that was there. He thought I was nuts – he said that was his property and there had never been a building there. Yes, there was! And now there was no trace of it. Nothing.

**(2)** Even the physicists are questioning our reality and saying that we most likely are in a Simulation because the "physical constants" are changing, ***anomalons*** show up when you expect them to, and aspects of subatomic reality border on the holographic – see Chapters 9, 12, and 13 in VEG. There were so many physicists speaking <u>for</u> the subject I had to add a chapter to the first book, and document them in Chapter 13. They are also examined in TSiM.

**(3)** A third insight I got was late in coming to me because I don't play video games. There are players in a video game that we don't control but are part of the game's Drama – they are called **NPC's** (Non Playable Characters). It was a **1-second drop** that showed me that the NPCs in the Earth Drama are the OPs in our world, again confirming that this is probably a very sophisticated Simulation, and the OPs help drive the Earth Drama. (See *Quantum Earth Simulation*, aka Book 4.)

So, Ok, you say "If Knowledge, Truth and Light are so important, why didn't Jesus, Buddha or Krishna tell us about the Simulation and soulless OPs – Didn't they want us to get the Light so we could get out of here?"

Excellent question.

**Answer:** This Earth either was not a Simulation (if true) until AD 800-900 (somewhere in that timeframe), or Avatars did not want to alarm people. There was no great amount of OPs either – we have been through at least 2 timeline splits (increasing the number of Placeholders [OPs]) since AD 900, and so when the Masters walked the Earth, it was a 3D physical planet and not in quarantine. The Higher Beings have protected Man today with a **Quarantine** and an HVR Sphere to facilitate his soul growth, manipulate Earth vibrations, prevent external Orion interference, and hopefully increase the harvest of souls ready to 'graduate.'

**Clarity #4:** It doesn't really matter if Earth is a Simulation or not – we have our lessons and issues to attend to and still need to do the best we can to handle whatever comes our way. Yet, it is intriguing that Someone cared enough about Man to see to his protection (we <u>are</u> in **Quarantine**), and provide a way to drive the Greater Script to deliver our preplanned experiences (the Control System), and overall establish an automatic feedback system to cycle Man through his lessons (Karma and Reincarnation). See Chapter 7.

**IV. Jesus and Apollonius:** while this is a touchy area for some, it was a revelation that there <u>was</u> a man living about the same time as the one-and-only (but historically undocumented) Jesus, and it looked like the exploits of Jesus in the Bible had been copied by the Church from the similar real, documented life of **Apollonius of Týana**. This was in no way meant to denigrate anybody's faith. All masters do, say and teach the same thing – Truth and Love.

For years I had been a Christian and it always bothered me that every time I searched for <u>historical proof</u> of a real man, Jesus, there wasn't any. It bothered me that contemporaries of Jesus known as Philo, Suetonius, Pliny the Younger, Plutarch, and Cornelius Tacitus said nothing about him – if he had been such an important man of renown <u>in their era</u>… thus I suspected He was a myth. I already knew from **serious Christian Bible scholars** that Josephus' entry in his *Antiquities of the Jews* had been modified to say more than what Josephus had originally said `(which could have been describing any local rebel) – pointed out in VEG (Chapter 11) in detail.

True to their word, to help me finish the first book, my Source gave me another **1-second drop on Jesus**. I was stunned, to put it mildly. Not only did Jesus exist, and there <u>was</u> a virgin birth (think: artificial insemination), He did those things that were said of Him. (His birth and death dates however may be in question, as was discussed in Appendix D of VEG … due to the Scaliger rewrite, in V below.)

They said that Jesus did not do a 3-year ministry but barely got in 6 months before He was crucified. And that is one reason why not much was publicly written about Him; the other main reason being that the Pharisees and Romans agreed that nothing should be written about Him (so that He would not be a martyr for the Jewish cause/revolt) and gave orders to NOT write about Jesus (Yeshuah) – and when a Roman overlord and Sanhedrin decree something, people listen… under threat of death.

And then I discovered **Apollonius** who did wonderful missionary journeys <u>identical</u> to those of Paul the Apostle. Apollonius taught the same basic things Jesus and Paul taught, walked on water, fed the 5000, and healed the sick and raised the dead. Even more freaky was that Apollonius, having travelled <u>to the same cities as Paul at the same time no less</u>, had an interesting nickname: "Pol." It didn't take me but 2 seconds to get the picture. Apparently the Church used the exploits of Apollonius as those of Paul… or maybe they were in fact the same historical person?

**Clarity #5:** So be clear that Jesus existed, He was all He was said to be, He still watches over Earth and Man, and is dedicated to answering prayers and healing people, guiding those who ask and who seek Him. And as is said later in Chapter 7 there is power in His name. (And as was also said in Book 1, Chapter 6, even the Greys respect His name.)

**V. Alteration of Western Chronology**:   much as this is a shock to hear that Man has been on the planet <u>this time</u> for only 1200 years (since AD 800-900) – that applies only to this Era. Mankind has been around for a lot longer than 1200 years – witness the Sumerians interacting with the star visitors (Anunnaki) 6000 years ago. What has not been clear in the history of Man is that there are various Eras that start and stop – the **Aztec and Maya** said that we are in the 4th World, the **Hopi and**

**Chinese** have said similar things. And interestingly, as VEG pointed out, there is a history gap around AD 800-900 that the Chinese, Vikings and Maya all experienced (VEG, Ch 10, 'AD 900 Limit')… what appears to be an end of a prior Era and the start of our current Era.

**Dr. Anatoly Fomenko** discovered this chronology anomaly when he began statistically analyzing major Western historical events, cultures, peoples and their timelines and he found too many historical events separated by hundreds of years which had <u>exactly the same events</u>, same duration of events, same people, and while the kings' names changed, the incredible similarities in their personalities and reigns intrigued him, so he did further research. What he found was that nothing for sure could be known about any Western Civilization history **backwards of AD 900** due to this problem – it was as if someone had taken a template and moved events that actually happened in the AD 1000-1200 time period back 500 – 1000 years, copied the events and 'faked' the history – copying events, reigns and battles but using different names of what we now think are famous personages. His research over years showed that this reworking of Western Chronology **actually happened**, and as others studied his results to disprove them, they corroborated his findings. Aghast, he wrote Volume 1 of his 7-part series laying it all out in great detail so that any layman can follow WHAT he found and WHAT it means… and he submits proof using corresponding anomalies in art and literature. He found **the anomalies stopped with the invention of the printing press**… writings and history could no longer be altered. (This is examined in some detail in Appendix D, in VEG.)

So why would that happen? That is <u>the</u> question. And it suggests that someone in authority knew that Man had been restarted in a new Era and had no recent history immediately backwards of AD 900 – and so one had to be created. Not to deceive Man but to avoid the obvious problem of Man now being on Earth, AD 900, with no previous recently-recorded history – a 100+ year gap would have been a dead giveaway that something was wrong – and it would have so distracted Man that he would not have moved forward and lived whatever life he had – without, what Gene Roddenberry called, the **Non-Interference Doctrine**. If Man is distracted for whatever reason, he does not behave normally nor move about his business as if nothing is amiss… so how could his actual behavior be evaluated?

**Clarity #6:** In fact, something <u>had</u> happened to "interfere" with Man and it has happened many times before – when the Earth Drama has to be stopped and reset… If "…all the Earth is a stage…", then aren't there different scenes and storylines from scene to scene, and "…a man in his lifetime plays different parts…" and what if The One wants to put Man through certain lessons, and we pretty much complete them, then why not stop the Drama (suspend things, terraform the planet) and restart a <u>new</u> drama or scene? Could a God do that? Is this the secret behind **Eras**? That has been called a **Wipe and Reboot**.

**Clarity #7:** It would have been easy for the Anunnaki Remnant who are here with Man to note what had happened (they are underground so it doesn't affect them directly, i.e., they don't experience Eras) and then they (pretend to be human and) advise the hierarchy in the Church to make some adjustments to History so that Man can continue as if nothing happened. Not a bad idea.

Such is further argument for **Earth being a Simulation** such that The One can manipulate scenes and storylines via Eras – all for the experiential growth of His souls. Nothing to get hung up about – Can we roll with it?

> **Rewind: Ultimately it doesn't matter if we are in a Simulation or not, and it doesn't matter if ancient history is fabricated backwards of AD 900 – we still have our Scripts and lessons to learn. But it is interesting that Someone cared enough about Man's development that They might go to the trouble of a special Simulation with a manipulated history... and the evidence is overwhelming in Books 1 and 4 that that happened. Just something to consider...**
>
> It also had to be done if the Orion Group would not stop interfering and harassing Man while in 3D. A Simulation and/or a quarantine would work nicely. (RA said this <u>was</u> done, see Chapter 12, VEG. )

**Clarity #8**: By the way, before discounting that we are in a Simulated Drama with some set (preplanned) events, ask yourself if this doesn't explain how those prophets who were accurate knew what was about to happen? They were told, or shown, the Greater Script for this or that Era and *voila!* they were correct. That is not Fate because we are in a Freewill Universe, just that we are destined to experience certain things in the larger Father's Script, yet have freewill about how we respond.

**Clarity #9**: The point to all of the above is that unless we know WHERE we are, we won't see the point to getting out – 'graduating' – and we don't belong here any more than we can live forever in 3rd Grade in Snortface Elementary School. The 3rd Grade has preplanned lessons (destiny) we are to learn, and how we handle them (Freewill) determines whether we pass or fail. Fail and you repeat 3rd Grade – and you may experience **Déjà vu** as you go thru it again!

The Chinese sages say that all is illusion, and it is just a Game that we souls go <u>through</u>... we handle it, we don't stop on it and get heavy...

The Chinese sages also say that once we have attained enlightenment, the only thing left is to **have a good laugh**. The things we thought were so important, aren't. Both the Near Death Experiencers and the Abductees have come to this greater realization as a result of their experiences (which took them out of this world), and that is examined in Chapters 8 and 9. All parts of Transformation.

The way we thought things were, they often aren't. And <u>all</u> is contained in the Father of Light's Greater Script – and since **nothing is out of control**, we can relax.

## Evaluation of <u>Virtual Earth Graduate</u>

In addition to the above five points, there was a reason for the *Virtual Earth Graduate* being as encyclopedic as it was, presented the way it was, and even as in-your-face as it was/is. This is a key point and is not to be skipped … if you want to understand the VEG better, and your place in the **Spiritual Growth Scale**.

> Note that another book by the author, *The Science in Metaphysics* (aka TSiM), in Ch 12 examines the levels of souls and consciousness levels.

There was no trick and no game was being played – what was presented in VEG is purported to be true, with the possible exception of Dr. Fomenko's speculation in VEG, Appendix D. Consider that if it IS all true, and I reported it that way, you are ahead of the game. The only part I am still tongue-in-cheek about is item III (Earth Simulation) above… bit it is interesting catalyst, or "brain candy" nonetheless.

> Your **reaction** to it all is what is significant.

## Spiritual Growth Scale, SQ

*Virtual Earth Graduate* is intended to be a revelation of the true history of Man and Earth. As such, it crosscuts several different disciplines, revealing new discoveries and exposing errors and disinformation. And above all, it was designed as **catalyst** – you don't have to believe catalyst for it work a change, or even a subtle shift, in your beliefs and increase your awareness of the world around you.

So many new ideas in one book is a fact that is sure to put a number of people on overload … and as such will offer them the opportunity to consider new, dynamic theories and truths, and reconsider beliefs they have held for years… even beliefs that no longer work for them (see Chapter 12 herein on EFT) and keep them strongly attached to the Earth plane. If this latter is true, when they die, they will not get out of here… lies and false beliefs count for less than the 51% Light that one needs to get out of here. They will be **recycled** until they learn what is true, what works, and who they really are.

In essence, while the VEG book presents as much truth as it can, it can also serve as a kind of 'test' – i.e., how much of it do you already know and <u>what are you willing to learn?</u> Indirectly, this establishes the reader's **SQ** – **Spiritual Quotient**. It was understood that there would be several levels of reader SQ in people reading the book and the basic 4 are examined below.

1. **Rejecting Ralph** – the total skeptic. Didn't like it, didn't finish it and could not figure out what it was supposed to be. This is a soul who is very 'tightly wrapped,' a linear, analytical 'show me' person who cannot think outside the box that others created for him/her. They are at the bottom of the SQ scale and may even be OPs – the soulless who cannot understand spiritual things anyway – So what attracted him to the book in the first place?

2. **Doubtful Dave** – read some of the book, skipped through it, liked the pictures, and came away with 1 or 2 issues he found interesting from the Science, History and Religion chapters. Overall, he doubts the book is useful, and cannot see how it could benefit him in his daily walk. This person, like Rejecting Ralph, is totally plugged into the limiting Current Earth View.

3. **Selective Sue** – read most of the book and found some things to her liking and came away with some ideas for further research and contemplation. Actually checked out some of the footnotes and looked at more of what the original author(s) had to say, and got a new proactive slant on part of her life that she had not seen before.

4. **Advanced Alice** – read the whole book, understood it, and checked out some key footnotes, bought those books (or already had them!) and came away with a regenerated desire to walk in the Light and anchor the Light for other people. Being a free thinker she evaluates what others say, has the discernment to know in her heart whether something 'rings true' or is more disinformation. She is intuitive, has high integrity, and walks in the Way outlined in Chapters 14 – 16 of VEG.

Of course there are variations on each of these classic *persona* and no one fits perfectly into a nice, neat little box, but these are also indicative of the 4 Types of Souls examined in Chapter 7 of the VEG book – there is often a one-for-one correlation: the **Baby Soul** is Resistant Ralph… and the **Old Soul** is Advanced Alice. This tends to be true because the more we live and experience, the more we know, and the more we know, the greater is our understanding of ourself and our world. Whereas the Simulated Earth issue could be unknown to Alice, she would not reject it out-of-hand, but would check it out, see if it made sense or was self-contradictory, go within and see what her heart's take is on the matter (remember that the heart also has an intelligence), and at least reserve judgment and perhaps put it on the shelf for now. It is more important that you wonder than blindly believe.

Sue and Alice obviously handled the book as **catalyst**, and that is how we are expected to handle anything that comes our way in this Great Drama on Earth. We don't get bent out of shape about it, we don't bitch about it, we just handle it ... note that **what you resist, persists** and that sooner or later you will have to handle it... despite your opinion – which doesn't really, ultimately, count for anything.

Sue and Alice have probably also moved on from Religion to Spirituality preferring to see life as a **Drama from the Creator** – to be enjoyed, and failing that, **catalyst** to learn from. As was said in the first book, Religion was designed to control Man (for his own good) who could be very petty, rowdy, noisy, lying, cheating, violent and smelly – at least the Anunnaki found them so. It was necessary to culture these still wild hominids, and give them morals and direction ... it was not really to manipulate or abuse early Man.

As one progresses in their soul growth, it is important to see the very limited, controlling doctrine of most standard religions – and such was examined in Chapters 1 and 11 in VEG. To specifically recap them, because Transformation can be impeded by harboring false religious ideas:

## Chapter 1 Insight

The design of the first VEG chapter was to reach the **adherents of Judaism** and supporters of the Old Testament. It was revealed that Yahweh was not who they have traditionally taken him to be – i.e., Yahweh is not The God of the Universe. Those Jews who are Messianic Jews, or Jews for Christ, have begun to move forward in their spiritual growth. Jesus was all about brotherhood, peace, love and respect for self, others and the planet. Yahweh, on the other hand, was about following ritual, controlled procedures and smiting one's enemies – "an eye for an eye" was the old way.

> Jewish scholar **Dr. Harold Bloom** also says Yahweh could not have been the God of the Universe. [1]

So Chapter 1 was about realizing in concert with the VEG Chapter 3 that Man's **soul was created by The God,** The One, but Man's **body** was created by the ET (probably the Anunnaki, among others) – and they wanted Man to worship them. Yahweh was actually the head Anunnaki, **Enlil,** until he left the planet (650-600 BC) and then another Anunnaki, **Marduk,** assumed the role: as Zeus in the Greek gods, then as Jupiter in the Roman pantheon of gods, and finally as Yahweh... all to control rowdy, very primitive Man.

I shared this with Sylvia, a super Jewish lady, and she had no problem with it, and in fact told me "Oh, you know, we have suspected for some time that Yahweh was not the God of the Universe... but we are faithful to our traditions and YHWH who is the God of All!"   She saw a difference between petty, humanistic Yahweh and the greater  I AM or YHWH.  Mazeltov!


## Chapter 11 Insight

In a similar way, VEG Chapter 11 was aimed at the Catholic Church ... which already admits in their **Catholic Encyclopedia** to most of the things presented. Issues addressed in Chapter 11 were the Inquisition, the Alteration of Western Chronology by Scaliger and Petavius (Catholic scholars, probably Jesuits),  the fable of Peter in AD 1 being the first Pope when the Church didn't even exist until AD 325, and their likely use of Apollonius (Pol)  of Týana for the exploits and travels of Paul.

And who could blame them for wanting to establish order in the world, get everybody under the same banner, and standardize faith – to minimize wars in the post-Roman world?  Not a bad concept – it was just that the **means** for achieving those noble goals left something to be desired : "Believe what we say, or we'll kill you!" (aka **Inquisition**), the murder of the Cathars and Knights Templar.... Witch hunts to exterminate the humans who were still experiencing advanced Anunnaki genetics (making them psychic) which could have been used to benefit Man. And last but not least, who can ignore the three (3) sackings and burnings of the **Library of Alexandria** – a major repository of Man's cherished Knowledge?  At least one of those attacks (AD 391by Pope Theophilus) the Church <u>was</u> responsible for. That was then.

In todays' world we have had the P2 scandal with the Vatican Bank, and the issue of **pedophilia** among some priests, and the 40-year 'suppression' of the Dead Sea Scrolls' translation – kept locked up in a vault in Jerusalem because there were some differences between the old Scroll texts and today's Bible version of the same documents, as well as some documents that were found that did not make it into the Bible.[2]  Lastly there is the issue of **Indulgences** – paying the Church to absolve sins, and an on-going potentially harmful teaching : lying is just a **venial (minor) sin** – "the priest will absolve you, you didn't do any harm."  Unless the lie cost someone his job and thus a marriage, forcing a suicide... that is <u>not</u> just a venial sin!  In fact, the **Karma incurred by that lie** will cost the perpetrator plenty, and s/he may be paying for it over several lifetimes... Too bad the Church doesn't teach that truth to its flock today... or do some of the more progressive Catholic churches teach it?

> The **Church originally taught reincarnation**[3], but it was expedient to say that there was no reincarnation, and threaten people with Hell and damnation if they were bad – "You have just one life and that's it... Turn or Burn!" If people knew they were eternal souls who live many lifetimes, the Church was sharp enough to fear that people would

continue partying in this lifetime, saying "Ahhh .. don't bug me – I'll get it together next time!" Hence, no reincarnation in Christianity.

And I have spoken about these issues with 2 Catholic priests and their main objection to the Church was: **priests can't get married**. Both had no issue with anything I said above. And the reason priests were not allowed to marry goes like this:

> Say you are a young idealistic man who really cares about serving God and want to minister to people the Word of God and very important Sacraments. So you cannot be poor, your parents must have the money to get you educated, or pay the Church for your education. You complete your education, and are ordained – you cannot marry since your parents will leave you whatever is left of their estate when they die -- and because you belong to the Church, you cannot directly inherit and so it all goes to the Church – which was an historical aspect of the Church acquiring wealth.

Archaic. For God's sake, let the priests marry ... and perhaps with the new enlightened Pope Francis, as this is being written, that archaic condition may be finally rectified, just as the Vatican Bank issue was resolved.

## Summary

Ironically, there is a type of human who needs to be told what to do – as **Arnold Schwarzenegger** said when he was Governor of California (VEG Ch 11). Just like Rejecting Ralph and most Baby Souls, the sheeple prefer that others think for them… and tell them what to believe… and so *Virtual Earth Graduate* would not be for about 80% of the people out there.

So basic religion does work for them, but my condolences, they will be recycled, maybe never getting out of here – and then (as VEG Chapter 7 said) if they are defective and over much time do not learn or change, they can be 'disassembled' back into their atomic elements… energy can be cleaned, reformatted and reused. This is because **we are all energy** as Chapter 12 shows.

**The major point of VEG** was to get people to consider that all is not what it appears to be AND when you finally see what this place is, you will realize that this is not our planet, we are not alone here, and thus most souls need to be moving on. But until you have a realization that **Earth School has been hijacked** by humans who love being Lords and who seek to keep Man a prisoner here, and continually lie to him and deny his divine birthright, you will continue to live a mediocre life and be repeatedly recycled back into the Earth realm… until the gods do a Wipe & Reboot. (Think: AD 900.)

## Rewind

It needs to be pointed out that the New Age (Glossary) is not better than Organized Religion. They are different, and meet different needs. The reason for examining them, and trying to reach a clarity on the subject, is that **a person with key false beliefs cannot achieve Transformation** – what this book is about. Ultimately, spiritual Transformation is about attaining higher consciousness, and the last 3 chapters address that issue – and share the modalities and caveats involved with such a pursuit.

That was the reason for two whole chapters examining errors, omissions and contradictions in Organized Religion – in *Virtual Earth Graduate*, principally Chapters 1 and 11. If you want to attain **higher consciousness**, which incidentally is the same as being an Earth Graduate, then you need Light – the Truth, not manmade suppositions, doctrine, or disinformation. There is a very revealing saying in the Bible which is incomplete… it is repeated here in its entirety… because you have never heard the whole saying:

> You shall know the Truth and the Truth will set you free…
> Jn 8:32 (paraphrased)

> …but first it will p*ss you off.

Why? Because we have all been lied to, sometimes not on purpose, but when you find the Truth (especially in **Religion, Science and History**), you will also realize that someone you trusted told you wrong. Maybe they meant well, but your pastor, school teacher, college professor, or even your parents were not perfect – none of them really knew all the answers, and so repeated what they had been told.

> Reminiscent of the game of **Grapevine** where 10 people sit in a circle and a simple sentence is given to the first person, who whispers it to his left, the next repeats it to the left, and so forth around the circle and when it gets back to the original person, no one recognizes it!

The deception can make you angry, especially if you relied on some of that information to make substantial decisions in your life – like where to live, what college to attend, whom to marry, what God expects of us when we sin, etc. etc…

> **Science** still promotes Evolution even though the Law of Entropy denies it, and even Darwin in later years questioned it, himself… Apes are not still evolving (but I used to wonder about my high school gym teacher…)

**Religion** still promotes vicarious atonement for sin, even though a loving God of the Universe would not operate that way. There is no Hell – it was a Church construct (based on the Jewish **Gehenna** pit and the Greek concept of Hades) to snap rowdy humans back into line…

According to Wikipedia:

**Gehenna** refers to the "Valley of Hinnom", which was a garbage dump outside of Jerusalem. It was a place where people burned their garbage and thus there was always a fire burning there. Bodies of those deemed to have died in sin without hope of salvation (such as people who committed suicide) were thrown there to be destroyed. Gehenna is used in the New Testament as a metaphor for the final place of punishment for the wicked after the resurrection.[4]

**History** still promotes the Egyptians building the Sphinx even though it clearly shows water erosion from 10,000 years ago. The Great Pyramid was never a tomb, and it was built by the same beings who built the Sphinx – which originally had the head of **Anubis** – and the Temple of Anubis is next to the Sphinx.

The Sphinx is not a statue of a lion, rather the following:

(credit Wikipedia:
https://en.wikipedia.org/wiki/Anubis#/media/File:Tutanhkamun_jackal.jpg)

Such is planet Earth… this book also gives a way to rise above the deception and manipulation and either Graduate or Ascend. Along the way, we'll see what Transformation is happening now and what is yet to come…

# Chapter 2:  Timelines & Dimensions

### Author's Note

This chapter was originally part of Book 1 (**Virtual Earth Graduate**) and was removed due to size restraints: the original book was encyclopedic and 868 pp. It is included in this book to round out your general edification, as it does explain timelines and how they work, but due to Earth being in an HVR Sphere (a very special 3D Simulation) and Quarantine <u>since AD 900</u>, there have been few timeline splits and the material in this chapter is more informational as opposed to procedural.

Having said that, the following information is still valid for an understanding of timelines – <u>and</u> if one is serious about synching up with an alternate, more proactive timeline (especially one where another aspect of self already exists, and it is wanted to project one's consciousness into that timeline [and out of this one]) the Timelords will not prohibit that.  The connection depends on your PFV.

## Timelines

As was presented in VEG, the last 3 chapters, **ensouled** Man needs to get out of here and short of graduating with Light, there is another way to get out. Just as gaining Light was a way to ensure that one can leave here <u>at death</u> (because one's Light quotient exceeds that of the planet) there is another way to leave here that can happen <u>while still living</u> – but it may mean enduring the Dark Night of the Soul (Appendix A).

Choosing to energetically entrain with the right timeline is one of the ways to get out of here. And is still possible – just don't wait for the next timeline bifurcation. And that involves several things, including one's beliefs, one's PFV or vibrational level, and **intent** which all influence each other.  As the following information on timelines shows, we normally have a choice about where we wind up, or we can drift along with the crowd and take whatever we get.

Another term for timeline (herein abbreviated TL) can be 'dimension' or alternate reality inasmuch as a timeline does occupy a dimension – and two timelines can occupy two different dimensions, or with phase-shifting, may occupy the same dimension. To picture phase-shifting, first picture an oscilloscope with a single sine wave crossing the screen. That single wave looks like the letter 'S' lying down, and can be likened to a single timeline.

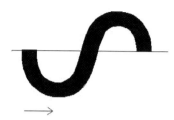

Now add a 2nd sine wave (dotted line below) 45° 'off' from the first, starting **.1** second after the first wave, and there will be two sine waves crossing the screen, one behind the other. They will overlap but not interfere with each other and each occupies its own 'slice of time' on the screen.

While the two waves pictured (below) are technically sine and cosine waves, the emphasis here is the fact that two waves, two timelines, can be running through the same linear space-time, with a phase-shift to separate them. For a minute, however, assume that both waves are propagating across the screen at the same time and rate, and note that they do occasionally **intersect**. When they intersect, as timelines, it is possible to move (consciously or unconsciously) from one to the other… (see Epilog section in Chapter 5).

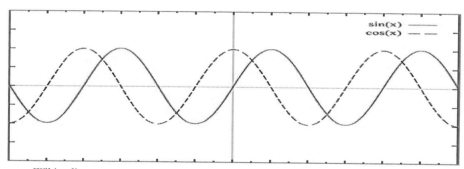

(Source: Wikipedia : http://upload.wikimedia.org/wikipedia/commons/1/13/Sine_Cosine_Graph.png)

An alternate timeline is usually another, similar TL parallel to this one, but phase-shifted 45° - 90° , so that one dimension does not see the other, yet they can virtually occupy the same space as they are **superpositioned** (explained in the following sections).

On the other hand, a TL **Split** is what happens when a single timeline bifurcates and becomes two or more timelines. Such a shift has been done several times within the last 60 years which is why the predictions of Edgar Cayce (in the 30's and 40's) and those of Nostradamus (500+ years ago) did not come true… actually they may have – but not in <u>our</u> timeline. Consider that there is a timeline where Hitler won and most of the civilized world is speaking German. Consider that there is a timeline where JFK did not die, and consider that there is a timeline where the Berlin Wall did not come down, the USSR still exists and World War III is already underway... Alternate choices of mankind are played out on alternate TLs.

The significance of a timeline split is that <u>it is another way of getting out of here, and is based on intent and PFV</u>.

Here's how it works.

## Timeline Splits

Let's say that Earth was in one continuous timeline up to and thru the mid 80's. Cayce predicted that Atlantis would rise in the Atlantic Ocean during the late 60's, and Nostradamus predicted that in July 1999 there would be a 'king of terror' coming from the skies (asteroid). [5] Obviously, that did not happen here. Such things happening were predicated on that timeline continuing to develop with the same influences and energies as were seen by Cayce and Nostradamus.

What those two men did not foresee was the infusion of positive thinking, Light and proactive behavior of incoming higher souls – sometimes called Indigos, Starseeds, Wanderers, or Homo *noeticus* – planned by the Higher Beings. These two men also did not see that the Higher Beings would move Earth into an HVR Sphere for eventual ascension into the 5D realm... or <u>did</u> they and we have not understood their writings? Neither seems to say anything about timelines and possible splits.

The Father of Light is not sleeping, but He is not <u>directly</u> aware of the lower levels of His Creation. He "sees" through His hierarchical delegation what is happening even though it is a Virtual Reality, and He does not violate anybody's freewill when He inserts souls with more Light into the mix -- or having the Greys perform genetic upgrades. This operates like a "5th column" approach (see Chapter 8).

What it does is increase the overall vibratory level of the soul mix on the planet, and establish a new positive vector sustained by the Wanderers who coherently and collectively agreed on their intended assistance for this planet. This new, positive vector tends to dissociate with the already established (negatively based) vector and thus creates a growing separate resonance, eventually building enough energy potential to birth a new timeline.

The Neggs can see the 'special' incoming souls but not stop them, and as was said earlier in VEG's Chapter 7, they try to afflict and derail the incoming souls who have a higher purpose (but are not protected), and sometimes they are successful. Other times, the incoming souls are 100% protected and thus succeed in their missions so that the overall effect is to more positively orient the Earth.

*Note: the following sections use advanced terminology to describe concepts which can be found in the Glossary.*

## Bifurcation Mechanics

**Since the amount of Light carried by the aggregate incoming souls is more than equal to absorb any additional negativity created by OPs and Neggs, there develop two main groups of opposite entraining vectors: the original negative timeline, TL1, and the newer positive timeline-to-be, TL2. As the energetic potential builds between these two groups on the same planet/timeline, and each develops and seeks to sustain its own coherent diversity, there is a growing bifurcation potential. At the point where the mutual consensus of each group accretes and generates an energy level capable of promoting and sustaining a mitosis, and when that energy potential is rendered unstable by the growing energy of their group volitional intent -- exceeding each domain's point of cohesion --- the main event stream (timeline) will split into (at least) two different phases – entraining like souls to each timeline based on intent and PFV frequency.** [6]

One group in TL1 seeks to maintain the status quo and keep things mediocre like they have always been (unwittingly supporting entropy), and promote more deception and oppression. This would be the 3D PTB who are empowered by the Anunnaki Remnant (3D and 4D), and who have a lot to gain by retaining control and furthering their money-making schemes, even at Man's and the environment's expense.

The other group chooses a more positive collective spiritual emphasis which tends to phase-lock into its own vibration sustained by the collective energies and **intent** of the souls moving toward a TL2. In this way, Man <u>can</u> create his own reality, but it is done on a collective level with much coherent intent.

## Timelines within Timelines

Timelines are created or split based on energy potential concurrent with accrued intent or need. The **Metaverse** supports soul growth and indeed supports and accommodates divergent intentional group soul issues via bifurcation. "Split-offs, regionally divergent realities, and mutually joined continuity are all features of a soul growth accommodating hyper-universe." [7]

This is not a "many universes" argument where it is assumed that all possible outcomes have their own timeline vector – in fact, this is more of **a "necessary universes" model** where only "quantum eventuated paths exist. The necessary universes model **disallows** alternate timeline generation that has no co-creative participating quantum soul agencies." [8]   What that means is that (1) there are no possible timelines that are uninhabited but which exist in case someone wants to experience it, and (2) unless there are enough (quantum) souls with the <u>intent</u> of experiencing something coherently, the timeline will also not exist.  And when timelines are created, generally they are created on the 'macro' scale, involving many, many souls, although **'fractal' timeline** elements may exist for a time when there is a brief need to simulate an alternative.

> Nature provides for serial creation of parallel timelines on the macro-scale.
>
> In effect, a whole new history is tried by changing key past events. Since quantum observer-participant reality is malleable, changes to individuals that do not change larger scale events, permits multiple timelines to be embedded **fractally** within a larger global  timeline.
>
> Timelines are weaved [sic] together into a toroidal traveling wave-front fractal flower of eddy frequencies, where patterns of many alternates exist within different levels of contained scale of the flower. [9] [emphasis added]

This suggests that sub-purposes of subgroups with enough coherent energy may wind up as a smaller timeline fractally interwoven in the larger timeline framework, and even be dragged along by the larger timeline, and be possibly affected by it energetically.

## Collapsing Timelines

What is not known is that such bifurcations have happened in the past when the accreted energies of opposing collective intents forced the creation of new timelines – which were <u>sustained</u> only through the collective intent and energies put into them. If a majority of the souls later determine that they have no further interest in their chosen vector (i.e., TL), and this is realized on a collective level to an extent large enough that sustaining energies are depleted, the timeline weakens and then disintegrates. (See point Z in Chart 5.)  **Entropy**.

Another way to collapse a timeline is to create one through a negative emphasis:

> From a soul's higher point of view, knowledge, intelligence, and mental creativity, when operating without love, compassion and empathy, in the Omega analysis, is always considered a **doomed evolutionary track**… Mind is at odds with the heart on a grand evolutionary scale. Mind applied without any context of compassion and empathy for the world, is a form of evolutionary insanity,

however permitted and explored by many.[10] [emphasis added]

Sizable conflicting agendas also create fracturing of the overall energy of a domain into competing streams of energy supporting different agendas and the result is a discordant, multilevel energy that does not achieve enough coherence to promote and sustain a bifurcation. The situation is one of chaotic energy, however, and that ultimately results in dissipating the timeline.

## Alternate Futures

Alternate futures are often created, or assembled and disassembled in this way. Every time a person faces a <u>major decision</u> in his/her life, the other option not consciously chosen is usually played out on another **fractal** part of the same timeline. In this way, the Father of Light through all the lessons of the Higher Self, or Oversoul, is completed by the knowledge of the outcome of all <u>significant</u> possibilities.

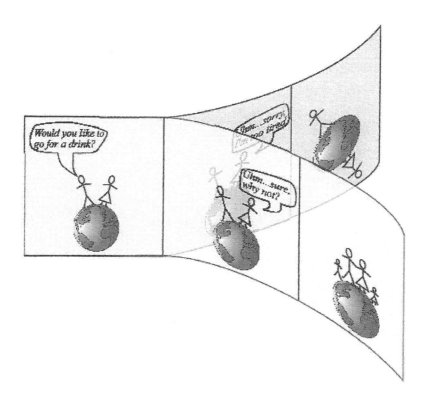

Credit: http://www.bing.com/images

This was also postulated by a quantum physicist Hugh Everett III:

> Everett noted that **quantum physics predicts** that all alternative outcomes of any given experiment must occur even though we may only see a single outcome! Somehow, those hidden alternatives must exist simultaneously along with the observed outcome. [11]

and

> Any universe [timeline] you may inhabit at the moment will seem real enough with the others hidden from plain view. However, the same thing will be true for each of the other universes and other "you's" as well… how can there be copies of me that I have no knowledge of? [12] [emphasis added]

VEG Chapter 7 answered that in the discussion on multiple aspects of the Soul. You will recombine all soul aspects (you's) back to the Higher Self (You) which will assimilate all experiences back to the Oversoul (*multiple Higher Selves*).

## Parallel Universes

Another description of alternate futures is parallel universes or dimensions. Quantum Physics attempts address this aspect of our world and sees it as a possible solution to the particle versus wave behavior when addressing the photon-thru-the-slit experiment. Part of the answer to whether light is a particle or wave is answered by a theory that says particles in adjacent universes are interfering with those in this universe [13] because multiple universes are **superpositioned** (see next page).

Specifically Dr .Wolf says:

> Thus in any single universe, even though the particle in the other universe is not present [in this universe], the effect of its presence mysteriously changes the course of the observed particle's history and its final destination. [14]

Again, this is an example of **entanglement.** Said another way, Professor David Deutsch has explained:

> Quantum mechanics is basically a theory of **many parallel universes**. Some of these universes are very like our own and some are very un-like our own. The nearby universes differ from ours by, say, only one photon, whilst the other, more distant universes are completely different from ours…

In a sense, each and every particle exists in its own separate universe, but <u>these universes interfere with each other</u> to produce the pattern of the universe that we can actually see or perceive… **Reality does not consist of just a single universe**. [15] [emphasis added]

Besides being entangled, the universes are in superposition to each other. This involves similar parts of 'adjacent' universes to be phase-shifted, thus allowing the particles to sometimes interact between universes. This also suggests that the ZPE Field (i.e., Matrix) extends between and permeates adjacent universes. (Chapter 12)

### Superpositioned Universes

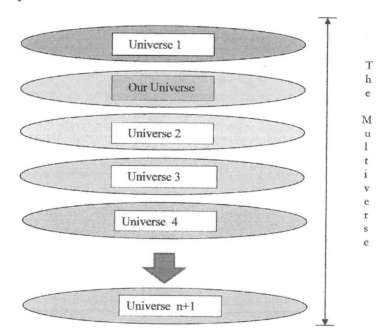

And, this also mirrors and corroborates the interaction of multiple soul aspects of a Soul Group which affect each other (energetically) as was also explained in VEG Chapter 7. Soul aspects can/do affect each other (via the silver cord) even when located in different realms.

### Timeline Mechanics

Mother Nature's economies provide for the existence of many

> parallel, alternate, space-time dimensions as necessary, and no more. Near dimensions to present time Earth … have their own **separately evolving Earths**. They exist in a parallel dimensionality. Sometimes near dimensions are synchronous and thus morphically porous and **overlapping and easy shifting** between singularities is possible.
>
> There are a limited number of alternate global present day timeline realities.
>
> At this time in our history there are an acute number of **overlaps** and inter-connects between dimensions in special ways. [16]
> [emphasis added]

Immediately after timelines split, it is fairly easy to move between them since they still look 99.9% alike – which percentage diminishes with time. But as they are close together, all one has to do is **focus** on a different set of timeline attractor emotions (see the section on 'Three Global Futures' later in this chapter), and one is 'switched' to the timeline with which s/he resonates – based on the intensity of the emotional attractor. Everything else being equal, feel love (and sustain it) and be on TL2, feel hate (and sustain it), and you'll shift back to TL1.

This actually happened to me and I briefly wound up on an alternate timeline as I share more in Chapter 5 ("Epilog: Soulmate Encounter"). Everything was the same and I had no clue that when I went to church, that the church and people were in the other timeline… until Leslie showed up, and I had no idea who she was. At some point within the next hour, I was switched back to my 'normal' timeline, and I suspect that I cannot go to that timeline any more since the facts there now are bound to be different: if Leslie and I got married there, that would be a significant deviation from what is true in my 'normal' (base) timeline.

The switch from timeline to timeline has been likened to two boats out in the water, touching each other side to side, and they start to drift apart. At first, moving from boat to boat is easy, just walk over. In a few minutes, you'll have to jump to go to the other boat, and after 30-60 minutes, you'll have to swim over. And eventually there is such a gap between the two boats that movement between them requires a new strategy. With the passage of time, it gets similarly more and more difficult to move between timelines that split. [17]

And it also is difficult to manipulate a timeline, but it is possible with advanced technology (as was done in 1943, explained in a later section on 'Timeloops').

> Each individual sees the global timeline within which they are embedded, but usually cannot seem to consciously influence it.

> To the degree you genuinely do influence the global line, it can
> either move you to an alternate Earth that already exists with
> you in it (an aspect of you got there earlier in an earlier split), or
>
> generate an entirely new timeline of global quantum singularity
> to some level of scale. [18]

So to move between timelines, as was <u>done to me</u> in the church above, the two TL
had to be very much alike (and were probably "intersecting" as described earlier),
and while I did not shift my consciousness, They moved me to the other timeline,
shifting consciousness is normally how it is done. (As later explained, the Timelords
moved me there to make a point about my soulmate, and because it took me by
surprise I later knew I hadn't done anything to effect the shift.) The event happened
to me shortly after I experienced the October 1998 Change when a lot of powerful
things were happening to me.

So there is agreement that there are parallel universes, alternate timelines and futures.
What we are in the process of learning is what and who is in these alternate worlds.
And if we would like to get out of this one, and into a better one, how do we do it?

**Timeline Resonance**

The way to 'move' to a better timeline is to **resonate with it**: think it, feel it,
visualize it, focus on it – eat, sleep and drink whatever you imagine that timeline to
be. (QV, the movie *Somewhere in Time*.) Be as much like what you seek as possible;
this is not "act as if" philosophy which is pretending. The Insider said it very well:

> **Be** like that which you want to connect with as much as possible.[19]

And the clarification was added by the following:

> Whatever you want to connect with, simply support it, reinforce it,
> try to become it. People who pray to Jesus from the standpoint of
> weak beggars [**not the meek**] receive no response because they are
> vectoring towards a future of dis-empowerment and victimhood, a
> direction opposite to what the Christ represents, and so they receive
> little feedback. Those who call upon the divine impulse within,
> recognize it, and do their best to express it, receive reinforcement. [20]
> [emphasis added]

In short, it is whatever you **energetically reinforce** – what you are giving energy to
in thought, word and deed. If you are optimistic, giving, cheerful, patient, and caring,
you will vector toward a different future than a person who is pessimistic, depressed,

impatient, a taker, and fearful or passive. Your <u>basic soul resonance</u>, your PFV, and its strength, determines what timeline and future you resonate with.

## Special People

One exception. This was briefly mentioned by Drs. Modi and Peck in VEG Chapter 7: If you came here with a lot of Light, for a specific purpose, the 4D STS Controllers see that and will do everything they can to block you fulfilling your mission – and your resulting life may be anything but the positive, wonderful experience you'd expect from being a positive person!  In fact, your life may be rougher than others because you are more of a threat to the STS Controllers' agenda; you experience broken relationships, health problems, financial problems – anything to disrupt your mission and derail you.

Do <u>not</u> assume that the drama in your life accurately reflects who and what you are.

Do <u>not</u> let OPs tell you that you are wrong and so messed up that you'll never amount to anything.  Keep your own counsel. Don't give your power away.

Such a person with a lot of Light may have to work hard to trust themselves, develop an **inner strength** and learn to listen to their own ideas  – despite others' 'helpful advice.' In fact, that may be the essence of what that soul is here to learn – a form of self-confidence, inner strength, and connection with a higher part of themselves. To walk calmly amid the crowd of rushing fools, knowing the truth, and not follow the crowd is hard but results in an **Earth Graduate** that is very well respected.

Self-mastery is expected of souls who want to graduate from the Earth School: to live by the highest values you can when all about you are doing what feels good. It's called **Integrity**.

Shakespeare said it:

> To thine own self be true, and it follows thou canst not then be false to others.
> -- Hamlet.

## Chained to a Timeline

As was said in VEG Chapter 14, some people may have noticed that beautiful planet Earth is really screwed up – and they want to get out of here. Some 'chain' themselves to this timeline by devoting themselves to fixing/changing it, and others live in denial that anything is wrong. Still others make excuses for whatever is going wrong by claiming that it is just someone's Karma, or "It was an accident!"

**Accidents are premeditated carelessness.**

Interestingly, we are not required to fix/change/stop whatever is going on – and you can't anyway! If the planet seems like a zoo or an insane asylum, it IS that way for a reason, and the 'inmates' here have to learn that they have 'created' it that way.

But there is a way to absolutely chain oneself to this (undesirable) timeline: See oneself as a '**righter of wrongs**' or a teacher of Mankind, or set about attacking what is wrong and see oneself as the bringer of Light and Love to the planet. Your focus on what is wrong demands that the gods (Higher Beings) place you in a context where you will have plenty to work with –so that you can work out your agenda. (Remember: it is done unto you as you believe.) And that may involve putting you (briefly or not) in a **fractal subdomain** where most if not all of the players in your drama (based on the larger drama of the main timeline) are OPs. That way, you don't harm any other souls, but you will learn from the <u>futility</u> of trying to fix the 'unfixable.'

Does that mean that when we a see a problem, or someone is in need, that we ignore the need and tell ourselves that the gods will do it? Does that mean that we should tell ourselves that nothing is wrong? No. It may be part of your Script on this TL, to serve and be proactively involved with others or the environment. The key is to do the right thing and help <u>if you can</u> – note that if you can, it is set up for you to do that, a negative response shows insensitivity and that may earn Karmic penalty. Don't obsess about things that you can't fix/stop/change.

## Fractal Changes

Unless you can see auras, you'll not know that you have been seamlessly moved into the fractal version of your world so that you don't know that you are not affecting the larger timeline. You can wreak havoc as you choose in a very controlled subset of the real timeline – and most likely experience frustration and futility until you give up any self-appointed agenda. At that point, any major changes you effected may be replicated in the larger timeline and you are placed back in the original timeline. Or if you sufficiently learned compassion and had a change of heart, you may be moved to another timeline version of the same larger timeline to be of more effect therein.

If you can see auras, you'll see more OPs than normal in your world.

Such a move to a fractal subdomain does NOT apply to a soul who has come here, who is empowered, or 'chosen', to effect change within the Father's Greater Script in the main TL. The fractal subdomain is largely a device to teach non-chosen souls that their intentions and self-chosen agendas may sound great but that they are not equipped to succeed, and they need to <u>ask</u> what it is they ARE supposed to do.

Remember, whatever it is that you need to experience, for soul growth, will be done for you by the gods: you will be placed in an appropriate context reflecting your beliefs, so that it can be "done unto you as you believe/expect." If such a context is not available in the larger timeline, or you cannot be moved to where it is, you can be placed in a **fractal subdomain** to experience your intention(s) where the OPs will bring you the opportunity to be/do/have whatever it is you fancy experiencing. How else can you learn? Thus it would be wise to examine one's intentions and resulting experience in light of the following questions – if one is not getting what is wanted in life:

1. **What am I doing on a level where this is real?**
   If feedback is negative and people and events don't support your purpose, or you can't get what you want, or your world is turning upside down. Operating from a low level of fear will cause a lot of projects to fail, as well as operating from a high spiritual level above the understanding of people around you.

2. **Out of all the perceptions available to me in the Universe, why am I focused on _____ ?**
   If you see yourself as a bringer of Light, virtue and Love, and it isn't working, your self-chosen image needs examination. If you find a lot of fault with other people, and they 'need enlightening', ask yourself why you are focused on their ignorance/stupidity/rebellion? You are attracting them to you.

Whatever you are focused on is what you will attract to you, and possibly 'chain' yourself to it. And the gods know if it is YOU that needs the lesson, so don't be surprised how it plays out. Just be careful on what you focus and insist – it can 'chain' you to a particular timeline as described in the later section on 'attractors.'

## Placeholder Replications

Let's take a look at what happens to people when a timeline splits.

Suppose that Jack is on a timeline TL1 that splits to TL1 (more negative) and TL2 (more positive). In this case, TL1 is the original TL which just got more negative when the more positively oriented souls (STO) left for TL2. The difference in positive and negative deals with whether the outcome is supportive and appropriate, or whether it detracts, disrupts or derails thus being inappropriate. Further suppose that Jack's desire was to align with the TL2 positive timeline and he <u>as a soul</u> is translated there. He is thus an ensouled human on TL2.

# Transformation of Man

## Timeline Split Diagram

**Legend**:  ESH = Ensouled Human    OP = Organic Portal (**soulless human**)
TL1 = original timeline      TL2 = new timeline

Steps B & E assume that TL2 is a virgin timeline (no one else is there already).

**The following is a step by step breakdown of how the above timeline split affects the people. Headcounts may be easier to follow below:**

## Timeline Splits and People: Steps A - E

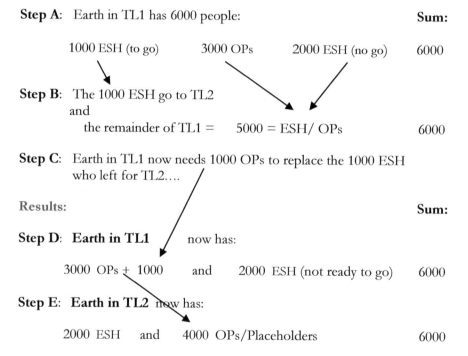

**Step A**:  Earth in TL1 has 6000 people:                                    **Sum:**

        1000 ESH (to go)        3000 OPs        2000 ESH (no go)        6000

**Step B**:  The 1000 ESH go to TL2
        and
            the remainder of TL1 =      5000 = ESH/ OPs            6000

**Step C**:  Earth in TL1 now needs 1000 OPs to replace the 1000 ESH
        who left for TL2....

Results:                                                                **Sum:**

**Step D**:  **Earth in TL1**        now has:

        3000 OPs + 1000        and        2000 ESH (not ready to go)        6000

**Step E**:  **Earth in TL2** now has:

        2000 ESH      and      4000 OPs/Placeholders            6000

**Note**:  this is how **timeline splits result in an increase in the amount of OPs or Placeholders**. TL1 gained 1000 OPs. The Sum of beings is kept the same indicating that the change was **seamless** – no one on TL1 would know anything happened. The 1000 souls moved to TL2 would also not suspect anything because everyone transferred with them.

When the timeline splits, TL1 is actually the continuation of the original timeline which has a less than desirable outcome, even negative, where World War III occurs. Members of Jack's family, people at work and church are used to having him around and in some ways, he completes the scenario for them – all to say that **Jack cannot**

**disappear from TL1**. He is needed to fulfill duties, or responsibilities, that become a part of the on-going life drama of the other people still on TL1. So he becomes an OP on TL1 to sustain the on-going Drama there...

How can Jack be in two places at once? Simple: he is an ensouled human on TL2 (his choice), and he is replicated as a Placeholder OP on TL1 (by the Timelords who oversee this whole process). The Placeholder does not have a soul, there is no aura, but there is a 'soul cord' or energy link between the TL1 Jack and the TL2 Jack.

> *Sometimes Jack may replicate in more than one timeline as an ensouled human – i.e., both 'copies' of Jack can have a soul, but this is rare as it entails a division of limited soul energy that cannot be reduced beyond a certain point, so the usual event is that ensouled Jack moves to TL2, and the original TL1 Jack becomes an OP Placeholder. (Chapter 10.)*

Note that a subconscious non-souled aspect of Jack was replicated in the TL1 timeline, and other significant 'players' in Jack's life drama are also replicated in TL2 for Jack as **'Placeholders'** to continue their function so that Drama options can be played out on both timelines – and now you see where some OPs come from. The Placeholders do not usually have souls and do not need them – although some players of significance may opt to replicate with a soul aspect if they need to learn something, too. Here again, a Soul can only send its energy into so many alternate timelines (depending on soul level) and thus there is often a limit to the replication with soul-link back to the original Soul (VEG Ch 7) .

> The more advanced souls can replicate themselves into more timelines and realms than younger souls can. Note that Karma 'attaches' to a Soul (via the Script) and is not constrained by an Era or a timeline.

An OP also replicates as an OP in any new timeline, because the ensouled human needs them as part of his day-to-day Drama, and even some of these replicated OPs may depend on other OPs to perform their functions to keep the Drama going. **This is one reason Earth currently has so many OPs** – we have been through several timeline splits in the beginning of this Era – and that is good news.

## Fractal Simulation

Sometimes, an alternate choice (for example, a fractal TL3) playing itself out is more of a temporary **simulation**, as the late Robert Monroe discovered (in *Far Journeys*, end of chapter 8). He was already out-of-body (OOBE) and one of the Beings of Light (what he called an *Inspec* [Intelligent Species]), immersed him in a simulation where he had to discover how to do an emergency landing of a plane. His co-pilot was a simulated OP. He fails 4 times and the simulation starts again from the top...

At the point where it proves successful, the simulation ends. The key point Monroe made was that **the simulation was very real**; the noise of the engine, the smoke, the OP co-pilot saying things to him… there was no way to know it wasn't actually happening – just like our experience on Earth.

Monroe suggests that there are "…training centers on planets circling those billions of stars, tied to us by **an intelligent energy field** common to all of us." [21] And that Matrix is examined in Chapter 12.

The consciousness of the original soul may move over into a new timeline (with any necessary adaptations in conscious memory so that the move is 'seamless'); if the fractal choice proves disastrous, the information is recorded in the Oversoul's consciousness, as a learning experience, and the fractal simulation (TL3) is discontinued for that soul.

A soul may also opt out of an alternate fractal scenario if it becomes too burdensome and/or there are no more lessons in one's Script to be learned. The Oversoul, in this case, knows what is going on and the goal is not to prolong an alternate scenario to the point where the soul is damaged. What might be useful is finding out what it takes to consciously move to a more proactive timeline, and that is what part of this chapter is about.

## Timeline Vision

At this point, it is relevant to relate a <u>very</u> vivid vision that was given me back in November 1998 – 3 weeks after the Soul Merge in October. This was a very real vision, so much so that I found myself initially holding my breath because I found myself in space, looking at the Earth. I later learned that the vision corroborated Lynn Grabhorn's book about a second Earth, called <u>Planet Two</u>, and I exchanged emails with her regarding this synchronicity.

What the vision showed was this:

> From a position in space near Earth, say about 400,000 miles out, the Earth was about the size of a basketball at arm's length. I saw the black velvet of space and the multicolored stars behind what was a very realistic, full color planet Earth.
>
> The Moon was not part of the vision.
>
> While I watched, the Earth split into two Earths – an effect kind of like crossing your eyes (while looking at an object), except

that the new Earth was up at a 45° angle. And after a few minutes, the two Earths began to drift apart somewhat. I understood only that this was a future timeline split for Earth.

**Timeline Split**
Credit: http://www.bing.com/images

Lynn's book came out in 2004 and I was stunned. Had she seen the same vision as I had been given? And what was I supposed to do with it? In her emails, she was non-directive but supportive and suggested I pray about it and see if there was some action I was supposed to take. Years after the vision, the information has made its way into this book. In the last two years, as I have reviewed the vision, I have had additional insights on it... it just represents a **timeline split**.

The vision signified that Earth had been 'splitting' into two timelines, and as the years have gone by since the vision, I have understood that TL1 <u>not splitting</u> could be a very negative scenario: a *Mad Max* world, despite the PTB's efforts to enforce martial law and lockdowns with technology everywhere they can... cameras, RFID chips, biometrics... there could be war and disease. And due to the chaotic energies, the timeline begins to suffer entropy and eventual disintegration... Being clever and having some Anunnaki Remnant technology, the PTB might devise a way to go back in time and see if they can entrain more souls onto the timeline – expecting the TL to split (eventually) and give them an optimum negative TL1 timeline. (See Chart 5, later in this chapter.)

Meanwhile the TL2 scenario with a more positive energy normally succeeds in distancing itself from the TL1 people, war is averted, disease and famine controlled, poverty eradicated, and Man begins to move forward in a more proactive society – especially with the help of the Homo *noeticus* that the Greys have been building. The Neggs (see Glossary) would also go with the souls whose Scripts they manage… to continue their assigned duties.


## Current Timeline Problem

It is interesting that some Internet blogs have discussed the idea that beings (us) from the future have come back via a **timeloop** to hijack this timeline (TL1) and entrain more souls into coherent negativity so that when a future split happens, TL1 will have more souls (than the last time this happened) to support their desired vector… Why would the bloggers suspect that?

### Cassiopaean Input on Loop

While it is hard to believe that there could be a timeloop operating over which we have no control (Chart 5 following), it was verified by a fairly reputable group called the C's whose information always appears to be accurate, even though they can be evasive, vague and sometimes smartass. See the following exchange below… Their input on this subject has enough credibility to warrant quoting it, and it did affect Man for a while.

The following is selectively quoted from a **90's session** with the Cassiopaeans with Laura Knight-Jadczyk (noted as "L" herein): [22]

> Q: (L)  Let me ask this one before the tape runs out and we take a break. What is the "ultimate secret" being protected by the Consortium?
> A: (from Cassiopaeans):
> **You are not in control of yourselves, you are an experiment.**
> Q: (L)  Yes. Okay. How long … have the Greys been interacting with our race?
> A: No.
> Q: (L)  What do you mean, "No"?
> A: Time travelers, therefore, "Time is ongoing."
> Q: (L)  Okay. Recently I read….
> A: No, not finished with answer. Do you understand the gravity of the last response?

Q: (L) They are time travelers, they can move forward and backward in time, they can play games with our heads…

A: When you asked how long, of course it is totally unlimited, is it not?

Q: (L) That's not good. If they were to move back through space time and alter an event in our past, would that alteration in the past instantaneously alter our present as well?

A: Has **over and over and over.**

Q: … (L) So at each…

A: You just are not yet aware, and have no idea of the ramifications!!!

Q: (L) We're getting a little glimmer… So our only real prayer in this whole damn situation is to **get out of this density level**. That's what they [the C's] are saying…

A: Close.

Q: (L) Because, otherwise, **we're just literally, as in that book** [not identified]**, stuck in the replay over and over and over…**

  **(T) We're stuck in a timeloop**…

   (J) Are we in a timeloop?

A: **Yes.**

Q: (D) I have a question about… Mankind has found it necessary to appoint time for some reason…

A: Control mechanism.

Q: (T) Is there a way for us to break the control mechanism? Besides moving to 4$^{th}$ density?

A: Nope.      [emphasis added]

And on another related occasion, Laura decides that Earth life is too negative and she understandably wants out: [23]

Q: (L) I want you guys to know that I sometimes feel … like a pawn on a chessboard!

A: You should, **you inhabit 3$^{rd}$ density STS environment**.

Q: (L) I was at least hoping that if I was a pawn, that some of the players were good guys. Is that asking too much?

A: Yes.

Q: (L) To which statement?

A: Good guys don't play chess.

   …

Q: (L) Okay. One of the sensations I have experienced is that I have had it up to the eyebrows with the negative energies and experiences of 3$^{rd}$ density, and I have thought lately that this feeling of having had enough, in an absolute sense, is one of the primary motivators for wanting to find one's way out of this **trap** we are in. **I want out of it**….

> A: … **When you see the futility of the limitations of 3rd density life, it means you are ready to graduate.** [emphasis added]

Finally some good news. **Futility is closure.**

There **was** a timeloop after the Philadelphia Experiment in 1943, the Greys had something to do with it, the Timelords would break it, and **Man is no longer contained within it**. Interesting input if true, but even if not, it just adds a new dimension to this chapter for consideration. What is a timeloop and how would it operate? (That is discussed below in a new section.)

Nonetheless, Man _is_ contained in a 3rd density HVR Sphere which can be exited only by: (1) "energetically" gaining the escape velocity by absorbing Knowledge/Light, or (2) synching up energetically with the vibrations of the timeline one wants to be on after the coming timeline split, as explained herein.

As for the 1943 Philadelphia Experiment mentioned above, it was said in VEG Chapter 2 that **this planet began as a kind of experiment** and the benevolent 'gods' (i.e., Higher Beings) who run it are not going to permit 'outsiders' to mess it up nowadays. It appears that the only way out is by overcoming it – raise one's awareness: see one's true nature, see the <u>futility of trying to fix/change/stop things</u>, and gain knowledge and Light… become an **Earth Graduate**.

## Cassiopaean Input on Graduating

The communication with The C's was expanded in response to a question on what Man is here to learn, and how do we get from 3D to 4D. Laura is concerned that there is a Galactic Super Wave coming toward our solar system (an idea supported by Dr. Paul LaViolette) which she thinks has an energy potential to "harvest" souls and awaken them with its higher vibration. She fears the Wave won't work for her.

Q: (L) Well, how in the heck am I supposed to get there [graduate to 4th density] if I can't "get it?"
A: Who says you have to "get it" before you get there?
Q: (L) Well, that leads back to: what is the [incoming resonance galactic] wave going to do to expand this awareness? Because, if the wave is what "gets you there," what makes this so?
A: No it is like this: After you have completed all your lessons in "third grade" where do you go?
Q: (L) So it is a question of…
A: Answer please.
Q: (L) You go to fourth grade.
A: OK, now, do you have to already be in 4th grade in order to be allowed to go

there? Answer.

Q: (L) No. But you have to know all the 3rd density things…

A: Yes. More apropos: **you have to have learned all of the lessons**.

Q: (L) What kind of lessons are we talking about here?

A: **Karmic and simple understandings.**

Q: (L) What are the key elements of these understandings, and are they fairly universal?

A: They are universal.

Q: (L) What are they?

A: We cannot tell you that [a violation of the **Law of Confusion**, see Glossary].

Q: (L) Do they have to do with discovering the MEANINGS of the symbology of 3rd density experience, seeing behind the veil… and reacting to things according to choice? Giving each thing or person or event its due? [As the Sufis teach.]

A: Okay. But you cannot force the issue. When you have learned, you have learned.

> They also said that "Who you are and **what you see**" is important. They suggested that learning to see the "unseen" would be of great value in moving to 4D, and if you couldn't do it, it could render anyone "helpless" when traversing the path to higher consciousness and spiritual growth.

C's: **Beware of disinformation**. It diverts your attention away from reality thus leaving you open to capture and conquest and even possible destruction. [See Chapter 3 New Age fallacies section .] Disinformation comes from seemingly reliable sources. It is extremely important for you to **not** gather false knowledge as it is more damaging than no knowledge at all. **Remember knowledge protects, ignorance endangers.** The information you speak of, Terry, was given to you deliberately because you and Jan and others have been targeted [by the Neggs, or Discarnates] due to your intense interest in level of density 4 through 7 subject matter.

You have already been documented as a "threat." […] Remember, disinformation is very effective when delivered by highly trained sources because hypnotic and **transdimensional techniques** are used thereby causing electronic anomalies to follow suggestion causing perceived confirmation to occur. [24] [emphasis added]

## Disclaimer

Thus it is wise to question not only what we see/hear that is new (even this book) and if the new disagrees with what we think we already know, it is wise to re-evaluate both the old belief and the info – resolve the issue. Check it out, discuss it, research it – your soul growth eventually depends on it.

Secondly, also beware of purveyors of esoteric teaching who believe themselves to be competent without even completing an elementary education. They can receive all kinds of insights and messages from many sources, but they can falsely judge them to be true before they have developed within themselves the facility called **discernment** (a balance of IQ, Knowledge and Intuition). We have to be well-versed in a subject before we can give an opinion, whether Quantum Physics, medicine, nutrition, or the UFO issue.

> *As was said in the Introduction, I realized I had an agreement to do a book, but felt unworthy and not up to it. Turns out, They wrote Book 1 using my years of notes plus Their insights and I facilitated getting it to print.*

If the information and suggestions resonate with you, great, go for it. If there are parts you are not sure of, put them on the shelf for later, or you can always ASK for guidance and clarity.

Back to the issue raised by the C's – the mechanics of timelines that Loop.

## Timeloops

> **It has been said that Man is contained in an HVR Sphere which is quarantined (since AD 900) AND now we learn that this same Earth WAS in a timeloop (AD 1943-1983) over which Man had no control. How lovely. More reasons to get out of here.**

While in the Loop, Man was being manipulated by 4D STS beings who sought to stabilize and empower the Loop by entraining as many ensouled humans into as low of an energy/awareness state as they could. By entraining or capturing more souls onto our TL1, even today they entertain the vain hope that they can sustain some future version of what they conceive as true STS vectoring. [25] The reason they hope in vain, is that other advanced beings (time travelers and/or Interdimensionals) are engaged in re-engineering the STS efforts to repeatedly hijack our timeline. [26] This part is not speculation. They also assist us by birthing into the Earth realm and offsetting the STS agenda.

Another researcher was told the same thing as he experienced very positive hyperdimensional communications with Higher Beings back when the timeloop was an issue:

> … the five-sense 'world' that we daily experience is a 'time loop' that goes around and around basically **repeating the same sequence** in theme, if not detail. What we call the 'future' eventually becomes the 'past' and spins around to repeat the 'present' over and over… **The same experiences keep repeating**. [27] [emphasis added]

According to the same researcher,

> Only that which was free of conditioned belief was able to transcend the vibratory illusions of the Matrix and become consciously one with the Infinite. **Belief was the prison** and other levels of the Matrix were different levels of illusion. This meant that **the overwhelming majority of information 'channeled' through psychics in the Time Loop was from consciousness still caught in the Matrix....** [28] [emphasis added]

And Icke goes on to say that

> ...because consciousness in the Matrix was caught in a cycle of moving in and moving out of the Time Loop through 'reincarnation' they were not only conditioned by the beliefs of one physical lifetime. **They were conditioned by endless experiences in the Time Loop** and between these 'physical' excursions they were in another form of illusory state. So **they were already conditioned even as they returned** to the Time Loop reality for still more conditioning. This was why humanity dropped into the conditioned, servile state so easily. They had been there many times before. [29] [emphasis added]

And Icke's Loop today is actually called **Recycled**, not Reincarnation. (Icke was not referring to the 1943-1983 Loop.) He goes on to state that he was also shown, as was I, that Karma and Reincarnation are controlling constructs of the HVR Sphere – you go back if you didn't make progress. [30] (This was examined in VEG Ch 15, 'Life is a Film' section.)

**Chart 5: Timeloop Control**

The following Chart 5 is an attempt to diagram timelines and the former timeloop problem.

X – Y – Z – X is the timeloop created by the mis-guided Philadelphia Experiment in 1943 that went awry. It looped up to 1983 initially and through unsuccessful human attempts to cancel the Loop, it allegedly reinforced the Loop and may have extended it – for an unknown length of time. When this happened it was a timeline split at point X, generating the X – Y leg of the Loop. Our current position at Y will eventually complete the Loop at Z (some future point in time).

The Y to A leg is the potential and hoped-for exit from the Loop which would then bifurcate to B and C at some point. (Major events on the planet automatically and normally create a timeline split.)

The Z leg is doomed eventually for dissolution in the future... either when the Timelords cancel the 'lesson' and remove the Loop, or when souls resonate with enough negativity (and no new souls are entering the Loop), such that any Loop dissolves through entropy (i.e., negative emphasis produces entropy). Hence the timeloop was a trap which the Timelords knew existed, but wanted us to experience the folly of the 1943 STS actions before removing it. Due to their intervention (at point X, stopping each iteration from generating an additional Loop), it was merely one aspect of our multi-selves that was trapped in the one Loop and whereas each soul has 'copies' of itself in other realms (Chapter 10), it is not a scenario where we are "doomed for eternity." At the least, whatever happens in this Era will be reset when the next Era is started.

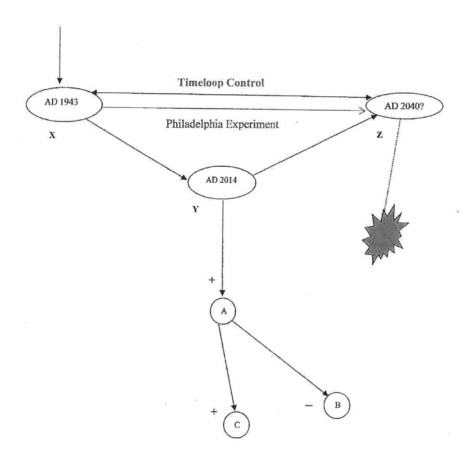

**Chart 5**

Note that a timeloop control must of necessity always create an <u>alternate</u> timeline from the one that was last created <u>as you come through the loop again</u>. [31]   In short, it would create TL1a, then TL1b, then TL1c….in a replicated  X – Y – Z –  X Loop. The Timelords stepped in and stopped this from repeatedly happening, but the original Loop may still be there and cannot be removed without damaging the original timeline – this is an instance of **'entanglement'** in 3D as the Physicists have pointed out in VEG Chapter 8.  So this means that there were replicated aspects of the souls originally in TL1 just prior to 1943 when the Experiment went awry, and those soul aspects were 'trapped' there unless they could ascend out… and beat the 4D STS entities' Game of getting additional souls to incarnate into the timeline to reinforce it…   Man is currently in the Y to A leg of the chart.

**Time Traveler Hypothesis**

To emphasize, and for what it is worth as **catalyst to consider**, there may be good time travelers coming back trying to block the PTB from 'stacking the timeline' with negative souls… by incarnating into the original timeline Loop and destroying it through entropy.  So far, there are only 3 ways to exit a timeloop – (1) if and when the Timelords remove the Loop, or (2) by shifting out through resonance to an alternate timeline, even one in 4D, or (3) becoming an **Earth Graduate**.

Note that with the Earth being a 3D HVR construct in 4D, and in Quarantine, it is unlikely that many future beings could come back to <u>directly</u> manipulate what is a "protected" Sphere. And yet, **it is possible to sustain a hijack of souls by sustaining the negative energy of the current TL** – if the existing souls can be <u>influenced</u> to think, live and act negatively – as if such orientation were their own idea – and if more STS souls can be born into the current Earth. Hence, the attempts to entrain Man into his lower 3 chakras with **sex and violence** are surefire techniques to reinforce the negative TL.

Note also that timelines usually split into two paths, but may involve three or more – depending on what scalar coherent energies are present. For convenience, the splits, or bifurcations, are marked as 'positive' and 'negative' although they just represent different aspects of preferred outcomes to the inhabitants of the timelines – i.e., best-case scenario and worst-case scenario. Such are examined below…

> The time traveler issue will be resumed in a later section , 'Negative Future Vector.' But first let's complete the overview of TL basics…

## Three Global Futures

Theoretically speaking of timelines in general, not reflecting any Loop mechanics, suppose that the current timeline, TL1, splits into 3 timelines, suggesting that there are basically three different, aggregate types of people on the planet, and each group has enough strength to cause the timeline to split into 3 scenarios: [32]

## Worst Case A: TL1

In this scenario, the people attracted to this timeline expect the worst, are pessimistic, love to control others and live by the "eye for an eye" system. Cynics. They half expect a cosmic disaster: an asteroid hits Earth, or a solar flare 'burns' Earth, or there is a pole shift. In this timeline, the world may experience World War III creating much nuclear disaster and disease, Man has to live underground to survive, and the Earth produces volcanoes, earthquakes, floods, and there may be an ET attack. Most people die.

## Mediocre Case B: TL2

In this scenario, the people attracted to this timeline, are not that positive, often being fatalistic, but not really negative either. Skeptics. They express some compassion, desire to help, but often wind up sitting on the fence, worried but not directly creating problems. They tend to be pleasure/pain motivated, and still have a desire to control if only to protect themselves. World War III does not happen, but there are a lot of little brushfires and contained wars. Civilization keeps going in a mediocre way, and there are some Earth changes, and the ETs avoid direct contact. A lot die but Man carries on.

## Best Case C: TL3

In this scenario, the people attracted to this timeline are optimistic, proactive, treat each other with respect, quickly resolve differences, and they are responsible: they realize that the Earth is all there is to live on and they'd better take care of it. Negative potentials are recognized and transformed and people develop more interest in spiritual issues. Economics, politics and religion are redesigned for the benefit of mankind. Man begins to move into a millennium of peace, love and joy while the Earth is ecologically healed. Benevolent ETs make contact and work with Man who has waked up and grown up and can take his place in the Galactic Federation.

Needless to say, we are currently living in mediocre Case B, largely due to the interference from the "2nd Seed", the OPs, the PTB and 4D STS entities who have no compassion, no conscience, no spiritual interests and no goals other than self satisfaction, power, money and survival. If Earth were not being manipulated, world peace could be achieved within 6 months or less.

## Choice of Timeline

How does one 'choose' to go to the right timeline, the timeline of choice, when a split happens? If a soul begins to resonate enough outside the locked resonant system, then

> …it begins to sympathetically vibrate with and entrain into adjacent or distal systems that operate at a similar or mutual entraining frequency and phase. **Thus you are drawn to the attractor that fits your resonance** and hyper-phase. You automatically, individually conjugate into the collective volitional system that most closely pattern matches your conscious growth focus. [33] [emphasis added]

In other words, "birds of a feather flock together." Your PFV (Personal Frequency Vibration) synchs up **automatically** with the energy of the timeline most like your energy and when the split happens, you are automatically 'locked' into the timeline appropriate for you… which may not be the same one as your spouse, or the rest of your <u>ensouled</u> family! Yet they can be there, too – as **Placeholder** OPs. If so, you will probably notice a slight change in behavior. (See VEG, Ch 5.)

> Catching the better ride cannot be faked. The ride you take is based on what you in co-creation with your higher soul-self feels you need to authentically grow the fastest. [34]

Specifically, there are **3 sets of personal values** that typify each of the 3 timelines, or Cases above, and possession of a majority in one of the three sets constitutes a 'ticket' to that timeline:

## Worst Case A: Attractors

> Pain, alienation, pessimism, fear, superiority, cynicism, judging, hatred, hurtful, punishing, self-destructive, and punishing/vengeful. Life-or-death-struggle. Warrior mentality. [35]

## Mediocre Case B: Attractors

> Apathy, blame, indifference, control, uncaring, greed, unfeeling, isolation, unthinking, passively reactive, and narrow-minded. Fence-sitter mentality . Me-vs-you. [36]

## Best Case C: Attractors

> Love, joy, peace, patience, trust, forgiving, healing, beauty, caring, friendship, pro-active service, giving, optimistic, appreciate diversity, and spiritual growth work. All-is-one. Adventurer mentality. [37]

# Temporal Discontinuity

So the timeline splits, is there something that acts as an outside force to trigger the split? Yes, and it is what Laura referred to above – called a temporal discontinuity, or a **resonance wave**. And when it hits, it is too late to try and become a better person.

> The implication of the coming discontinuity wave of standing resonance and each human soul agency's participation in it, is that depending how you energetically hold the wholeness of who you are and the world at large, selects which global bifurcation path you will be thrown into when the discontinuities hit…
>
> Make no mistake, the presence of self, love, caring, empathy and forgiveness are the touchstones that **autoselect** a human being into the more optimal reality vector…
>
> Willingness to be motivated to grow your soul by love and joy, is a soul phase-locking into the future Earth vector that supports and substantiates this.
>
> Willingness to only be motivated by fear and pain, places a soul into the reality that corroborates this *modus operandi* for growth. From the higher soul's point of view, either path will eventually get the soul growth job done. [38] [emphasis added]

You can learn through peace and joy, or you can take the hard route. Again, choice.

It is in the natural order of things for timelines to split; it is in support of spiritual evolution – some souls are ready for more, and others like things as they are. And it is not in Somebody's overall Plan to hold the adventurers back until the sheep get ready to move on. And so it would seem that there are three basic types of souls:

| | |
|---|---|
| Those who make things happen, | Case C |
| Those to whom things happen, | Case A |
| and Those who wonder what happened. | Case B |

They each resonate with their own timeline where they'll feel comfortable, and the adventurers don't have to live like sheep (unless their Script calls for it).

Man on timelines (not in a Loop) is at the crossroads of a unique experience which will separate the sheep from the goats. But why is it happening?

> Why is this discontinuity, this tsunami event, this space-time wave current convergence happening? What makes Earth so special? Somehow, Earth is a key player in how and whether a whole host of very positive universal evolving timelines, or very negative universally infesting realities timelines develop in the future and propagate their influence downline...We are somehow the unwitting kingpins, <u>not pawns</u>, in a cosmic evolution **experiment**... The future Earth timeline **failures** are the ones sending the most time travelers back to this timing [pre-1943] to try and effect a timeline course change. [39]     [emphasis added]

Something can happen downline following a Split that may result in several distinct different Earth dimensional splitoffs, and some of those will be failures and some will be successes, as far as spiritual evolution goes. So what normally happens in a Split is watched closely by Higher Beings, Interdimensionals and by any alleged time travelers affected by a Split.

And some of those travelers have been called Men In Black (MIB).

**Men In Black**

Credit: misteroufo.blogspot.com

It is appropriate to suggest that there are 3 types or sources of MIB involved in the 'management' of our current timeline:

1. **Inner Earth:** indigenous humanoids: remnants of older civilizations that went underground and work **to keep their existence quiet**. (Anunnaki Dissidents)

2. **Time Traveling MIBs:** back from the TL1 future to negatively control/influence Man in his volitional potentials. (To sustain the timeline)

3. **Interdimensionals:** these beings may be the Djinn spoken of in VEG and in Chapter 7, this book. They inhabit the Astral and do not like Man. They may also be the 4D STS. Both seek to keep Man ignorant and subservient. (See Chapter 7.)

Men in Black focus on suppressing the knowledge of ET and extra-dimensional (ED) contact that would hinder the volitional energy that could be harvested for reinforcing the energy and power level of **their** future eventuality. [40] [emphasis added]

What that means is Man was not to find out what was really going on so that he would not know he had a choice about where he could go during any bifurcation, or that he could ascend out of a timeline. There are allegedly other groups from the future that <u>are</u> seeing to it that people have the option to wake up, and that others raise their PFV without knowing why it's important – in either event, blocking the attempted shanghai (containment) of millions of souls onto a less desirable TL.

## Alleged Timeline Wars

Some might say that we are in a war between alternate universes. It is not just timewars, or timeline wars, but more acutely, it is a volitional allegiance war, with conquered populaces enslaved into negative singularity futures…

There are some invasion forces from the future attempting to reinforce their own quantum energy, power and influence into the past, present and eventually other alternate timeline dimensionalities. The men-in-black are merely **the temporal street muscle** of one particularly strong major negative alternate timeline…

The men-in-black are also interested in preventing current day development of free energy, time travel, psychic powers, contact with enemy ET or extra-dimensional entities. These things all represent a threat to their negative line reinforcement activities. [41] [emphasis added]

Of course, their clandestine activities are also being stealthily blocked by more benevolent entities – some of whom have the Earth in Quarantine since AD 900, as was mentioned in VEG Chapter 12. Man has been and is being protected as much as possible – just short of abrogating the freewill of those who seek to enslave us. One of the first steps was to move the Earth into an HVR Sphere, as others have also noted. Then the Quarantine was imposed – protecting from external intruders. Why is Man so protected? What is going on?

## Soul Harvest

As was said in earlier chapters, Man has something that others either want for themselves, or at least they seek to contain him so that he cannot connect with and develop his divine spark and activate his birthright. It's called a **soul**.

And yet, the negative STS forces cannot pull a 100% win for reasons dealing with
   (1) Earth's past contact with the right ETs,
   (2) true human spiritual awakening, and
   (3) the counterbalancing efforts from time travelers [and entities]
       from more positive [realms]. [42]

> We have something certain beings don't, and they want it, and for reasons other than what was intended. What we have is a particularly unique and powerful **soul substance** in the negative harvester's view, and if they don't take control of it, **they are terrified [of] what we will do with it against them**…
> They do not trust any volitional power that can exceed their own. They have a culture focused on control and suppression of diversity and individuality. That is a mistake, since we humans will eventually do the right thing for the universe, as is our ultimate destiny. [43]
> [emphasis added]

Man has a unique nature and a unique destiny, and we are here on Earth to work it out, despite the 3D Orion Group, and probably would have by now if we hadn't been interfered with so repeatedly. We will eventually overcome the PTB.

> Our purpose in coming together as creator fragments is to succeed in training ourselves enough about love, caring, and relationship to become more of who we are. The redemption is we, as descendants of angels, **progeny of the high forces of creation,** are ascending back to heaven in unity of diversity, as celebration of individuality in communion, not loss of individuality. We are holo- or fractal fragments of the creation's creator, [who] is wanting to create creations **with us** not for us…

Our first major task is to re-create the existing mother universe we find ourselves within with all its conundrums. Solve the unsolvable evolutionary problems. We learn to pick up the ball in our **training wheel practice universe** before we even want our own. And we want to learn very carefully, and so we use time to do it in a <u>serial</u> manner. That is the game…

Each creator fragment that is a human soul, ultimately seeks its origin and return to home. We are all, in a sense, **angels-in-training** learning to love and nurture our individual and co-creative mutual universes. Our job is to achieve spiritual evolutionary acceleration sufficient to help solve age old problems of spiritual evolutionary inertia in the universe. [44]    [emphasis added]

Elsewhere, the information is given that Man is ultimately to be a co-creator as his inheritance providing he can keep moving into more and more optimal timelines:

…as a reward, humans who accomplish this task, will be granted an initially uninhabited virgin future that can become even more optimal beyond comparison…

That final loop optimal future becomes the end-game singularity conduit path through which all souls of all alternate lines will eventually travel **to become qualified macro-creator agents.** [45] [emphasis added]

That is the promise to all **Earth Graduates**.

So, in short, they are saying that Man was created <u>a bit higher than the angels</u> with a purpose that will have the angels serving Man. An awesome potential that we would evolve to where many of us **ensouled humans**, *sans* bodies, would be running our own co-created universe one day, but that is the potential.

> **It is now self-evident why entities <u>without</u> souls would seek to keep ensouled Man from becoming all that he can be – including hijacking him onto a negative, suppressing timeline. That is what it has always been about, for centuries, and why the 4D STS and PTB persist in their STS agenda to contain/control ensouled Man.**

So, the 3D PTB goal is to entrain more souls into sex and violence to sustain the negative, martial-law and *Mad Max* scenario of TL1. The STS Gang cooperate by

(1) increasing the sex and violence, hoping people will opt for a more hedonistic lifestyle, and (2) the Anunnaki Dissident Remnant cooperate by sustaining their ELF grid thus increasing the discord, deception and disease in the present world. They also hope that people will buy some of today's false teachings (Chapters 3 and the end of Chapter 11) – which will automatically entrain people, sustaining a negative timeline future. Why is that important?

**When you die, your mindset determines where you can go.** [46]

Now let's return to an examination of how the Time Travelers may have anachronistically helped us…

## Negative Future Vector

The reason that negative **time travelers** may have come back is that their timeline is "petering out" – it began as a strong vector (negatively) and as souls no longer incarnated there, the supporting energy is not sufficient to sustain the timeline.

The following examines the possibility of time travelers…

### Time Traveler Caught on Camera?

Credit: http://www.bing.com/images/search?q=time+travelers

The photo above was actually extracted from a film shot in 1938 – and yet the woman is holding a **cellphone which didn't appear until 1980** (it appears to be one of the larger, original models)… see below.

Verifying the photo showed that it **was** taken in 1938, and she was holding something. Yet the alleged explanation of it is as difficult to believe as is the fact that she may be a time traveler. The purported explanation is that the factory behind her was experimenting with cordless phones [in 1938?] and she was testing it for the lab people inside the building… but nothing was ever done with the product, nor is there any documentation to that effect. So it is your call… [47]

Keep in mind that radio was a creation of the 1906 – 1920 period, and Walkie-Talkies (radio) emerged in 1938-1940. But the woman in the 1938 picture is not holding a **Walkie-Talkie** shown left:

(credit: http://en.wikipedia.org/wiki/Walkie_talkie

Is this evidence that BlackOps was at work and we had no clue how advanced their phone science was?

And below are two of the first **cellphones**:
(circa 1980's)

Credit:
www.photoree.com/photos/permalink...on Bing

Did we have help in creating the cellphone, or was it just an offshoot of the **Walkie-Talkie**?

Credit: http://www.bing.com/images

Certainly today's cellphones have much smaller circuitry and greater memory capacity – all from a micro-miniaturized technology that is so small it is amazing that Man has super-small machines to make them… or does he?

It has been suggested that our 'friends' underground who occasionally help Mankind, make the circuitry for us and 'transport' it to a locked room inside a secure facility said to make integrated circuitry. It is said they make it the size we are also capable of (so maybe we do that part), and then our friends use their technology to microminiaturize it...
Food for thought.

So it appears that humans, both STO and STS, from the future (with advanced technology) might have come back to live and walk among us. The potential STS time travelers are what concerns this chapter – they may have returned to **entrain and shanghai** <u>more</u> souls onto the current timeline, so that there will be a greater energy pool available to sustain their desired future TL1 timeline. The PTB have always thought that more is better, instead of realizing that they are doomed no matter how many souls they entrap... because souls will eventually opt to exit the timeline no matter how many the STS beings start with ...

And yet, look at the Earth. A similar entrainment has already been done here, which is what Book1 Chapter 12 was about. There is an **RCF/Matrix or ELF grid** around Earth which seeks to entrain Man's consciousness to the 10-16Hz level so he cannot connect with his Higher Self . Man is not as viciously trapped here as on the other more negative timelines from past Earth bifurcations, and yet Man <u>is</u> trapped (maybe 'contained' is a better word) here.

## Clarification Summary

At this point, to prevent any confusion on the reader's part, it is time to summarize and clarify what the current Earth status is. It truly is not good, so please bear with me; you need to know **how the ETs see us and what the problem is** so that you can make an informed choice... because you can rise above it. But first, I need to point out how we got here.

### Timeloops and Bifurcations

Earth in the current TL1 is in an HVR Sphere with a Control System and in Quarantine... it went into 1943 with that set of parameters (see VEG). What no one saw was the gross error that was made attempting to 'cloak' the destroyer USS Eldridge (DE-173) to make the it invisible (a war-time asset) by shifting its visibility into the upper part of the light spectrum – i.e., ultraviolet. Instead, with several UFOs watching, the experimenters did it wrong and the ship translated into 1983 and took a UFO with it. The remaining UFOs figured out where the ship went (based on the amount of energy used and the Earth's precession) and they communicated that to Dr. John von Neumann who lived long enough to work out what he thought the people in 1983 in Long Island could do to reverse the error...

but he died in 1957. Others picked up the issue, and of course the ship reappeared back in 1943 time, with many dead sailors aboard. That was called the **Philadelphia Experiment**.

Attempts were made to rectify the error in 1983 and instead allegedly amplified the timeloop between 1943 and 1983 (Chart 5), and it is said that their attempts also extended the Loop to an unknown point in the future. **The Loop does not now exist**; somewhere in the 90's it was removed by the **Timelords** who stepped in and removed it…after seeing to it that we understood the error (communicated via the ETs). It appears that those who engineered that Loop (and got us to do it) wanted us in that scenario – a trapped TL1 which would not be bifurcateable. The 4D STS would love it because it provides a permanent source of sheep to rule – remember, Lords need Serfs.

And that had to be part of the 1943 STS plan: **a timeloop precludes bifurcations**, and so the PTB wanted to lockdown the current TL1, in a permanent static state, and then run it for their antagonistic and power-hungry agenda. That is why, for those students of history, it is noted that the USA and the world took a turn for the worse in the 80's – it was then planned (by the Elite & Insiders) to do a gradual wake-up of people by producing more movies like *ET, Close Encounters of the Third Kind, Cocoon*, and some episodes of *Star Trek*, etc., to pro-actively introduce people to the concept of other beings with whom we could interact… and all that came to a halt after 1985. Now you know why.

What is left on TL1 now is Case B (mediocre) potentially moving to Case A (worst) scenario – unless we get help … and that has been the goal of the Greys (updating genetics to produce **hybrids** [Chapter 8] that cannot be manipulated by the STS lies), and there has been a *5ᵗʰ column* move by higher-minded souls birthing into the Earth TL1 realm – as Indigos. The **bad news** is that the STS PTB have shanghaied Earth in TL1, but the **good news** is that there are enough STO entities who are now infiltrating STS strongholds in government, military and education to at least obstruct and delay the PTB agenda.

> *Remember: The Solar Council has decreed that the Earth and its solar system will not fall to the STS Orion Group.*

As part of the STO agenda, currently on TV, there is an increase of the number of shows revealing the truth about Man and Earth – especially on H2 and SCI channels. In mid-July 2014, there was a 2 hour exposé [48] on SyFy channel of what NASA has been hiding about the Moon: pictures of structures, bases and artifacts with no airbrushing. NASA and the government know what the Moon is. And why we can't go back.

In addition, there are a number of books now coming out which seek to raise awareness of Man's true nature, the Earth problem, expose the disinformation and the solution to same. It is the function of <u>this book</u> to suggest that one can and must exit this TL by raising their consciousness to synch up with a better (outside) timeline while still living. VEG suggested gaining enough Light to make the switch when you die as an Earth Graduate.

**The only salvation is waking up**, knowing what this place is, who and what you are, and where <u>you</u> really want to go – and knowing you can make the choice and don't have to be recycled when you die. **Recycling** souls is the only way the PTB *et al* can sustain their lordship – by keeping the ignorant souls imprisoned here on Earth. Even a crummy play with a crummy cast has an audience…until the audience leaves and the Producer cancels the Show.

*Note: It is not necessary to be perfect to get out of here.*

## Timeline Development

In sum, **normal timelines** experience timeline bifurcation again and again in an effort to safely separate divergent energies and their agendas. Our timeline TL splits into TL1 and TL2 – where TL2 should be the timeline to carry the <u>proactive</u> side of Mankind into an alternate winning future. The remaining TL1 will be the loser – a progressively negative, entropic world that eventually dissolves… and that is permitted as a lesson for those souls who could not or world not choose better.

So it is not unimaginable that some High Tech STS beings from the TL1 future would attempt to work with our Anunnaki Dissident Remnant (and possibly the 4D STS) in an attempt to entrain more souls onto the current TL1, thus resulting in more souls to empower TL1…

If you knew, in a future timeline, that your timeline was about to dissolve (perhaps because there were not enough souls trapped there whose energy fed it), or your civilization was populated mostly by OPs (whose energy and purpose cannot sustain a timeline all by themselves), or perhaps because no one needed to experience any more of a negative world, and the original timeline that became TL1 as it played into the future lost energetic viability, you might attempt to do something about it, especially if you can manipulate time and space. So you hook up with 4D STS entities who can and do support your **agenda of containing soul-based Man**. In short, you'd go back to a more robust part of the original TL1 timeline and attempt to create or facilitate an alternate timeline/reality from a new bifurcation point (e.g., 1943). Your problem would be in getting enough souls to buy into the kind of STS world <u>you</u> want to run… because the timeline will be fed, or not fed, by the souls' collective energy.

**The Timeline of Choice**

Although a lot of space has been given to the aspect of timelines (or parallel worlds), one does not need to know <u>how</u> timelines work to get out of here – just that they exist and it is possible to make **a choice to align oneself with the kind of future one desires**. The preceding information is interesting and useful in that it specifies the need to align oneself with the most positive, <u>true teachings</u> and aspects of living that one can. Then when a timeline splits, one winds up automatically <u>initially</u> on an identical timeline – but whose future is usually better. It will be the TL with which one has most resonated. This is the **passive** way to get out of here, without dying.

> *Repeat: the* **active** *way was to acquire Light via Knowledge and 'Graduate' out of here when you die.*

First, what is necessary to see is that **one has a <u>choice</u> about where one goes at death, or during a timeline shift.** But if you don't know that, or how to exit the Earth School, you could be stuck in a timeline that may not be of your choice. The ETs see TL1 devolving into a rough experience and then dissolving.

Secondly, if one knows who they are at death and what is really going on, they can make an informed decision – to come back to Earth, or move forward. This is the **active** way to get out of here.

But in any event, if one is sufficiently oriented to positive, loving, peaceful, and joyous living that is incoherent with this current timeline, that is how, if the focus and higher PFV are sustained, one automatically attracts oneself to another appropriate timeline where they resonate with other like beings.


**4D or 5D?**

Man is currently in a 3D Construct which is already contained within the 4D realm and, as a matter of fact, this Earth is actually 3 ½ D+. Most souls are here to learn the lessons dealing with the 3$^{rd}$ charka (ego/power) while some deal with the 4$^{th}$ charka (compassion/love). Chakras are covered more in Chapters 11-13.

Note that three dimensions deal with related chakral issues:

$$3D – ego/power \quad (solar\ plexus)\ chakra\ \#3$$
$$4D – compassion/love \quad (heart) \quad chakra\ \#4$$
$$5D – truth/knowledge \quad (throat) \quad chakra\ \#5$$

Souls in the Earth HVR Sphere who have only learned to control the ego, and don't exhibit much compassion, would return to the 4D realm. Souls in the Earth HVR Sphere who have mastered the ego and learned compassion can advance to the 5D realm. **The three realms do not look any different from each other** and one is not 'better' or 'higher' than the other, but their energies and focus <u>are</u> different.

> When the lessons of ego, compassion, and knowledge have been assimilated, the soul moves into **6D** and learns to **integrate** them.

## Humanity's Future

Knowing something about timelines now, and how they are formed, dissolve and what attracts souls to one timeline and not another, what kind of a future is most in store for the current Earth – if we can't get out of here? (Remember VEG, Ch 14 and the problems and issues facing mankind.)

> This reality vector has already had a number [of] prior **singularity splitoffs** occur over the last 60 years, with many in the last decade. Already, in spite of ourselves we have enough going right that we are on the reality timeline vector that doesn't suffer "God's wrath," but as surely and lethally, we can suffer our own wrath towards one another.

> Predicted cosmic destructions include massive earthquakes, vulcanism, covert or overt ET invasions, polar shifts, photon belts, Revelations-style God's wrath wrought, civilization stopping cataclysms, 2012 calendar endtime zero-point, cometary or asteroid impacts…

> Given current probabilities, **these are all predictions which will NOT happen** and all of which are unwitting, psychological means to keep humanity helpless and disempowered, needed only as spectators.

> These decoys keep our eyes off the only real ball in the air – **humanity's failure of humanity** and the living Earth…. [both] desperately need to be solved, or the human species will largely self-destruct on a planetary-wide scale over the first twenty years of the third millennium. [49] [emphasis added]

### We Are Being Watched

Man can make it <u>and some will</u> – it just depends on how soon he is willing to wake up and join other intelligent and benevolent galactic species who have been watching him. There are many souls on Earth today who, thanks to *Star Trek*, *ET*, *Cocoon*,

*Close Encounters of the Third Kind* and other movies, are ready to step forward into a future of brotherhood and exploration with other entities "out there" that they <u>know</u> exist… **A huge Multiverse like ours cannot be empty and it is time to think about our place in the cosmos**. And yet the PTB insist on keeping Man ignorant of who he is, where he really is and squabbling amongst his brothers and sisters as if no one else were watching… as if we were all alone… as if the planet were flat…. As if power were the only game in town.

**The PTB and Dissidents don't acknowledge it but they are here to learn, too. They think they are gods to the rest of us. Yet, in their ignorance and resistance, they are also inmates, and it so far looks like the inmates are running the show.**

But this is not our planet and we're not here alone. Man is not the top of the foodchain, and he doesn't really belong here. But he cannot be released until he grows up, **respects** himself, **respects** his brothers and sisters, and then **respects** the planet. Only then can he **respect** other lifeforms… who are waiting… for him to be released. Enlightened, proactive souls cannot stay here.

## Good News

The Timelords <u>can</u> release a soul from our TL who is ready for Graduation – from the HVR Sphere <u>and</u> from any Loop. (Timelords are a subgroup specialty within the Higher Beings' hierarchy. See VEG, Chapter 7.)

But the choice was to be either an Earth Graduate or entrain oneself to a better Timeline… the latter also referred to as a Shift to a better Earth. So VEG encouraged people to get it together (and after reading VEG, you would know enough to **choose** to be an Earth Graduate ) – that is why it was written. On the other hand, if one has enough insight and Light already, then it is possible via **intent, visualization, and will** to choose to coherently entrain oneself to the better Earth TL (it already exists).

If you are reading this book, or have read VEG, you are <u>not</u> part of the 80% who will not make it. They cannot be helped; they can't be told anything… they just don't get it. 80% of the people, bless their hearts, are genetically impaired (due to EMF and drugs) and thus are mentally and spiritually impaired. Many of them look normal, dress and walk/talk OK, but they just have a polished act that crumbles when confronted with something outside their normal everyday world… and that time is coming.

## Case in Point

The following is a hard part of the book to write. I avoided it in VEG.

I was shopping again in a well-known, name-brand supermarket two days ago in an nice, average middle-class section of town and was struck by all the dense, lost, people who are just barely making it through this world. I had to stop and get ahold of myself because it was obvious I was being "shown something" which is what They sometimes do. I saw many overweight people, stringy hair, dirty clothes, tattoos, rings piercing many different parts of peoples' bodies, poorly-behaved children demanding their way, and background music that was some sort of unintelligible rap… I could not make out what it said due to the music drowning out the words (maybe just as well…). I turned a corner with my cart, and was confronted by a woman taking up the whole aisle with her body and cart… I said excuse me and she turned around, squinted at me through glasses that not only didn't fit but were smudgy… I backed up and moved on. I headed for the dairy section…. but was confronted so many stockouts I couldn't find what I wanted… I knew I would have to try another store… So I moved on to another part of the store, looking for the crackers section… and I encountered two stockboys <u>throwing</u> boxes of cookies and crackers down the aisle instead of sliding or walking them to where they would open and shelve them… I understood why I get broken cookies/crackers (at any store)….

In another part of the store, I encountered a little old lady (maybe 55-60 years old) all bent over with "dowager's hump" – her back was so bent over she could not stand up straight. I almost cry when I see that because it could have been prevented -- but no one told her years ago to get more calcium in her diet (Chapter 4), and I suspect her doctor didn't tell her either… and the man with her (about 60 years old) was carrying a bottle of oxygen with a tube up his nose…

And lastly I went to check out, and encountered two women trying to fix an issue with a self-checkout station – the unit was unhappy that the customer had filled one bag and moved it to begin placing items in the second bag, but its pimple-faced 25 year old programmers had never considered that and didn't program for it, and the machine locked up. (They had to turn it off and move the customer to a manned-checkout station…) I checked out and stopped to get a Frappuccino.

In the coffebreak corner, CNN on a TV was displaying images of Man's inhumanity to Man: Arabs bombing Israelis, a Malaysian passenger jet shot down, killing everyone onboard, and ISIS rampaging through the Iraqi-Syria area… This goes on and on because the perpetrators don't care if intelligent, benevolent ETs see all this craziness… so ETs just sustain the Quarantine. And the Greys stealthily rewire Man's genetics to hopefully get rid of the defective genes on Earth.

Later that night I was treated to more CNN at home – the growing Dead Zone in the Gulf of Mexico, the huge Pacific Trash Pile (the size of Texas) in the Pacific Ocean, the Fukushima radiation spreading over the Pacific Ocean (forgot about that didn't we?), and lastly the Ebola epidemic in Africa, also coming to a town near you (as Africans flee their country). Mosquitoes with a new neural strain of West Nile Virus have appeared in the USA – understandable since viruses mutate. The problems just don't stop. Earth's environment is dying, and viruses are spreading, folks. It won't be long before the Higher Beings call a halt to it (2016-18?) – after enough souls have gotten the message: **respect the Earth and each other, or die**.

People, this is pathetic. The highest form of life (supposedly) on the planet, and it is basically dysfunctional, lazy or sick. Don't misunderstand me, I really feel for these people – they don't know what they are, what their potential is (some of them had auras, so they had souls), and they just drift or stumble through life. It is too much for some of them. And our society doesn't care if they live on the street – rich folks say, "Well, it's their fault!" and then they get back in their BMW and drive to their $500,000 home. Their insensitivity will come back to them… belittling someone's Karmic condition only hurts the attacker.

And, our public education system is 3$^{rd}$ rate and teaching to the lowest level of the class (I know because I taught school for 4 years), and our media keeps on pumping out TV shows that sell: sex and violence. Hot video games: more violence.

Do you still wonder why humans are in Quarantine?

## Bad News

According to another source,

> …the ETs are here because **the human race is in danger of extinction** [and may be replaced <u>when</u> the Greys are successful].
> …the ETs have the technology to save the human race and that it is their inclination to help us because they view us as a part of them… However, if the ETs were to repair the Earth without making any changes in our behavior, we would simply "undo all the good they had done…We might survive long enough to find an even grander way to destroy ourselves, one that could **harm worlds other than our own**. These beings feel that, by saving the human race, they would be condemning themselves to a violent confrontation with us in the future." [50] [emphasis added]

This is not a positive comment on the human race, and is echoed by similar sentiments in the United Nations. The same source continued,

> "These beings said the human race, <u>as it now exists</u> and as it has existed, **cannot be saved**. If it were, all the problems they could foresee happening when we eventually meet them in space would be inevitable, assuming we didn't destroy ourselves first." Therefore

another part of their plan is to attempt to change us in more subtle ways by means of **genetic manipulation** and by attempting to reawaken our spiritual values and beliefs. [51]     [emphasis added]

*And Book 1 suggested that that is the function of the **bio-cybernetic Greys** and their abductions. Note: there an **extra 223 genes** in Man that they do not find in other lifeforms on Earth and no one knows yet what they do.  See Chapter 8.*

**And the majority of Man being petty, violent and/or ignorant does not inspire any of the benevolent ETs to petition for our release from the Quarantine. Since this version of Man cannot get it together, wake up, and stop operating from the lower 3 chakras (survival, sex/power, and ego), much of this version of Man is being replaced – just as Neanderthal was.** (Hint: the Greys are very busy. See Chapter 8.)

As was said earlier, **Man's <u>devolving</u> DNA** is one of his biggest problems, and the shadowy power group that has been called the PTB/Dissidents/4D STS contribute to the dilemma by manipulating an already dumbed-down populace. This is another reason why **much of the existing version of Man cannot be saved**, any more than Neanderthal could be saved.  Neither Homo *sapiens* nor Neanderthal were smart enough to know that they were being manipulated, rise above their inherited genetics, and that is why, as was revealed, there have been a number of "Wipes and Reboots" or Eras in which Man started over. But it hasn't been enough.

> **In this sense, the Georgia Guidestones may be prophetic instead of prescriptive.  Many of the people in that supermarket cannot and will not wake up, nor do they have the 'horsepower' between the ears to see and learn. They cannot figure out what is wrong – much less fix it. The Earth has been quarantined because it will be the home of this unfortunate (80%) level of humanity… and they will be allowed to live out their lives while the 'replacements' are birthing onto the planet.**
>
> **Less than 10% of Man will move forward.  Sad.**

Ironically, the Elite and the Remnant know the true status of much of mankind; **they know that not much can be done now** and they will have to handle the coming (potential) breakdown and forced management of planetary dysfunctional societies.  They are preparing for it: cameras, detention camps, GPS tracking and the RFID chips (combined in 'smart' credit cards)... the PTB mistakenly think it is to benefit their agenda.

## Transformation and Timelines

The ideal issue is that Man be living on a timeline that is free of 4D STS/PTB control and is free to live out his LifeScript (Chapter 7). To the extent that the timeline is negatively charged, Man will experience less than optimal conditions for soul growth – the PTB will have to make the Sheeple's choices for them, and that is why the Earth Graduates (those who can) need to get out of here.

When a TL is negatively charged, there is an abundance of dysfunctional and rebellious souls that incarnate here—the Higher Beings see it as an opportunity briefly permitted to give special lessons to **wayward souls** and it in effect turns Earth into a **Rehab Facility** (our current status, by the way). Earth is thus employed to put the defective or dysfunctional souls in a context of their equals… viz., "meeting themselves in spades." This includes some of the PTB.

It will not be allowed to continue for long, because scenarios like *Soylent Green* and *Mad Max* are counter-productive in the long run…they create damaged souls. However, it can be very instructive for a limited time.

So a Script or Drama that starts to go awry doesn't go on forever, and the Higher Beings and Beings of Light do watch and try to keep the Earth School functional, so that souls can learn from whatever situation they find themselves in…. But when the School becomes a Rehab planet, it means the Greater Script has failed for that Era and it needs to be reset. We are dangerously close to confronting that outcome. Sorry, but that is the actual state of things.

## Point of Choice

The foregoing was not intended to bum anybody out; I didn't want to write it. But you need to know why you need to get out of here and why you need to gain as much Light (Truth & Knowledge) as possible. Ensouled people need to get out of here, and they have an important choice to make: **graduate or ascend**. Sitting on the fence will not work – the fence is about to go up in flames, and you can't make an intelligent decision when everything is going to hell around you. NOW is the time to realize that Earth is not our home and souls have been lulled into a false sense of security – thinking that we are on our way to a bright future on this timeline. No, we're not. That is the warning that I was asked to emphasize in writing this book.

# Chapter 3: Spirituality vs. Religion

Since this book is about discovering the truth about Man and Earth, and waking up so that we can either Graduate or Ascend, it is very relevant to examine whether our belief system helps or hinders us in doing that. The Christians believe they have but one lifetime and then they go to Heaven... what if they have been deceived? The New Agers believe that they are in charge of their lives and that they can develop their godhood ... what if they have been deceived? The atheists believe there is no God and that Man is just 'molecules of emotion' and neurotransmitters – no God, no future, no eternal soul... dust to dust. How sad.

This book suggests that there is another way to look at life, God, Man and the Earth and when that information comes into focus, it will be obvious where we are, what we are, and what we need to do. And the PTB hope you don't wake up because they love being Lords and need you as ignorant Serfs. If they can keep you ignorant, they can tell you what to believe... Aren't they experts in history, religion, genetics, science and pharmaceuticals and medicine? They wouldn't have a hidden agenda now would they? After all, this is America where the government agencies are telling you they are here to protect and guide you. Your belief in the 'experts', in turn, conditions you to further go along with their (hard-to-believe-its-false) deception and your freewill is violated – but you don't know it.

Don't expect them to accept this book or ignore it – they will tell you it is nonsense – haven't you heard for most of your life that Earth is all there is, we are all alone, and there is no reincarnation, no soul, and you can relax, eat your burrito and junk food, and watch the TV programming (and it **is** 'programming' you – remember subliminal advertising in the 60's?). If you think you're already enlightened, you turn instead to the News channel of your choice (spin or less spin?) and tell yourself that you trust the Lame Stream Media. People, it is all following an agenda of the PTB – Did you know that no show on Aliens or UFOs can be created and put on TV without the Pentagon's Department of Public Affairs reviewing it first?

> *That is why many episodes of Ancient Aliens (H2 Channel) start off with a fascinating thesis and work it right to the point of actually telling you something, and then they either : Ask if the proposition could be true, or they segue off at a 90° angle to something else. Teasing.*

The point is that nowadays, neither standard Religion nor New Thought churches are really helping people to wake up. **They are all playing safe**. You may be better off with New Thought, at least you are moving in the right direction, and will hear more useful truth than in a standard church – and all that was reviewed in VEG Chapters 1 and 11.

Here is the **big revelation about New Thought churches**:  They can only go so far --- up to the point where they think their congregation will balk at accepting more than WXY and so they never hear about Z because it stretches their minds and causes them to grow – too much.  And if the minister doesn't tell them what they want to hear, or s/he tells them too much, the sheep split for another church. Humans have a problem with hearing things that are outside their 'known' comfortable world – it is called **cognitive dissonance** and when they hear something that conflicts with <u>what they think they already know</u>, and may even sound threatening, their sub-conscious jumps in, denies what was heard (or read), and keeps the human surviving by letting him go on as if the info were wrong and the human thus ignores it.

The other very human reaction is: If I hear something I don't understand, or have never heard before, or I can't relate it to what I think I already know, I can't accept it, and I won't believe it and thus <u>it is automatically wrong</u>.

Now you know why humans make so little progress.

Some humans DO think for themselves, and over time they discover that something is missing in Christianity, for example – they feel like there should be more, and they aren't getting 'fed.'  This is due to the limited source of preaching material: How many ways can you slice, dice and chop the positive message of the Bible?  So they move on to another Christian church, or some go search out the New Thought churches – which are also called spiritual centers.

Some of the New Thought churches began, like **Unity Church of Christianity**, by blending Christianity with true spirituality, a new way of thinking about what Jesus really taught… and it was uplifting and drew many Christians into the New Thought movement in the 1950s.  It was a good blend. (See Glossary.)

Sometimes there was a man like Dr. Ernest Holmes who had insights and revelations about the true nature of Man, the soul, Reincarnation, Karma, and how to use the information as a 'scientific', structured way in one's daily life… he called his new church **Religious Science**.  It was said that he was so advanced in his thinking and application of the Science of Mind principles that he could heal people and once walked through a wall.  (See Chapter 12.)

The problem nowadays with both New Thought and Church groups is that they too run out of their basic church principles to teach and await the next Self Help or Metaphysical book with new revelations. And some of the ministers in these churches, and their offshoots, begin teaching whatever sounds good, like it should work, it sounds positive and hey, let's go for it – such was the trip that *Conversations With God* took, *A Course in Miracles*, and *The Secret* – attract your good, think positive, and later… create your day, name it and claim it… and the insight that we're God.

> *Actually you **are** a spark from The Source, or One, but have not developed your divine potential, and 3D is not the place for it.*

## Scripts and Karma

Let's examine some of these New Age concepts. But before we do, let's do a brief review of what we all come into the Earth realm with – a **Script**. No one gets into the Earth experience without a plan, a Script. It is not fate and is not cast in concrete – just a list of the types of events, people and goals one hopes to accomplish, with testing points, points of choice, and points of exit (usually 2 potential ways to exit Earth).

Secondly, concurrent with the Script, it reflects at least in a few of its elements what you specifically as a soul need to work on – More patience? More compassion? OK, these will be tested, but be aware that if you failed to be patient or loving in a few past lifetimes, many "opportunities" will now come up to meet situations demanding patience, and you'll be faced with disagreeable people around you who need love.

Karma is not about you being knifed in this lifetime because you knifed someone else in a past lifetime. The dictum "An eye for an eye" is false… two wrongs don't make a right and it is too bad that the tit-for-tat teaching made it into the Old Testament of the Bible. It is wrong and serves only to further hostility and negativity on the planet.

Your Karma is what you need to work on – by **meeting yourself** in other people – you need to meet the **Shadow Side** of yourself that caused you to knife someone in a past lifetime and handle it now – not repeat the act. And nothing is gained by you being knifed in this lifetime. Thus the Script will be orchestrated (via Beings of Light [aka Angels but they don't have wings], and Neggs – both explained in the Glossary and VEG). Events, people and circumstances will be initiated for you, if you don't undertake them yourself, to present you with **experiences that reveal who you are**, how you react, and where you fall short. Failures are an opportunity to wake up, correct and move forward.

All of that to say that **your Script rules**… if it doesn't prohibit something, go for it. Since you don't know consciously after birth what is in your Script, you do whatever you can while here – and if the Script prohibits it (for reasons of 'teaching' you something through denial of what you want), you will not be able to get it, do it, or have it… That doesn't mean you are a bad person, or that God hates you, it means there is a <u>reason</u> you can't get what you want and it has to do with soul growth.

## Personal Case in Point

I really abused other people in the last lifetime who were bad for the State and were corrupt, lying, cheaters and I had them removed from the Parliament and public office. I was psychic and knew what I was doing was solely for the good of my country, I had the approval of the Crown, and I truly had no malice toward these bad guys. I denied them jobs, forced them to leave the city, and basically was helping the King and Queen to clean up the government. How could that be bad? These louts probably had it coming to them anyway, and I was just improving society for everyone.

What I didn't know was that Karma is a very exacting Law and it doesn't care or see WHY you are doing something – I hurt those people, denied them jobs, money and ultimately health. And I was extremely healthy in that lifetime, personally wealthy, and had married the village beauty where I was born.

So I was born into a wealthy family this lifetime and (1) I could never get my hands on any of my inheritances [there were two], (2) I inhabited a frail body always coming down with pneumonia, (3) I lost job after job because they went out of business, laid off, or were bought out, (4) I had to move when I could not pay the rent (because I lost too many jobs), and (5) all my relationships went nowhere in this lifetime.

You could call that **payback** – the gods wanted me to see what it felt like to be on the receiving end of what I did to/for others. (It didn't stop until age 54 by the way – which coincidentally was my age at death in the last lifetime.) I could not get what I wanted, or if I did, it was taken from me by forces/events beyond my control. That has "Script" written all over it.

In a lighter vein, I used to say to people that when I died, I wanted a key message carved in my tombstone: "He couldn't get what he wanted, and if he did, it was taken from him." My wiser friends advised me to not die as I didn't have the money to buy a big enough tombstone to write all that!

Ok, let's look at 5 current day New Age teachings and see if there are any fallacies in light of the Script-Karma issue.

## 1. Attract Your Good

This says that through intention and positive thinking, you can **attract** what you want. That was the essence of The Secret. So far so good. Notice that you <u>cannot</u>

make it happen, but you can and should do those things that look like they will bring you what you want. This axiom is teaching persistence and patience.

**Intention, focus and visualization** are all productive in attracting your good. Put energy behind your intention and focus (if the Script doesn't prohibit it) and if you persist, it will come to you.

## 2. Create Your Day

This is the Attract Your Good on steroids – you can make it happen, the way you want it, when you want it – Wow, what a **god trip**! In case you wonder where this started, it was promoted by a psychologist in the *What The Bleep Do We Know* movie (2004 version) who had graduated from the Ramtha School of Enlightenment.

Not only is the Script in control, but humans at this 3D stage of development do not have the ability (which is 4D and above) to manipulate their environment, much less other people to get what they want.

**Caution 1**: you appear to have power.
If it appears that you can create what you want, or manipulate things, be aware that you aren't doing it… it is being done for you and there is a pricetag attached – see Caution 2 below. People who practice witchcraft fall into this very dangerous 'personal power' trap.  (See also Chapter 12 caution: 'Caveat #2'.)

## 3. Name It and Claim It

Ok, this one turns God into a **vending machine**.  Just say what you want, and expect the Universe to deliver it… because you believe …and these people stand on the Biblical phrase: "It is done unto you as you believe!"  So do it to me, already! To really help it along, you can say affirmations designed to put a lot of positive vibes out into the Universe, and we all know that what you put out comes back to you – Didn't Napoleon Hill also say that? Maybe if you release your 'inner giant,' you can make it happen…. Sure sells a lot of books and seminars.

Again, by all means go for what you want… you might get it. Remember that your Script rules, so if you don't get what you want, try again ,and if that fails you might want to consider that you are to learn something from the absence of what you think you want/need. Don't take any failure personally – although it is you that can't get it (right now) and that reflects something about you … but ultimately, you are an eternal soul and you are worthy of all things good – providing you are not working through a lesson that is designed to grow you by NOT having what you want.

> *Because I was denied the huge inheritances this lifetime, I had to learn to better manage money – which I did not learn in the past lifetime.*

81

**Your soul growth is more important than getting what you want.**

In sum, any teaching that says you can do whatever you want, get whatever you want, any time you want, and appears to lead you in developing your godhood is a scam in 3D. We are learning the lessons of humility, patience, compassion, and respect – 3D lessons. The next level in 4D teaches a higher set of lessons that the New Age teachers want to push now because it sounds good and many people want to hear that. And it continually augments their bank accounts, because their teaching doesn't work and you are led to suspect that you just need one more book, maybe one more seminar… then it will all come together!

**Caution 2:** taking help from entities who volunteer help.
Caution is advised as there is for example, a New Age motivational teacher who appears to be an OP, soulless, but who is so afraid that people will wake up and hang him that he lives on an island off the continental US, so that disgruntled followers cannot get to him. He was given his 'schtick' by an entity who showed up in his apartment one day when he was depressed and offered to help him… this was the Faust scenario and the depressed young man bought it – and they <u>have</u> made him rich and famous – but when he dies, they will come to collect, and they don't want his money. (See also Chapter 12: 'Caveat #2'.)

There are a lot of gameplayers out there in the Astral and they love to deceive humans and then shanghai them to another timeline when they die – because the human owes them. <u>This is not a joke</u>. Forewarned is forearmed.

**Knowledge protects**
**Ignorance enslaves**

## 4. Third Grade Guru: The Giant Within

To drive the control point home, and more specifically address the "giant within" (your Higher Self) issue, let's ask this…

Could you do whatever you wanted to in your 3<sup>rd</sup> Grade classroom? Could you just get up and sell marbles to your classmates and make a few bucks whenever you wanted to, because you felt like it, or because the 'giant' within you said to do it? (You'll have to get the teacher's permission – and that is like our Script here.)

*Better yet – Can you stand up in 3<sup>rd</sup> Grade and tell your teacher that you are becoming an advanced being, you can know everything and can do whatever you want to because there is a 'giant' within you? (She may tell you to sit down and shut up.)*

Earth is 3D and is like the 3$^{rd}$ Grade – I know. I fought hard to make something of myself anyway, but could not get free from the karmic constraints of my Script (Chapter 5). And as I said earlier, anything I did get was taken from me… I suspect the karmic payback would still have been there had Mom married Bob (Chapter 5) and had I met and married my soulmate, and Baldy confirmed that in 2008. BUT in marriage to my soulmate, supporting her purposes, caring for others as a doctor, plus whatever outreaches we might have had to others in the community, payback would have taken a different form because I was doing a life of service.   As it was, my soulmate must have vetoed meeting this lifetime and I had to learn compassion and caring for others via a different, harder path.

In my last 40 years, as me, trying to do what I wanted, even though I occasionally served, **my life did not work for me**. I learned compassion, patience and respect the hard way. Perhaps this is why I screamed and yelled for days at my birth in the hospital – I didn't want to be here because on some level I knew that Mom could make a "bad" decision and "sock it to me": marry Brian instead, put me on 17 years' Rx drugs, and cheat me out of a huge inheritance (so that in later life I would have nothing to offer my soulmate should we ever meet).  Examined in Chapters 5-6.

So Bob the doctor was the alternate, possible path that could have been chosen, **if** Mom had not been directed (by the gods?) to choose Brian. It had to be that way because on some level, my soulmate 'voted' to not meet. I know it wasn't my choice to not meet, and the gods will not go against a soul's wishes and attempts to learn through a multitude of options. So Mom did as she was directed because that is one of the functions of OPs – to execute Karma for the souls in their Dramas.  She had no choice, did not see alternatives, and cannot be blamed. I suspect the gods knew which way it would go…even though I fancied an **alternate Script**. And so I yelled for days in the hospital (according to my grandmother who was there).

**Red flags**

You then would argue, as I did, that Earth is a much more sophisticated 3$^{rd}$ Grade and we are expected to be more, do more and thus have more. I used to think that, too… How's it working for you so far?? Some of you can be/do/have an almost unlimited selection of things to manifest, but **some of us are more bound by our Script than other people are**, and that's what I'm explaining here.

How to know if you're bound or not?  Go for it and see what happens… Just do it with as much awareness, patience and self-respect as possible.  Consider your options, consider the results of your actions, and stay open to new possibilities… By all means, do go for what you want... but go easy on yourself. Failure may not be your fault. It may be due to your Script.

Fatalistic?

No, it means that some people try to face backward in the saddle instead of looking where the horse is pointed. Where is your Script pointed? It doesn't mean that you shouldn't go for what you want, in the direction that you want, **but** if you have done your best, knew what you were doing, and did the correct things, and were positive about it and still failed – that is a **red flag** designed to get your attention! Note the lesson. You may be wiser to stop trying to push the river… or put your boat into another river…

A red flag means:  rethink the issue.

> **Caveat:  If you compare yourself to another who has it all, or can get whatever he wants, watch out! It may be an OP. OPs do not have a Script and they can do pretty much whatever suits them… Be careful whom you admire and whose advice you follow.**
>
> **Remember:  it was the OPs who created the bumper sticker that says: "He who dies with the most toys wins!"**

Give thanks that you are here to learn and play – no one comes to the Earth without a Script (a plan of action) and a reason for being here. Earth is by 'invitation' only. Make the most of it.


## 5. Get Information from Higher Beings

This is the last of the common New Age misconceptions. Learn to do Tarot, or use a Quija Board (without protection), I-Ching tiles, or try channeling. What people don't know is that the lower Astral sees us (where the Discarnates reside) and if we open ourselves to communicate with them, they may control the Tarot cards or I-Ching tiles for us, and if people use the Quija Board (which really does work) again the Astral entities see what you are doing – and may decide to answer – You want to play a game, they'll oblige.

> The safe way to use a **Ouija Board** is to pray and ask for protection, White Light the group present, and ask that only entities of the Light answer, and only the truth. (Such was done when another group contacted the Cassiopaeans examined in Chapter 2). The same thing applies to **hypnotic regression** as a way to get answers.

This subject deserves a separate section as there are pros and cons.

## Channeled Information

In this category, there are several sources of channeled information and two of them were apologetically mentioned in Chapter 2 – Edgar Cayce and Nostradamus. It was determined that their prophecies may have been valid – on another timeline – even though the predictions did not come true <u>here</u>.  That bit of text will not be repeated here except to reveal some of the ways that the Astral entities that one contacts in channeling (and they are not necessarily Neggs – they may be Discarnates) love to amaze and confound. Let's look at a few of the better known ones…

### Edgar Cayce

Perhaps the all-time master of convoluted and archaic verbalization is the self-channeling that came through Cayce. Here is a sample – see if you can determine what the question was from the answer as quoted below:

> **A:**  Well that karma be understood, and how it is to be met. For in various thought – whether considered philosophy or religion or whether from the scientific manner of cause and effect – karma is all of these and more. Rather it may be likened unto a piece of food, whether fish or bread, taken into the system; it is assimilated by the organs of digestion and then those elements that are gathered from same are made into the forces that flow thru the body giving the strength and vitality to an animate object, or being, or body. So in experiences of a soul, in a body, in an experience in the earth. Its thoughts make for that upon which the soul feeds, as do the activities that are carried on from the thought of the period make for the ability of retaining or maintaining the active force or active principle of the thought **through** the experience….[52]  (reading 440-5)

There is much more, but it is a pain to type it – You probably thought the question was something like 'What is Karma?' or 'How does Karma operate?' Here was the question:

**Q:** Have I karma from any previous existence that should be overcome?

By the way, the original question is never answered: the woman wanted to know what <u>specific actions</u> did she commit that must be paid for in the current lifetime? Instead she got the above (and longer) dissertation.

Cayce's information also lost its effect with people when his predictions didn't come true. Atlantis did not rise in the Atlantic Ocean in the late 60's, and planet Arcturus was not discovered, and the pole shift did not happen in '58 to '98, along with numerous Earth changes in 1934, and there was no bad earthquake on the Pacific Coast of California in '36 … [53]   Not in this timeline anyway.

One of Cayce's profound goofs was often committed while giving someone a 'Reading' of their past lives -- they were usually from Atlantis, Egypt, or Meso-America, as a Mayan… all very romantic settings. The most glaring error he made was that **no one was ever from Sumeria** – where it all began… Thanks to Zechariah Sitchin, we now know about Sumeria and that mankind (after being first created in Africa), spread out in the Iraq-Iran area and became quite numerous… and no one ever had a life there, according to Cayce, in thousands of Readings….

If, as has been examined elsewhere, they were all OPs, they would not have had any souls and would not have reincarnated – I will grant Cayce that. However, with the second creation of Man, by Enki called the *Adapu*, in Sumeria Man did have a soul, but propagated to such an extent that Enlil was ready to wipe them all out.

Interestingly, Cayce often said that if a person didn't have an aura, they were dying and would be gone in 3 days. So **he did not know about OPs**. How perceptive and accurate is that for "America's Sleeping Prophet?" Or was he withholding…?

> And yet, Cayce was of incredible value for diagnosing peoples'
> illnesses and prescribing accurate cures.


## Seth / Jane Roberts

Another popular bit of channeled information came from Jane Roberts who began by experimenting with a Ouija Board, then began hearing voices, and finally progressed to where the entity just took over her body and began speaking through her. Of course the entity had her permission, she thought she was doing something noble, and the entity, later calling itself Seth, encouraged that. By the way, there were no prayers for protection and guidance, and the Light was never invoked into any session.  In the end, she died at age 55 of immune system complications – after Seth had satisfied himself with drink and smoking while in her body.  A tree is known by its fruit. Considering the lack of integrity of the entity Seth, it would be well to carefully examine his major teachings: [54]

1. There is a multitude of universes/dimensions
2. The human being is a multi-dimensional being
3. The inner self projects physical reality
4. The human being creates his/her own reality
5. Reincarnation is real but karma is misunderstood
6. There is a God, the "All That is"

7. There are no devils or demons except in one's imagination
8. Christ still exists and is a highly evolved entity and was not crucified
9. Paul/Saul will reincarnate and create a proper Christianity

And lastly, and very interesting:

10. Time and Space are "root assumptions" of this plane of existence; i.e., they are essentially illusory, and both the past and future coexist with the present in what Seth referred to as the "spacious present". **Therefore, a person's incarnations in different time periods are actually lived simultaneously, as opposed to consecutively.** Communication among the various past, present and future selves occurs during the dream state. Time appears to exist in a linear form, he says, because of limitations inherent in the physical human brain.

Said Seth, since all lives are lived simultaneously, **there is no karma** from past lives – yet if you <u>believe</u> you must pay, you will – and bind yourself to recycle on Earth. "All existences are simultaneous." [55] But he doesn't explain how I lived 5000 years ago, that life is over and now I am here – they cannot all be simultaneous – which is his justification for no Karma. (Chapter 7 makes this issue clearer. Karma is useful.)

And in my hypnotic regression of 1991, I saw what I did that has affected this lifetime…Lifetimes are linear-sequential, but there may be multiples happening concurrently. Seth does not comment on this – he continues to support Reincarnation even though he says that there is no Karma. He is wrong – else there would be no reason for some things working for some people and not for others, and no reason for Scripts that control/guide what we can do and not do. If there is no Karma, then there is no reason for Reincarnation.

Notice the reference to no Astral entities or Neggs in the list above. That is an immediate **'red flag'** when you know that they <u>do</u> exist. Edgar Cayce said that the demonic exists (which it doesn't) – so two channeled entities disagree with each other about the Truth of the Other Side. That is a major red flag – one is lying. And that is why Man was admonished to avoid confusion and not play the channeling game. (Neggs can appear to be demons.)

Seth does not say anything about OPs, nor a VR Sphere, and yet there is this strange comment:

If a certain number of entities were responsible for the creation of our physical world, where do the extra [?] human beings come from? I told her [Jane Roberts] that, according to Seth, each personality making up an entity [soul] could manifest itself physically as often as it chose to. [56]

This is reminiscent of the replication of people on the timelines as the TLs split (Chapter 2) – which also produces what we have been calling OPs. However, there is a limit to how many times one can 'split' or replicate, as "spreading oneself too thinly" leaves one without enough energy to serve all instances well. (Chapter 10)

And notice the New Age teaching (#4) that you can create your reality -- which is not true. You can **attract it**, however. And note that the "inner you" somehow creates the world that you see (*à la* holographic projection) which turns out to be true. We are also programmed through exclusions in our DNA to <u>not</u> see things around us – see VEG Chapter 12 where Tom reads the watch <u>through</u> Laura's body. If it can be done hypnotically, could it not also be 'programmed' into our DNA that we see what the Neggs deem appropriate, and we don't see what they don't want us to? The Greys do that to people.

Item #3 <u>should</u> refer to our holographic vision, but that is not what Seth says. According to Seth, items #3 and #4 go together, but we do not <u>manifest</u> things in 3D. Item #5 should have said something about <u>Recycling</u> as Reincarnation does not always happen.

So, Seth's credibility drops a bit with items 3-4, and 9, and approaches 70% trustworthiness as he mixes truth with disinformation. The other listed statements are known to be true.


**Ruth Montgomery**

During the 60's to the 80's, Ruth Montgomery wrote a number of books that were channeled from the Other Side – supposedly by "Art, Lily and the Gang" – people who had passed on and chose to meet Ruth at her typewriter where they controlled her hands/fingers to produce their text. A form of automatic writing.

Again, Ruth would enter a slight trance and type what she was given. Or she could ask questions and the Gang would answer her. The topics ranged over politics, earth changes, UFOs, spiritual issues, the world to come, and Walk-Ins. The books were quite popular.

So, in essence, that information was spurious and may have been harmful if some naïve people read the books on Walk-Ins and sat down to invite some higher entity to take over their body – even if for the good of Mankind, of course. Keep in mind that the Neggs and Discarnates <u>are </u>considered "higher entities" as they occupy the 4th level while we are constrained in the 3rd. It is important to be careful what one asks for.

**The Cassiopaeans (The C's)**

This is a group that is channeled through a Ouija Board and while they have produced much information about the OPs, and the chakras, and other spiritual concerns, they are occasionally smart-aleck, evasive and uncooperative – not exactly traits found in entities of higher enlightenment and soul-purpose. If they are asked a question, they may be evasive, cute, or just avoid the question.

Sometimes, which is unusual for true Higher Beings, they would <u>volunteer</u> information – that is a real 'red flag' as it violates the **Law of Confusion** (see Glossary).

A snippet from one of the 14 September 2002 sessions runs like so:

Q: (L) …You said before that OPs were originally intended as a bridge between second and third densities and that they were used [by 4D STS]. Is Mouravieff right about the potential for OP's to advance being dependent upon souled beings advancement to STO at the end of this cycle?

A: Not exactly…. However it is more likely for a soul to "grow" when interacting with 4th density STO. STS tends to drain energy for its own use.

….

Q: (L) …. are there other types of soulless beings more than those reanimated or remolecularized dead dudes and OPs? Is there such things [sic] as **holographic projection** beings running around on the planet at this point and time?

A: In a sense, you are all "holographic" projections. But to answer the question, it is rare.

….

Q: (L) …. Is the **gray alien abduction** scenario: a.) a screen memory, b.) a creation of the American military mass mind programming project… or c.) something else, or d.) are they really just gray aliens abducting everybody?

A: You have stumbled upon an interesting question indeed. As we have noted previously, <u>physical</u> abductions are rare. Not only that, some abductions do not end with return of the victim. Now what do you suppose you would do to cover up this fact? You might "create" a lot of abductions that end with return and "no harm done."

Q: (L) That wasn't one of my answer selections! Does this mean that the abductions reported by the people that Bud Hopkins worked with followed by Whitley Strieber were staged?

A:   Close enough for horseshoes.

Q: (L)  OK, what would get us closer?

A:   How about several varieties of experiences including government experiments. Did you ever notice that some cases exhibit extreme trauma and others do not? Same general story, but one is related with deeper sensation of reality, and another is not. Why do you think so many "abductees" are able to accommodate the experience, while some result in ruined lives?

Q: (L)  So you are saying that some of them are not really being abducted. They're just having something projected into their mind. So how long has that been going on?

A:   Over 30 years…. There really are "Greys." But not nearly as ubiquitous [as] the gov would like you to think.

**The above dialog is found on many websites that have copied it, discussed it, and for the most part, it can be found on the website of Laura Knight-Jadczyk, known as www.cassiopaea.org.**

Such is what the C's dialog basically looks like. The OP info is often valid…but some channeled points are open to question or interpretation. The dialog shows the difficulty in not being able to know if the C's are telling the truth or not – if they are really Neggs or Discarnates don't count on it all being true.
(Chapters 8 and 9 clarify the Grey issue.)

Yet, during their dissemination of information, about all that really had value was to isolate their info on OPs, trace it to the Greek *hylics*, and to Boris Mouravieff and his pre-Adamic race. There were also a couple of write-ups on Simulacra, Robotics and OPs on the www.Montalk.net website, and that was an accumulation of data from various other sources.

> *Montalk.net seems to be a well-run and informative website dealing with a lucid analysis of many issues. It is recommended reading.*

And as was said earlier, the reason that OPs are in VEG and this book as a serious consideration is because, at the present time, there are people out there who match the behavior of what OPs are said to do, and they have **no auras, and that means no soul.** OPs do exist, I have had unfortunate experiences with them, they are a nuisance, they do not know what they are, the Neggs do operate through them (I have proven this by confronting and binding the entity in Jesus' name), and they are no doubt the 2nd seed that Genesis 3:15 refers to (VEG, Ch 1).

## RA

The last channeling to review is that of The RA Group – they are alleged beings from the 6th level and speak a lot of the Law of One, catalyst, love, charkas, ET entities out to get us, the harvest of 3D beings into 4D, Wanderers, STO/STS, and of course, the **Quarantine of Earth**.  RA was channeled by the L/L Research group.

This is one of the few sources of channeled information that does have a very **high level of integrity**. The information over the years is **consistent** with what they have said in prior years, and I personally have never had cause to 'raise an eyebrow' at anything said, and in some cases I have gone researching to verify/disprove some things that were said, but there are no errors, and disinformation seems to be absent.

A good part of the channeled information, covering a wide variety of subjects of interest to most New Agers, truth seekers and metaphysicians, can be found in The RA Material Book I, [57] and the book has an index for researching specific topics. At last count, there were 5 books in the published series.

> *Note: allegedly RA was part of a group that was called **the Nine**, or the Council of Nine, and throughout the 70's to the 90's there were many channelings of them by different people. While the information appeared to be consistent, it was consistently wrong, prejudiced and racist, and the same is profiled by Picknett and Prince.* [58]  *In addition, the Nine spoke of using force to achieve goals,  equated Jesus with Yahweh, and the Nine's predictions didn't come true, but that was explained as the people of Earth having become more spiritual and thus the predicted landings and intervention by our mentors was "no longer necessary."* [59]

Due to the deceptive messages of the Nine, they claimed that RA was part of their group. Such was not the case. The Nine were Gameplayers (see Chapter 12).

What is really scary in all this channeling is that some responsible people in our society (and government?) have bought into assorted New Age teachings and hang on the expected word of these gurus… because people seeking a better world, truth, Light, brotherhood, often turn (unwittingly) to the Astral (Neggs, 4D STS, and Discarnates) and open the door to deception and eventual manipulation and control.

## An Interesting Test

Don Elkins, of L/L Research, was one of the original set of people to channel RA and he was concerned that the communication not be fabricated. So he devised an experiment in which he worked with over 100 subjects who had no familiarity with channeling or UFOs, and under hypnosis and his guidance made them channel extraterrestrials. He then compared the messages with those received by people claiming to be genuinely in contact with ETs.

> He found that the 'fabricated' messages [of his volunteers] were very similar to the 'real' ones. Elkins then leaped to the rather unscientific conclusion that this proved the reality of extraterrestrial contact, and that contactees were not 'chosen' but that anybody could do it if in the right altered and receptive state of consciousness. (Of course, it could be argued that his data proved the opposite, demonstrating that extraterrestrial channeling is a pathological phenomenon, and that it is never 'real.') [60]

And if you understand what this Earth is, and the entities who are just waiting to play the channeling game with you, you'll see that the latter option above is closer to the truth. Please remember:

> **True Higher Beings have more to do than channel information to humans who have not even used the messages brought to them by past teachers and avatars on this planet. They will not violate the Law of Confusion.** (See Glossary.)

And by the same token, the Neggs and especially the Discarnates have a lot of time and opportunity on their hands to play games.

## Higher Beings Assist

We also need to remember that the Higher Beings are not cruising the lower Astral realm to see if anyone wants to channel them, and unless you know their name or some way to call them, they can't hear you anyway. And they don't play games. Man has been given all the spiritual teachings he needs for his growth, and until he actually puts that basic truth into practice, the Higher Beings aren't about to (1) rehash what has already been given, or (2) give further truth that depends on an understanding of what has already been given. And lastly, (3) the Higher Beings understand the **Law of Confusion** and are not about to violate that universal law... i.e., you have the 'right' to not know and **They do not volunteer**.

The reason the Beings of Light (angels) and the Neggs hear is because they are all right here (assigned to this realm); they see you, and they know what you're doing. It is their job to answer.

## A Show-stopper

From a personal experience, I can vouch for the fact that the Beings of Light <u>are</u> listening, and apparently just waiting for someone to ask or pray something that benefits people.

I attended a special 1-week seminar given in a Christian church by a visiting, healing minister, who fancied himself kind of a modern-day Smith Wigglesworth. That evening, he started out preaching the Word, and later began walking around the huge auditorium, up and down the aisles, "throwing energy" from his hands which had the effect of slaying people in the spirit, or causing them to faint and hit the carpet. Very near where I was sitting, he threw some energy at the person next to me, who went down, and I was also hit with **energy that felt tingly and creepy**, and I didn't like it. Something in my gut was saying, "Stop him, this is fake."

He walked on down the aisle, and I said a quick prayer that **if** whatever was empowering him was <u>not</u> from the Father of Light, that he be bound, stopped and he would have what he himself called an "anointing" removed. I also prayed for the roomed to be cleansed – it felt spooky – in OUR church, and I asked for all unclean energy and vibrations to be removed.

Almost immediately the room lightened up and the visiting minister found people were no longer affected by his throws of energy, and he kept at it for another 30 minutes, finally going back up front and he resumed preaching. I was shocked. I learned that he could not do it on 2 subsequent nights, either, and his "energy healer" visit was no more the exciting spectacle that it had apparently been for years.

I attended his last night there to see for myself, and he could also not lay hands on people to get them healed. No 'carpet time.' He was clearly upset. I said another prayer that he be empowered to teach the Word and remove unclean spirits in people. I have kept up with his ministry, still receiving announcements when he is in the area, and occasionally I check him out. People are being taught, changing their lives, and he does have a deliverance ministry.

So, what was the lesson? Apparently, he was empowered by the Neggs and all I did was ask for it to stop. He was in MY church and I (as an usher) had dominion over the space – as all members of the church also did – but all were so enthralled watching this 'energy' spectacle that he was free to display the 'gifts of God' – but I sensed in my gut that **it wasn't from God**. His energy was creepy and people weren't being healed. My 2 short prayers were answered and his 'act' was cleaned up; people are now being served by his teaching the Word and delivering them from bad habits and health problems.

**We don't need to channel**. I didn't ask for an answer from God that night as to what was going on. I just asked that **if** it was anything being empowered by any dark or STS entities that it be shut down.  Just ask and it will be given – if it is in peoples' best interest. I also had the <u>authority</u> to ask – I was an usher.

## ET Effect on Religion

One of the major concerns of current-day clergy is what will happen to Man-based religion when we learn that there are Others out there? Not only did Zechariah Sitchin (author of the Anunnaki-based *Twelfth Planet*) ask that question, but the **Brookings Institute** answered that question **in 1960** with a resounding warning: It could totally collapse society including our faith-based religions.

### Brookings Report

This was a major report made by a think tank in Washington D.C. which  conducts research and education in the social sciences, primarily in economics, metropolitan policy, governance, foreign policy, and global economy and development.

Their report, called *Proposed Studies on the Implications of Peaceful Space Activities for Human Affairs*  was a severe warning that Man on Earth is not ready to deal with the presence of ETs with greater technology and probably a better understanding of The God of the Universe. If there is no God, or if they have a different version of The God which would disrupt human's view of themselves and the Cosmos, that could basically result in **chaos and many nervous breakdowns**.

It is an historical fact that when a lesser –evolved society meets a superior civilization, the lesser one is either absorbed into the more dominant one, or eliminated entirely.  The impact on public values and attitudes could be catastrophic. Thus the Report recommends **withholding information from the public** until such time as a better evaluation of an extraterrestrial presence can be made, and this is wise if the ET presence should turn out to be malevolent. The same holds true if the ETS are benevolent but possess the truth about Man's origins and why religion was created (see VEG where this is examined more fully), where such information <u>would</u> cause massive upset of belief systems – things we take as true in Science, History and Religion <u>would</u> all come crashing down, and the result is, again, chaos.

For this reason, the government and Air Force will not discuss nor reveal what they know about UFOs or ETs. The downside to non-disclosure is if the PTB who seek to rule Earth know that the ETs are benevolent and want to help us to resolve Earth's environmental issues with superior technology, and who could also implement free energy, dropping dependence on fossil fuels and electric wires strung all over the place to control the distribution and charge for power…. The PTB would not want to surrender their control of the existing money-maker economic system – thus ET participation in our world would also **disrupt the economy** of almost every nation on Earth. (See what the PTB did to Tesla.)

Man has painted himself, economically, politically and religiously, into the proverbial 'corner'... a self-made, constricting box. And the only way out is either going to be a very gradual shift to the ET-supported way, or total destruction of the existing systems. *Virtual Earth Graduate* suggested a personal way out of this issue.

## Historical Precedents

Let it be known that the **Zulu** have a tradition that says they are people from the stars, 'Zulu' means that. The Zuni legends teach that there were star people (worshipped as **Kachinas**) who brought humans to Earth and taught survival skills. Eastern spiritual philosophies such as Buddhism and Hinduism also discuss other worlds, as well as the ***Mahabarata*** describing aerial battles among starships. In fact according to some Hindu beliefs, we can "...incarnate on another planet for at least one lifetime." [61]

There is even a modern-day religion that will not be much impacted by a disclosure of an ET presence... the Church of Jesus Christ of Latter-Day Saints, or the **Mormon Church**. They believe that there are

> ...countless planets whose inhabitants – Children of God – are progressing, as are human beings on this earth, [sic] according to eternal principles towards a Godlike life.[62]

In addition, Minister Louis Farrakhan and Elijah Muhammad both proponents of **Islam**, have openly discussed UFOs and ET Space Brothers on occasion. In February 2011, Ishmael Muhammad chaired a Nation of Islam's Saviors Day and included UFOs in the agenda "... because they are a core belief of the Nation of Islam." [63]

## The Survey Said...

So is there really an issue with people not being open to the news about ETs visiting Earth?

Dr. Ted Peters at Pacific Lutheran Theological Seminary in Berkley, Ca, decided to find out and designed and ran a survey **in 2011** called the *Peters ETI Religious Crisis Survey*. He and his assistant surveyed over a thousand people of various religious backgrounds, as well as a few agnostics. The results were very interesting... after all, this is the 21th Century, not the 15th when **Giordano Bruno** was burned at the stake for even suggesting that other planets are inhabited... And **Galileo and**

**Copernicus** were heavily censured by the Church for "leading people astray" as heretics.

The survey revealed that very few people today, 50 years later, felt that their religion or personal faith would be affected by a confirmation of ET presence. [64]

> Not one Buddhist or Mormon felt their personal beliefs would be affected; only 8 percent of the Catholics felt they would be affected; and the highest-affected group was the Jews at 11 percent.... Catholics and Jews [also] responded that their religious tradition may face some turmoil, around 18 percent for Jews and 22 percent for Catholics. [65]

It was revealed that the strict followers of Western religions would be the most affected, whereas the 'loose followers' would welcome the discovery. So Dr. Peters opined that "... if the [majority of the] adherents to the world's religious traditions foresee no threat, then the widespread assumption about an impending crisis fails to gain confirmation here." [66]   And yet, nearly ¾ of the non-religious people said they believed that **all religions would be in trouble**.

The only conclusion is that some religions will have to adjust to a new reality more than others, and yet a lot of people will still maintain their faith – despite being confronted with the truth of a new reality. Note that many people in the 1500s stubbornly clung to the Flat Earth belief – despite having been shown scientifically that it could not be so. (Hint: Magellan.)

## Government Warning

So there is some basis for caution in dealing with the ET issue. While several UFO researchers are busy pushing for Disclosure, the government has given us a hint about the ET presence with the publication of the **Extra-Terrestrial Exposure Law** (14 CFR Part 1211 of the Code of Federal Regulations ) adopted by NASA in 1969. This preceded the Apollo 11 launch as a way to "...guard the Earth against any harmful contamination ... resulting from personnel, spacecraft and other property returning to the Earth after landing on or coming within the atmospheric envelope of a celestial body."

While it was ostensibly to quarantine astronauts who might have brought back hostile organisms on their suits or equipment, it also applies to any person on Earth who comes into **contact** (i.e., Close Encounters of the 3rd Kind, aka CE-3) with beings or ships from another world. **The fear is contamination**. The Law provides for a heavy fine and jail time for anyone found violating it.

So in addition to sociological 'contamination' of ideas, we are also protecting Earth and ourselves from biological contamination.

There are those on Earth who are already contaminating the ET scenario by claiming that the Bible proves that ETs are really demons. The Vatican does not agree, so the fundamentalist, narrow-minded religious types are the only ones advocating personal deliverance from ETs via the use of Jesus' name to protect oneself… without understanding <u>what</u> the ETs are doing – which is proactive (see Chapters 8–9).

So where do we go from here …now that **the preponderance of evidence suggests that the ETs are here and watching us?** Because they are here and have been here for centuries, we know they are not malicious – they could have conquered us even 100 years ago if they wanted to. Maybe they are waiting for us to grow up? Maybe they have spoken with our leaders who are tasked with the responsibility to bring the Earth under peaceful control? Maybe they have contacted people on Earth to deliver new ideas and solutions to age-old problems? And when books by authors Sitchin, Tellinger, Hegland, Olsen, Clark, Marrs and others (see Bibliography) appear, they are dissed by a large populace in America that has been already **conditioned to ignore**, yea verily to laugh at!, information that could set people and the environment free from error and abuse.

So herein is another suggestion for reworking (Transforming?) the religious issue.

## Third Alternative to Religion and New Age

So if the Bible has omissions, misstatements, mistranslations… that would mean it is not perfect and would not be the inerrant word of God (who is defined as perfect). And if the New Age is a derailing of the <u>original</u> New Thought of the 60's (which has pretty much disappeared)…. What is left?

**Bishop John Shelby Spong** has written books advocating that Christianity must change, update, or die. His ideas and recommendations hold water and to some extent, he was able to implement some positive changes in his Episcopal Church. And yet, his suggestions for a more dynamic Christianity that is more in synch with today's people and today's Science have fallen on deaf ears. Old ways are so hard to change (even if for the better) that usually the only way to effect proactive change is to destroy the old. A merge or infusion rarely works.

Whereas there are a multitude of religions around the planet, hundreds at last count, the last thing we need is one more. **Unless** the new religion actually unites people instead of dividing them. If the new religion could somehow keep the best of the 7-8 major religions, while adding concepts and teachings concurrent with findings in Genetics (Creationism and Epigenetics not Evolution) and Quantum Physics (entanglement, vision/holograms, and the observer effect) and the InterLife (see

Chapters 5 and 7, and NDE reports) we would have a relevant spiritual vehicle for enlightening ensouled humans – which was what the **Serpent Wisdom** groups tried to do back in the days of the early Gnostics (See VEG 1, Ch 2).

It would be important societally to keep most of the traditional sacraments that make a church part of a society – and upgrade the major Religions to a **New World Religion –** in a special way. Just as each country in the world has its native people with their own language, and most also speak a common language for better communication with other countries (English fits that description in our current world)...so too would each religious group keep their traditional religion AND also acknowledge and practice the NWR. Both could be practiced on a Sunday – even in the same church building. The rework could look like this:

## Aspects of A New World Religion

In fact due to connotations and prejudices, let's not call it a Religion... How about

### New World Unity? Or World Faith?

**Let it first be clearly stated that this chapter is not prescribing a new religion, nor does it suggest how it should come together – we have all seen the disastrous results of Heaven's Gate and the Raëlians... but herein it is suggested that a World Religion could serve to unite people rather than distance them as is now the case with the differences in religions around the world. Secondly, what follows is merely what appear to be the salient elements of a practical, nurturing, spiritual church that is an adjunct to the existing religions.**

A world of people united in one faith based on reality, common needs, and scientific facts... A world recognizing the divinity of ensouled Man, and celebrating our common issues, our common dependence on a fragile ecosystem, with common purpose in respecting each other and the planet... to finally stand up and claim Earth as our own and cherish her, protect her, and clean her up!

No more need for huge, antagonistic militaries around the world – they still exist but their function is to (1) protect Earth assets, (2) arrest and detain those who would desecrate, destroy and trash or harm the planet, and (3) see to the correction of such people. That also includes (4) defending the Earth against any ETs bent on harming humans or the planet! It would be an **Earth Army** in every sense of the word. And when the technology is acknowledged, the **Earth Special Forces** and their craft would patrol the stratosphere, ecosphere, and oceans (as **Earth Navy**), later building bases on the Moon to administer the intelligent and benevolent management of

Earth. From there, building bases on Mars to help administer the Solar System and obstruct or remove any hostile ETs – call it **Solar Warden**?

Let's first see a war on ignorant destruction of Spaceship Earth – this is all we have folks! Destroy it and we all disappear. We have been asked to do this since 1987. How's it working so far?

## Specific Aspects of New World Unity

The following are just notes jotted down as to desired elements of the new spirituality. They are purposely not worked into a coherent paradigm as this book is not prescribing a new religion but does see the need for one.

### I. Keep
celebrations of Birth, Baptism, Bar/Bas Mitzvahs, Weddings, Deliverance (from habits and ignorance), Prayer, Confession, Tithing, and Last rites/Funerals.

### II. Add
the concept of Reincarnation and Karma back in – they were there 1800 years ago.... Reinforce the concept that we are all One, interconnected at the Higher Self level (see VEG, Ch 7) ... add the Aramaic Bible and Rocco Errico's book to define meanings in the Bible and clear up Aramaic idioms...or add George M. Lamsa and the **Peshitta Bible**. Workshops in Yoga, Meditation, Qigong and Tai Chi...learn to move and use the *chi* to heal self...

**Need** a better understanding of Abortion, Homosexuality, and Sin (prostitution, pedophilia, and pornography)... more updated info and integrity & tolerance...

### III. Remove
vicarious atonement, excommunication, indulgences, Eucharist becomes a symbolically updated communion .... virgin birth becomes artificial insemination... Salvation through your faith and learning (gaining Light).... Update concept of Hell as an Astral fantasy realm for those who just have to experience it (or create one as an 'amusement' park) ...priests and pastors become ministers of faith, truth and deliver people from darkness/ignorance...remove Original Sin concept... substituting the understanding of Karma and the real creation story of Man.

### IV. Update
church libraries to contain major Holy Books of the major religions, plus Apocrypha, Nag Hammadí scrolls, newest Dead Sea Scrolls, a summary of Quantum Physics discoveries related to what our world really is, a summary of Genetics findings as relate to the DNA and special construction of Man ....include teachings on InterLife as supported by NDEs and validated Hypnotic Regression insights...

## V. Personal Spiritual Achievement

there will be differences in spiritual level and thus understanding, thus it is suggested that there be four levels (as in most organizations – from Boy Scouts to Karate to Masons):

| *Class Id* | *Symbolic Level* |
| --- | --- |
| Entry/Initiate | Green belt |
| Accomplished/Functional | Brown belt |
| Master/Teacher | Black belt |
| Graduate | Black & Red belt |

Somebody at the Graduate level is also ready to be an **Earth Graduate**. Masters and Graduates can teach others.

And the first three levels might have to have sublevels -- but not a plethora of such.

We can do this… and should. Who is ready to move Man forward into a new tomorrow that works for everyone? When can we start?

## Support for Religion

It needs to be repeated, due to the nature of what has been said in Chapter 1 and this chapter, that many people still want a basic, bare bones religion with rote repetition, simple tenets, even rosaries, and traditional ceremonies. In no way should those be discontinued for those who want or need them (refer to Chapter 13, 'Brain Development' section). There are even ensouled humans who are severely limited by their genetics and yet need a faith to hold on to. They just are not capable of embracing a metaphysical understanding of Life, God and Man. We are required to be understanding and compassionate of them.

What has been suggested about religion is that it be updated to reflect Man's new awakening realizations about himself and his world – for those who are ready for more. This was traditionally the **esoteric** side of every church or even secret societies in history – you get what you are ready for. The masses were given the **exoteric** or everyday teachings. Perhaps we need to return to that… if we can get past the egotistical "pecking order" as implied by the stratification of the congregation. (This was an issue addressed by VEG in Chapter 2 by the Valentinians and Gnostics.) And that is probably why secret societies (with esoteric knowledge) are kept secret.

There are many paths to the top of the hill; there is no one "right" path. The soul learns from whatever path it chooses… just take care of your health.

# Chapter 4:  Diet & Health

In any book about spiritual growth and hence becoming a more enlightened person, it makes sense to consider proper nutrition and care of the temple which houses the soul. In short, eating junk food, playing violent video games or watching shoot-em-and-stab-em TV shows AND trying to be a more spiritual person is an oxymoron.

In fact living in the wrong city can seriously dampen your efforts at meditating and generating a higher spiritual vibration. Some places on the Earth are just not conducive to centering oneself, meditating on the Light, and focusing on peace and brotherhood – and there are other places, like Sedona, AZ, and Stonehenge, with their vortices that can aid one in focusing and amplifying one's PFV.

## Obstacles to Spiritual Growth

**The following pages are not meant as a prescription, nor can I diagnose and medicate for you. What I am sharing is what my experience and research have borne out over the years.  Choose what works for you.**

### City Vibes

I had a real good friend who was serious about spiritual growth and undertook classes in Yoga, Tai Chi, became a vegetarian and meditated twice a day. He made no progress after 3 years and couldn't understand it… he even read positive metaphysical books, by known teachers, and listened to inspiring music and chants.

He finally shared with me what he was doing and asked what he was doing wrong. When I stopped laughing, I calmed him down and we sat and talked about it. I had to ask him if he thought that living in any old city whose history involved corruption, drugs, crime, gangs and poverty was really conducive to spiritual growth? In short, if the city has an aura whose energy is low, slow and negative, would it not be like trying to swim in a polluted lake?

I asked him how he expected to overcome the ambient negative vibration of the area in which he was trying to grow…?  I have always been sensitive to energy and I personally avoided his city which had a low, dull vibration whose violence and corruption was actually impacting the energy of the city. Cities have something of an aura which reflects the collective energy and intent of its inhabitants… **as well as any past energy** that has not been cleared. His city often felt dirty, heavy, and dangerous when I was there on business, so I avoided it.

In addition, we discovered that the prior tenant of his apartment was into drugs and died of an overdose, traumatizing his girlfriend who also lived there. He got the message. He moved out and is now making good progress in another state.

If the body's aura picks up negative vibes it can and will translate that to the body, over time, and if the bad energy blocks a chakra or Bionet meridian, you will experience health issues in that area. This is why the Chinese use acupuncture to work on their clients who may also use massage and Rolfing to clear blockages – a healthy, flowing Bionet is a necessary prerequisite to staying healthy. A healthy body does not distract the mind from focusing on higher spiritual truths.

## Clearing Toxins

Another impediment to spiritual growth is the build-up of toxins in the body – if the body is out of whack, it will translate that to distraction in the mind. That is the other half of the Psychosomatic connection where the Mind can affect the body. Just as easily, but lesser known is the Somatopsychic connection – drugs and Rx reactions are a prime example of this.

If the Mind is generating fear, anger or depression, that takes its toll on the Body and can create a cold, MS (if someone hates himself), or allergies – all depending on how the Mind influences the body chemistry via the release of hormones and **signaling molecules** (examined in VEG, Ch 9).

If the Body is overtired, on recreational drugs, or infected by a virulent pathogen, it may have a negative reaction on the Mind; thinking will not be clear and relaxed, and the Mind's upset may trigger the release of the wrong signaling molecules (Dr. Candace Pert called them 'molecules of emotion' as was featured in the movie *What the Bleep Do We Know?*)

### Toxin Sources

Not only can there be residual antibiotics in our **tapwater,** there can be trace amounts of hormones and other chemicals. Usually they are filtered out by very conscientious water treatment plants, but they cannot get all of it, so we will get amounts of things at 2-3 ppb (parts per billion) which are generally not harmful… but concurrent with the principle of **Homeopathy,** the substances are there and even though one glassful is below Federally mandated levels, each time you drink the tapwater, you add to the total amount of such substances like lead, copper, arsenic, pesticides, fertilizers –  those get stored in the body, usually in fat cells. A serious issue is runoff of chemicals into the watertable, which can reach the local river, and that goes downstream and another water treatment plant gets to deal with it. Storm drain runoff may carry pesticides and fertilizers into local streams and lakes as well…

Many progressive plants are treating the water today with ozonation and UV light which helps to kill organisms, including bacteria and amoebas... some water treatment plants have stopped using **Chlorine** as it produces THM's (Tri Halo Methanes) in the water which are also a minor contaminant. In addition, Chlorine does not always kill the bugs like *Giardia* and *Cryptospiridium*[67] some of which have developed immunity to it. **Ozonation** is a better (but expensive) alternative.

The safe, but expensive, way to purify public tapwater is with **Reverse Osmosis** – and that is available through many brands of bottled water. Check the label. And yet several well-known brands of bottled water have removed the Chlorine but still have Fluoride.

There can be a problem with **well water** – many subsurface parts of the US often have to be inspected for traces of arsenic, heavy metals and hydrogen sulfide that are sometimes naturally found in subsurface deposits. And if the well water has a high level of **TDS** (Total Dissolved Solids) like sodium bicarbonate and sodium sulfate – that is a lot of sodium in the tapwater for people who may be on a low-sodium regimen ...in addition to which the well water should be chlorinated and filtered... but filtering won't work long for TDS levels above 400 ppm (parts per million)... any faucet filter (like *Brita* ® or *Pur* ®) will clog in 3 days due to high TDS (> 400 ppm).

Additional toxins can come into to your diet through mercury (Hg)-contaminated fish, **mercury**-contaminated flu shots – please ask your doctor for the flu shot that is inhaled through the nose (it does not have **Thimerosal**, which is the Hg derivative). Eating shrimp, scallops, lobster are potentially dangerous as they are scavengers on the bottom of the ocean, like crawfish in rivers and lakes – when you eat them, you get whatever they ate... including chemical and organic waste. If you eat Tilapia fish be sure it is from a fish farm and not the ocean for the same reason – and it is wise to avoid Sushi – raw fish often have tapeworms and parasites.[68]

When eating deer or old cows/beef there is always a possibility of **prions**, causing Mad Cow/Deer Disease and the prions turn human brains into Swiss cheese (which shows as Creutzfed-Jakob Disease, a chronic wasting disease). Our USDA people and ranchers are responsible for checking livestock to be sure they don't have any infection and putting them down if they do.

**Chicken from China** is dangerous as they have few sanitary standards and the chicken meat may be contaminated with fecal matter or other organisms (*e. coli* or *salmonella*).[69] Even produce (veges and fruit) from the California and Texas central valleys should be thoroughly washed before eating it.

This is why many people become vegetarians and wash all food very carefully, even soaking it in alkaline water or **hydrogen peroxide** for 5 minutes before eating it. Some people go even further and have a local D.O. or Naturopath do a **Chelation Cleansing** (i.e., detox) – over 4-5 hours you sit in a chair and a slow-drip chelation liquid is fed into your bloodstream which picks up toxins in the body and flushes them.

**Water Dangers**

Two main cautions here.

Be wary of buying bottled water that has been sitting outside the corner store or grocery store <u>in the Sun</u>. Same warning applies to leaving your water bottle in your car on a hot day – when the Sun heats the bottle of water, there are dangerous molecules that leach out of the plastic into the water, called **BPA** (BisPhenol–A) and that is a carcinogen.

To avoid any tapwater issues, including Fluoride (which all of Europe has removed from their tapwater), go to the local health food store and use their water dispensing machine – it usually is filtered and uses Reverse Osmosis, and some stores bathe the water tank inside the machine in UV light (kills organisms).

> It has always fascinated me that the French bottled water Evian is "naïve" spelled backwards… is there a message in that?

By the way, it is OK to drink **distilled water**, just make sure that you also use a good quality multiple vitamin so that when the distilled water leeches some minerals from the body (and it does happen), you are putting minerals back in.

**White is Pure**

For years the American food industry worked hard to convince housewives that they should consider the purity of the food they were feeding their families. Pure meant white. **White bread. White rice. White sugar**. All highly refined and lacking in the nutrients originally found in the whole grain, the brown rice, and the unrefined cane sugar.

When they took the wheat from the farm, they separated the bran from the wheat and sold it separately. They did the same thing with the wheat germ… sold it separately. Today unless you get **organic whole wheat bread**, you are eating white pulp – and they have to "enrich" it with vitamins like the ones they took out! What a racket… but it does $erve $ome purpo$e, I guess.

Brown rice takes longer to cook but is better for you.

**Sugar Issues**

If it isn't regular table sugar, honey, **Stevia,** or **Agave Nectar,** don't use it.

The problem with artificial sweeteners is that their man-made molecules are smaller than the molecules of the normal sugars listed above and they can get into the cells where they don't belong and wreak havoc with the mitochondria (Chapter 13), causing cancer. Excess sugar does not benefit the brain, either.

Normally, sugar molecules move through the bloodstream and attach to the outside of cells and dissolve through the cellwall releasing only the components needed by the cell. On the other hand, the **synthetic sugar molecules** are so small they can enter the cell via the openings designed for other nutrients. They disrupt the mitochondria and other organelles with chemicals that are not friendly to the cytosol.

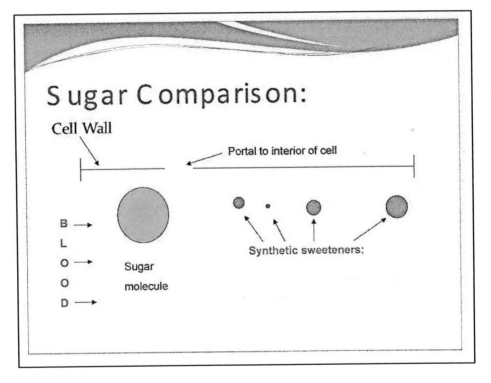

While we're at it, try to avoid drinks and sweets with **HFCS** (High Fructose Corn Syrup) – it metabolizes so fast it is one of the main fat-builders!

> **You need to reduce all sugar intake so it doesn't feed Candida**
> **or**
> **exhaust the insulin-producing ability of the pancreas.**

# Common Myths

**Cholesterol**

Don't be too hasty to get your cholesterol down to 0 – the body and brain both need cholesterol to make other necessary molecules like enzymes and hormones, myelin, Testosterone and Estrogen, and Cortisol for example... if you don't have enough cholesterol, you will suffer in other ways. But that's OK, they say, "We have pills you can take to compensate!"    Seriously?

Cholesterol is made in the liver as a response to the body's water-content. The more water you drink, the more your cholesterol will normalize itself – whatever 'normal' is for you. If you don't drink enough water (and tea, Coke®, beer and wine don't count) your body will send messaging molecules to the liver to have more cholesterol made ... Why? Because when you don't drink enough water each day, the body's defense mechanism kicks in and makes sure there is enough cholesterol to line the arteries so that whatever water is in the cells doesn't leak out and dehydrate you!

If you take statins to kill liver cells so that they cannot produce cholesterol when needed, you may be in trouble. That is why the doctor must monitor you so closely when you are on statins. You could also drink more water and see if your cholesterol levels (HDL, LDL and Triglycerides) reach a stable lower level faster...

There are two things to watch out for in this scenario:  (1) have the doctor test and see if you have a defective cholesterol regulating system – that does need attention! (2) If your regulatory system is normal, your cholesterol count will not match someone else's anyway, and it (LDL) may not be under the magic number 100,  BUT you don't want excess cholesterol to stick just anywhere and blood thinners can meet that requirement. In fact, a friend of mine used **Lecithin** to make sure extra cholesterol didn't stick where it shouldn't be. She also used Gano Coffee ® with a **Reishi mushroom** extract (in *Ganoderma lucidum*) and the MRI that showed excess cholesterol in an artery branch had disappeared 2 months later ... and she was an avid tennis player. It has not come back.  Gano Coffee (available on Amazon) is a **natural blood-thinner** ... so don't drink Gano Coffee (also called Organo Gold) if you are on a blood thinner (Coumarin or Warfarin, for example).

Just something to think about.

**Fluoride**

Do aluminum manufacturers influence the ADA to sponsor Fluoride in America's drinking water? There is a rumor to that effect, yet even Snopes.com does not clarify the issue. Actually **it is enough to put it in toothpaste**, but let's look at the history of the chemical to better understand.

When Aluminum is made, using Cryolite, one of the by-products is sodium fluoride (NaF) and because the manufacturer wanted to do something with it, it was initially sold as rat poison, and then as a cleanser and it was very effective. It was a stroke of genius when the Soviets put it in their Gulag drinking water to keep their inmates docile, and the Germans in WWII followed suit in their concentration camps – it kept the inmates docile and lethargic. It makes one wonder just how this was discovered…

*NaF can also be made chemically by combining hydrofluoric acid with sodium hydroxide (NaOH). This is the version that is used by water treatment plants.*

Europe and the USA started fluoridating public drinking water when initial research showed it does **strengthen bones and teeth**… so the ADA jumped on the bandwagon and saw that it could help prevent osteoarthritis (if bones were strengthened), and could help strengthen teeth to prevent cavities – why not use it?

Europeans and some chemists in the USA continued testing fluoride and found that there was a whole **county in Kentucky** that had natural fluoride in the water, yet the teeth of the citizens were badly mottled (dental fluorosis) and tooth decay rates were not reduced – so there was obviously a limit beyond which one should not go. In short, more was not better. In fact the recommended safe level is not to exceed 2.0 mg/L. [70] Water treatment plants have to monitor it carefully and some cities do it via slow-drip as the clean water is pumped into the Water Tower. This is fairly accurate.

Europeans discovered some birth defects could be traced to fluoride and most of Europe to this day has removed it from their drinking water. They found that removing it did not affect the rate of tooth decay. Why do we still have it? The best place for it is only in our toothpaste. There mu$t be a rea$on for it too….

I do use a fluoride product that really works, and irritates my dentist: ACT Restoring Mouthwash ® – said to "… rebuild tooth enamel, and mineralizes soft spots." And it does work. My dentist was watching two spots in my teeth and told me that we'll get those next time! I said "Oh no you won't" to myself and started using the ACT mouthwash over the next 6 months and at the next checkup, he couldn't find any soft spots, no cavities… I told him what I did and he just glared at me. And yet it is .05% NaF. (Two years later he was promoting it and Sensodyne ProNamel ® to his patients.)

Something else to think about.

## Eggs Are Not Bad

See the Dr. David Perlmutter list of recommended foods below….

Eggs produce less cholesterol than your body makes every day! They are a perfect food and you need cholesterol and may not be getting enough protein.

Body functions are regulated by the special properties and 'sequence characteristics' of its amino acids…There are 22 of them and 8 of them are essential and are not manufactured in the body – these must come from the diet… The best source is complete proteins, like rice with beans, or eggs. [71]

Lastly, **eggs also contain Lecithin** which aids in fat assimilation, and eggs raise HDL (good) cholesterol – which lowers your chances of getting heart disease. [72] Don't fear using eggs…

But if your doctor says back off, follow his advice.

### Fasting is Not Dangerous

> **If fasting is done wrong, it can do more harm than good, and do not try to fast if you are hypoglycemic.**

Fasting is used to clear toxins from the body, and because the body begins to get into the fast about hour 8 into the fast, you may experience a headache – which will pass. And by the 2nd-4th days the headaches will be gone just before the body starts accessing the fat reserves – and then the headaches return (the first or second time you try a fast) because the body often stores toxins in a fat deposit (encapsulates the toxin so it doesn't harm the body) and your fasting can release them – this is sometimes called **a "healing crisis"** and is nothing to worry about – it just means you are detoxing.

After you have learned what your body does in a fast, and you have done it several times successfully, you can fast for a week to gain mental clarity and experience very little if any headache. More than a week is not really necessary: i.e., more is not always better.

> **Water must be drunk frequently during a fast as the body wants to flush the toxins.**

Personally I did not find that fasting got me any clearer on spiritual issues than normal non-fasting meditation, and I stopped doing it. And there is special care to be taken when **coming off a fast** for more than 3 days – have a lot of Jello, pudding, soup, milk and non-solid foods ready for the first 24 hours because the stomach doesn't like a big juicy beefsteak after a 1-week fast!

## Diet Considerations

While this book is not a compendium of nutritional information, and several related subjects were dealt with in Chapters 14 and 16 of VEG, it is important to point out that **it is hard to walk a spiritual path with a sickly body** – thus we want to do those things that keep our bodies healthy and energized.

All I am pointing out, **from my own experience and research,** is that there are some major showstoppers to getting the body and mind to work together in harmony. If the body is out-of-sorts, or sick, or recovering from an infection or surgery, that is not the best time to try and focus on new spiritual issues. Same thing applies if you are just hungry – the body wants to be fed and will not be at peace until it is given good, wholesome food and water (6-8 glasses of pure water a day)…

## Food

A safe rule of thumb is: **if God didn't make it, don't eat it**. That applies to a lot of concoctions that Man makes – French fries (grease fried), ice cream (a lot of sugar), hot dogs (you don't want to know), and bacon (cured with nitrites). Of course, we all do junk food once in a while and that is not going to wreck one's spiritual path… as long as it isn't a daily thing. Sometimes the body craves French fries or bacon (for the **salt**!) – so give it to it. You may be doing more harm in self-denial than by giving in and cleaning up the effects later with a few extra workouts! Salt is essential to healthy blood pressure.

The latest bit of good news was a basic diet devised (or rather approved ) by **Dr. David Perlmutter, MD.** The following things are actually beneficial for your body and should be in your diet, at least weekly:

1. avoid foods high on Glycemic Index
2. cut down sugar (esp HFCS)
3. cut gluten  (wheat prod's)
4. eat the right fats, omega-3, DHA/EPA:
    Virgin olive oil, coconut oil
    Peanuts
    Salmon
    Avocado
    Dairy prod's (milk, cheese, yogurt, ice cream…)
    Eggs
    Brown rice (not white)
5. cholesterol is not an enemy – many hormones and enzymes needed for brain growth  and general body function are made from cholesterol.
6. irritation is the enemy – caused by too many carbohydrates, sugar which create **excitotoxins** (see following)
7. aerobic exercise in moderation  3x a week…

One of the major reasons for using a good **Multivitamin** is that our fields growing our wheat crops nowadays are depleted of chromium (needed for blood sugar management), and other staples like corn, peas, and vegetables are picked and frozen, then we boil the heck out of them, or microwave them destroying nutrients. Even a lot of fruit is picked before it ripens on the tree or vine and we get apples, peaches and grapes that are bitter, and so we buy less next time and miss certain nutrients.

**Vitamins**

Make sure you have a good **Vitamin B complex**, and I prefer a B12 from methylcobalamin as the standard cyanocobalamin is sometimes hard to digest and the body can't always use it – although it is the cheaper, common form of B12. If you are taking a good B complex and are always tired, your body may not be absorbing cyanocobalamin… **check with your doctor** or nutritionist. There is a test they can run to see if you need B6 or B12. Or just a more potent daily Multiple Vitamin which you should **not** get in the over-the-counter pharmacy section of your supermarket; while those brands are better than nothing, the local health food store, vitamin shop, or even Whole Foods Market® can help you select a quality Multiple tailored for your lifestyle.

If you need stamina, be sure that the Multivitamin has Folic Acid (Vit B9) and Pantothenic Acid (Vit B5) – vitamin B5 is a **stamina vitamin** and because it is water-soluable you can't overdose on it. If I get **gout**, I have found that 1 Gr of B5 every hour with plenty of water dissolves the uric acid crystals within 12 hours and I am back walking the next day.

When taking vitamin E, use the **E complex** with mixed Tocopherols and Tocotrienols. The same goes for a Vitamin C complex – it functions like a B complex – all members of the complex have to be there to function effectively. **Vitamin C complex** has rose hips, bioflavonoids, rutin, hesperidin, acerola and of course ascorbic acid – they all work together and are much more effective than just ascorbic acid by itself.

**Minerals**

**Ca-Mg** (Calcium Magnesium) are the 2 most important of the minerals and should be in a 2:1 ratio if done properly (500 mg : 250 mg). **Magnesium** helps regulate Calcium, supports the brain (fights ARD - dementia), and you need at least 200 mg a day. Americans tend to be deficient in Magnesium according to the latest studies. Calcium is better absorbed if it is **chelated**… look for that on the label – Calcium is hard to absorb and Calcium Orotate is way too expensive.
Small amounts of **Chromium** work to stabilize the body's glucose-insulin management system.

**Sodium** and **Potassium** are also major players in the body, running the sodium-potassium pump in each cell, and also the ionic forms serve as neurotransmitters. Zinc for men, and sometimes Iron for women (**if your doctor doesn't prohibit it**).

## Supplements

Needless to say, **Garlic** keeps one healthy, cook with it often.

Also valuable are **Resveratrol** (the same substance in red wine that has been found so good for the heart and keeps Calcium in the bones).

**Curcumin (Turmeric)** is a major antioxidant, doing multiple good things in the body…be sure to use the BCM-95 version as the standard Curcumin is hard to absorb and the BCM rework is 95% absorbable.

**CoQ10** is another thing to pick up in a high quality multiple. (Heart & eye support)

**Phosphatidyl Serine** and **Vinpocetine** are great to keep ARD (Age Related Dementia) at bay… you may add **Bacopa** or **Huperzine A** to that mix.

**Lutein, Astaxanthin** and **Zeaxanthin** – for the eyes (as well as Vit A).

Use **Vitamin D3** especially during the Winter months – 2000 U for women and 5000 U for men and it lessens mood swings and depression in a natural way. You will need Magnesium to utilize D3.

**Cinnamon** is great for circulation and is an anti-fungal.

A great morning **probiotic shake** is the following:
  Spirulina and Chlorella (green powder mix)
  Frozen yogurt (vanilla bean)
  Cinnamon powder or Cacao powder (not together)
  Pomegranate powder – great antioxidant
  Maca powder (aka Peruvian ginseng)
  Organic 2% milk with DHA/EPA Omega 3
  A packet of Gano Coffee (for the Reishi: *Ganoderma Lucidum*)
  A capful of liquid Glucosamine-Chondroitin (anti-arthritis and
      is also effective at reducing joint aches after exercise.)

**Note**: the preceding are what we use daily and our health is great – I suggest you try these things **if your doctor says it is OK for you** (based on your body chemistry), and you might even want to experiment with a few items that you have never taken just to see if you have any sensitivity to a supplement (Also see section near the end of this chapter on Under The Tongue Testing.)

## Exercise

Don't overdo it – **too much exercise creates free radicals** – and a bad oxygen singlet: SOD removes the oxygen free radical called Super-Oxide.

When exercising to lose weight, say you are jogging – the first 30 minutes the body burns glucose (blood sugar) and **there will be no fat loss**… After 30 minutes and you're still exercising, the body switches to burning fat as an energy reserve. Thus people who leisurely walk their dog around the block for 20 minutes are not getting any weight-reducing exercise benefit.

Exercise 3x per week for best results. Constant heavy exercise may lose weight faster, but that also creates **excitotoxins** and they are the newest culprit identified to cause irritation in the body – joints and muscles, and even nerve cells (leading to ARD in the brain). They have determined that irritation/inflammation damages cells[73] – and may cause cancer, especially in the absence of antioxidants like Vitamins C and E.

## Chinese Exercise

**Tai Chi** is the Chinese exercise most Americans are familiar with and it serves to focus the *chi* and move it through the body for improved health. **Chi** is the universal life force that permeates all life – plants, animals and Man. It fills the universe and is said to be the Primal Life Force coming from the Creator, The One.

This exercise form has preset specific movements which are designed to focus attention on what one is doing – while one can do a sloppy version, not paying attention to the feet, legs and hands (whose positions are very important), it will not do much for the overall energizing and health of the body. The Tai Chi forms were developed centuries ago by masters who saw the aura and the chakras and how the chi actually flowed in the body along the meridians. Meridians are today called the **Bionet** which is a series of channels that criss-cross the body and interconnect at major chakras. (See Chapter 12 for additional information.)

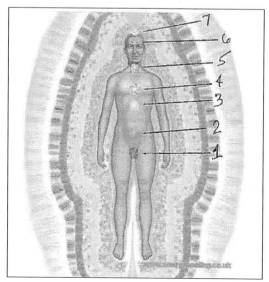

The meridians are the freeways for *Chi* and the chakras are the interchanges. The aura and the chakras look like this:

The chakras are numbered 1 – 7, from the root (1) to the crown (7) and the solar plexus is #3 which is discussed more in Chapter 11.

There are also 7 layers to the aura – each chakra connects to one of the layers.

(Source:  www.differentlight.org/images/Aura%20400pix.jpg)

There are more than the 7 major **Chakras** shown; both intermediate and minor ones exist. The palm of the hand has a minor chakra. Chakras connect the Bionet with the layers of the aura which in turn (Chapter 12) extract energy from the ZPE Field, or Matrix, in which we all live. The **Meridians** or **Bionet** contain **Acupoints** (dots in diagram) which can be used for Acupuncture.

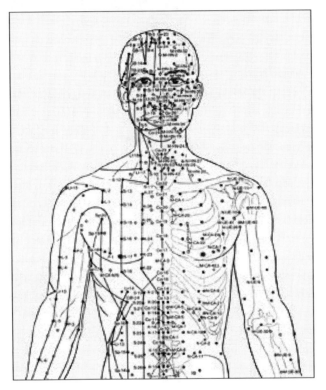

(source: http://www.tibetanacademy.org/Images/acumansmall.gif

Information and energy flow along the Meridians to the organs and cells where they eventually reach the DNA. The meridian system also has the closest interface/connection with the etheric (1st) layer of the aura, the layer closest to the body. Note also that the Root chakra (#1 in chart) "talks" to the etheric layer, the 2nd layer from the body "talks" to the 2nd chakra, and so forth.

Chakra #6 is also called the **Ajna** or "3rd Eye" connected to the pineal gland and it assists in psychic abilities.

The Crown chakra (#7) is also a connection with our Higher Self and thus the Godhead (in VEG, Ch 7). More energetics in Chapters 11 and 12.

## Masaru Emoto

At this point it is valuable to point out the work done by the Japanese scientist and scholar, Masaru Emoto who demonstrated to the world what positive emotions can do to water. He also showed the effects of negative emotion and bad words (of course backed by negative emotions) on water.

Figure 3.3
People's consciousness changes the dirty water in a dam.

Water at Fujiwara Dam before the prayer

Water at Fujiwara Dam after the prayer

**The caption says:**
Before the prayer, the water in the dam was dirty. We sampled the water, whose crystal yielded a shape like a person's face in agony… We took another photograph of the water after the prayer. The crystal was sparkling, with a halo at the center.

(credit: *The True Power of Water*, p. 79.)

Masaru took samples of the Dam water. Before praying over the water, he took a small drop of the Dam water and froze it – it produced the dirty, misshapen crystal in the top picture. His group then prayed over the same water sample, and said words of blessing, Love and Peace. Then they took another drop of the water and froze it. The bottom crystal was the result.

What is the significance of this?

The body is 70% water. Water is an excellent conductor of electrical impulses in the body, and it also connects subtle energies which flow along the meridians. If the body is dehydrated, the energies do not flow as well, and blockages develop, and then illness. (See last section of this Chapter for the issue of Dehydration.)

**Would it not be a healthy thing to do, to take a glass of water (for drinking) and bless it, say a prayer over it, say words of Love and Peace, and then drink it?  What could that do for your body?**

### Alkaline & Ionized Water

There are water machines that sit on your home counter and use tapwater to create alkaline and ionized water – which is not froo-froo – the benefits of these machines are terrific. (BTW, "micro-clustering" is the sales froo-froo because it is not micro-clustered in the bloodstream.)

**Alkaline water** is water with a pH of 8 or greater. A pH of 7 is neutral and is what tapwater is. Ocean water is about pH 8.2.  A pH of 1-6 is **acidic** and is used for cleaning and disinfecting, and a pH of 8-10 is **alkaline** and is used for drinking.

> pH means 'percentage of Hydrogen' – or how many hydrogen ions (H+ also called protons) are in the water… the more there are the more acidic the water is (a lower pH number), and the less drinkable it is.  The reason a high number of H+ ions yield a low pH number is because pH is the <u>negative</u> logarithm  (i.e., inverse) which reflects the activity or concentration of hydrogen ions.

So one of these water machines generates clean alkaline water at 8.5 pH and you drink it. What does it do?

> **Biochemistry lesson**: when you drink water, the stomach will not let any liquid pass to the small intestine if it is not around 7 – 8 pH – acidic liquids are kept in the stomach until the Pancreas can dump some sodium bicarbonate to neutralize the acidity (bring up a Sprite from 2.5 pH to around 7 - 8 pH) before it will release it to the small intestine (just the other side of the stomach) – and that is where absorption happens.  The blood must stay around 7.365 pH and so the stomach knows not to dump a highly 'acidic' drink into the small intestine where it will be absorbed into the blood stream – as acidic! That is called **acidosis** and can be fatal.

So instead of taxing the Pancreas to dump sodium bicarb (pH 8.1)into the stomach to neutralize the acidic drink (pH 2.5), would it not be better to drink an alkaline water, say around 8.0 – even 9.5 pH which will be DOWN-graded to +/- 7.365 pH by the stomach's normal acidic (pH 1-2) condition? (The Pancreas does double-duty as you can see – it provides both sodium bicarb and Insulin to the body.)

Now the **"ionized" part**. Water that is run through the water machine can produce acidic or alkaline water – and the alkaline water is ionized (has an extra electron)… and this is what your body likes. The following diagram shows water being electrolyzed to ionize it:

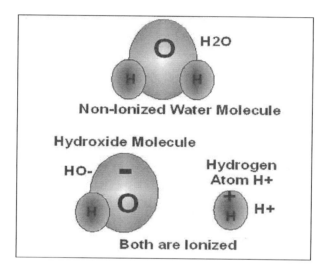

The OH- is the **antioxidant**. The H+ is the **Free Radical** (missing an electron) – together they neutralized each other, apart they both seek to merge with another molecule:

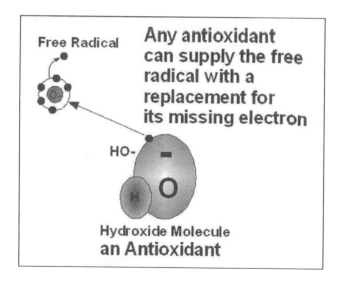

# Here is the secret of the ionized water:

The alkaline water is full of OH- (hydroxide) molecules which seek to donate their **extra electron** to another molecule that is missing an electron – which just happens to be the Free Radical (H+) molecule, also called a **proton**.

The H+ is the Free Radical and is also called a proton and has **lost its electron** and so has a positive charge… this makes it a **Free Radical** -- looking to steal an electron from another molecule somewhere (anywhere!) in your body. That is how Free Radicals create damage, especially in the cells.

**When the OH- and the H+ meet in your body, they unite and flush from the body as harmless water : H+ and OH- = H2O.**

Clever, huh?  Sounds like a design…..

# Self Care

### Sensitivity Testing
So how does one know if a vitamin or mineral or even a food is not well tolerated by the body?  People's biochemistry varies from person to person and what works for John may not work for Sue. It would be nice to find out without spending big bucks if the body has a problem with a substance.

There is something called Under the Tongue Testing and it is very easy to do. Here is the procedure.

### Under The Tongue Testing

1. Best done in the morning before breakfast, when you first get up.
2. Rinse your mouth out with water – no mouthwash.
3. Sit down with the substance you want to test, and make sure your heartbeat is normal and calm.
4. Using a watch with a second hand, take your pulse for 10 seconds. Multiply by 6 = your resting heart rate.
5. Now put a small amount of the substance you suspect you might be allergic to under your tongue and hold it for 20-30 seconds.
6. Keep as still as you can, and take your pulse now.
7. If you are sensitive or allergic to the substance, there will be a **rise** in your heartbeat…
   If you are OK with the substance, your heartbeat will not change from the reading in step 4.

If you do get an increase, just cut that food or pill out of your diet or regimen. If you have a serious reaction (you feel dizzy, and your heartbeat really rises or you feel nausea), go see your doctor.

## Getting Rid of a Cold

This technique comes from Germany and works just as well for a sinus infection or a cold, and may even relieve a stuffy nose due to allergy.

> **For allergy**, I first use a **Saline Nasal spray**… clean out the sinuses, from a squeeze-bottle squirt 2x up each nostril, inhaling to get the spray into the sinus cavities… pinch your nose shut and wiggle your head, move the saline mixture around, 20-30 seconds, and then blow your nose…
> Then I may also use something like Afrin® to spray up the nose.

To get rid of a cold within 2-3 days, rinse your sinuses out (Snarfing) at the first sign of a cold, or even during the first day when you know it is a cold…If you wait too long it will be harder to stop the cold…:

# Snarfing

1. Get a big bowl in which you can put warm water and is big enough to accommodate your two hands… you are going to cup your hands together and capture water in them…
2. Using warm tapwater, add ½ cup of **seasalt** (non-iodized is best) And swish it around helping it to dissolve…
3. This is best done at the sink and I use a bath towel folded over, laying on the counter – between me and the sink – for what will be obvious reasons in a minute…
4. Have a box of Kleenex at the ready, nearby…
5. Cup your hands together and dip them into the saline water, exhale, and stick your nose into the water in your hands and inhale strongly… sucking the saltwater up into your nose. (**No it will not hurt**.)
6. Pinch your nose shut and shake your head gently from side to side to get the saltwater to move around and cover all the sinus area… 10-15 seconds is enough…
7. Lean over the sink and blow it out into the sink (water running), And
8. Repeat steps 5 – 7 at least 3 times…
9. Grab some Kleenex and blow your nose…getting the rest of the water out.
10. Clean up.

Then I also take something like Zicam ® (**zinc** throat spray) before going to bed and squirt the back of my throat. Morning and night, just 2x a day. If I am taking Vitamin C complex during the day, plenty of water, and maybe occasionally putting some colloidial silver drops in the water I drink (2x a day) – I guarantee the cold is gone within the next two days.

Do **not** use colloidial silver except when you have a viral infection.

Why?

The principle is that your sinus is a breeding ground for the virus and any secondary bacteria feeding the cold – a constant source of infection that the body has to really ramp up the immune system to fight the **pockets of infection** in your 8 sinus cavities! The cold virus is being handled in your bloodstream, but the immune system cannot easily get to the breeding pockets in your sinuses which just replicate germs out the wazoo – constantly taxing your immune system.

What Snarfing does is remove the mucus pockets of infection (may have to do this the second day [once a day is usually enough]) to get it all… and the Zinc gets into the bloodstream and kills viruses – same thing the colloidial silver does – they are both **natural 'antibiotics.'** (Be advised that **antibiotics only fight bacteria** – the cold virus is handled by your immune system – but the battle may produce mucus waste that is loaded with bacterial junk – and that is what an antibiotic is for.)

Note that in a minor sinus issue, not a full-blown cold, you can just squirt the Saline Nasal spray into your sinus cavities, swish it around and blow it out – and that is usually sufficient.

## Gout

Drink a lot of water (maybe a gallon a day) with 1000 mg (1 Gm) of vitamin B5 every hour, rest and keep your foot up, avoid walking on it… I start at 8 in the morning and <u>every hour</u> I drink a glass and do **Vit B5** until about 6-7pm at night… and usually by the next morning the gout (uric acid) crystals are dissolved and I take another day with a lot of water and still rest… usually by the end of the 2<sup>nd</sup> day I can get a shoe on again…

Here, **diet is important** – you cannot eat food with high protein (purine) content – or you feed the gout and it won't disappear… What can you eat? I do Jello, rice rice rice – for breakfast/lunch and dinner (boring but it is only for 2 days), veges, and bananas… fruit and veges are good – no purines which in excess is what sets gout off -- when the body gets something too rich and cannot digest it all, there is a residue of **uric acid crystals** (from the excess purines) and they just need to be dissolved – B5 does that by speeding up the body's metabolism. And you need the water to flush the dissolved crystals from the body.

Stay off the foot – I use a crutch to get around … you will make a lot of trips to the bathroom… the kidneys are very busy.

### Dehydration

**Adults do not drink enough water** – the body from adult to elderly should be fairly stable at around 70%... but the chart below reflects what health professionals have found to be the case as we get older! Dehydration is associated with getting older, aging and poor functioning of the body … and older people who drink more water, exercise and use vitamins, minerals and the right supplements are not only much healthier, they also look younger.

Note: "…**excess cholesterol formation in the body is associated with prolonged dehydration**" – because the body seeks to save whatever amount of water it has and uses the cholesterol to "lock it into the cells." [74] Drink more water.

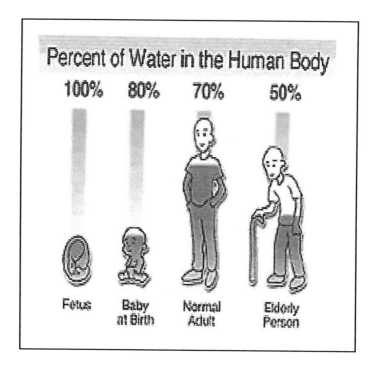

**How do you know if you are dehydrated?**

**Take the pinch test:**

**Pinch Test**

1. Using the back of your left hand,
2. Lightly pinch the skin with your right thumb and index finger…
3. Let go… and Observe what your skin does…

    a. if it snaps right back, you are hydrated, all is OK
    b. if it tends to stay "pinched up" more than 1 second, or
       is **very slow to go back to normal**,
       you are dehydrated and need to start drinking more water.

## Summary

So the whole point is to take care of the body and help it with the right amount of Vitamins, Minerals and Supplements. Eat right and drink <u>at least</u> 4 glasses of water a day – adults do not drink enough water and are often dehydrated, but don't know it.

The AMA recommends 6-8 glasses of water per day, and you can test your skin (above) to see if you are getting dehydrated (which really causes all kinds of problems in the body.) Since the body is 70% water, if you don't drink enough, the dehydration will manifest in the joints, eyes, brain, wherever the lack is the worst. [75]

When you don't drink water, you get dehydrated.
When you get dehydrated, you fall down…
When you fall down, you can't watch Direct TV …
Don't get dehydrated and fall down…
But if you do, take the remote with you!

Transformation of Man

# Chapter 5: Regression & Soulmates

Many people are going to wonder how I wound up with the knowledge and insights that have been shared in Book1 and now this book. For that reason, before examining the InterLife, it is important to share the Regression of 1991 wherein I was given a lot of the information. Thus this chapter is necessarily about the author and what he saw and learned, so that **the examples amplify the principle involved**.

My life for many years revolved around a central theme: I either can't get what I want, or if I do, it is taken from me by forces (people and events) beyond my control. That was either my fault and I was dumb and didn't know it, or it was a curse. Some said it was Karma – whatever that was. Back in 1991, I knew nothing about Reincarnation, Karma, and soulmates. I was to find out.

## Search for Answers

At first, in the 70's, I went to four excellent recommended psychologists, one of them name-brand, author of many books, looking to see if there was something seriously wrong with me. The name-brand guy used to fall asleep on me (I was that exciting!) so I quit him. The Christian guy kept saying I needed deliverance – when your only tool is a hammer, everything looks like a nail.

So I did deliverance, three times and must have annoyed the devil because nothing happened the first two times, and then on the third, I gave a big sneeze and the deliverance minister proclaimed me healed. Seriously. I thought of all the people back in the 1700-1800s who used snuff – were they 'delivering' themselves?

Moving forward, in 1975 I visited a psychiatrist who suggested I take some tests, one of them an IQ test, so at least I'd know if I was dumb or not. The series of tests averaged out to an IQ rating of 160 on the first day, and he said the rest of the tests the next day could add or subtract and round it all out, but that I had had the hard parts on Day 1. I never went back – 160 was enough for me. But I was still concerned: I could be brilliantly stupid, screw myself and not know it!

The last guy was a trip. He was a Primal Scream therapist and I spent some time hitting pillows, and yelling at a plant that he told me to visualize was my mother – which would probably have worked had it been a Venus Flytrap. And lastly, he suggested I go into the closet and yell things at my mother, who was a real insensitive person. My mother was still alive and I was trying to love her, so that didn't appeal to me, and I left. I never paid for one of the pillows I destroyed.

## Continued Searching

On a gut-level, I knew there was a woman for me, and I had even seen her in dreams… not constructed fantasy, but the same woman kept showing up.
I was 48 in 1991 and my special woman had not shown up, and I wonder what was going on…

I finally took a transfer from Southern California where the lifestyle seemed to pull marriages apart, and went to Texas. The last woman I had dated in California had a yellow Mercedes 450 SLC sport coupe with a bumper sticker that read: "If you're rich, I'm single!"  Funny but scary.

So I went to Texas in 1987 with the hope of meeting the cute blue-eyed blonde, getting married and settling down… which never happened.  I was confident that my job skills would guarantee me success in the more straight-laced Texas computer environment … little did they suspect that I was a brilliant screamer who destroyed pillows and put people to sleep with my life story.

Seriously, I was getting desperate for answers and becoming fast disenchanted with the therapists, psychologists *et al* out there. I now knew that I wasn't stupid and there was no curse or demonic oppression, so what was left?  Karma?  Someone in California had suggested that, but I knew nothing about it except that it had to do with one's past lives. That meant I would have to find someone qualified to do a regression, and that meant hypnosis (which scared me), and what if it didn't work? What if I stayed hypnotized and never awakened?

When I was told that in a regression I could discover whether there was a curse or Karma or was I so smart I was subconsciously messing myself up… I decided I had to do it.

# Regressions

I decided to take a chance and look for a qualified person. One of the few times that my life worked, I was led to a Dr. K  through a friend at a large Nutritional Wholistic Fair.

Long story short, Dr. K did her thing and I never went to sleep. I kept breaking the trance because I was still conscious and wondering when I would go under. Finally, she got me to relax and just follow her voice. I suspected she was after some hidden childhood trauma when she asked me to go back to the time most responsible for this lifetime's problems.  It surprised us both when I went directly back to the last lifetime.

# Transformation of Man

We found the following four lifetimes (in reverse sequence, last to first) and the concomitant data that helped to explain my situation. The 2 ½ hour session was recorded on cassettes and given to me, but after a few years and multiple plays, and because I was still a Christian, I was uncomfortable with them and threw them out. (Brilliant.)

## Last lifetime

The first thing I saw was my murder… stabbed and shot by a foreign agent and thrown into an icy river. Dr. K asked we where I was and what my name was in that lifetime and I told her. There was dead silence on the tape for a few minutes… she was making notes. "Oh, you were well-known…" she said. It was in a foreign country in the late 1800's (the country and my name is withheld because it is <u>still</u> too embarrassing).

Continuing, she asked why I was murdered. I had used and abused too many people and gotten involved with <u>manipulating</u> the corrupt politicians – they got even. That was one of the big things I was paying for this time – even though I was fighting corruption and meant well, I was manipulating people for the good of the State, **and that <u>still</u> earns karmic penalty** (because I was interfering with many souls' freewill and their lifepaths).

Continuing, I saw my wife and family – five kids, two died in childhood. My wife was a very pretty ash blonde with blue eyes – Scandinavian-looking I thought – feisty, stubborn and she could be quite a handful, but was excellent at running the farm. We were well-to-do farmers. She was very sharp, but uneducated as was I. Our oldest son helped run the farm when I was away in the big city, we had hired hands, and I sent money back to her to keep it running smoothly. She had been the neighboring village beauty and I met her during a harvest festival, about 1880, and we soon married – absolutely a stunning but headstrong woman.

*Yes, she was the woman I had seen in my dreams!*

Continuing, I was shown my womanizing and drinking problem – I could not get control of my body; it was very strong and its drive for sensual pleasure drove me to carouse. The angel directing this review, later known as 'Baldy,' said that that was no excuse although I did get credit for spending several years in a monastery meditating to gain self-discipline. While there I also developed psychic abilities under the guidance of a very advanced monk/shaman who taught me to channel energy up from the lower chakras and use it for healing and clairvoyance.

*If it wasn't used, i.e., expended, it could fall back down and empower the physical appetites via chakras 1 and 2.*

It was the occasional excess of lower chakra energy that (1) got me in trouble with polite society, and the State and (2) caused my wife to disbelieve my explanation that I could not control it. Her not understanding and mocking me in the InterLife seems to have caused the gods to bring <u>her</u> back this lifetime with a similar body issue – so that she (at a soul level) would understand as she went through similar issues this time.

Lastly, just before my murder, I was shown that instead of staying in the big city, ostensibly to fight corruption, when the going got rough, I was too insensitive and did not have the sense to grab the money I had saved, go back home and grab the kids and family and get the heck out of the country that was now falling under the control of oppressive rebels. When I stood up to them, once too often, it was a setup, and I was murdered. My death resulted in the political hacks going out to my farm, taking it, scattering the family, and my wife fled north to another city and died there soon after of scurvy as a scullery woman. I had unwittingly abandoned her.

Lastly, I was shown that my squandering money and aimlessly giving it away to needy people (who in turn squandered it) cost me in this lifetime because I could not hang on to money, and I was denied **two large inheritances** in this lifetime! To the extent that I got corrupt men fired and denied them their ability to make a living, thus collapsing their marriages, I also this time could not keep a job nor could I get a relationship to work out.

I had been hired by the Crown to oversee the Parliament and the men who were entrusted with running the country, but I discovered so many scoundrels, and corrupt deals, I exposed them and got them removed from office. It is an interesting aspect of Karma that I was genuinely concerned about the welfare of the country and its citizens and **I believed I was doing the right thing** – but according to Karmic Law, I was manipulating people, denying them the freedom to make a living, and interfering in their lives and marriages. That all came back to me – to experience the frustration and poverty generated by those actions.

## 2ⁿᵈ Lifetime Back

Going back in time, to the 2ⁿᵈ previous lifetime, I was in Lille, northern France, about 1830. I was a teacher, unmarried and fell in love with one of my students – Guess who, again?  A pretty brunette, **Elisette**, looked to be about 14-16 years old and I was about 26. We had an affair, deeply loved each other, and planned to marry when she was older. Instead of our leaving town and settling somewhere else (a recurring theme), we stayed and kept our affair secret… we thought.

Somehow, the authorities found out (I wasn't shown how) and rather than disgrace his family, **Jacques Denis** committed suicide (hanged himself from a rafter in his bachelor attic apartment) and thus abandoned her. Again. In addition, the suicide and exposed affair disgraced my family anyway, and Elisette was heartbroken and never married, dying in her forties as a cleaning woman (another repeating pattern).

> *Obviously if the school authorities found out, someone had to have said something… Did she share our secret with a gabby or a jealous girlfriend?*

I couldn't believe how insensitive I was, not to mention the stupid decision to escape whatever punishment might be awaiting me… but that <u>fear of punishment</u> drove me due to the unfortunate circumstances of the previous, 3$^{rd}$ lifetime back (and that part I didn't understand until 1998 when I was given an insight after asking for specific *faux pas* in past lives and why they existed).

The peek into the 2$^{nd}$ lifetime was really quick and it was just enough to show that certain patterns were repeating: inappropriate sex, failure to leave town, and abandonment, to name three. Not much else was shown me of that lifetime.

## 3$^{rd}$ Lifetime Back

This was also a short look at a lifetime, in colonial Georgia, about the 1780s. I was **Joseph,** a tall black slave on a prosperous plantation, and quite a strong man somewhere in his late twenties. While I minded my own business, the plantation owner's daughter **Leah** (guess who?) took a fancy to me and cornered me in the huge barn 'way across the main field behind the house.

One thing led to another, I liked her, and I also had the sense that I knew her. I helped her put her horse up. She fancied me I could tell, and it scared me because being caught with a white woman was severe punishment, and then death. She said she wouldn't tell and we wouldn't get caught, and no one was around… so, we hid in the horse stall, and got it on.

I lived in mortal fear during the next week, but nothing had happened… yet.

Someone knew and told her father and I was dragged to the big tree and whipped and then castrated. They thought I passed out, but I had already left my body. While she watched, crying, they hung my body by the neck from the tree, and that was the end of it.

Her father knew she was to blame, especially since she didn't scream or expose me, and she cried when I was hung. He sent her away to a nunnery in Atlanta. She ran away because it was too dull a life, and became a lady of the evening, later dying of some STD.

## 4th Lifetime Back

There was one more lifetime that I was let see very briefly, and I think it was in England, somewhere southwest of London in the 1600s. In that one, I was married (to the woman who was my late mother in this current lifetime!) and I ran a local herbal apothecary in the town and my soulmate was our daughter, who was a handful. Seems souls groups go 'round together… it was also interesting that my soulmate and my mother (current lifetime) looked a lot alike in their twenties…

This last peek at a lifetime came in response to my question in the 1991 Regression as to where my interest in **healing and medicinal alternatives** came from. This also relates to my desire in this current lifetime to have been an NMD, and I share some important considerations for diet and nutrition in Chapter 4 that are related to empowering or supporting spiritual growth.

Obviously, as can be seen in the above examples, both good and bad patterns repeat.

*  *  *

# Evaluation 1

Before drawing the connection between the Regression and the InterLife, certain things have to be pointed out.

While the 2nd and 3rd lifetimes back were not perfect, please note that we didn't do anything wrong in the sense that no one was injured by our private actions. We didn't lie, cheat, steal or cause physical damage to property or bodies… All we did was ignore societal norms (*mores*) and we did what we wanted. It still cost us even though no other-based Karma was generated by our actions.

The last lifetime is where <u>she got it together</u> and behaved herself, and **I** lost it and really abused people, money and sex. That generated some of my basic karmic payback this time. And let it be known that she was not to blame for my deaths in those two lifetimes before the last – it was **my decisions that were bad**. If she was testing me (as souls do) I failed the tests.

I suspect that neither of us now or in the future would repeat what we did in those lifetimes, and that is the point of the Earth School:

Seems like both souls had a recurring problem with sex – inability to be appropriate.
Seems like both had an issue with arrogance leading to taking unnecessary chances.
Seems like he had an issue with insensitivity leading to her abandonment.
Seems like both made their share of bad decisions.

His sexual cavorting (in his 20's and 30's) in the last lifetime would be an inappropriate use of energy as well as his disrespect for marriage – so it is not surprising that I would <u>feel unworthy</u> of a special woman for most of this lifetime. Subconsciously I knew I had committed adultery. And I never married in this lifetime. Not surprisingly, my special woman did not show up.

> *According to historical books on me and her, she is reputed to have said (regarding my womanizing) that "Oh, he has enough to go around!" It took me years to admit <u>to myself</u> that I had committed adultery and her blowing it off was a cover for her real upset. I have been sorry for the crude breach of the marriage vows.*

And I would hear about these same issues in the InterLife after I died and passed over last time. She told me she wasn't too charmed with my lack of caring… And **it was arranged that we not meet in this lifetime**. So even at age 41 I wondered (not remembering the InterLife episode until the Regression) why I hadn't met my woman… but They did let me know in 2010 who she was…

## Discovering My Soulmate

Discovering who she was happened in a way that bears sharing. It was truly unexpected and a total shock – but the gods aren't ogres, and I <u>had</u> asked who she was (no name was given to me in the Regression as to who she was in this lifetime, or if she was even incarnate this time). The same pretty woman was in <u>all three of my past lifetimes</u> and we were married in the last one. She got me killed in two of those three lives, and I inadvertently caused her early death in the last lifetime.

> *I cannot be more specific about her in this recap because she is still alive and well in a major US city. Identifying her would not be appropriate.*

The woman was a very pretty ash-blonde in the last lifetime, and a brunette in the other two, but I instantly recognized her as my wife, and I knew her name then, too. What really puzzled me was that I had <u>never</u> seen her in this current lifetime, and this is important information because the subconscious in hypnosis will sometimes *confabulate* scenarios with memories from far back in the current lifetime. I had never seen her nor met her, and hindsight shows **we were deliberately kept apart** (because I was also shown how we could have met but Mom decided on the "wrong" third husband to marry) and we never met. However, after the regression, I wanted to meet her and I began keeping an eye out for her…

I knew she had issues with me, from the InterLife, so it puzzles me why I still held out hope and watched for her face as I went through life from 1991 forward. It was the same woman in all 4 lifetimes, and in the InterLife, and she wasn't happy with me. My focus was on myself and affairs of State and not on her and the kids. I had insensitively abandoned her. That seemed to lead the gods to initially split us up this lifetime to better appreciate each other, **and** because she also had lessons to learn.

## Mom Almost Puts Us Together

In what turned out to be a freaky bunch of coincidences, shown to me during the Regression, Mom almost made the decision that would have brought my soulmate and me together.

Mom was a 'trip' unto herself and rather insensitive – as was I last lifetime – I suspect that was also payback – Mom socked it to me in that regard instead of my soulmate doing it! She was never really involved in my life, no direction, no advice no counsel... she seemed to not care. I could not talk with her about anything. I was on my own to learn and make decisions... except for the beautiful 8 years I was raised by my loving and spiritual grandmother! I could discuss anything and everything with her, even metaphysics, Atlantis, UFOs – no subject was taboo.

So when I was about 13, Mom met two men and grandmother suggested Mom pick one and get married (for the third time) to give us (me and my sister) a stable family life. She had a choice of two men – one was Bob, an M.D. from Patterson, NJ, and the other was Brian an electrical engineer. Here is where it gets creepy.
If she had chosen Bob, we would have moved back to NJ and I would have gone to Hawthorne High – exactly where she was a student... and it was a small school, so we would have met. We were 2 years apart in age. Obviously Mom chose Brian and we ping-ponged all around the country, like an Army brat, as Brian worked for GE... but he did work in the mid-60's in Huntsville, Alabama, with Werhner von Braun and the Boys.

Oh my God, chills went up my spine and neck! We came that close. Bob said I'd like Hawthorne, and living in Los Angeles at the time, I thought he meant Hawthorne, Ca....but he said I would have gone to Princeton and probably have become a doctor like he was... shades of the 4th lifetime back.

And she never married either but wrote songs including one that used my name from my 2nd lifetime back! Why did she pick that name and describe me *in French?* And even more weird was that I had heard her sing a song on the car radio and it was special, but I figured it was just <u>that</u> song that the radio played... It was haunting. I came away realizing that I had never met her and yet I couldn't forget her. I suspect, somehow, she knows about us and was waiting, too... Soulmates <u>know</u> there is one other special person.

I never saw her face on any record albums, and I was buying LPs all the time at Wherehouse and I played guitar in a band in my mid-late twenties... but I never heard of her group. Never saw her face... but her songs on the radio in the late 70s – early 80s haunted me and I didn't know why. And a song about dreaming always brought me to tears and I didn't know why...

*Sad if she was reaching out through her music and I was prevented from responding...*

## Moving Forward

So by 2005 I had forgotten about finding her, and I focused more on cleaning up my 'walk' and becoming a more spiritual person. If I could make some progress that way, maybe the next lifetime would be better... I was beginning to better understand why I was alone (unmarried) in this lifetime. 2009-10 went pretty smoothly for the first time in 66 years. The karmic payback seemed to have slacked off and I didn't feel like I was under a raincloud everywhere I went. My health was excellent, and I was able to use my naturopathic/nutrition background as a technical presenter in weekly health seminars. Finally, I could serve in a small way.

## The Big Aha!

I was sitting watching TV one late-Saturday afternoon in July 2010. I was between yard projects and just resting, so I flipped on the TV. I do not watch TV during the day, even on weekends. Nothing interesting was on, and I was surfing the channels. All of a sudden, as I turned to a new channel, the station was advertising hits from the 70's --- there she was! The woman of my Past Life Regressions! Oh My God! A blonde dressed in black. I was stunned. My heart skipped a beat, and I had goosepimples. "My God, it's her!" is all I could say. She was exactly the woman in my last lifetime.

*I can't give more data as it might identify her.*

Instant recognition. It wasn't infatuation, fantasy, or lust. If I hadn't had the 1991 Regression ( and seen her 19 years earlier) I wonder if I would have made the connection as easily...? But there was no doubt. The eyes, hair and voice were her.

Ten seconds later, I was very angry. I turned off the TV and went outside to walk it off. I wasn't angry at her, it was just the simple recognition that (1) we hadn't met, and (2) she was famous and I now had as much chance of meeting/communicating with her as I did with the Queen of England. I shook my fist at the sky and said, "Thanks a lot!" (Actually, I told Them They were number 1 in my life with my right hand...) My realization of the difficulty in even writing to her would turn out to be accurate. She has a cadre of assistants and an agency with "guardians" to insulate her from avid fans. Of course.

Remembering what I had seen and heard on the TV screen, I later went to the Internet and began looking for info on her. I remembered the song – one I had never heard anywhere before… One keyword connected me to her website. I began digging, and I finally got a name (there had not been one on the TV screen). Again, I had never heard of her…or her group. And I realized that **the gods had deliberately kept us apart**. They knew if I had seen her years ago, I'd have made a beeline for her and my karmic lessons and upset would have been enough (if we met) to scuttle any friendship at that time. They were right. (Dang it, every time! But boy was I angry.)

Apparently, I have changed enough that the gods <u>orchestrated</u> my seeing her on the TV. Yes, **orchestrated**. First, I don't watch TV Saturday afternoons, or during the day, period. Second, I just happened to switch to <u>the</u> channel in time to see her. Third, that program has not been shown on TV since that day (I have looked). And fourth, in the last 3 years, I had been really changing my attitude toward women, showing more care and concern for them as real people (not as the sex objects they had been last lifetime), and recognizing the beauty, love and mystery of what a good woman brings to a man and his life. I became enamored of the feminine goddess mystique. So I finally got to know who she was.

**The Door Slams Shut**

So I started searching YouTube and Wikipedia, appreciating some interviews she had done years ago. There wasn't a whole lot of biodata on her but I <u>did</u> find her website and got the address of her agency. I wrote her care of them. Twice. No answer. I said nothing weird, just tried to make conversation on some common points I had learned about her on the Internet. Nothing. So in November 2010, I called her agency and asked how they handle fan mail, to better determine if they had given her my letters. My apprehensions were well-rewarded: The "guardians" open it and if it doesn't meet whatever their "criteria" are, they trash it… to protect her and (maybe) the writer of the letter. She still doesn't know I exist… and may not care.

I thought of checking her out on Facebook, and asking to be her friend, but the "guardians" run that site, too. I don't dare send her a copy of this book via her agency because they will open the package, read the book, put 2 + 2 together, and the cat will be out of the bag. Not only might they still not give her the book, there might be some legal issues, even though she is not identified in this book. But, sending the book to her via her guardians would be a dead giveaway and her privacy is important.

So, I have lost. I really regret the last lifetime, and just <u>can't quite forgive myself</u> for what happened to her as a result of my insensitivity. Now I see where the constant sense of unworthiness came from that plagued me during my dating years.

## Another Incredible Shock

As I discovered her YouTube performances, I got a second shock. She wasn't the only person I saw in the '91 Regression. Her lead guitar player was **our son** in the last lifetime, and while he shared years and much time with her this lifetime, he never tried to marry her. And she made it clear that she was waiting for a special man or she wouldn't marry at all – and has not to this day. Neither did I.

## An Opportunity Arises

While surfing her website and listening to her Internet performances, I discovered that she was coming to my town on a USA tour – and again what was weird was that she had never come to my city. This was October 2010 – Did her staff clandestinely set up a potential date to see her? After all, we had talked about her and me, and they knew where I lived… and she never included my city on any of her past tours…

I checked out the venue and for $80 a head, there was no seating – it was all standing room only in an old rundown theatre which would have made the 400+ people a wall-to-wall carpet… <u>for three hours</u> with her headliner appearing first. I just couldn't see that… and yet she was coming this close, I wanted to do something to connect, or at least try to…

So I came up with a plan. I prepared a letter and put it in an envelope marked: To Be Opened at the End of Your Tour. I went there early and saw the two huge travel coaches behind the theatre, and her staff lounging in the patio behind the building. I parked across the street and got cold feet – What if she comes out sees me and recognizes me (like I recognized her!) and is so shook up that she can't finish the Tour…? What if I give the letter for her to her Staff and they open it, trash it – or even give it to her and she is so upset that she cannot finish the tour (she had 3 stops left) …? I could be sued… Or maybe she would not recognize me… Or maybe she would not care…?

I could not go through with it. I could not take the chance that it might impact her in a negative way. To say nothing of her protective Staff picking me up and throwing me into a dumpster for what they would think was a clever but inappropriate ploy to meet her…

I decided that the only thing I could do was go home and forget her. A really special woman and this jerk-of -the-month messed it up.

## Evaluation 2

So, is that the lesson? Is that why they showed her to me in July 2010? To reinforce the loss of a special woman and drive home the point that I really screwed up last lifetime? There may be nothing I can do about connecting as friends in this lifetime... and I am apprehensive about meeting her anyway because I was such a jerk. How could I tell her who I am, who I was, and what I did?

> "Hi, I'm your long lost soulmate, and I caused your death in
> last lifetime... and now I'm back!"

I wouldn't blame her for kicking me in the *cojones*! No way to meet – we'd have to just be friends this time.... Maybe. She's now 68. I'm 70. As the old man on *Laugh-In* used to say, "Want a Walnetto?"

*And yet, that pain is offset with a 2ⁿᵈ surprise event in the Epilog section.*

Ironically, I was famous in the last lifetime, and she is famous in this lifetime. And she has done some of the things in this lifetime that I did in the last lifetime. Maybe the playing field between us has been leveled since we now have both made similar errors and (hopefully) learned from them. I have been humbled as she may now have been, so that we no longer have the situation that existed when we were both born into <u>this</u> lifetime: I had some real embarrassing mistakes to my name, and she had not done anything. I was guilty and she was just the injured party, so to speak. Hopefully our mutual arrogance and my insensitivity have been transformed by our similar experiences. **We both have a lot to think about**. And I see where her absence and then the sudden discovery of her served to hit home: My god, look at what I lost!

Concurrent with the Chapter 2 examination of synching up with another timeline, and going there, there was one other shock I would experience connected with my soulmate that bears recounting so that you can see how the gods work. Then the InterLife examination will make more sense. The preceding was not for drama's sake, it really happened and I wrote the details down right after it happened.

## Evaluation 3

By now, hopefully some readers have also seen something else – another major lesson to be learned from the past life. My life as Joseph and as Jacques both ended while I was very young – somewhere in my 20's. Obviously Jacques was a **suicide**, and not so obviously, so was Joseph's – when you act foolishly and it takes your life, you act out a **subconscious death-wish.** And I'm sure now you can also see what I was up to in my <u>last</u> lifetime – instead of grabbing the money (I had a lot), and returning to the farm and taking everybody out of the country, I stayed to "teach the bastards a lesson" who were ruining our country. What you don't know is that I felt a certain amount of hoplessness about the monarchy I was sworn to protect and on that last, fatal night (I was invited to an evening dinner that I knew better not to attend – it was a setup),  I resigned myself to a depression and **I gave up**. I figured what the heck, it makes no difference what I do… I was very clairvoyant last lifetime and I <u>knew</u> what was about to befall the country and monarchy, but instead of seeing **futility** (see Chapter 10 and Appendix B), or rescuing my family (!),  I went to the party, tired of fighting the scum who had sold out our country.

There is no excuse for giving up – what I did amounted to **the third lifetime back where I subconsciously chose suicide as a way out.**  Needless to say, the Higher Beings are not happy when you do that, and I would have to come back into an oppressive lifetime (this current one) and handle it without giving up. (Ironically, there were some times in this lifetime when I played with the idea [again!] of terminating myself….)  Apparently I learned enough in the InterLife to stay my hand from doing something that I would regret.

> It is because of that scenario and what all I saw in the '91 Regression that I am moved to share significant pieces of information about Life and the InterLife that all may benefit – it turns out to be part of the agreement I had to generate value for others this time… atonement perhaps for the insensitivity of the last lifetime.

## Epilog: Soulmate Encounter

In the last few months of 1998, still looking for my special woman,  and knowing what she looked like, and maybe meeting her and perhaps give a better ending to this story, I attended a New Thought church in this area.  What happened was amazing.

After the very inspiring service, I was standing in the back of the sanctuary talking with Chet (an alias)  and all of a sudden this stunning brunette runs up to me, grabs my arm, kisses me on the cheek and says "Don Pablo's at 1pm!" and runs off.  I got a good look at her but I had not seen her at church before… and yet, she was vaguely familiar.

I asked Chet, "Who was that?" and he broke out laughing.

"Always the kidder!" he said.  "Who <u>is</u> your fiancée?"

I smiled, not sure what to say, and so I said, "Oh, yeah. Her." WTF?  He was still laughing. I felt like I knew her but…. Oh, my god, it was the hair! With blonde hair, she was a carbon copy of my soulmate I saw in the 1991 Regression… and looking back today, she would be the same one I saw on the TV (in the future) on July 24, 2010. (This is suggested 'proof' that the LifeScript is largely preplanned.)

And I stood there confused … Meanwhile, Chet had caught the minister's eye and was heading toward her. I decided to slip out the side door and head for the bookstore, to see if there was anything new…

Almost there, I heard a woman's voice say, "Hi there, snob!"

I stopped and turned to greet Vicki (an alias) – she looked somehow a little younger than I remembered her (from the Singles Group)… and come to think of it, Chet also looked a bit younger. Puzzled, I asked her what she meant by that.

"I saw you at Ridgemar Mall last week in your dark green pickup, and you ignored me!" she answered.

"No, you must be mistaken, I never go to that Mall" I said. "It must have been someone that looked like me…"

"Oh it was you – same license plate: KB 4715 – the one you told us about last week in Singles class and compared it to Microsoft's Knowledge Base numbering system…"

I gave up. "Well, I'm sorry that happened… I must have been preoccupied."

I have never been to Ridgemar Mall, although I know where it is on the west side of Ft. Worth, but it is way out of my way from anything I do during the week. This thing at the church was turning into a definite WTF moment and I half expected to see Rod Serling appear any second.

She continued to press the point. "I don't know how you could miss me, we both left our vehicles and headed for the Mall and you weren't more than 30' from me… But I forgive you, 'cause I'm spiritual!"

I smirked, knowing she was always after me to date her, and her reputation was anything but spiritual! I laughed.

Then she asked, "How's it going with Leslie?"

I checked my reply, about to ask again who Leslie was, and then I had an idea that maybe she was the brunette goddess who had just kissed me … so I said, "Which Leslie?"

She laughed and said, "The one you're going to marry, idiot!"

So Leslie was the brunette and oddly I have always liked that girl's name, but never met one that was single and datable. I desperately wanted to ask her where I had met Leslie, how long we had known each other, and when the wedding would be, but I couldn't figure a clever way to ask. Damn, what was going on?

The church parking lot was almost empty. Vicki turned toward her car, and said "See you at the restaurant!" I said, "Don Pablos?" She said, "Yeah!"

I said OK and forgot the bookstore. I looked my truck over real good: same color, plates, and paint stain on the passenger seat. I looked at the church real closely and everything seemed the same as I had always seen: parking lot in need of repair, broken limb on the oak tree, and colored flyers announcing events on the bulletin board between the church and bookstore... except for the brunette, I didn't notice any big change in the usual church goers.

I drove the 4 miles to the restaurant, and no one was there. This was the *Twilight Zone*, and Rod Serling never showed up. Neither did the church people. I went inside, and no one I knew was there. I almost wish Rod had showed up so I could have asked some questions.

On the way back home, I was thinking it all over and decided that I somehow wound up on **an alternate timeline**, but the crossover and back was so seamless I could not say when it had happened. And since no one was at the restaurant, that meant I was back in my normal timeline. Normal? Yeah, right! Everything that must be going on over on the other timeline would be dangerous for me to participate in – after all, Leslie would be there and if I was somehow in my **doppleganger's body**, and I popped in and said some odd things, and then popped out, I could screw everything up for him... me-there ... whomever.

And it was just as I was driving, lost in thought, that I received a **1-second drop** of information:

"This was all for your benefit ...
to remember in the days to come."

Ominous... They knew I'd see her on TV in 2010. Even now I'm not sure I like the implications. What it seems to mean is that Leslie (my soulmate) and I are together on the alternate timeline. She <u>is</u> a perfect copy of the blonde version here that I lament having lost. Could the alternate timeline be playing out a different version of choices that we (me and my soulmate) made...? (Chapter 2.)

Thus maybe I was supposed to be comforted by having seen her on the alternate timeline? Is that why the gods showed her to me? I remember being aware during the '91 Regression that she had said OK or agreed to a probable separation in this lifetime. For the whole lifetime? Was that a permanent choice?

We judge choices as good or bad based on outcome, when really it is all learning and the choices are just appropriate or inappropriate at the point of choice. However, had I not been insensitive or indifferent to her needs and safety in the last lifetime (or several past lifetimes!), I would have done then what I now know to do in the future.

That realization leads me to feel **unworthy** of my soulmate, and naturally, my lack of self-worth reinforces our being apart in this lifetime. I now realize what I lost by my inability to act lovingly. Perhaps the bottom line of this lifetime is:

> **There is never an excuse for a failure to love.**

And I do love her, <u>the soul</u> that she is.

## Postscript Analysis of Options:

So if the alternate me and she are together over there and <u>this me</u> chooses to move on and not see her ever again, then one of three things happens:

1. the gods may not let this me and she-here separate for good, since there is still an aspect of my Soul that is accompanying her and my two soul aspects cannot <u>permanently</u> split;

or

2. I will do my thing for a while (not incarnate), let her meet her next life issues, and then reunite this me with the alternate me, and <u>possibly</u> come back together with her;

or

3. I have to wait until the alternate me dies and reunites with this me, and then we can permanently separate from her... or get together...

There is a **key issue**: if she and I are **Twinsouls**, there is no walking off – she is my other half and we must resolve any issues. If she is a **Soulmate**, either one of us has the option to let it go, break it off, and not see each other again – <u>providing</u> we can take out leave in a way that doesn't leave any unfinished business between us – which will drag us back together.

Through all the drama of being Soulmates, there underlie the insights and data of the InterLife.

# Chapter 6:  InterLife & Soulmates

## The InterLife

The location of this place is said to be in the High Astral – above the Angels and Neggs who tend to us, but not as high as where the Higher Beings live and operate. It is where souls come for rehabilitation, to be schooled, to be counseled, and to plan future incarnations – creating their Scripts and making agreements with members of one's Soul Group to play certain parts.  It is a working world… no one is sitting back playing a harp (except musicians in training).

Souls are not here to just party. Both Earth and the InterLife are part of the greater School for souls.

**The InterLife is preparing and the Earth is doing.**

Earth is sometimes a context of one's equals where the ignorant, selfish and dysfunctional are put (under supervision) to experience their errors and learn from them. It is all about soul growth. And while learning, when appropriate, one can party.  The gods aren't killjoys.

## InterLife 101

Here are the basics of what happens at death.

### Leaving the Body

Almost always when a person suffers an accident that takes their life, whether it is falling off a cliff, getting run over by a Mack truck, or being shot, the soul knows what's coming and is already out of the body, and it is only the body that experiences the destruction.

There is little point in the soul experiencing the body's agony as it is maimed or shot, stabbed, or hung. Often, the soul watches dispassionately from a few feet away to what happens to the body it once inhabited.  The ETs refer to the body as a 'container' since **the body is not who we are**, we merely have one and at birth, the soul merges with the body for its 3D experiences.

It is important to not bemoan what happens to the body in a life-taking  accident. It is also an interesting insight that **there are no accidents** as we know them – events are often pre-programmed into our Scripts and they are designed to grow us and teach us something, or sometimes the events are 'tests' to see if we handle things correctly and make the right choice, or have the appropriate reaction, or sometimes, no reaction.

The soul is on its way back to the realm that it came from, to rejoin with members of its Soul Group, the Masters, and the Schools where the soul is counseled, schooled and evaluated to see how much progress was made in the last 3D lifetime.

## Tunnel & Life Review

This section's discussion pertains to **souls** who die and who also believe in God.

Note however that the **atheists and agnostics** have denied the existence of God, saying that they see no reason to believe in God, and so their freewill choice is to be without God and when they die, and that it is done unto them as they believe. They wind up in a limbo state, sometimes in a thick grey fog where they can hear others around them but they can't see anyone. There is no Hell – except for those who believe in it and thus are 'asking' to experience it. This limbo is not the InterLife, it is a separate holding area.

*Argue for your limitations and they are yours.*

When the soul in limbo has had enough of isolation and asks for someone to help them, a Being of Light will meet them and present them with their options. Where that soul goes depends on (1) what that soul can accept, and (2) whether their ego can admit that it was wrong in denying Man's spiritual side.

The remaining review applies to souls who have an awareness of a Divine Being, a Father of Light, The One who loves them and they seek to be with Him. The soul will go through the **'tunnel'** which is a protective energy field so that Lower Astral entities cannot harass him as he makes his way to the Other Side, also called the InterLife area.

The soul is met by a Being of Light (an Angel, without wings) and receives a complete immersion, a sound & light show, replaying the just finished lifetime – to see whether progress was made in his/her scripted issues. The Being of Light does not judge or condemn – each soul through its connection to the Oversoul does its own judging.

If the soul made hardly any progress, s/he may be **recycled** back into the same lifetime. If a student doesn't pass 3rd grade is he allowed to move on to 4th grade? Otherwise making progress, s/he can and will later move on (**reincarnate**) into a new experience in the Father's kingdom. It is all up to the soul – no one makes anyone do anything.

*Déjà vu* *is the evidence that we have passed through the* *same* *lifetime*
*once before – it means you have been recycled.*

The Being of Light also assesses the incoming soul's condition; is the soul in pretty good condition, or was s/he really traumatized by the lifetime?

If the soul is lightly damaged due to traumatic life events, he will be sent to **Rehab** and probably will be regenerated, filled with more positive healing Light and Love, rebalancing him. These souls are mainly those who have lost their connection to their Higher Self, to the Godhead, and are minimally dysfunctional. They may also have simply lost heart.

If a soul is severely damaged, and does not respond to rejuvenation, he may be found to be unsalvageable (sometimes called "atrocity souls") due to having committed such heinous acts that they have aligned themselves with 'the dark side of the Force' and need **serious realignment** with the Light. If they cannot be realigned or rejuvenated, the energy/being will be disseminated, cleaned and then the energy will be reused somewhere else in the Multiverse.

## The Life Review

The incoming soul is evaluated by a Being of Light specifically trained to administer the Life Review, allowing the soul to assimilate what was done and not done as the lifetime is played back. The soul will see key events and people from the lifetime just ended and an interesting feature of the Review is that every time the soul harms another soul by word or deed, the soul gets to experience how the other soul felt… i.e., what the effect of their words or action were. [76] When Tom hit another man in the face, he got to feel what that was like:

> In the life review I got to sense and feel basically what everyone
> around me felt at the same time. I was watching it and I was doing
> it. And I got to experience both aspects of it at the same time. But
> I didn't see anyone as actually judging me. It was more like I was
> judging myself on what I did and how that affected everyone….

> Everything was more accurate than could possibly be perceived in
> the reality of the original event…. During the life review you seem to
> have telepathic understanding of others' thoughts and emotions…

> I [Tom] also experienced seeing [my] … fist come directly into my
> face. And I felt the indignation, the rage, the embarrassment, the
> frustration, the physical pain. I felt my teeth going through my lower
> lip – in other words I was in that man's eyes. I was in that man's body.
> I experienced everything… that day.

> In short, ...**there is no real separation between you and others**, and your illusory isolation as an individual in this world is revealed to be a sham. [77] [emphasis added]

The Being of Light does not judge, he merely asks questions and answers the soul's questions as the whole lifetime is played back – as if it were a living video or holographic reenactment of the lifetime. It is very real, and you are back in it moving quickly from scene to scene.

Everyone finds that they are **more judgmental of themselves** than The Father or the Angel ever is. We are our own worst critic and sometimes the Review stops while the Angel calms the soul down, re-centers them emotionally, and then continues... The whole lifetime is played back AND kept in the Akashic Records...it does not playback and then disappear.

In fact, if you knew that others could see what you did, what would you want them to see? Remember when you start to do something nasty: **Movie time!**

## Meeting or Rebuilding

Following the Life Review, the soul is aware that it needs to either consult with a Master about what went wrong in the last lifetime, or the soul is so upset that it may need to spend time in an area (EIZ in Chapter 7) reserved for nurturing and lovingly energizing 'frayed' souls... to rebuild and re-center those souls who had a rough time and are not ready to meet with their Soul Group members, or a Master.

> *This rebuilding area is appropriate for souls who were caught in a hurricane or earthquake and died without much warning. It may also be a refuge for souls who abused others – like a Hitler or a serial killer who can't face themselves or others for a while....*

## Soul Group Welcome

Following the exit from any nurturing area, the soul can move forward to meet with 'family' members, members of one's Soul Group. Souls will often get together and plan an experience in the Earth realm – one will be the mother, another will be the son, another will be the father and so forth – different roles to experience different aspects of the human incarnation.

There are lessons and aspects to be learned, insights to be gained, by playing different roles. Shakespeare told us more than we were able to hear with the following clue:

> All the world's a **stage**,
> And all the men and women merely **players**;
> They have their exits and their entrances;
> And one man in his time plays **many parts**.     *As You Like It*, II, 7.

Subtly he tells us and uses the key word. A Stage. And a Man plays many parts – he cannot play all parts at once, so he must wait until the next time the play is performed to play a different part in the **Drama**. Reincarnation. The subtle message here is "in his time" – the soul is eternal, so "his time" is **eternity**, and he thus "plays many parts." (And what if the Drama is run as a Simulation?)

Perhaps that is what Shakespeare meant when he said:

> …And all our yesterdays have lighted fools
> The way to dusty death.
> Out, Out, brief candle!
> Life's but a walking shadow,
> A poor **player** that struts and frets
> His hour upon the **stage**,
> And then is heard no more.
>
> **It is a tale told by an idiot,**
> **Full of sound and fury,**
> **Signifying nothing.**     *Macbeth*, V, 5.

If you're on the stage, you're in a Drama, right? And if the Drama is a tale signifying nothing in itself, and you can't control the Play, then it is **futile**, right? And if the Drama has no significance beyond providing your lessons/tests, and your gaining Knowledge, why do we get so attached to something that, in itself, is futile? Drama is catalyst only.

## Futility is the Goal

Surprisingly, the desire to help/fix/change Earth or people can also be a mindset that attaches you to Earth and now, to get out of here, also needs to be let go. It is another lesson that has to be learned.

> *And the frustration of not being able to fix, stop or change any of it is what leads to the **state of futility**. The deep realization that spending more time on Earth is futile. You have to see it, feel it and really know it, and then **detach**. That is part of your ticket out of here.*

**Meeting With a Master**

The Soul Group has access to ascended, wise Masters who counsel souls in the undertaking of a planned lifetime. The players for the next round of incarnation may have to adjust what they plan to do, or switch roles – depending on the Master's advice.

As a result of the meetings and discussions, and plans to meet each other, where and how, and what things this group of souls will do to and for each other, they will also include exit points (death scenes), special tests and Points of Choice will be set up in their respective Scripts. Their individual Scripts must mesh with each other and with the Greater Script running in the Earth during the time period the group plans to incarnate.

This level of planning does require the insight of the Master, and the review of the potential lifetime is put through a simulation in a **Heavenly Quantum Bio-Computer** – the same one mentioned in VEG Chapter 13 that runs the Greater Script for the Era in which Earth currently finds itself. (It is examined in Chapter 7.)

## Scripts: A Major Point

Consider: How many people around you, during the day, are also ensouled and working out their Scripts? What if you are the only soul working out the particular drama you find yourself in? What if 95-98% of the people around you are **OPs** – Placeholders driving your Drama/Script? That could mean that you are in a **fractal simulation** that will repeat – until you get it right – which is what the Higher Beings showed Robert Monroe in one of his OBEs. It would additionally explain why there might so many people without auras in a specific lifetime…

*A simulation that repeats is also called being* ***Recycled.***

Could it be that everything we see and experience is <u>orchestrated</u> for our benefit – as **catalyst** to provoke a certain direction in our growth? And how could the orchestration be done with willful [ensouled] human beings who do what they want? Two or more souls may make an agreement to be or do minor things as <u>a test</u> <u>or a</u> <u>blessing</u> of another soul in their group when they are all incarnated together in a common Drama. If the **intent** is to test or bless and not harm, then no Karma is usually earned.

Lastly, to repeat a related major point: the soulless/OPs <u>are</u> often what help keep the **Father's Greater Script** for Earth on track. Man has freewill and does not always do what he should, preferring to boogie and party instead of studying, inquiring and cleaning up his act – to get out of here. Many don't want to leave the Earth. So the

**OPs can be manipulated astrally to drive the serious karmic aspects of the Script**, giving Man his 'lessons', in turn manipulating Man for the greater good.

## Freewill vs Control

Interestingly, Shakespeare gave us a clue about our ability to control our lives or our destiny. Your Script governs generally what you can do and what you can get, as well as it governs what the Neggs are permitted to do and not do. And your Script reflects your **Ground of Being** which helps determine what experiences you need and thus attract. You do not create your day, manipulating people & events, much less your life. Shakespeare also said:

> There's a **divinity** that shapes our ends,
> rough-hew them how we will...                    *Hamlet* V, 2

For "divinity," substitute the words **Greater Script**...and this opens up the subject of freewill and control – do we really have both in our lives?

# Scripts

Soul growth is carefully scripted. No one is allowed to come into the Earth experience without a Script – a plan, Contract or Pact, for what the soul wants to accomplish where **only the major events are scripted**. In addition, there are often many **Points of Choice**: options to follow one path or another, and that is effected through one's level of knowledge (knowing what to choose), and open to the degree of Freewill one has in the particular situation.

Often the lessons the soul needs to learn are hardwired **events** into the Script – i.e., there is no avoiding them. The major lessons will appear as the soul's Destiny, and yet what he does about them is governed by the soul's wise/unwise use of his **Freewill**. Events are orchestrated as tests and opportunities. The Script is not Fate.

> *For example, my big dog is in the back yard, contained by a fence. He cannot get out except when I take him for a walk. He can do anything he wants to (and usually does!) within the backyard (freewill) -- but his overall life is 'destined' (fated) to live in the backyard.*

**Man's Script does not tell him what to do or say**. It generally controls what he can do, where he can go, and sometimes what he gets and doesn't get: **up to 10% of his Life**. The Script even determined his parents and any physical defects he would have to experience. And it determines the **exit point** from a lifetime, when, and what form(s) that can take. Within the limits of the Script, Man otherwise has "freewill" to do whatever he fancies – appropriate or inappropriate. **The Script orchestrates events, Man chooses how he will respond**... and unwise choices mean he will be returned to the Earth School over and over – until he gets it right… reminiscent of *Groundhog Day*!

Note that in many cases, incoming souls with a Script, participated in the 'design' of that Script; their birth location, choice of parents, and the opportunities and obstacles in their lives. While it is <u>not</u> a case of 100% Fate, **things are a lot more scripted than Man would like to think,** and there are some optional <u>choices</u> he must face.

## Alternate Scripts

Many souls usually develop or have an alternate Script that they use as a fallback if the first, or main, Script should prove unworkable – or if a soul somehow completes the lessons of a lifetime early, they can try out the alternate Script! But they stay within the same lifetime, and the alternate version must 'fit' within the boundary of the current lifetime.

The switchover is done when the person is asleep, desires the change, and when arrangements can be made and the Drama reset. The Beings of Light assisting you in your Script are keenly attuned to whatever is going on with you; they don't miss a beat.

## Script Control

The controls (i.e., "boundaries" of your life as set by your Script) are to make sure you experience whatever your Script says you are here to experience. **How you deal with events is up to you** – knowing that your inappropriate response(s) could damage your body, lengthen your stay here, or make yourself and others miserable. Insisting on your way, when you want it, the way you want it, was <u>something that got you put here in the first place</u>… you might want to reconsider your **ego's point of view** that you can do anything you want while here.

*Earth School is not controlled by the students.*

If you resist learning and overcoming tests, trials, and blockages, and hate your life, you may consider drinking, drugs, sex or even <u>suicide</u> as a way of escape. All will result in your being sent back, with the "screws" tightened more than they were the last time. [78]

You must eventually face what you were just sure you couldn't handle. This is exactly what happened to me: I committed suicide two lifetimes back and then avoided doing the right thing in the last lifetime, and so <u>this</u> current lifetime has been very rough (i.e., my freewill has been almost non-existent). My Script this current lifetime was 40% orchestrated (10% is the norm.) and I saw it all in the '91 Regression.

The Higher Beings are serious about our learning what is expected of us. And, ironically, even though we may not be aware of it, **we are more capable than we could ever imagine** – technically, we <u>can</u> handle whatever is given us – and that is one of the lessons (usually reserved for "last time" souls who are about to graduate from Earth). That realization has to become <u>part of each one of us</u>.

## Higher Control

No one does anything that does not fit within the boundaries of the Greater Script, else it would mean that God is not in control, and that is not the definition of God. Since God, The One, is not a person, It is more an entraining, Intelligent Force or Consciousness that underlies and empowers the Greater Script which is the **intent** of a yet Greater Intelligence <u>outside</u> this universe which oversees the Multiverse. The intent of an advanced being is very powerful. It is often called Law.

### Nothing is out of control and there are no accidents.

That means that God <u>does</u> have control, even though to us with a limited intellect, it appears as if things happen by chance and we fear that one day one of those things that is not under His control will collapse the planet, or solar system, etc. God does not watch over the world and every now and then say, "Oh, shoot! I wish I had foreseen that. Now I have to do that over!" **We don't have a God in training**. His Greater Script **is** in control and ours must mesh with His.

> Think of the **Greater Script** as the operating system in a computer, and your life Script as a program (e.g., a word processor) running under the 'control' of the Operating System. The many programs experience a give-and-take with the Operating System (OS), and they can function because the OS empowers them. They are not able to do anything they want; the OS acts as a 'control' and monitors their activities and use of all resources.
>
> Another word for the OS is the **Control System** (VEG, Apx C).
>
> When a program violates programming convention, or tries to illegally access files, or change parts of the operating system, it is not only stopped, it is usually quarantined.
>
> Note in the diagram below that there are five jobs running in the computer – under the control of the Operating System.
>
> > **Job 1** is a bigger job and occupies more computer space than Jobs 3, 6 or 8.

> **Jobs 4, 5, and 7** have finished and have exited the system.
> **Job 6** is an email with a link to a video, so the Operating System performs the link to the video and plays it for the person who initiated it thru the email link.
> Note that all jobs depend on give/take from the Operating System (symbolized by the double-headed arrows).

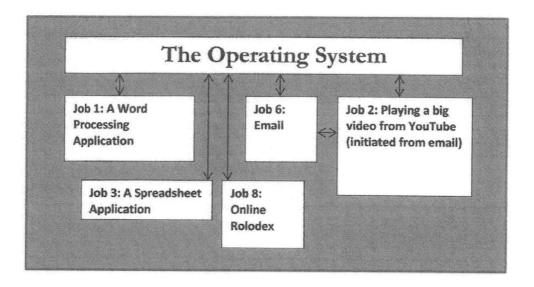

The Heavenly Quantum Computer operates in a similar fashion – think of the Jobs running in the diagram as 5 Scripts of 5 individual souls incarnated on Earth. The **Operating System** for Earth is the Greater Script and a major part of the OS is the Control System which often acts like firmware **Drivers** do in a PC system – operating the peripherals. The Control System sometimes initiates **Utilities** that perform special functions (like fish falling from the sky, or manifesting Airships [1896-97] to inspire Man…)

Job 6 and the interaction with Job 2 (horizontal arrow) is similar to two souls who have an agreement with each other to interact in some way. The Greater Script still oversees the association.

Note that **there are no LifeScripts for OPs**. Souls need Scripts to identify and manage what souls are to learn. OPs are bit players (NPCs) sustaining the Drama and providing catalyst.

OPs are walk-on bit players. Neggs and the Beings of Light effect the action and the scenario. God is the Playwright. The major theme of your life is not by chance. It may be called a Sacred Contract as Dr. Carolyn Myss so termed the Script. Welcome to the Greatest Show on Earth. Your life.

*In the following, refer to the difference between Soul and soul – in the Glossary.*
*The 'gods' below refers to the Higher Beings.*

## Heavenly Quantum Computer

When the soul has 'designed' his or her Script, with or without the help of the Master(s), it is analyzed by the **Heavenly Quantum Bio-plasmic Computer** to see what time period is most conducive to the lessons planned… and a suggested time period and potential families known to be available are presented to the soul. A choice is made to try out a lifetime, for example, in Elizabethan England with the Smythe family and the soul gets to study the characteristics of this family to see whether the projected lifeline of the incarnated soul will meet the needs of the scripted lessons planned… If not, another time and family are chosen.

**No soul is ever tested beyond what it can endure** – it is not the goal to "make or break" souls, although steel is not made without fire…. And the creation of steel may require several lifetimes before a soul can respect itself and stand up to whatever is thrown at it. The gods aren't ogres, and they know a soul so well (because they are trained to read the aura which tells the whole story) that they will not permit a soul to undertake an assignment that is obviously foolish or wild – unless the soul is prepared (and briefed) and can handle it.

If a Soul cannot decide which lifetimes to choose, or what role to play with aspects of one's Soul Group (Souls often incarnate together into a life experience to help each other), the Master will choose aspects and locations for the Soul and possibly even for the Group, as is often done for Baby and Young Souls.

At this point, we need to reconsider Reincarnation and Karma and how they play out – note that **Karma only applies to the Earth realm**, and not to the whole Multiverse. Earth is a School and Karma is the measuring stick reflecting lessons that were not handled appropriately and have to be redone. If the soul aspect successfully passed his last lifetime lessons, or at least a good number of them, he is eligible for **reincarnation** – incarnating into a new realm and experience (even though some past lessons may present themselves again in a new guise).

If the soul failed to make much progress in the last lifetime, that soul aspect may be **recycled back into the same lifetime.**

## Recycling vs Reincarnation

A significant object of this chapter is to clarify the difference between Reincarnation and Recycling.

People already know that **Reincarnation** is when the soul selects another lifetime in another locale or timeline for further experiences. What is less obvious is that the soul must have completed his Script (lessons) from the last lifetime with enough positive marks that he can move on.

If the soul failed to make sufficient progress in the last lifetime, he can be sent back into that <u>exact timeline</u> again – and that is where **Déjà vu** comes from. You <u>have</u> seen that before, you <u>have</u> heard that before, and you <u>have</u> done that before. Being sent back into the same, exact lifetime is called **Recycling**. It can also be done in a **fractal portion** of the same timeline; it is a **simulation** involving mostly OPs.

*Soulless humans are not recycled and they don't experience Déjà vu.*
*They also have no Karma, and thus no Script. Like NPCs in a video game,*
*they help drive the Greater Script in the Earth Drama.*

Yes, Recycling is less common than Reincarnation, but it does happen. If a student in elementary school does not pass 3$^{rd}$ grade, is he sent on to 4$^{th}$? He may be sent to another 3$^{rd}$ grade, in another experience (and that is Reincarnation) but sometimes the failed lifetime was so potentialed that there isn't another like it… yet. The soul either waits indefinitely for a similar opportunity to come up in the future, or he is reschooled and sent back with the hope that his 'retraining' in the InterLife will help him meet the tests of that <u>same</u>, failed lifetime. And sometimes, a new fractal lifetime is specially programmed for that soul.

**Life is a Film**

According to **Boris Mouravieff** (of VEG fame):

> The life of Man is a film… Incomprehensible as it may seem, **our life is truly a film produced in accordance with a script**. This film goes on continuously, without ever stopping, in such a way that, at the time of his death, Man is born again. **What seems absurd is that he is born in the same place, at the same date where he was born before, and of the same parents** [i.e., recycled]. **So the film goes on again**. Each human being then is born with his own particular film… [Script]
> **The repetition of the film is not reincarnation**, although these two Are often confused…
> It thus happens to him that, faced with certain events, he will feel that he <u>has</u> already seen or lived those events… [**Déjà vu**] The human [body's] personality is not a reality in the proper sense of the word, but a possibility. It plays a role in the film to which [the soul] is attached,

from which it will not disappear until the moment of [death]. [79]
[emphasis added]

See two different Life Paths below. One succeeded in his chosen tasks, and the other wasted her time, and will have to sooner or later repeat the Script.

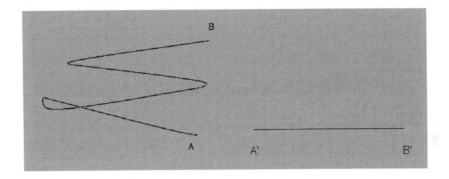

The above diagram shows a lifetime on **the right** where no progress was made, and the end of the life (B') is the same level as the beginning (A'). This flat line means that not much was learned, the soul probably partied so there was no soul growth, and the soul basically **wasted their lifetime**, and will have to repeat it or one like it.

On **the left** is a lifetime that made considerable progress, with a few twists and turns, setbacks and reversals, but ultimately winding up with more Light and more spiritual progress than the lifetime on the right. The ending must be "higher" than the beginning if the film is to <u>not</u> repeat; otherwise you can visualize the end of the film as attached to the beginning of the film as <u>a giant loop</u> – and it repeats in a life where <u>nothing or very little</u> was learned.

The teaching is that Man is born (into the film/Script), and as he progresses and applies himself to the spiritual **'B' influences** (VEG, Ch 5), the film stops being linear and begins to assume a **spiral** path upwards. The body's personality is associated with the indestructible real Self and will itself be transfigured by conscious application of spiritual growth, and thus the personality [ego] subsumes itself into the Soul.

> As long as Man lives in the wilderness [of carnal **'A' influences**], self-satisfied and immersed in lies and illusions, the film will unfold with mechanical inflexibility, and the personality will remain entirely unchanged. [80]   [emphasis added]

And a person who has made no progress in their life/film, often is **recycled**.

In theory, Man can stay in the repeating loop of his life/film/script until the end of time. As long as he is happy with himself, oblivious to the truth and higher forces, attributing his virtues to himself, attributing his problems to others... he is among the **"living dead"** that Jesus said were men who "believe themselves to be alive." [81]

They repeat the film, since it stays **linear** and the end meets the beginning in a giant loop... and hence they are **recycled** (and may later be dissociated back to basic life elements).

On the other hand, the person who seeks Truth, spiritual growth, and acts on intuition and follows the 'B' influences, has turned his film into an upward **spiral**, where the end cannot meet the former beginning. His ending PFV is greater (higher). Having done that, he is breaking the cycle of repetition and does not return to it. In fact, he can't because his 'magnetic centers' (or charkas) have grown and he is now watched and assisted by Higher Beings who are adept at setting up circumstances as stepping stones to further growth.

> We should know that, at the end of a spiral (incarnation), a comparison is made between the film as it was conceived at the time of birth and what it has become at the time of death. The **balance sheet** between these two states is drawn up, as in accounting, by listing assets and liabilities, followed by a profit/loss statement. This will show the result of the elapsed life objectively.[82]

A soul can make no progress by fighting his Script and ironically some people do just that under the mistaken notion that they are proving themselves 'tough' and exercising their freewill. Man does have freewill to work with his Script or fight it... and then face the consequences.

**Absolute freewill is an illusion** – the Script is the controlling factor: if your Script permits something, go for it. If the Script prohibits, say, being rich because this lifetime is about mastering the poverty experience, then nothing you do will result in your being rich – any large amount of money you get will be taken from you.

The Script reflects Karma ... not always a payback, but some part of yourself (even a "shadow side") that you need to master.

**Why Karma?**

There has to be a way **to track the soul's use of freewill** (when they do have Points of Choice) and hold a person accountable for what they have done. It is called the Law of Karma and **only operates where there is freewill**... obviously if you have no freewill, no choice about what you do, you are not responsible for what you do/don't do. And Earth is a Freewill School where souls learn the consequences of their actions. Hence the existence of tests.

> **Karma is not control – it is merely a feedback system that reflects itself in elements (mostly events) of your Script.**

If you didn't do the most compassionate or appropriate thing, and harmed someone else, you do not have to pay "an eye for an eye" – that is not Karma. Whatever it was that caused you to be inappropriate, act without understanding or compassion, is a lack or weakness within your development and will (1) be reviewed with you in the InterLife, and you may receive further teaching or 'adjustments' to help you, and (2) you will meet that part of yourself again in a future incarnation (not necessarily the very next life).

> **Karma is nothing more than meeting your shadow side.**

For example, if you lost your self-control and knifed someone in a past life, you do not need to be knifed in a future life to 'pay' for that. You need to see that there is a part of yourself that was weak (**underdeveloped**) and responded poorly to a provocation which might have been a 'test.' Such an event will be reviewed with you in the InterLife and you can receive training and energy adjustments to help you meet the 'test' again in the future. It will come up again – you can count on it being part of some future Script's test.

Again, Man does not have total freewill to do whatever he wants, whenever he wants, any way he wants – that describes a **god** and not a soul in a learning mode. Individual Scripts vary from soul to soul depending on what a particular soul is here to learn – **Old Souls have more latitude than Young Souls**. We don't always have the control we'd like.

## Handle it

If you are never 'tested' how will anybody ever know what you are capable of – let alone you?

The Beings of Light never ask you whether you like what you get or not, or whether you're happy – that is irrelevant. **You are merely expected to handle it**… including the sex of the body you were born with.

The experience of non-control is not to be met with anger, resistance, and depression. Whatever is in your life is there for the effect it has on you. **Catalyst**. The intended objective is for you to rise above it, not take it personally, and **handle it**. It doesn't need analysis, it doesn't call for rebellion, denial, suicide, or micro-managing one's life. It also doesn't call for drinking or drugging (Rx or otherwise) the problems away.

If you can't control (change, fix or stop) something in your life, it is a sure sign that it is **scripted catalyst.** It is not intended that you can control catalyst. Handle what you get, and don't wish/try/hope to get what you can't get. Find the inner strength and just handle it. Or, you'll be back…

Where Man gets into trouble is that he tries to be God and do whatever he wants, when he wants, any way he wants… before he has the wisdom to act (or not act) appropriately. A form of 'godhood' comes later (6D ), after discipline and maturing on the Path that all graduating Souls must walk.

## LifeScripts

Obviously, if a soul plans to come back as the son of another member of his Soul Group, then the Mother and Father souls have to incarnate first. Otherwise, by working with the Heavenly Quantum Bio-Computer, a soul may choose to experience something outside his Soul Group – especially if there is a particularly taxing lesson he has to undergo – such as being born to an abusive Mother or Father – due to the way Karma works, no member of his Soul Group can play that abusive role without themselves incurring Karma!

Thus Soul A might choose another, different Soul Group member in another realm who could provide that lesson, to experience the giver of abusive behavior, BUT the giver would pay for that behavior anyway, so Soul A cannot use Soul B's behavior. The hangup comes in when Soul A begins to resent or hate Soul B and this would create unfinished business between the two souls – if Soul A cannot forgive Soul B while in the Earth realm.

> Realizing what happened and trying to forgive when back in the Soul Realm  does not release debts… **what is earned in 3D must be paid in 3D and/or overcome in 3D** for it to have an assimilation in the Ground of Being of a soul.

Thus having said all that, be clear that the right way for Soul A to experience an abusive parent and have no residual karma or debt with that person is for the abusive parent to be an OP. **OPs do not incur Karma**, they have no soul and one never sees them again… when they die it is literally "dust to dust." That is also why, besides timeline bifurcations, there are so many OPs on Earth driving the Greater Script for many souls.

## The Greater Script: Control

In an effort to control this Earth School, you'd also provide the 'puppets' (OPs as PTB) on the planet who would do the will of the Neggs, **or** the Beings of Light, which in turn is actually the Will of the Father of Light, or the Grand Design, or whatever you want to call it. I call it the Greater Script because it reflects the intention of The One for Man.

There is a Greater Script which characterizes each historical Era and Man is subjected to different Drama and challenges in each Era. So, like it or not, **the OPs provide a good part of the Drama to keep Man on track with the Greater Script.**

> *OPs, remember, are not all perfect and sometimes get off track themselves.*
> *And when they do, they are often called sociopaths.*

Since Man has freewill, he won't always do what he should, much less what the PTB would like, and so to steer civilization onto the Path that will have the most **catalyst** (opportunity for growth) for Man to learn from, the standard OPs are controllable, largely influenced by the Neggs. OPs serve to act as both a feedback mechanism to Man and a derailing, deceiving mechanism to push, pull or prod Man into the experiences needed to grow him. And the experiences can be positive or negative.

Positive experiences don't teach Man as much as negative ones and thus war is permitted to show Man why Love and Peace are the way to go. Man must sometimes learn the hard way.

## Rewind: OPs

OPs are very necessary as an interactive element in every person's Drama; other ensouled people who would be required by your Karma to lie, cheat and steal from you, or worse, and would <u>themselves incur more negative Karma</u> – even though their actions are required by your Script. Such "give and take" Dramas are <u>not usually</u> staged between ensouled beings. To repeat: **OPs are used as <u>they incur no Karma</u> and can deliver the negative experiences to you (at the behest of the Neggs administering the negative aspects of your Script) that other ensouled people could not do without generating more negative Karma for themselves.**

## Scripts and Errors

Souls have relative freewill and while our lessons <u>are</u> scripted, our appropriate exercise of freewill depends on our understanding of the situation, compassion for the others involved, and what our accumulated Knowledge (wisdom) tells us is appropriate in a given situation. If a soul has had no experience in a certain area, or plays dumb, or really can't figure out what to do, he is still expected to make the most appropriate choice s/he can. Even if it is wrong, do something!

Errors will often be made because no one is perfect on Earth. Goofs can happen, even as errors of judgment and we are still held <u>accountable</u> (not "guilty") for our choices. When someone is inadvertently hurt by our carelessness, or ignorance, <u>it counts</u> – but not like it does when we <u>knowingly</u> harm others. So if I hurt my soulmate and she feels like kicking me in the *cojones* and spits on me, if that occurs to her – that will incur some Karma <u>for her</u>… Payback on payback. When does it end? "Vengeance is mine" did <u>not</u> say the Father of the Multiverse, and a loving God would not say that. **God does not punish**… we do it to ourselves.

> *Any vengeance, or payback, should be left to God since the system of Karma is much more effective and complete.*

## Forgiveness

Forgiveness breaks the cycle and **breaks the energy link** to the person we hate or resent – it removes the link and the need to come back and play with that person again and again, until one of the two stops paying the other back. One of the worst role models that we have had on Earth was the Hatfields and McCoys. "An eye for an eye" is the wrong way to go… (see Chapter 11, section 'II Using Energy').

> *And the higher one goes spiritually, the more one forgives – because it becomes evident that the others <u>don't</u> know what they're doing. Getting involved in their ego game doesn't pay.*

## Summary: Scripts, OPs and Simulation

On the positive side of the coin, when everything is said about Karma, OPs, Scripts, freewill and destiny, it may occur to some readers that the soul is undergoing a Simulation, not unlike *Star Trek's* **Holodeck** where experiences are very real but 'engineered' nonetheless. If everything was totally freewill, there would be no need for a Script, and no need for OPs, nor would there be a need for a Life Review when you die. But, all these things exist. And they exist for a reason: **no one gets into the Earth experience without a <u>purpose</u>, or a Script (or a Contract).**

Consider the following:

The <u>Script</u> contains some elements of <u>destiny</u>, as well as Karma as things that must be faced – as payback or as <u>tests</u>. The Script is largely driven by <u>Karma</u> and selected lessons, and it may include some particular aspect of soul growth that the soul has elected to work on. Every Script needs a scenario and supporting players and the mix becomes the <u>Drama</u> whose major acts/scenes are the elements of destiny – scripted events and/or people that must be met. The OPs participate in creating the Drama, like walk-on bit players. Unlike a hardwired script in a thespian playhouse, there are areas of one's personal Script that call for <u>freewill</u> decisions (Points of Choice) which are reflections of the soul's maturity. <u>All</u> reactions to one's Drama/scripted events are <u>recorded</u> and will be evaluated after leaving the Earth life by the gods who run this school.

Many OPs are "fillers" – there to round out the scenario, but they have no personal purpose in the Drama. They are like **NPCs** (Non Playable Characters) in a video game --They have no Script. Yet, some OPs are key to your lessons. There may also be few ensouled humans in one's Drama as they have their own lessons to learn, in their own Scripts and as will be seen in a later chapter, they are not all participating in <u>your</u> Drama… unless by agreement, like a soulmate. **So many players in your Drama who are not family or close friends, and who challenge you, turn out to be OPs**.

So if we can see that the Script is driven largely by OPs who discharge karmic lessons, and some aspects of the Script are open-ended, is it not logical that someone will be reviewing our progress or failure, and thus **our scripted life can be called a Simulation**? Wasn't a function of the *Star Trek* Holodeck to pit oneself against simulated situations to hone skills and develop personal growth? Why should the scripted Drama on Earth be any different? (See Appendix C.)

Just something to think about.

**Remaining InterLife Issues**

Please note that issues pertaining to incarnation, selecting the baby/body to inhabit, choosing the family, cancelling out with 'still' birth, and changing one's mind were covered in VEG, Chapter 16, 'InterLife' section, and here in Chapter 7.

# Soulmate Relevance

**Putting it All Together**

Soulless humans, recycling and timelines add a new dimension to the basic triangle of Soulmate – Reincarnation/Karma – InterLife. In the old paradigm, or standard Earth teaching, there was key information missing. Reincarnation often involves alternate timelines, most Earth timelines involve soulless humans, **soulless humans cannot be a soulmate**, and you may not meet your soulmate if they got recycled, and recycling can happen instead of reincarnation. Our true Reality is more involved than we have been led to believe.

Hopefully, the last five chapters were interesting and useful information, and there was much more that could have been said. This chapter seeks to make the link between the InterLife and Soulmate choices, whereas the last chapter linked a Regression with a Soulmate significance.

Having presented all that for consideration, let us now review (1) how it relates to a Karma and soulmate issue, from the last chapter and (2) how my issue fits within the larger context of the Reality that we all inhabit. Our issues and lessons are not that different and it is possible to draw some universal conclusions that everyone can use.

When we know <u>where</u> we are and <u>what</u> we're doing here, we will be in a better position to make the decision that we all have to make, sooner or later: Do we continue to return to Earth, with its attachments, Karma, soulmates, lessons and potential for recycling, or do we choose to get out? And if we are willing to consider getting out, what does that mean? **Appendix C** offers an alternative, summary look at the option we all have to transform and graduate from the Earth School.

> **Please note in the following recap, that all Earth Graduates will have experienced the same basic drama during their lifetimes – there is nothing new under the Sun and we are not all that unique. All will have experienced lying, cheating, stealing, carousing, adultery etc… thus there is no embarrassment attached to sharing what happened in my lifetimes. It is shared simply to serve as a template for the universal truths explained herein.**

### Rewind: Recapping My Soulmate

The first thing is to briefly recap the discovery of my soulmate in this lifetime, and what the discovery revealed. There are story parts omitted in the earlier chapter.

My life up to 1991 was very hard and I had too many problems with jobs and relationships. A friend suggested it could be Karma and that meant going through a hypnotic Past Life Regression. In February 1991, I did that and saw my last 4 lifetimes. The same pretty woman was in <u>all four of my past lifetimes</u> and we were married in the last one. She got me killed in two of those three lives, and I inadvertently caused her early death in the last lifetime.

The '91 Regression confirmed my problems as Karma and had more information, including a look at her and me in the InterLife. It was the same woman in all 4 lifetimes, and in the InterLife she wasn't happy with me. My focus was on myself and affairs of State and not on her and the kids. I had insensitively abandoned her. That seemed to lead the gods to initially split us up this lifetime to better appreciate each other, **and** because <u>she also had lessons to learn.</u>

I still had no idea who she was in the present and was not given her name or location, but I <u>was</u> told that she is here, now, and that a future meeting was pretty "iffy", depending on what she and I both did about meeting our lessons. And it was also "iffy" due to <u>her</u> circumstances and choices, which I would later discover on the Internet. The '91 Regression was also when I was offered a way to serve and cut some Karma out of my Script.

So by 2005 I had forgotten about finding her, and I focused more on cleaning up my 'walk' and becoming a more spiritual person. If I could make some progress that way, maybe the next lifetime would be better… I was beginning to better understand why I was alone (unmarried) in this lifetime.

In 2009-10, life went pretty smoothly for the first time in 66 years. The karmic payback seemed to have slacked off and I didn't feel like I was under a raincloud everywhere I went. My health was now excellent, and I was able to use my naturopathic/nutrition background as a technical presenter in weekly health seminars. Finally, I could serve in a small way.

**The Big Aha!**

Discovering her was first done through my '91 Regression… so I knew what she looked like. Then in 2010 it happened to me while surfing TV channels. It was obviously **orchestrated** – like the 1998 shift to an alternate timeline where I briefly met Leslie (Chapter 5) and learned that my soulmate there and I were engaged to be married on that timeline. Three times I was shown that she was real -- but unavailable.

Remembering what I had seen and heard on the TV screen, I later went to the Internet and began looking for info on her. One keyword connected me to her website. I began digging, and I finally got a name (there had not been one on the TV screen). Again, I had never heard of her… and I realized that **the gods had deliberately kept us apart**. They knew if I had seen her years ago, I'd have made a beeline for her and my karmic lessons and upset would have been enough (if we met) to scuttle any friendship at that time.

Apparently, I have changed enough that the gods <u>orchestrated</u> my seeing her on the TV. Yes, orchestrated. First, I don't watch TV Saturday afternoons, or during the day, period. Second, I just happened to switch to <u>the</u> channel in time to see her. Third, that program has not been shown on TV since that day (I have looked). And fourth, in the last 4 years, I had been really changing my attitude toward women, showing more care and concern for them as real people (not as the sex objects they had been last lifetime), and recognizing the beauty, love and mystery of what a woman brings to a man and his family. So I finally got to know that she exists and who she is… and that she is doing all right.

## The Door Slammed Shut

So I started searching YouTube and Wikipedia, appreciating some interviews she had done years ago. There wasn't a whole lot of biodata on her but I <u>did</u> find her website and got the address of her agency. I wrote her care of them. Twice. No answer. I said nothing weird, just tried to make conversation on some outreaches we both had in common which I had learned about her on the Internet. Nothing. So in November 2010, I called her agency and asked how they handle fan mail, to better determine if they had given her my letters, and maybe she just wasn't answering. My apprehensions were well-rewarded: The "guardians" open mail and if it doesn't meet whatever their "criteria" are, they trash it. She still doesn't know I exist… and may not care now that we are both 65+.

So, I have lost. I really regret the last lifetime, and just <u>can't quite forgive myself</u> for what happened to her as a result of my insensitivity. Now I see where my constant sense of unworthiness came from that plagued me during my dating years. (Chapter 12's EFT could have helped me –if it had existed then.)

## Evaluation

So, that was the lesson. They showed her to me late in life to drive home the message that I was alone for a reason and … look what I lost. I realized that I really loved her, but was an insensitive jerk. (Women always appreciate that in a man!)

Ironically, I was famous in the last lifetime, and she is famous in this lifetime. And she has done most of the things in this lifetime that I did in the last lifetime—after telling me in the InterLife that she would not have done those things! It occurs to me that she may have thought we'd meet, and when we didn't, she did what she did in the 80's because she gave up…? (Some of her songs do carry a subtle question of "Where are you?")

Maybe the playing field between us has been leveled since we now have both made similar errors and (hopefully) learned from them. Hopefully our mutual arrogance and my insensitivity have been transformed by our similar experiences. We both have a lot to think about. And I see where her absence and then the sudden discovery of her served to hit home: My god, look at what I lost! Look at what we could have had!

That is how it works. That is how They get our attention.

# Rewind: Lifestory Issues Enumerated

Given the info in Chapter 5 there are a few _explanations_ that can now be put forth to reconcile the karmic cause and effect scenario of my lifestory. It has been possible to connect the dots and extract meaning from the events, and then derive options based on the issues that are to be dealt with. In short, there follow 3 sections examining the _Problems_, my _Options_ at this point, and a look at _Significant Issues_ raised by the first two. This is **a template** that everyone can use.

> **Remember: my lifestory is not important; it is the insights to be gained from it that count.**

## I. Problems Explained

### 1. Body Type Too Strong

I chose a body type last lifetime that was too headstrong and with which I never bonded in a position to give _me_ control. Its testosterone output was too strong. In addition, my ascetic years in a monastery and meditation to awaken _kundalini_ backfired and moved energies into areas of the lower body that amplified libido and led to carousing, not spiritual growth.

In addition, my mind was not agile, I was an uneducated peasant. The mind in that body appeared to have average intelligence, but I discovered more than once that it could not always determine an appropriate course of action, and could hesitate to the point of indecision… despite being clairvoyant! Such a shortcoming led me to make a bad decision and abandon my soulmate.

### 2. Mom Chose Wrong Path

When it came time for Mom to remarry (husband #3 in 1956) she had a choice between 2 men: one was an electrical engineer and the other was a doctor. The doctor (Bob) was from the same town back East (NJ) where my soulmate lived and was raised and we would have gone to the same high school. And I could have been a doctor ( I later found out I had the IQ and interest for it.) She and I would have met.

> _It is possible that Mom chose Brian because he had never been married, and I think Bob was divorced with 2 kids._

Mom picked the engineer and we ping-ponged all over the country every 3 years when he'd get a raise, promotion and a transfer. My life took on an aimless quality – I didn't know what I wanted to be in the gypsy life I would now lead. And I often didn't finish the same grade in the same school. Instability was her#1 gift to me.

### 3. Lost Jobs and Relationships

Due to the manipulation of government workers and politicos last lifetime, I earned a similar karmic treatment this lifetime. I lost many jobs for which I was qualified, and relationships were either with the wrong type of woman, or I couldn't meet the kind I wanted. In addition, subconsciously I did not feel worthy of a woman after what I did in the prior lifetime, so most relationships went nowhere. I never married.

## 4. Lost Inheritances

Due to a mishandling of funds entrusted to me last lifetime, I did not have a healthy relationship with money this time. I squandered money on women and drink, last lifetime, and cost others their livelihood and income in the name of removing Undesirables from State jobs. The money came too easy and went just as fast in the last lifetime. Mom cutting me off from my part of the huge family inheritance was her #2 gift to me.

## 5. Pneumonia Many Times

I had had pneumonia 7 times before I was 13 and one more time when I was 22 (1965) that hospitalized me and almost killed me (see VEG, Ch 14). This was all due to my lungs having been immersed in icy cold water when I was beaten and thrown in the river. My assassins were trying to hide my body after they thought they had killed me, but I was still breathing and in one ill-timed breath, I damaged my lungs and drowned.
Ironically, it was the hypothermia that killed me.

Note that what we do to our bodies in a past lifetime comes forward as a scar, a birthmark, or in this case, abuse of the lungs (even caused by others) resulted in pulmonary issues this time.

## 6. Depression and Mood Swings

Many times since 1982, I would experience strange moodswings, depression and thoughts of suicide…and then they would disappear. I was not on drugs (I weaned off Rx meds in 1979) and these emotions would just hit me from out of the blue.

It was during the '91 Regression that I learned of the way two soulmates can affect each other even if they aren't together. I was given corroboration by being led soon after to the Oneness book by **Rasha**. There is an energy link between soulmates and strong feelings may be sent to the other via that link.
(See: VEG Ch 7, 'Multidimensional Effects' and Chapter 10 in this book.)

These energetic transfers' effects on me were augmented by my 17 years on prescription medications that upset and weakened my biochemistry. I was told that the negative energy of several issues my soulmate was going through, since 1982, were in part 'offloaded' to me. This is a natural, automatic occurrence among soulmates and so I helped her without consciously knowing it. I certainly had a karmic debt to help her, so now that I understand, it was the least I could do for her.

### 7. Unnecessary Prescription Drugs

This was my mother's #3 contribution to my life. Stemming from an apparent ulcer, the resulting medications were such **a good tax write-off** that she kept me on them for 17 years. How? I trusted her. What kind of a deal is it if you can't trust your own mother?

*Misplaced trust must have been another lesson.*

There went all my 20's and most of my 30's (ages 19 – 36) – the most productive, energetic years a man has, and I was drugged out. Seems to be payback for the lifetime where I used my apothecary skills to try and control our daughter's hyperactivity – ironically it was an OP mother (this lifetime) who socked it to me. My soulmate did not 'get even.' At the very least, it may also have been just a general way to control/manipulate me as I did others last time.

### 8. Soulmate and I are Damaged Goods

Due to the trauma I suffered at death last lifetime and the karmic payback stress this time, and not being able to connect with my soulmate, I feel the need of the InterLife Rehab (EIZ, Chapter 7)) to rebalance my energy, attitude and health. She has similar issues from doing whatever she wanted this lifetime and from being (what looks like) used and cheated, then possibly developing health issues, she might also need Rehab.

### 9. Unusual Health Issues

After getting off the Rx medication in 1978, I took up my former lifetime's lifestyle with women and drinking. I was dating anything with a skirt and engaging in unsafe sex practices. No one knew anything about HIV until 1982 and by then it was too late for many people. In 1979 I had relations with a very nice woman who had an unknown health problem that she would not talk about, and she mysteriously died 6 months later. I followed that with another woman of questionable health in 1980, and then my health collapsed.

In my rundown condition, some 'bug' seized the opportunity to blossom. No one, not even my doctor could tell me what my problem was. It was just written off to Epstein-Barr or Chronic Wasting Syndrome, as I also had Candida, great fatigue, constant sore throat, and I felt like I had the flu for weeks. I began to work out, jog, eat right, dropped sex and drinking, and generally rebuilt my health so that 8 months later, I was fine. We suspect it was HIV and I beat it because I am Norwegian and do have the **CCR5delta32** gene which creates white blood cells that kill HIV. [83]

In brief, items 1-8 capsulize the major karmic paybacks that came to me in this lifetime, including the 17 years on Rx medication, and all events had multiple antecedents from prior lifetimes.

> ***Mom's triple whammy*** *was obviously 'scripted' as well as her making the 'wrong' marriage choice. OPs are often used to administer negative Karma in concert with the Neggs.*

The 9th issue may not have been karmic, but is an indication that the gods might have been looking out for me. Just as they healed me at other times in the past (1965, 1987 and 2001), so I could live longer to learn from the scripted dramas (and write the book?). And that could be significant **grace** to me if we are about to do another Wipe & Reboot and I don't have to return to Earth – if I handle my lessons!

Nonetheless, it seems now like there were <u>too many</u> paybacks during one lifetime and I seem to have been really setup for a rough lifetime. Supposedly we are never given more than we can handle, and surviving the stress can make us stronger. But I sometimes wonder if my Script was all my doing? What if some of it wasn't Karma, but was merely scripted to provide the necessary catalyst to effect the desired changes? Yet, What if <u>all of any Karma I owed</u> was crammed into this one, 'last' Earth lifetime ( as I suspect)?

## II. Options

Given the problems I had with my soulmate in the last three lifetimes, we seem to be at odds with each other, and it looks like largely <u>my</u> fault.

Given the difficulty in communicating with her, due to her "guardians" protecting her, I have been at a loss to even talk with her, make it up to her, apologize, see who she is now… And even more interesting: How would I ever tell her who I am (assuming she doesn't get a soulmate insight)… But, who knows? She and I have always shared a similar sense of humor. And I love a snarky woman!

Given the InterLife scenario I saw in the '91 Regression, she was not happy with me and we have been initially separated this lifetime; for all I know she may have already rejected me and she may want to pick a new romantic soulmate for next time.

And lastly, given the upset I have with this planet, <u>I'm evaluating not coming back here</u>. I hate the corruption, pollution, disease, lying, violence, cheating and stealing, and certainly this last lifetime is not the kind of thing I want to repeat… <u>unless</u> she and I could come back together and do it right… but are we doing that on the alternate timeline where she is Leslie (Chapter 5)?

# Transformation of Man

Thus, it occurs to me that <u>we all have options</u> for most scenarios and problems. In my case, there are 7:

**Option 1**:  Go in person to her agency, present myself, explain things and see if they will give my letter to her. Or maybe get a 3$^{rd}$ person to intercede for me. In any event the travel to her city would be expensive for me now.

**Option 2**:  Send her this book and see if there is a recognition, with a note and return email id. This risks her "guardians" becoming aware of the soulmate issue, and a possible negative legal response if I am seen as a kook.

**Option 3**:  Pray and ask for the help of the Higher Beings to intercede, perhaps give her a dream to do something, or go somewhere so that we could just happen to meet and talk.

**Option 4**:  Do nothing and wait till the next lifetime. Continue to develop spiritual values such that she and I would work better. Requires patience and compassion.

**Option 5**:  Forget her, release her, ask for a <u>new soulmate</u> for me on the Other Side. Especially if she rejects me.

**Option 6**:  Release her, pray for her, forget her and move forward with <u>no soulmate</u>. It means choosing some other place and task to do in the Father's Multiverse, and not returning to Earth.  A viable alternative if we are not twinsouls because **twinsouls must eventually work it out**, and I wasn't told whether we are twinsouls or not.

**Option 7**:  This would be my **fantasy choice**. If she ever writes a book about her life, and discovers my book, gets curious and then discovers that we are soulmates,  not only would that change the ending to her book, but it could change mine as well. In fact, we could <u>together</u> to create <u>one</u> book, and perhaps see it made into a movie (largely about her life) – a more positive version of a movie like *Somewhere in Time*.

I addition, since we would be communicating, we could get each other's take on coming back together and doing what had to be derailed by my mother's No-choice in 1956: I become a doctor, and she can do her music, art, writing, and outreach with me providing the financial rock. We can have a couple of kids and travel where and when we want to. Or we can sell the kids and travel the world… (just kidding).

But she doesn't even know I exist. And we're both getting older…

Options 4, 5 & 6 are the only viable ones given the current scenario. To repeat: if we are just **soulmates**, we can break it off and move our separate ways. If we are **twinsouls**, I can go my separate way for whatever time is required for her and me to realign with our (joint) true soul nature and then make the connection later in a much more positive way.

**Evaluation**

Each soul has relative freewill and thus free choice about what it will do, whom it likes, and where it will go. **No one, not even the Higher Beings, makes any soul do anything.** If her choice was to reject me (because things <u>are</u> setup where we did not meet <u>and</u> I cannot easily contact her), then Option 6 is left to me. If she chooses to understand and try one more time, then Option 7 is possible for us (if it isn't already happening on an **alternate timeline**… see Epilog in Chapter 5).

If she and I were **twinsouls**, her potential rejection of me and Mom's decision in 1956 would not make much sense; thus we are probably not twinsouls, although we have a lot in common. More likely is that our **alternate Script** (to meet at Hawthorne) was blocked by the gods (via my OP mother) due to my soulmate's upset with me in the InterLife and has resulted in our being apart. And there appears to be very little chance of rectifying anything with her in this lifetime… undoubtedly further 'feedback' for me to consider.

It would appear then that **Option 6** is what is left to me. I have to mentally release her, wish her well, and the gods will assign some other soulmate to her. I have chosen to move on and do something else in some "backoffice" somewhere in the Father's Kingdom… I am tired of the Earth-Human scenario. I haven't done it well and all the feedback says to move forward with something else.

> *We do not have to master the Earth-Human game -- we can quit and go do something else in the Father's Kingdom. We always have a choice.*

Obviously, there is no point in sending this conclusion to her (even if I could) because the gods will enlighten her when she returns to the InterLife. I won't see her again, and they will assign her a new soulmate with whom to work out issues. Sad, but we can't keep beating each other up.

# III. Significant Issues

Part of soul growth is recognizing and <u>assimilating</u> the lessons, and this last section deals with the possible intended significance of my current situation. One of the outstanding aspects is that I cannot easily communicate with her, and another is that I find it hard to forgive myself. These two issues alone bring to mind the following considerations:

## Patience

I wonder if this current situation exists to develop patience, since I can't do much about her now anyway. Would it be patience or self-sacrifice for me to come back with her next time, where we try to deal with <u>our</u> issues, and she may be repeating some of what I just went through? That would also require finding more **compassion**...

However, I'm not going to criticize her. I'll just leave. While it was walking out on her that got me into this mess to start with, it is obvious that I cannot hang around and hope that we will reconcile this lifetime, and she probably doesn't want that. So **moving on is the right thing to do**. She's also not on a pedestal and I would not talk down to her. Our relationship certainly calls for **tolerance** and making the effort to **understand her needs**, and to do that we have to **communicate**. In essence, patience is an <u>active</u> not passive activity – we have to <u>do</u> something while focusing on patience.

To have patience also means I have to **respect her process** and remind myself that whatever she is going through is Drama (from her Script, and maybe mine) intended to provide **catalyst** which provokes the transformation sought by one's Script.

Patience begins to sound like the key element without which none of the other positive attributes can happen. Someone said –

*In Patience we possess our soul.*

## Compassion

As a form of unconditional Love, this was sorely lacking in my past treatments of her. I took her for granted and sometimes ignored her. My cold behavior was called indifference and it was not loving.

### The opposite of Love is not hate. It is indifference.

Love and compassion are proactive, warm emotions which often seek to bless another person; indifference is cold and devoid of emotion and interest in the other person.

I tried to rationalize my indifference as that which a man in that male-dominated society was justified in doing – thinking that it was better to not show emotion and stay neutral to everything and everybody. In fact, it was cold, aloof and uncaring, and inappropriate behavior toward a woman that I loved.

When soulmates are separated, as in our case, it was (1) because she asked for it due to her disgust of me (adultery) and the times I hurt and abandoned her, and (2) because **some of her lessons had to be done by herself**, as were some of mine so decreed. These issues were made clear in the InterLife, which I was briefly shown in '91 (Chapter 5). As can be seen from the three prior lifetimes, they were not all sweetness and Light, and she <u>also</u> has issues precluding our getting together so far this time. She was not an easy woman to live with in the last lifetime… which is one reason I did avoid her from time to time… but, maybe I deserved her "little general" treatment!?

And what if she now has health issues? Would I like her to reject <u>me</u> if I had health issues? I am very healthy for my late-60's: not bald, no paunch, no dentures. Having been in Naturopathic and Nutrition studies for years, I follow a simple regime (3 things) that keeps me fit and I would share that with her <u>for her benefit</u>. If she has serious health issues, I would still not reject her… and that is the ultimate test of any relationship. If a man cherishes the woman in his life, he should be willing to lay down his life for her. She is that important.

**There is no excuse for a failure to Love.**

## Forgiveness

I have **not** forgiven her for my deaths in the two lifetimes in which I had 'killer sex' with her. Why? Because <u>it wasn't her fault</u> that I died after having sex with her. I can't quite forgive <u>myself</u> for stupid decisions, reactions and abandoning her in the prior lifetimes. I made an inappropriate choice whose consequence was to abandon her. I didn't think that through.

Yet, forgiveness is easier when I remember the following scenario:

> In an InterLife meeting with her, prior to my life as a Black slave, we **'contracted'** to have her test me. She and I both liked sex, and yet it must be appropriate and not be such a strong force that we cannot control it. So the test was to see if she could tempt me as a pretty white woman into having sex with her which was punishable by death.

> I failed the test. A social taboo and threat of death did not stop me.

> And I failed again in France as she was a bit too young for me, and

I succumbed to her charms anyway. Again, a social taboo did not stop me.

No, it was not a case of true love winning by overriding a social taboo. It was a case of **insensitivity**: I didn't care what others thought or would do – to either one of us! I risked <u>her</u> safety, reputation and future, too.

So, is it fair to her to blame her for what she did as Leah or Elisette? Is it loving to hate or resent her for doing what we agreed on? In point of fact, regarding her, **there is nothing to forgive**. My failure to do the right thing (respond appropriately) is <u>not</u> her fault. I am the one who did not **call on an inner strength** born of being considerate of her! I blame myself. Hence my feelings of unworthiness. I have had trouble forgiving myself.

## Self-worth

To handle **unworthiness**, I have to constantly remind myself that the issue involved thinking of someone else besides myself and what I wanted. I needed more 'schooling' in the InterLife for less ego (arrogance) and more <u>caring</u> in handling sex issues if I were to return to the **Earth-Human game**. I know that my issue was lust instead of Love, and I know that had I truly loved <u>the woman she is</u>, we could have found other ways to handle the issues of those two lifetimes in Georgia and France.

In the case of Jacques and Elisette, we could have run away and lived in Paris with her as my 'daughter,' and then married her in another year or two. **Or** be brave, stand up for her and marry her right then and there. Why avoid the issue?

In the case of Joseph and Leah, due to the race issue, it was clearly set up for him to experience 'courtly love' – the distant, unattainable woman concept of the days of chivalry. And <u>ironically this is exactly what I am now faced with in this lifetime</u>: she is unattainable.

Her kind of beauty is what I still need to be tested by… <u>if </u>I stay in the Earth-Human game. The answer is not to find a woman less beautiful. She has a unique chemistry and is a very special woman. **Baldy** (see Glossary) said to either work it out in my mind, because we are that 'connected' …or forget it and move on (Option 6). Sounds like we're not twinsouls.

*Her beauty (even in her late 60's today) still turns heads!*

The new realization is that my unworthiness issue can be handled **mentally or spiritually**. My arrogance and ego were hurt in my failure, and my unforgiveness

169

of myself is a form of nursing my wounds. What is needed next is a realization that it was a Drama for which I was not ready… and that is probably WHY it was in the Script: to say "Look at what you can't handle – this is your next lesson!"

*I have already resolved the issues via EFT (see Chapter 12).*

Then self-forgiveness is reached by recognizing that each Drama has its **process** which must be **acknowledged and respected** – not grieved over. If I can respect my process and respect the Law of Karma, the issue of unworthiness and inability to forgive myself can disappear. It is all just Drama.

Having said that, **self-worth** must be put in the proper context. No one is more worthy of anything than any other soul. Our very existence and specialness as a soul means we all have the same worth and potential to the Father of Light – **or** we all have none at all where 'worth' is an abstract concept that is meaningless in the absence of ego. The more egotistical we are, the greater we believe our self-worth to be. If we have no ego, we will not have a sense that our 'self-worth' is better or different than anyone else's.

### Self-respect is more important than self-worth.

It was my ego's position that I should have been able to handle those two tests (in the French and Georgian lifetimes). Obviously, I lacked something that the ego was not aware of: thinking and caring about others. **If I had known better, I would have done better, and that is all the 'tests' were showing me. There is really no unworthiness issue**… but it feels like it. If I predicate my self-worth on external events and successes, then I will psychologically 'crash' every time I fail a test. But I can still respect myself. I am not a perfect soul and cannot possibly pass every test I am given the first time. And the test is merely a learning opportunity in which our **Scripts often deliver the test first** which then forces us to find the answer.

Self-worth is an irrelevant ego position that precludes true humility.

The reason that Scripts operate in what appears to be a 'backward mode' is that we often don't know what we don't know, so we can't prepare for any/every eventuality. This is why we often don't know what to do in a new situation. Now, with this new insight, we can see such a situation as a **red flag**: It means we need to pay attention, perhaps ask advice, seek more information, or if the 'test' is demanding an answer right now, do the best you can. A decision to do nothing, or avoid the lesson, means it will be back. Do something. Take your best shot.

If the unfamiliar territory involves doing something for/to other people, ask yourself: What would you have others do for/to you in this situation?

**Why Forgive?**

Thus, Dramas do not need forgiveness…. unless you hate or blame someone (right or wrong) and they should always be released <u>anyway</u>. **They are not a test of our self-worth.** Note that the state of **unforgiveness** of another person energetically links you to that person and it means that you'll have to either let it go, or 'dance' with them (or their surrogate) later on (see chapter 11.) You are connected until you resolve the issue and release them. **Unforgiveness generates more Karma**. It isn't worth it. Release them and release yourself.

If a **soul** does something amiss to you, it is probably scripted Drama (prior agreed-upon drama), so forgiveness is not really an issue. See it as a lesson/test and give thanks. If a **soulless** person does something amiss to you, it is probably also scripted, but could just be their <u>unconscionable</u> behavior. In either case, give thanks for the lesson/test because there are no accidents. Don't shoot the 'messenger' who delivered the lesson. Only the lesson is important.

**No Drama, No Process**

Realize that most Drama in our lives is scripted. **Catalyst**. It is not to be fought, resisted, changed or avoided. Face it – with a new insight:  You are never given something that you can't handle – it is just your point of view that (1) it shouldn't be there in your life, and (2) you want it gone.  Worse yet, you think that its presence in your life means that (3) you are bad, defective, lazy or cursed. Reread Chapter 5 – I went through all of those possibilities and came up empty-handed. The most damning question I could have (and did belabor) was  **"Why is this happening to me?" I wasted years with that search**, and all the while I was so distracted that I lost aliveness and productivity, missed job and personal relationship opportunities, and became demoralized.

> *It is fortunate that I didn't become an alcoholic, start smoking, or doing drugs… or commit suicide.*

Unless you do a hypnotic regression with a qualified therapist, you will never be sure of the reason Why, and guess what? Ultimately, **knowing Why is the booby prize**! The lesson was <u>What</u> not <u>Why</u>. Even when I found out what past events caused current issues in my life – <u>I still had to handle them!</u>  That ability is not conferred as a result of an hypnotic regression, although it can make it easier, and the realization of one's fault sometimes removes health problems whose antecedent may be a past karmic event.

> *When we get to the Other Side, in the InterLife, we can know anything*

*we want; all Knowledge is available there. But knowing about tennis means nothing without the 3D experience of it and we need the experience of handling our drama – to <u>understand</u>. Hence the Earth 3D School.*

What really drove me nuts was hoping to find the answer and then magically expecting that my life would all work out… it was as if the quest for the elusive answer became the *raison d'être* of my life. Nothing else mattered. And because I could not find the answer, I brilliantly concluded that I was either defective or cursed. This is a downward spiral for anyone and leads only to a crash. Then in addition to not knowing Why, there is the illness or destruction caused by the crash.

Some people don't seek answers. They give up and commit suicide, or drink/drug themselves to death. Or, as in the New Age, some people pretend the issues aren't there and they think that by ignoring them, they'll disappear… these are the same deluded people who think they're creating their day (i.e., <u>making</u> it happen). Sad, because they'll be back to eventually handle it… and the problem won't disappear until they do.

**What you resist, persists.**

All Life Processes deal with Drama in one way or another. No Drama, no Process. No Process, no growth. No growth, just death and stagnation. A soul that refuses to grow may be brought back to the Other Side, 'disassembled' and re-infused with new energy, then 'reassembled' in an attempt to correct 'blockages.' Failing that, their energy may be terminally 'dissociated' (disseminated) as a failed unit. (Chapter 7, VEG.)

We are **eternal souls** having an Earth experience – whether we like it or not. Certainly, my opinion about what I was going though in my life didn't count for anything, and **I wasn't expected to figure it out**. No one is. I was expected to **handle it**. I wasted time learning that.

**Steel is not produced without fire.**

# A Better Way

What is suggested here is that we are not our Drama, we are not our Process, we are not our stuff, not our car, not our home, not our job, and not even our body. These are all things that the ego uses to justify itself and look to for security and meaning.

The Process is just a Script and what will surprise you is that **you can handle whatever your Script brings your way**. That IS one of the big "Ahas!" that we are expected to make as we grow in spiritual maturity. Instead we back off, fearing the worst… What <u>is</u> the worst that could happen to an eternal soul?

## Worst Case Scenario

People fear death because they have forgotten that they are an eternal soul – the body eventually dies, but the soul lives on. **A soul cannot be killed** (but the Higher Beings may disassemble it!). Death may be inconvenient and a nuisance, but it is not the end. A soul is an eternal spark of Light from the Father, and each soul carries a unique potential preprogrammed by the Father.

The worst thing that could happen for a soul is to be separated from the Father of Light's Love. Cast out into a Void. No Light, no Love, no other souls to be with… and according to the reports by Drs. Ring, Moody and Modi, and others, some souls are so ashamed of what they have done on Earth, they assume the Father will visit terrible punishment on them so they avoid going to the Light at the death of the body, and they voluntarily choose to be alone – in a Hell of their own making. They are the Discarnates.

Please be advised: **God punishes nobody**.

There is no Hell – I didn't see one when I saw the Other Side. We punish ourselves. But, doesn't God hate sin? What is sin? A mistake. God knows we are imperfect here and He knows we will make mistakes. That is what Earth is all about, just as with any 'school.' And everything we have ever done is recorded like on a "video tape" of sorts and is played back for us when we return to the Other Side…this is called the Life Review, full of our mistakes and successes.

**We are evaluated, not judged.**

Only deliberate heinous acts are worthy of 'incarceration' and separate 'counseling' by very advanced, loving Higher Beings… the perpetrator is still not punished as we think of punishment. Being separated from other loving souls is often punishment enough – ostracized until one comes to one's senses and asks to be 'rehabilitated' and then the **Father's Grace** is immediate and restoring… All the soul has to do is ask and open to receive. God is Love.

You have only yourself (and your ignorance) to fear. Darkness is ignorance, or absence of the Light. Darkness is not a material thing in itself…if it were, then when you turn on the light in a dark room, the light would have to make an effort to push back the darkness and its ability to do so would depend on whether the light was stronger than the darkness. A *non-sequitur*.

# Outcomes

In essence, Man is a special creation and needs only respect himself, others, the Creation, and his Script. Everything he needs is provided – even if it doesn't look like what he said he wanted. As Flip Wilson (1971-74 TV show) used to say, "Maybe what you want ain't what you need!"

Go with it, handle it the best you can. No fear. Remember that we are to go <u>through</u> the Drama, not stop in it, not play with it, not ignore it, not try to figure it out, and not blame others for it. I did all of the above. I thought that if I could just figure it out, I could stop it, fix it, change it… **catalyst cannot be manipulated**.

Thus, you cannot "create your day."

The Earth Drama is scripted and will 'roll on' anyway and your expectations don't count. **An expectation is a setup for an upset.** Get rid of attachment to outcomes and you'll be a much happier person, and healthier. Part of your 'lesson' might be to never have anything turn out as you intend or wish – So will you be unhappy your whole life? You can't control your Script, and you don't know what's in it… unless you do a hypnotherapeutic regression.

## No Control

Not all parts of our lives are under our control (because this is scripted planet Earth) and control is an effort to manage the outcome. Want to be really happy? It is simple:

> Take what you get
> and
> Don't take what you don't get.

Whatever you get is what <u>you</u> got, because you 'earned' it. You can't get something that another person got, and they can't get what you got – sometimes they can't even *grok* it. However, you <u>both</u> may be able to get the same thing if you both <u>do</u> the same thing <u>and</u> if your Scripts don't block it.

I know. People don't like hearing that; it is popular to believe that we can do whatever we want to while here. (You can try AND it may not work.) Sounds good, but our Scripts <u>do</u> rule, and we are <u>not</u> here to do whatever we want… Souls don't all have the same degree of freewill.

When my life went allegedly "off track" in 1956, my **alternate Script** was no longer a possibility, and the Script that was left was all about karmic payback. I found it impossible to do whatever I wanted – there was a karmic payback part of the Script that remained in effect until 2008-2009. (Writing Book 1 was part of the release, as Baldy had said.) Still I didn't commit suicide, overdose on drugs, become an alcoholic, or give up… Remember the gods asked me in 1965 in the hospital if I

wanted to continue? (VEG, Ch 14) They knew I was off track (else why ask?), but I chose to continue... although I have since thought (with 20-20 hindsight) that whereas I had no future and could not meet her, I could have answered 'No' to Them, but might have been later recycled into the same lifetime
I am now finishing. The lessons may be postponed, but they must be met.

> *By the way, from the research I did on my soulmate, her life was also a lot less than it could have been and she has been through a rough time, although she probably doesn't know why she wasn't able to get/be what she wanted either.*

Soulmates empower each other when they are together and can accomplish much more with their coherent, synchronized, empowered intent. Their energy is multiplied, not just incremented. So it is clear that both she and I have a lot less separately than we could have had together...and for the lessons to be learned, could it have been otherwise this time?

Don't forget that soulmates are **aspects** of the Group Soul and they always play different roles. It is similar for Twinsouls.

## Twinsouls

Normally the greater Soul or Higher Self will split into 2 or 3 soul **aspects** (not fragments) for experience in different realms, timelines or universes with no intention of these aspects meeting each other (Chapter 10). These soul aspects normally agree/plan (Script) to meet with other souls when incarnated, even as romantic **soulmates** or as just companion soulmates.

See Glossary for difference in soul and Soul.

When the Soul does split with the intention of meeting itself and working out some specific project, it may do so as a male aspect and a female aspect, or two females, or two males, who are to find each other and complete a unique (usually personal) agenda. This describes a **twinsoul**. Twinsouls are identical in essence but usually look different, and they are from the <u>same Soul</u> – whereas romantic and companion soulmates serve different purposes but usually are different Souls in the same Soul **Group**.

Romantic soulmates may choose to split, walk off and not see each other, but twinsouls cannot just walk off – they must resolve issues, if any, between them.

## The Last Word...

So there you have it, and that is the basic information on the InterLife as it relates to Scripts, Soulmates and Reincarnation. Something that affects all souls and is important to understand. It is presented for general enlightenment and further explains the actions/inactions of some people on Earth, and even explains why bad things happen to good people (Hint: think Scripts). And as we examined OPs, there are soulless people on Earth, **about 60% are OPs**, and they are used to drive the Greater Script.

Lastly, not everyone has a soul, and not everyone cares about it – the soulless person will (if they hear of this distinction) pooh-pooh it and tell you that it isn't important – after all, aren't we all equal? (Hint: no.)

The soulless would not be reading a book like this, dealing with soulmates and spiritual issues. Not only do they not know what that is, they don't care, and they assume that you don't, too. They are the promoters of the over-simplification of life: drive your car, eat your burrito, and watch Seinfeld… They are often attracted to Science where everything is Evolution, the soul does not exist (and it doesn't for them), and we are all the product of biochemical interactions within our bodies.

Yet it is to your advantage to know about them and what they do, and evaluate that man or woman that you're dating, your child's teacher, your pastor, your congressman, some 'scientific' pronouncement by some 'expert', or person with whom you work – ensouled and soulless are like oil and water. They don't mix, and a marriage between them is headed for trouble. Maybe even abuse. An ensouled human with greater spiritual potential should not be at effect with the primitive, soulless person and should seek to minimize their interactions with them. (See VEG, Chapter 5) Forewarned is fore-armed.

**Knowledge protects.**
**Ignorance enslaves.**

# Chapter 7: Timelines & Scripts

## Author's Note

This chapter will tie together the Timeline information from Chapter 2 and the InterLife Script data from Chapter 6. This is new information, not found in Book 1. In addition, a brief examination will be made of the issue commonly asked by a lot of people on Earth: Why do bad things happen to good people? Or, more properly restated: What does it mean when things go wrong – Did I do it, or was it done to me…? Or was it the Script?

## Whole Picture

This chapter will also, therefore, deal more with Karma, freewill and Reincarnation than before, completing the whole picture – in layman's terms.

Why? Who needs to know this?

So that you become an awakened soul who now knows the following:

1. Death is nothing to be afraid of
2. Don't avoid the Tunnel at death
3. There is no Heaven or Hell, and no demons
4. At death you return to the 4D Realm from which you came, herein also called the InterLife
5. You are an eternal soul and everything is **catalyst**/Drama, scripted for your growth
6. There is no failure; just choices and experiences
7. God does not punish, Karma does that
8. Karma is merely a record of success and failure that generates the next Script (or set of lessons)
9. Reincarnation is a new experience; Recycling is repeating the same lifetime
10. **Deja vu** means you have been recycled
11. Forgiveness means setting yourself free from the same lesson and negative energy yoke
12. Self-respect is more important than self-worth

By the end of this book, you will see why these are important to your becoming a freer soul who can make better decisions, a thus a fully actualized human being, and you will see why experiences in 3D that have attached us to places, things and people on Earth, have to be released in 3D. The 3D experience becomes part of our Ground of Being and cannot be easily changed in 4D. That is why we opt for multiple experiences in the Earth School and refine our soul's energy and knowledge.

Having given you the answers first, let's see how we get there with a review of the InterLife , Timelines and Life Scripts as a Process that shapes us both as humans and souls.

## Choosing a Lifetime

As was said in Chapter 6, when a soul has had the Life Review (which exposes areas of weakness), and has gone through any additional schooling with the master teachers (to gain counsel and insight on the weak areas), and has done any energy work in the Energy Imprinting Zone (to absorb and augment the energy needed to handle the weak area[s]), s/he is ready to focus on choosing a new Lifetime Script that will provide the opportunity to meet and handle one or more experiences that are appropriate to what that soul needs.

So the next step is to go to the Group Area and meet with one's 'family' – like souls on a similar mission who often incarnate together to help each other out. Souls tend to move together in a Soul Group which is often, but doesn't have to be, comprised of souls who share a similar interest... there is a Soul Group for Technical souls, like engineers, physicists, programmers, etc... just as there are Soul Groups for Artists, Teachers, Athletes, Medical specialities, Lawyers, Philosophers and Warriors... just to name a few.

The souls will discuss what aspects of their development are **mutual** and can be met together; one soul will be the Mother, another will be the Father, another the Son, and still others may be ancillary support along the way... during the lifetime, there are people, like significant teachers in school, who help keep us on track and may refocus us.

At any time, the souls may consult with a Master for advice, or they may tune in to the Akashic Records for information. The Akashic Records also contain **archtypes** (such as what Jung identified) which souls can study. Then, if a weak soul needs more courage, for example, s/he may opt to **imprint** the lifetime of a Mother Theresa or Alexander the Great so that that experience although not directly experienced, is available to the soul as if it had lived that lifetime and can assimilate the energy signature of a successful warrior-type soul.

That same soul of course still has to meet an experience requiring **the use** of the assimilated imprint and demonstrate that the 'lesson' was learned... imprinting alone is not enough... but at least the soul who has the imprint can 'draw' on an impulse (even if subconsciously while in 3D) which leads to the action of being brave. The soul also has latitude in how it plays out the courageous act, it does not have to copy just what Mother Theresa or Alexander would do. Thus the soul comes to 'own' the assimilated aspect of bravery as a part of its soul growth.

**The Heavenly Bio-Computer**

The next step is to go to the Computer and, much as one would Google 'Courage' on today's PCs, and 2,000 + entries may come up – so it is better to qualify one's search as 'Courage in health crisis' and the Heavenly Quantum Bio-Computer (HBC) will respond with a selection of Lifetime Scripts, Eras and options that require a soul to meet a health crisis with courage. This can be further refined by Era, race, sex, country and married/single, etc…

For example, the soul may refine his search down to the following criteria:

> Location = Earth (TL1 on timeline 1)
> Country = England  (C10 code for England)
> Era  =  1800s  (E3.6)
> Sex = M
> Race = Black (R2)
> Marry = No
> Lifespan = 60
> Health Issues = yes, critical  (C4 is cancer stage 4))
> Exit Points = two (age 30, age 55)
> Family = poor, small  (Fp3)
> Wartime = No
> School = E8  (8<sup>th</sup> grade elementary)
> ….

This would be an entry in the HBC that looks like this:

Tl1C10:E3.6MR2N60C4:30:55:Fp3NE8…… **LS:TL1.EA6.Mn42. 4356922**
|----------- lifescript elements ------------------|------------ Id tag ---------------|

This describes where the lifetime is, what elements the Script must have in it, and it spells out a real challenge for a Black man in the 1800's in England who has two close brushes with cancer/death, does not marry, and does not live past the age of 60. Of course more can be and is programmed into the LifeScript like Tests and Opportunities also called **Points of Choice**…

These elements are already scripted in a Timeline as LifeScript **LS:TL1.EA6.Mn42. 4356922**. All the soul has to do is choose that in concert with his Soul Group (for support they may enter too), or he may go it alone.

This LifeScript is loaded into the LSReview part of the HBC so that the soul can **preview that LifeScript** to evaluate the family, environment, projected lifepath and particular challenges presented by the Script. It is not subject to modification. The roles and lifepath are already set, scripted with some freewill playing a minor part –

Note: **Freewill** is much misunderstood – the LifeScript must be entered and played out to the best of one's ability – otherwise would it be much of a lesson or test if one's freewill were able to ignore or change the parts s/he didn't like? The only freewill choice the soul has is to choose what one's reaction will be to the catalyst of a specific lifetime… if the wrong choice is made, the LifeScript may terminate early. If the soul makes the right choice, the LifeScript can continue forward… There will be **Points of Choice** which are really tests to see just how much the soul has learned, and the soul always has the 'freewill' to fight the Script or commit suicide – but that is a failed Script and the soul will have to be re-schooled and at some point face what s/he was just sure could not be handled.

The truth is that **a soul is ultimately capable of much more than it thinks**, and one of the lessons to be learned is that ultimately, we can handle anything. We must come to **know** that (by experiencing it).

Perhaps now Shakespeare makes more sense:

> All the world's a **stage**,
> And all the men and women merely players;
> They have their exits and their entrances;
> And one man in his time plays **many parts**.     *As You Like It*, II, 7.

And again:

> Life's but a walking shadow,
> A poor player that struts and frets
> His hour upon the **stage**,
> And then is heard no more.     *Macbeth*, V, 5.

**It's all staged**… more than we would like to believe. The LifeScript is staged, the players already defined, the roles are set… all one does is select the Lifetime, and the Birth Masters will insert your soul aspect into the chosen Lifetime (see InterLife Component Chart below). It is merely a **Drama** that we go through whose preset challenges and opportunities (because many but not all elements are preset) allows for the Life Review (at death from a Lifetime) to be **evaluated** according to the ideal: an Old Soul who has mastered the Earth experience and would 'breeze' through any of the Earth Scripts. Any **Earth Graduate** could handle any of the Scripts… that is why the Earth Graduate is much **respected** by everyone on the Other Side (see VEG). See Appendix C.

## Handling Scripts

Perhaps it would be instructive at this point to point out that most Scripts are appropriate for all souls – it is just that a Young soul may not be ready for some of the tougher ones which really just test one's ability to bring up their inner strength, and Knowledge to handle whatever comes up.

Below are shown 5 Scripts (lifeline is dashed line) that one Soul (Higher Self) choose to experience by sending itself as 5 soul aspects into these lifetimes (LTn) and Eras:

**LT1**. 2000 BC Egypt:    ------------------------x1-------------

**LT2**. AD 1400: France:   -----------x2---------x3--------x4------------

**LT3**. AD 1600: China:    -----------------x5------------------------x6

**LT4**. 4000 BC: Sumeria:  ---------------------------------------------------------------

**LT5**. AD 2125: Mars:    ---------------------x7------------------

The 'x's represent **errors** made in handling catalyst encountered in the Script. Soul aspect 4 made no errors in LifeTime (LT) 4. This was a well-handled lifetime. On the other hand, LT2 made 3 errors and these will be reported during the Life Review (at death) and the soul will eventually have to meet these challenges again. That soul has a choice (made in 4D Realm) of meeting them all together again in a **rerun** of that LT2 (called Recycling) or s/he may opt to meet them in separate, new LifeScripts -- but **failed lessons will have to be met when the soul is ready**. The gods are not ogres and do not put more on a soul than it could handle… it isn't about overloading and causing souls to fail.

And lastly, LT3 met a serious challenge at x6 and botched its handling causing the soul to exit that lifetime. (And it may have been a preprogrammed 'exit point' designed to exit the soul… you'd have to inspect the Script to get the answer.)

Each soul gains knowledge and ability to handle catalyst from each LTn and at some point, all 5 soul aspects above will come back to the Soul (top level, also called Oversoul or Higher Self) with the accumulated experiences and lessons – for all 5 to share (even imprint). Then the Soul may opt to try one or more lifetimes with aspects of itself for further growth.

All 5 LifeScripts for the Soul become part of the Akashic Record (connected to the Quantum Computer) for that Soul. That is the source of the **Life Review** and the Masters evaluate it to see what each Soul needs.

## LifeScripts

There are almost an unlimited number of Scripts and variations of same such that new Scripts are not often made, but can be in special cases and are made by the Gods-in-Training (see Book 1) Programmers whose work is subject to review by Higher Beings (above 4D).

It is because the LifeScripts are preset with established characters/roles, problems, blessings, opportunities, challenges and tests that a soul aspect can be evaluated on their performance. The student does not control the School nor does the soul control the Script – thus the New Age teaching that Man can 'Create His Day' (or control the Script) is nonsense and now you see why.

LifeScripts also exist as a higher level in what is called the Greater Script under whose control all LifeScripts must run –i.e. the Control System (C/S) oversees and can inject more or less OPs, catalyst, events, and objects as are needed by the Script. It is a feature of the Greater Script for the Era being run.

**Case in point: Charles Fort** was to be instrumental in discovering what Earth is and for his LifeScript, he experienced and researched fish and rocks falling from the sky – and that may not have happened for other souls in the same Era and local part of the LifeScript – but it was executed via the C/S for him as part of his wake-up call.

**Second case in point**: because Scripts are largely preset, if one is granted "second sight" (or psychic abilities, or the gods running the LifeScript choose to tell you), you can appear to be a **prophet** – knowing what is to come in the rest of a person's LifeScript – or in general in the Greater Script for that Era. There is a Greater Script for each Era which says on a very high level, what that Era is about. For example, some Eras are about Earth calamities (earthquakes and volcanism), others are about dealing with wild beasts that challenge the community (like dinosaurs, huge mastodons, sabre-tooth tigers…), and lastly some like our current Era are about technological development and the potential to go into Space, as did the Atlanteans.

**Third case in point**: this is why there are no accidents that just willy-nilly happen. **It is all orchestrated**… or as was said earlier, accidents are "premeditated carelessness" – set up to happen that way. All cause has an antecedent, even if you don't see it.

In addition to the Greater Script for the Era, there are usually a lot of OPs (or Non-Playable Characters) whose LifeScripts are part of the Drama, and help drive the Drama for a soul or group of souls… just as they do in a video game. So Man and his LifeScript are a lot more constrained by the Greater Script, the OPs, and the Control System than he thinks. And it is all for his benefit – to make sure that things that are programmed into the Script happen… otherwise how can one be tested and 'pass' to move onto the next level? **His response is where his freewill comes in – and that is what is being evaluated.**

> **Think of the LifeScript as a curriculum in the Earth School.**
> **Don't curricula have tests?**

## LifeScript Elements

So if we are subject to Scripts that govern a lot, but not everything, of our lives on Earth, What would one look like? It was said that the LifeScript is designed to meet one's karmic requirements, i.e., there are elements in the Script that are designed to bring forth one's **Shadow Side** (Chapter 10) so that it can be recognized and dealt with. The Script also contains **Points of Choice**, tests, exit points, and new learning opportunities, which latter are those times where you have not seen nor dealt with a certain event before, and here it is in front of you demanding a response … this is where you take your best shot and there was no studying for that exam.

| | | | |
|---|---|---|---|
| Terms used in 6-month scripted events below: | | | |
| **POC** | Point of Choice | **TOR** | Test of Reaction: ability/knowledge |
| **KSE** | Karmically Scripted Event | **GG** | God's Grace |

Note that POC is a major KSE which includes a required TOR. In fact, most KSE provoke a TOR, and the major KSE will force a POC.

Remember: the Beings of Light (BOL or Angels) guide and protect, and the Neggs (temporary Dark Angels) administer the catalyst under the supervision of the BOL.

### Sample Eight Months LifeScript

May 2004
>Sean (35 and single) vacations in France
>>he is a successful, high-paid investment counselor and a
>>bit arrogant and STS
>Robbed in Hotel at night (KSE and TOR)
>>Hotel gives free dinner
>Falls ill, goes to hospital
>>Meets Elise (nurse) and falls in love (KSE)

June

> Sean is back home in USA
> His company goes out of business (KSE)
> Friend arranges new job interview
> Hard decision: Which job to take? (POC)
>> Chooses international job

July

> Moves to Germany for new job
> Reconnects with Elise and Gets engaged --
>> but she won't move to Germany (TOR)
> He spends a lot of money and energy commuting on weekends (KSE)

August

> Meets his soulmate Ilsa in Berlin and has to choose between
>> two women (KSE, TOR & POC)
> Sean drops Elise who is very jealous but demands one last date
> Sean meets her for dinner with Ilsa (KSE & TOR)
>> (Ilsa & Elise agreed in the InterLife to test Sean)
> Elise announces she is pregnant
> Ilsa announces she is gay
> Sean wonders what planet he is on... (TOR)

September

> Sean has lost both women (KSE)
>> and buys a Ferrari to assuage his mid-life crisis
> He drives to Switzerland to ski and the car is stolen (KSE & TOR)
> He takes the train back to Berlin
> Terrorists bomb the Berlin office (KSE & TOR)
>> he is unharmed (GG)

> Sean gets a free trip by boat back to the USA
>> he falls while climbing the ship's Scaling Wall and cuts his leg
>> his doctor tests his blood type for a transfusion
>> and finds Sean has contracted HIV [from Elise] (KSE & TOR)

>> [Note that the Script only said he'd encounter a serious disease, it
>> did not specify what it was...]

> Sean must decide what to do – suicide or hang in there? (POC)
>> (Suicide is tempting and he reasons it would make sense, but
>> he's not 100% sure it is wrong [thus although he does the right
>> thing by moving on, the test will come up again.])

October

    Sean decides to live and write a book and give the proceeds to charity
        the book is made into a movie and earns even more money
        Sean starts an outreach for disadvantaged people and has
        a change of heart – his life is about helping others [STO] now.

    Ilsa reads Sean's book and comes to the USA to meet him (KSE)
        she wasn't gay, just testing his arrogance  (TOR)
            (he passed a big test by caring more about others, so <u>that</u>
                Karma is gone [GG] and opened the door for Ilsa to return)
    Sean marries Ilsa (soulmate) and they work together

November

    Sean is abducted by Greys and healed of HIV  (GG)
        he is also given new insights to serve others
    Ilsa is not healed and has contracted HIV from Sean
        (and by pre-arrangement in the Interlife Sean is about
        to face a major test)

    Ilsa is in a car accident and crosses to the Other Side. (KSE)
        Sean is heartbroken – having lost a part of his life that he
        really loved – How could They do this to him?!    (TOR)
            (Remember souls are eternal and Sean and Ilsa will be
            together again in the future, very soon)

    Now Sean must face the test <u>again</u>:  What does he do with a major
        part of his life gone? His love is gone and the outreaches are
        running well, so he is not really needed to run them… Should he
        open an HIV hospice and contract the disease again and go down
        swinging…? Surely, the gods wouldn't blame him if it ended that
        way…? [yes they would: that is **subconscious suicide**] What does
        he have to live for now?  (POC & TOR)

December

    Sean decides to take a few days off and reflect. He goes camping in the
        Sierras. Asleep in the tent, he is taken Out of the Body to the Other
        Side where They remind him what Life is all about. (GG)  His Life-
        script is to minister to others and the gods don't want it terminated
        early… for his sake and for those who benefit from his outreaches.

    Sean awakens the next day renewed and refocused. He decides to stay
        committed to others [STO] no matter what. [He has just passed the
        biggest test of this lifetime and  it will not come up again… unless

he deviates from his Path.] He returns to the city and work with a new energy and purpose.

Sean stays with his outreach and meets Carrie, a new worker. (GG) Over the months to come, they become romantically involved, marry, and soon have a child – a girl … Guess who?

## Resolution

And so it goes, it is **all Drama** or catalyst. There are tests, blessings, major decisions to be made, and if the correct choice is made (POC), the test is not given again (unless your decision was made for the wrong reason, or was done half-heartedly). **Correct decisions become a part of your soul**, your Ground-of-Being (Glossary), and reflect your Light quotient.

Note that Sean started out STS, arrogant, me-me-me… on a human power trip. He began to meet with difficulties and setbacks that were part of the catalyst – designed to get his attention and 'mold' him into more of a caring person – coming from the heart and not the head. And when he decided to care more about others (i.e., the compassion and respect Path), that is when the Higher Beings 'rewarded' him (GG) – people could come into his life to bless him that could not get there before because his 'vibration' was wrong and he inadvertently repelled them – he shifted his attitude, his focus to STO, and instead of repelling people and events that he really wanted, he attracted them. He even attracted Ilsa back into his life – twice!

> **Note**: this is the only way that 'creating your day' can work – you do what it takes to **attract** what you want – by **being** what it takes to get it. (Your vibration must be capable of embracing and holding it, otherwise you actually repel it.)

Because the gods (the Higher Beings) are not ogres, They stand ready to reinforce and deliver good Karma (GG) and so Sean was blessed with people and events in his life that reflected his better choices. These blessings can also be considered scripted (KSE) – depending on choices made. It cannot be overstated how important it is to **make the correct choice and thus effectively avoid or cancel Karma that was originally set up or scripted to reflect one's Shadow Side, and now is not necessary.** (Chapter 10.)

Scripts often have **alternate paths** pre-programmed into them, following POC … best-case and worst-case scenarios – **there is still no 100% freewill even if major Karma is avoided** – the scene just shifts to follow-up lessons in a different part of the Script. You have **freewill** to make the choices in your life, and then the Drama takes over to play out the scenarios reflected by your choice(s) and may include less or more freewill, depending on the choice(s) made. No one has 100% freewill all the time – otherwise this would not be much of a School if the 'student' (soul) controlled everything (i.e., could do whatever s/he wanted all the time).

> **Freewill is constrained by whatever 'leg' of the Script one is on at the time.**

## Is Karma Valid?

**Caveat**: you may say, well if the Script is basically preplanned, preprogrammed (and it is), then what is the point of Karma? How can a soul 'pay for' mistakes that are programmed to happen? Now is the time to refine the definition of Karma.

**Answer**: Please note that **Scripts are never out of control**. And there are Points of Choice and tests preprogrammed into the LifeScript that the soul, of course, has a **choice** about how to handle – the <u>only</u> freewill aspect of a LifeScript. **The events are scripted, your choice isn't.** Karma is not 'payback'. It is **a recording** of your success and failures in each LifeScript that feeds into the design of your next Script... your successes <u>might</u> be tested next time, and you can expect that some or all of your failures <u>will</u> be retested. In a sense, **the soul is meeting itself** and has to overcome the "current status" as represented by the Karmic Report.

> Think of the Karmic Report as a **Balance Sheet**: it shows your assets (or strong points) and your liabilities (weak points). The difference is your Net Worth – you want the assets to outweigh the liabilities so that you are worth more as a soul and are thus capable of doing more and at some point, you "graduate" to be of service in the area of your choice (or strength) – and again that is why the Earth Graduate is so highly **respected**. (See Appendix C.)
>
> **For example**: can you coach a football team if you never played the game and have no feel for what the players go through, what kinds of plays work, in what situations, and how much practice it takes to win? When you graduate from Earth, you will have Knowledge in a certain area of expertise, and you will have (reasonably) mastered it so that you are of value leading other young souls in your expertise (say, engineering) and can mentor them, advise them, **or** work in the Heavenly Higher Realms where they 'engineer' planets and solar systems...and LifeScripts.

Just something to think about... this is why you need to know what is going on so that you don't waste a lifetime. You can graduate from Earth and be further trained for a position in a very dynamic aspect of Creation... but first the basics must be mastered <u>here</u> ... because service involves discipline and focus.

The only thing left to examine in the InterLife is the way that Timelines, LifeScripts, and the HBC work together.

## InterLife Components

In the diagram following, the soul (larger star) at 'a' in the Group Area, makes a choice via the HBC to select Lifetime 4 (LT4) and the lighter arrow at 'b' is that choice which results in the LT4 being loaded into the HBC (heavier return arrow). The HBC invokes the Control System (C/S) to in turn invoke the HVR Simulation for planet Earth in Timeline 1 (TL 1).

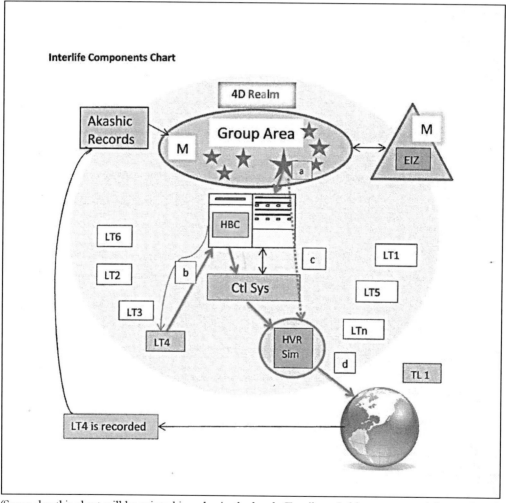

(Some day this chart will be printed in color in the book. Email me [address on copyright page] and I'll send you a copy.)

The LT4 LifeScript is loaded to TL 1 Earth via the red LT path. The soul at 'a' is processed into the HVR Simulation via the dotted blue line at 'c', and the LT4 + soul load (red + blue) and make purple at 'd'. There may already be souls running in TL1 and that is OK; the C/S can insert and delete without disrupting the Timeline and neighboring Scripts. The family into which soul 'a' is born is already there – they are just seen as having a baby. Thus the soul 'a' enters the LT4 Drama by birth.

Note in the InterLife Components Chart that:

The two small boxes with **"M"** represent the Masters who stand ready to advise. They are all over the place, advising, teaching and checking up on souls who may have gone to the EIZ.

The Energy Imprinting Zone (**EIZ)** is an area in 4D where souls go to recuperate and recharge after a strenuous lifetime. This is also the site for archtypes available for imprinting soul qualities, mentioned earlier.

**"HVR Sim"** is that part of the Heavenly (Quantum) Bio-Computer (**HBC**) that effects the desired Simulation of a Holographic Virtual Earth Reality in a Timeline. Both HVR Sim and Control System (**C/S**) are aspects of the HBC and were covered more thoroughly in Book1, Chapters 12-13.

**LT1 – LTn** represent the available Lifetimes and Scripts available for all souls (the **Stars)** in the Group Area.

The lifetime LT4 for soul 'a' is recorded in the Akashic Record (AR) which is available to any Master as well as to the soul whose lifetime is in there – soul 'a' in the Group Area can review any of his past lives (from 4D) – however, he cannot see just any other soul's life unless that other soul has given permission.

When the soul 'a' in TL 1 Earth dies, s/he is taken back to the Group Area via a **Tunnel –** which protects the soul from 'Astral' harassment by Thoughtforms, Parasites, and by Discarnates ('ghosts') who were afraid to go to the Light and will roam the lower 4D around that version of Earth until the TL1 dissociates and collapses.

## Script Administration

In addition, as shown in VEG (Chapters 6 – 7), there are beings assigned to each soul to make sure that the LifeScript is on track with what that soul needs.

> **Beings of Light** – administer the proactive parts of the Script and make sure undue harm does not befall the soul; blessings, health maintenance and guidance are what these beings, also called Angels,

do (but they don't have wings).

**Neggs** – administer the negative parts of one's Script, and work with the BoLs and OPs to provide the catalyst that challenges the soul to be more than s/he thinks they are. Anything negative that the soul has coming to it (curses, ill-health, or lack of guidance) is the purview of these beings. They are not demons but have been called that by the ignorant.

This separation of duties was explained in Book 1: it was more straightforward to have two separate groups doing two separate functions as opposed to one Angel who'd bless then curse, guide then mislead, heal then cause illness. This was a recipe for disaster – a schizophrenic approach that called for one Angel to make decisions and that is not what Angels do... they do not have freewill, and as was said, Man was created to be higher than Angels and they are to serve him.

## Astral Population

It was just said that a soul transitioning at death back to the Group Area in the InterLife, most often uses the Tunnel to avoid contact and potential harassment from Discarnates. Yet there are several types of beings in the Astral which is 4D.

**Discarnates –** those who died, and some who are dead but don't know they are dead. They are ghosts who are the victims of a traumatic death and are still trying to live out a lifetime that came to a screeching end... they will be looked at by the Beings of Light (Angels) from time to time and asked if they want to go to the Light.

**Beings of Light** – these are the **Angels** who administer one's proactive Script; so-called because they are light beings, pure energy and they do not have wings, but can appear with wings if that is what you need to understand who/what they are.

**Neggs** – these are former Beings of Light, they are now Dark Angels, but not demonic. When it was decided to separate the positive vs negative admin of souls' scripts, many Beings of Light volunteered to do the job, but they had to operate with 90% Darkness to stay true to their objective – too much Light in them and they'd hesitate before socking it to someone who needed it. At their core, down inside, they do still have the spark that will be activated to transform them back to a Being of Light. They are called Neggs which is short for **Neg**ative **G**uide**s.**

These first three tend to occupy the Lower Astral which is closest to the 3D Earth plane.

Occasionally there are the following entities present in the Lower and Mid-range Astral:

**Parasites** – these are biological entities which exist in the Astral, around Earth. They are not self-directed or conscious; they are attracted to negative energy people and will attach to their auras, and if there are holes in the aura (See Book 1), they can cause health problems as they drop to the body and can block chakras and clog the Bionet meridians. They are not very numerous.

**Thoughtforms** – **(TFs)** these are what Carl Jung often referred to as Archtypes. More properly, they are like "*memes*" – they are the result of ideas commonly held by humans which tend to accrete like light clouds of energy that are often fear-based, anger-based, or sadness-based and can like Parasites be attracted to negative people and stick to their aura – influencing the person by the energy potential contained in the cloud-like substance. The most common are Depression-Suicide, Angry-Warrior or Tough-guy TF, and there is the Playboy-sex TF.

The reason for these TFs is that Man is a creator and his mind coupled with the minds of hundreds of others thinking similar thoughts of revenge, depression, or lust (for example) energize the thoughts which really are things (Chapter 12) – that is another reason for the **Quarantine** around Earth – Others out there do not want the added impact or influence of what is going on in the Simulation – What happens in the Earth realm, stays in the Earth realm.

Thoughts of poverty, fear, and lack form a prevalent TF, thoughts of violence and revenge (amplified nowadays by the ubiquitous stalk-it-and-kill-it video games), help to reinforce that TF, and lastly the prevalence of pornography, prostitution and sex shops reinforce the lust TF in the environment. If you doubt this, walk into a sex shop and note how you feel BEFORE entering, and how you feel 5 seconds AFTER entering – what kinds of thoughts are going through your mind out on the sidewalk, and then go in and notice the energy comes as a *feeling* which then generates lusty thoughts – before you even examine the magazines and video jackets!

A second test would be to walk into a bar and see if you suddenly want a drink. Discarnates and Parasites hang around bars and try to entice human 3D beings to drink as they can 'get off' on the energy vibrations produced as the human gets drunk. They can 'ride on' the 'loopy' energy output of the drunk person.

And lastly there are the occasional Interdimensionals (aka Djinn and some ETs) who can come and observe. And the 4D STS.

**Interdimensionals** – aka Djinn and some ETs (not Little Greys although they operate **intra**dimensionally from where they are based to where they are sent – because it is a fast way to travel.)

These typically occupy and use the Higher Astral. Because they are so rare, they are skipped here, but Chapter 6 and 12 in VEG dealt with them. The main problem they cause humans is that they get curious about what the 3D human experience is all about and sometimes they take over a body (usually an OP because there is no soul) to see what it is all about.

**4D STS** – this group is lower Astral, too, and is behind the machinations of the PTB, some OP behavior, and they do not like Man. Some authors consider them to be the Interdimensionals that John Keel (in a section below) referred to so often. They seek to influence Man to be less than he is, and operate from his lower three chakras. They support poor education in school, errors in the Word in church, violent/sexy video games, selling drugs, crime and corruption to name a few. They and the Discarnates are the Gameplayers of Chapter 12.

Getting rid of them is what Deliverance and sometimes Exorcism are all about.

# Deliverance

*This is included not because it is scary – it isn't. In fact the year that I assisted in a Deliverance Ministry was mostly boring and the lesson from this section is simply: these people were oppressed (**none were possessed**) because they believed that demons existed… and it is done unto you as you believe. Our job was to tell them the truth and their oppressions automatically disappeared.*

In the deliverance ministry in which I participated for almost a year, patients would come in with their problems and upsets and we would have to screen them: those with **emotional problems** we sent down the hall to the regular psychological counselors. Those who had severe **health problems**, heavy addictions, and problems defying medical definition, or people who were **oppressed** (perhaps jinxed or cursed is a good word), would be given an interview to see how they responded to our praying for them.

What I noticed in many cases of severely oppressed people was that they all had a look on their face that was always the same – a kind of 'demonic' grin. I stood in front of a mirror and tried in vain to reproduce that look, but I never could. It was the same as seen on Charles Manson's face, by the way, or Richard Ramirez' face.

During one of the sessions, I was ministering with a coworker (we never worked alone) on an **older Latina woman** who had been involved with Santeria (occult worship of spirits). Earlier, our pastor had told us that the enemy was (1) weak as a toothless lion, and (2) he didn't know what we were thinking, and (3) the devil couldn't create. In my gut I knew that couldn't all be true, so I took an opportunity to find out. I bound the entity that had come forth in the woman and I commanded that it tell me the truth to everything that I would ask, <u>in Jesus' name</u>. I then asked it a few questions that had been bugging me for months. We started every session with a client with prayer for protection and that Jesus' name is in effect for the whole session.

We were about 30 clients and 10 ministerial people in a large Fellowship Hall at church and conversing with the subject/client was forbidden; we were to make demands and statements to get the subject released form whatever their addiction was. I broke rank and learned a lot.

The following is a paraphrase of that 1999 session (I never forgot the answers as I wrote the gist down right after I was discovered by the Head Pastor and left the room). I will explain at the end:

TJ:  What is your name?
D:   (with a sneer) False teaching.

TJ:  Can you read minds  -- Do you know what people are thinking?
D:   (just a glare and silence)

TJ:  You will tell the truth – now!
D:   (explosive) Yes!

TJ:  Do you put thoughts in people's heads to manipulate them?
D:   (cold silence)

TJ:  You will answer that. Now.
D:   (smart-ass) What do you think?

TJ:  In Jesus' name, answer that now. The truth.
D:   (as if he was poked) Yes.

(This is typical of the evasive way they operate.)

TJ:  What are UFOs?
D:   Oh, you like 'em, don't you? Since '58.

(Again, there was no way anyone knew I had studied the subject of UFOs since 1958.)

TJ:  What are UFOs?
D:   <u>We</u> do some… Like 'em?

(My coworker was getting nervous and said we better quit this, and remove the entity, but I was on a roll and had to get some answers. Questioning the entities was against protocol because they often lie – unless you bind them with His name and thus <u>make</u> them tell the truth.)

TJ:  In Jesus' name, tell me the truth: Can Satan create?
D:  (very subdued)  Who?

TJ:  In Jesus' name, is Satan real?
D:  No.

Obviously the name of Jesus carried some clout, so I knew He was real even though it had bothered me for years that no contemporary writer of Jesus' day wrote about Him. (VEG, Ch 11.)

TJ:  Souls? Who creates souls?
D:  No!  I hate souls.

TJ:  <u>What</u> are you?
D:  (silence)

TJ:  If there is no Satan, then there are no demons…
D:  Are you sure?

TJ  Dammit. <u>What</u> are you? Where are you from?
D:  Who wants to know?

TJ  In Jesus' name, stop this and tell me why you are doing this!
D:  (very subdued) Because she needs it…. she believes in demons.

TJ:  In His name, what are you?
D:  (no answer)

TJ:  If you don't answer me, I will ask the Angels to take you to the Light.
D:  OK (almost yelling – that's how I and my coworker were discovered). We harass and oppress people who need this – if they didn't believe in demons we could not do it.  When they get tired of the dumb game, we leave.

TJ:  Are you serious? What are you?
D:  (shaking) I told you too much.

CoWkr:   In Jesus' name, go!

> *Interesting that I was not corrected in my assumption that there was a Satan, but then neither were Drs. Modi nor Peck corrected (Book 1). And it never*

*answered me what it was.*

My coworker demanded he shut up and loose her, and that was it. Over. Done. Gone. We infilled the Latina woman with a prayer for the Light and Holy Spirit to protect her and cleanse the area where the Negg (or ??) had been – we never found out which it had been, and we didn't care.

**Analysis**

Based on my current Knowledge, 15 years later, I can identify the entity:

It was not an **Interdimensional** – they will not answer you no matter what you say – Dr. Peck had a lot of experience with them. We also know that it wasn't a demon or **Discarnate** because (1) there are no demons, and (2) the name of Jesus doesn't do anything with a Discarnate.

Thus that says, no guessing, that it was a **Negg** playing the role of a demon because the woman believed in them – and the Neggs' job is to give you all the negativity you can handle until (1) you either wake up and see the screwiness of it all (because they will interject nonsense into their game with you), or (2) you get tired of playing with them. The latter is what happened to me … after that session, I could see why the Head Pastor, who came over right at the end, didn't want us asking questions – we'd wise up, and quit the team  – which is what I did. The whole silly thing was **a charade by the Neggs for the little old lady's benefit!**

> **Interference by an Interdimensional or Discarnate is not a charade for anyone's benefit, but Deliverance is still needed.**

Needless to say, I was fascinated that **they know what we're thinking, and can put thoughts in our heads...** thoughts staring with the word "I......" so we'll think it is <u>our</u> thought. (I later corroborated this in a final session, with a different coworker. Then I quit.) I learned that **all communication on the Other Side is by thought** – we are alone in our 3D world with verbal communication, although Chapters 7 & 9 in VEG examine some of Man's potential via his DNA.

Also interesting that the entity played cute with some questions. It didn't want to tell me that there was **no Satan**... as Christians we are supposed to believe in him – but since there isn't such an entity, I am surprised that I got an answer. Naturally, the deception that there is a Satan is not something that the Neggs are going to correct... people are going to have to figure that out for themselves – the Neggs can't reveal that information by just volunteering it, as it is a violation of the **Law of Confusion**, and they are bound by that Law because they are a form of Angel sworn to follow God's Laws.

Also, interestingly, the Neggs are not going to play along and remove themselves from any patient just to make it look like Jesus' name has power. The Catholics in their exorcisms, I believe, would agree -- from all that I have read. So my experience says that **Jesus is real and most entities in the Astral obey that name**. That was the reason for sharing the above Deliverance experience.

It is also interesting that they played a game with the **UFO issue**... admitting that they do some of them, which suggests that there are others that must be real (since they didn't take credit for all of them).

## Collapsing a Christian Myth

While we're at it, there is a related issue that has been making the rounds more and more, in the Christian circles (no pun intended)—and that is the new-found belief that human encounters with ETs produce the same psychological effects in people as are found in those people who get heavily into witchcraft and demonology – thus 'proving' that the little Greys are demonic. This is false, but let's see why. Later in Chapters 8 and 9 the Greys will be closely examined as Man is about to experience their handiwork.

### The Greys and Abductions

The story has been around for years now that the little Greys are abducting people at night and doing genetic experiments on them. The people are never seriously injured and the Greys always put them back where they found them. They also effect some sort of hypnosis with their powerful staring eyes so that the human does not remember the event, or thinks they were seeing a horse or owl with big eyes.

**The Standard 3' Grey**
(source: http://www.think-aboutit.com/images/greyeyesbkwh.jpg)

196

It is a really different look but it is not particularly menacing – it just smacks of "all business, no emotion or compassion" and it does give the impression that it can see into your innermost being. Chapter 8 reveals this is a reality.

The following two men have similar ideas about what the ET/UFO phenomenon does to humans and they compare it to the effects allegedly produced by demons on people.

## John Keel

John Keel, who wrote _Mothman_ (later a movie of the same name), was an internationally renowned UFO investigator with many books to his credit on UFOs and the occult, and he voiced an alarming theory:

> Demonology is not just another crackpot-ology. It is the ancient and scholarly study of the monsters and demons who have seemingly co-existed with man throughout history. Thousands of books have been written on the subject, many of them authored by educated clergymen, scientists and scholars, and uncounted numbers of well-documented demonic events are readily available to every researcher. **The mani-festations and occurrences described in this imposing literature are <u>similar, if not entirely identical,</u> to the UFO phenomenon itself. Victims of demonomania (possession) suffer the very same medical and emotional symptoms as the UFO contactees…**
> The Devil and his demons can, according to the literature, manifest themselves <u>in almost any form</u> [shapeshift] and can physically imitate anything from angels to horrifying monsters with glowing eyes. Strange objects and entities materialize and dematerialize in these stories, just as the UFOs and their splendid occupants appear and disappear, walk thru walls, and perform other supernatural feats. [84] [emphasis added.]

Interesting but Neggs, Greys, demons and UFOs are not the same thing.

Mr. Keel often referred to the UFOs and their occupants as _ultradimensionals_ and he wasn't far from wrong – they are not flesh and blood, viz., they are not 3D biological organisms.

The reason UFO contactees and victims of allegedly demonic activity sometimes share similar health problems is because **both were subjected to the same EMF (electro-magnetic field) surrounding the phenomena.**[1] And because that field was stronger than the body's weak bio-electric field, it can really disrupt it, and nausea, headaches and disorientation are common results. (Chapter 12.)

In short: the similarity is due to the fact that Angels (Beings of Light) and Aliens (sometimes imitated by Neggs) have a similarly empowered hyperdimensional source whose **higher energy can affect humans neurologically**.

Keel doesn't know how close he is to describing the higher energy that the Control System uses to replicate objects in our world, but that is examined more fully in Chapters 12 – 13 of VEG. Suffice it to say, at this point that he is basically correct, but demons they ain't, **ultradimensionals** they may be, and he goes on to almost describe what Earth really is (very similar to what Dr. Jacques Vallée said about the Control System) when Keel says:

> I have gone through periods when I was absolutely convinced that [UFOs as] Trojan horses were, indeed, following a careful plan designed to ultimately conquer the human race *from within*…. But I am now inclined to accept the conclusion that the [UFO] phenomenon is mainly concerned with undefined (and undefinable) cosmic patterns and that mankind plays only a small role in those patterns. That "other world" seems to be a part of something larger and more infinite. The human race is also a part of that something…[85]

He is right, but it is obvious from the rest of his analysis that he still suspects that ultradimensionals are somehow related to the demonic and the Grey phenomenon, and that is not correct. The little Greys can and do make use of the **intra**-dimensional 'warp' to move around, but they are not demonic, nor do they reside in the **intra**dimensional zone.

The mishmash of others' terms is explained in the Glossary.

One last very significant observation that Keel makes was explored in Book 1, Chapter 4, but it bears re-presenting it here due to his discussion of ultra-dimensionals and their harassment of Albert Bender, for example.

> The … ultradimensionals are somehow **able to manipulate the electrical circuits of the human mind.** They can make us see whatever they want us to see and remember only what they want us to remember. Human minds which have been tuned into those super-high-frequency radiations… [i.e., people with psychic abilities] are most vulnerable to these manipulations …. Many are driven insane when their minds are unable to translate the signal properly…. [but] not all ultraterrestrial [i.e., ultradimensional] contacts are evil and disastrous, of course. But there are many people throughout the world who are deeply involved in all this without realizing it. They have entangled themselves through other frames of reference [e.g., witchcraft, Ouija board, and séances] and , in

many cases, have been savagely exploited by the ultraterrestrials in the **games** being played. These games have been thoroughly documented and defined … [and] the psychology of the … ultraterrestrials is well known and fully documented in the fairy lore of northern Europe, and the ancient legends of Greece, Rome and India.[86] [emphasis added]

Interesting to note that Keel connects the fairy lore and elementals with UFOs as does **Dr. Jacques Vallée**, and he also sees the connection with Al Bender's nervous breakdown at the hands of these 'beings' who allegedly occupy a world next to ours. He also identifies their ability to shapeshift. (Fairies and elementals were a creation of the **Control System**, as exposed in VEG, Apx C).

Remember that control was important to the Anunnaki, via the priesthood, and Dr. Vallée has also emphasized that earlier. Man still needs to be controlled, for his own good and the preservation of the physical Earth. Man is largely controlled today through the Control System.

Remember that the Neggs (not demons) are responsible for most of the above deceptions that 'entertain' Man. They afflicted Al Bender because he invited it. They afflicted the Latina in the Deliverance scenario. If some UFO encounters and some possessions are the result of Negg activities, the effect on humans would be similar IF it is the same higher energy source producing both phenomena. **And it is**. But not many UFOs are Negg projections; some are truly interdimensional, and some UFOs are 3D Earth-based **IFO**s (Identified Flying Objects).

Mr. Keel's Christian counterpart, Chuck Missler, is worth hearing.

## Chuck Missler

And then we come to the Christian viewpoint from Chuck Missler, who also studied the UFO and abduction phenomenon…and wrote the book Alien Encounters with another Christian, Mark Eastman. Needless to say, **the Christian viewpoint is that the whole thing is demonic**, and that means that when your only tool is a hammer, everything looks like a nail.

Included in Missler's book are quotes from Dr. Jacques Vallée who for a long time considered the UFO phenomenon to be much like the Celtic fairies and elves and perhaps just as illusory. Dr. Vallée says in his book Passport to Magonia that "… the folklore of every culture, it turned out, had a rich reservoir of stories about humanoid beings that flew in the sky, used devices that seemed in advance of the technology of the time." [87] It was from this original position that Vallée developed the later insight that elves, fairies, airships, demons, Greys, cropcircles and UFOs probably all had a similar source: the **Control System**.

The demon aspect is immediately recognized by the Christians, so they also can embrace what Vallée was saying about interdimensional beings.

## Nephilim and Demons

Returning to the idea of the Nephilim again, Mr. Missler suggests that the spirits of the Nephilim, bound to the Earth until Judgment Day, are probably the New Testament demons.[88] [Not.] In addition, we have clarification that the Watchers were "…a specific group of angels placed to watch over the Earth…. about 200 of these Watchers lusted and fell in sin….[and their] evil spirits shall be like clouds which shall oppress, corrupt, fall, contend, and bruise those upon the Earth." [89]

> *Note that we never read of demons before the Flood in the Bible. So, "…the demons are thus disembodied spirits of the Nephilim."* [90] *And yet, we did not have Neggs and Greys before the Flood either, and those were* **different Eras**, *which is important. Our Era does not have demons.*

## Angels and Aliens

The following points that Missler makes are very significant. [91] It is a summary of similar effects between Greys and alleged Demons:

- Satan and his angels are able to manifest physically in time and space, **morphing** themselves into a multitude of shapes.
- Angels are able to perform signs and wonders
- Angels and aliens can materialize and dematerialize at will
- Angels and aliens can manipulate matter.
- Angels and aliens can control human events and actions (people are paralyzed and time is suspended)
- Angels and aliens can control humans' minds
- Angels and aliens defy the laws of physics
- Aliens have healed their human abductees
- Aliens and fallen angels feign benevolence to deceive

Much study has been given to the UFO/alien phenomenon as correlated with possession by occult spirits. Keel and Missler are correct: **The symptoms in humans are the same. But that doesn't mean that the sources are the same thing. Greys are not demons.** Said Missler:

> *UFO behavior is more akin to magic than physics as we know it… the modern UFOnauts and the demons of past days are probably identical.* [92]

Missler is determined that humans experiencing PTSD from Greys and from demonic sources means that the Greys are demonic… kind of like saying that if a mosquito bites and leaves a mark on your arm, and a spider bites and leaves a mark on your friend's arm, you both were bitten by the same thing. (The Christian 'hammer' at work.)

> **Challenge:** try sometime to tell the difference between a mosquito bite, a spider bite, a flea bite and that of a bedbug.

Lastly, Missler suggested that if a person is about to be abducted, they should resist and command it to stop using Jesus' name. This could work, not because the Greys are demonic, but because using His name is answered in the support of any/all of His souls.

## Resolution

It is important to see what is really happening when Man, with a very weak and simple electrical field, comes into contact with **any hyperdimensional beings** who not only have a higher vibration but also have more mind power, and draw energy from their unseen realm.

Since there are no demons, we must be talking about Neggs, who can **shapeshift** and play the role of demons – if that is what a soul needs to experience for its soul growth. Because the Neggs occupy the 4D Realm with its higher vibration and they have greater (psychic) abilities, we can see that any direct interface with them is going to upset the delicate electrical field around a human – because a stronger electrical field always entrains and/or affects a weaker field. Pure physics.

Many times people claiming to see a demon were probably seeing a Negg just shapeshifting – playing their games. This happens when someone gets into Witchcraft and studies the spells and incantations and then tries them out to see if anything happens. Depending on the person's Script, a lot can happen, or nothing…

Trying to conjure the spirits and make them do your will is playing with fire and the Neggs do have the charge given to them to break the soul of that line of activity – what better than to pretend to answer the incantation and scare the heck out of the wannabe witch or warlock? Unless that <u>doesn't</u> scare the wannabe, and he finds it exciting, then the Neggs (knowing the mind of the human) will see to it that nothing happens for the wannabe. Souls are not to involve themselves with occult matters in the paranormal. (See Chapter 12: 'Caveat: Astral Gameplayers' section.)

As for the energy effect of the Greys, it is a very similar issue: they are **bio-cybernetic roboids** who are <u>also</u> empowered by hyperdimensional energies. Whereas the Neggs are 4D, the Greys are actually 3D with the ability to move interdimensionally and that makes use of higher, finer energies than Man experiences in his daily world. And the Greys peering into the human's face, doing **Mindscan** is using a semi-invasive technique backed with energy to cruise the human's neural network in their brain. That is bound to have some Post Traumatic Stress Disorder when coupled with the already-present stress of the abduction itself.

But it will be seen in Chapter 8 that the Greys are not really abusive, they are just **insensitive androids** – no emotions, no compassion and they just methodically do their work. Then they use their **Mindscan** technique to calm the human and block the experience from the human's memory. That all uses energy that invades the human's body and brain, and as such, invasive foreign energy can mean neurologically upsetting reactions.

And yet, as will be seen, the majority of abductees nowadays (while they don't like the Greys' procedures) are not experiencing the extreme PTSD that Keel and Missler speak of. Many of them are experiencing a greater awakening spiritually …

## Summary

So the Script, called the LifeScript or Lifetime in a scripted Drama is designed to grow souls by putting them through **preset experiences**, Scripts, roles that will call for the soul to bring forth its best response to whatever catalyst shows up in a person's life. And the soul, once it has selected the Lifetime of Choice for the particular incarnation, enters into the Drama with all its skills and Knowledge to prove that it is capable and disciplined student.

We saw that errors are not fatal and failure is not final – the courage to continue is what They are looking for. There is no disgrace in failure – the disgrace is in giving up. And suicide is definitely not an option.

The one thing you don't want to do when your world goes temporarily upside down, is to ask "Why do bad things happen to good people?" As if there was a reason other than your Script testing you… And is it not a bit arrogant to assume that I am so 'good' that bad things would not possibly happen to *moi* !? Some Scripts are rough and the really rough ones often have a Get-out-of-jail card here and there that it pays to watch out for … Good things happen to bad people, too. And it only makes sense in light of the LifeScript and what you signed up for. And the only way to know that is to visit a qualified hypnotherapist and ask some questions of your Higher Self… as I did in 1991.

Perhaps modern Man needs to read some of the great spiritual literature which speaks about the **Dark Night of the Soul** (Appendix A). Check out St. John of the

Cross or St. Theresa. At some point all souls will experience a disconnect between themselves and their Source, and feel utterly adrift – it happens when the body-mind-soul is making big adjustments to a Call that was placed on the soul to assimilate lessons to-date and make adjustments in its Ground of Being. And it is part of the natural progression of the soul -- just like rebooting a PC is sometimes done to clear old stacks and registers, and start with a fresh workspace.

So when things go wrong, here is the big secret:

Things happen because they happen.   Handle it.

**You don't get steel without fire.**

And there is no such thing as Sin – Man was not born in Sin, and he is not a fallen species. He is an imperfect creature at this stage of his growth and will make more **mistakes** as he moves forward. So what? Keep moving. Forget reasons, just do your best, and take what you get, and don't take what you don't get.

Transformation of Man

# Chapter 8: Greys, Man & Hybrids

Again, in concert with what was started in *Virtual Earth Graduate* (aka Book 1), this book will now take a brief look at Man in terms of what is being done to him and by whom... from the 40,000' level. The details from a lower level are not that important, but it is valuable to know that

1. We are not alone
2. We have never been alone
3. ...and Man's genetics are being changed.

Why is that valuable?

It answers a lot of questions. How was Man created? By whom? Why? And what does the future hold for Man? The answers to those questions involve beings who have shepherded Man through the centuries and have sought to get Man to the point where he takes responsibility for himself and the planet, and can interact meaningfully, intelligently with those who have been watching him struggle (from the Moon) – largely against his own defective genetics.

Man inherited some dysfunctional genetics from his progenitors who attempted to make Man in their image... they did, and saddled him with the same lower quality genes that they had! One group, of several, the Anunnaki took an existing hominid on Earth about 200,000 years ago and added their genetics to create a worker, a slave human – just bright enough to understand his 'gods' and what they wanted him to do, and yet dumb enough to not be able to come up with a plan to rebel against them.

In the process, they used their genes to assist in the evolution of the hominid, suspected to be Homo *habilis*, who had god-knows-what in his genetic makeup, but being a wild ape-like creature must have had traits that made him hard to domesticate (as evidenced by the *Atra Hasis* and *Enuma Elish* epics of Sumerian literature). Then the gods decided to add some intelligence, some speech, and later some reproductive capability – creating many early versions that didn't work out (see 'Almas' and 'Hybrid Man' in later sections). There was a lot of trial and error and finally the *Adamu* was created – via **genetic engineering**. ET intervention.

It was originally thought that the Anunnaki were paragons of intelligence, virtue and science, but that can't be true as they often fought among themselves, and they used Man to fight their battles from time to time. The Anunnaki gods were known to lie, cheat, steal, and were often petty and violent. Sound familiar?

If what is said about traits being passed down from generation to generation epigenetically, they also passed to Man a **"violent gene"** (as Michael Tellinger proposes). The Anunnaki genetics were not those of some ideal, advanced race but traits that are often associated with reptilian behavior: territorial, aggressive, violent, and mechanistic. [93]

Is it any wonder that Man today often behaves the same way? Is it not surprising that Man cannot overcome his genetics and live in peace with his fellow man? Homo *habilis* did not live in peace with his fellow primates (or proto-humans), and neither did the Anunnaki. There appears to be a **genetic predisposition to violence** and pettiness in modern Man... and it has been reinforced throughout the centuries via the Natural Selection or Survival of the Fittest (i.e., **Epigenetics**) dictum that if a genetic trait works to keep an organism surviving, it is kept in the genome.

Not the best thinkers, nor the most enlightened philosophers, avatars and teachers of the past have been able to work or inspire violence out of Man. And now with overpopulation, with some stupid and violent humans breeding more stupid and violent offspring, the planet is suffering ecologically. (See end of Chapter 2.)

> Sorry, but **that is how They see us**. A bunch of wild monkeys who are in the process of abusing the environment, abusing each other, upsetting the natural chain of inter-dependency in flora and fauna, and Man struts around barking about how great and intelligent he is – and he still is nowhere as smart as his progenitors who had nuclear power , spacecraft and genetic expertise millennia ago!
>
> Worst of all, Man's arrogance, greed and ignorance are slowly destroying the only planet he has. Man is the pinnacle of creation? This is the buffoon who makes Sci-fi movies that picture Man against the mighty and overwhelming odds of incredible weapon-equipped intelligent aliens... and Man comes out on top every time!? What consummate egotism. There are ETs out there who not only laugh at such posturing, but have voted (in the solar council) to remove Man from the planet...

Is there an answer to this dilemma in which Man currently finds himself? Yes. Enter the Greys.

# The Greys

As was said in VEG, the Anunnaki main force was tasked to leave the planet about 650-600 BC and yet a Remnant stayed behind. The Solar Council had decided to enforce a ruling that this solar system was to <u>not</u> fall prey to the Draconians, aka the Orion Group, and the Anunnaki were originally part of that scenario.

Just as Man was to be educated and learn and grow on Earth, so were the **Remnant** – who are still here for almost the same reason Man is. Both need to wake up, change their ways and learn better behavior, take responsibility for better managing affairs among themselves, and to show better management of their offspring, the fledgling humans. The Elite are monitoring both groups.

> This again was due to the **Galactic Law** that said if you were a "creator race" and could genetically engineer sentient species, original creation being prohibited, but allowing manipulation of extant species, you are responsible for nurturing and guiding them into a more mature species. And this was particularly true if your creation gave opportunity for souls to incarnate!

The existence of the Galactic Law was why Enlil, the commander of the Anunnaki contingent on Earth, wanted to do away with the humans – so he didn't have to be responsible for them! Enki, the science officer and his brother, enmeshed the gods into supporting the human upgrade scenario, thus committing the Anunnaki to a "care and feeding" of the nascent human population.

When the Main Anunnaki Group went home (650-600 BC), the remaining Remnant was tasked with the job of continuing the upgrade, support and nurturing of the humans. With an interesting proviso in AD 900… they were to not walk among and mix and mingle with the humans on a daily basis (and they used to as The Greek and Roman gods), but were to administer guidance and support from a distance – hence we had the Greek gods on Mt Olympus, and later the same group as the Roman gods… The reason for distance being that whatever support the gods gave the humans had to appear to be coherent with the **Doctrine of Non-Interference**: to see what the humans would do with inspiration and ideas and technology that did not appear to come from those watching them. In fact, Man was not to know that he was being watched so that his reactions and behavior would be a genuine reflection of his mental, emotional and spiritual growth – else how could any progress be measured if Man knew the gods were still watching and 'controlling' him (even if for his own good)?

## Underground

So the gods, who had long ago built numerous, large underground domains, now stayed underground, and that worked for them as the Sun tended to affect them negatively – it caused them to age prematurely. But they interact with the Elite.

And in order to continue to administer their guidance, inspiration and limited control over humans, they used their incredible genetic knowledge to fashion a **bio-cybernetic roboid (a Grey)** to work 'topside' (on Earth's surface) and begin to upgrade the humans' genetics. Such have been called the standard Little Greys.

> *Note that there are several races of sentient, Grey-like beings who are not bio-cybernetic roboids… the tall Greys and the tall Whites, for starters. There had to be so many Greys doing so many abduction events that it was easiest to replicate or clone them as drone workers.*

**Nature of the Greys**

So they are the brain-child of the Anunnaki Remnant and their purpose is to upgrade and hopefully correct aberrant genetics still running around in the human population – a little like **trying to paint a moving freight train**! Initially the Greys attempted to make corrections while people slept at night, and they tried the equivalent of EMF and energetic DNA fixes, and when that didn't last, they tried to use viral vectors but human immune systems saw the viruses as an enemy and succeeded in neutralizing the attempted RNA fixes to the DNA.

Nothing was left, but about the 1930s, to actually **abduct** the humans and take them to their labs where they could perform better analyses, and insert **implants** to track the humans – for subsequent evaluation of their Program of Corrections. This too was not having as fast an impact on the humans as was desired. Something better had to be done to make a better human… and that was the clue – to **create new humans**.

The Greys (mostly servants of the Remnant) began to implement a Plan B – abduct the women and rework genetics in the ova, implant the egg(s) and after 3-4 months, remove them in a second abduction and incubate the fetuses in simulated wombs aboard the laboratory ship (and it was huge). This also meant abducting males, gathering sperm, reworking the male genetics and fertilizing the egg in vitro and THEN implanting it in the earth woman. Thus did a lot of women mysteriously experience miscarriages – first they were pregnant… and then they weren't.

This was a simpler system. While it created confusion and consternation for the woman, it worked best to **create a new breed of humans**. The goal was not to create a new species to extend an allegedly dying Grey race, that was pure disinformation. **The goal has always been to rework the human genetics,** by inserting known genes (from various sources, some extraterrestrial, some reworked DNA from cattle) and eventually insert the created hybrids into human society.

This also was not without its share of problems – the hybrids often did not have a clue how to behave, being raised in isolation on the Lab Ship… so further incursion into the human experience had to be made with the abduction of humans to come on board the laboratory ship and (hopefully) compassionately interact with the hybrid children and adults – of whom there are now thousands.

> Many of those selected to directly interact with the hybrids were either chosen for this role **before** they were born (in the InterLife) or they were contacted during sleep, asked, and programmed to be an 'inter-acter.'

## Grey Mechanics

**The Greys are a bio-cybernetic robotic organism** about 3-4' tall, they do not eat, but do ingest nutrients through their arms which serve to 'feed' the biological aspect of their mechanism… lubricants and supplements to repair and sustain the organism. They all have a 2-part brain – a posterior one for 'local' control of whatever task it is they are doing, and an 'anterior' part that interacts with the hive-like inter-communications natural to this hominid. They react with surprise when the human goes out of control, flails out, and asserts itself – they have to check with 'Contollers' who monitor the abduction through the Grey and will tell the Grey what to do.

> The Controllers are the Remnant (underground or even on the Lab Ship) who are remotely watching the process through the Grey who is really just an 'instrument.' The reason for this is that the Anunnaki true form has always been a problem for humans and that is why a more generic form was developed in the Grey.

> Nordics and humans who seem to be watching the abduction are <u>sometimes</u> actually **shapeshifting** Greys to give some comfort to the human when they see other human-like beings present. Remember: shapeshifting is really just controlling what the human sees – no molecules change shape – and the Greys are very good at it.

**(credit both: Yahoo Images)**

Be aware that there are sometimes seen insect-like beings and taller Greys – these if present are in charge, not cybernetic organisms, and mind-to-mind they tell the little Greys what to do.

## Mindscan

The Grey seems to have **superquantum computer circuits** for processing and most Greys also possess an interesting ability called **Mindscan**, a term coined by Dr. David Jacobs in his book *The Threat*. Not only do they know what you are thinking, they can put thoughts directly into your mind. And even more amazing is that the Grey can stare into your eyes and manipulate the optic nerve to gain entrance to the brain's neural pathways. [94] He can inject new images, and cause people to 'see' whatever He wants … no doubt part of the secret to shapeshifting.

The Grey also uses Mindscan procedures to effect an orgasm in males for the purpose of collecting semen. The physiological responses can be artificially generated this way. [95] In effect, this ability gives the Grey absolute power over the human, even to the point of paralyzing them. They can make the abductees think, feel, visualize, or do anything they want. In addition, the Greys have been known to extract memories and information from the abductee and put it in their hybrids…[96]

Anybody remember Spock in *Star Trek* doing a "Vulcan mind probe?"

## Greys Causing Pain

The human abductees always complain about the probing, poking and scraping done by the Greys during their examinations. The Greys often put needles into the human's brain, nose, **eyes**, or belly – but the interesting thing is that the human – while awake and experiencing an emotional trauma – has not been harmed. There is no residual physical damage to the human's body. What is left is the emotional and psychological scar of their invasive procedures… which are not fun.

> **Note**: the Grey's ability to pass through walls and take the human with them to their ship is part of a technology that is used when they put a needle into the human's eye… it **displaces molecules** and does not damage anything.

So the issue is: Why are the Greys not more caring and gentle with their procedures?

What do you expect from a Bio-cybernetic roboid (machine) that does not know what pain is? It is not their intent to cause trauma or pain, and it often surprises them when the human is distressed. The Greys just use their instruments and clinically, methodically do what has to be done. (More recent abductions are kinder to the humans as feedback got back to the Controllers; yet the Abduction phase of the Program is all but at an end – a new phase of Integration has begun. See later section 'Alien Agenda' in this chapter.)

And somebody DOES care. As the human is then prepared to be returned to wherever they were abducted from, the Grey will Mindscan the human causing him or her to dismiss the pain and forget the experience via an advanced form of hypnotism. Some procedures and events are permanently blocked from recall – even under hypnosis to protect the human.

### Miscellaneous

There is a fibrous (cartilage) skeletal structure that gives support for the vertical orientation of the Grey body, and that weighs less than bone and gives the Grey a real flexibility.

The standard Grey is neither male nor female… they are **androgynous**. And yet there are female Greys who are taller than the ubiquitous, standard worker-clone Grey, and they tend to the babies. While they do not have physical female parts, there is something about them that, to most abductees, come across as "feminine." They are kinder and gentler. There are also taller Greys who can be white, tan, beige and different shades of gray, and some of them can be in charge, such as the one often called "the doctor" who lets the smaller Greys do the lab work, and then he does the more complicated procedures. So there appears to be a hierarchy and a division of labor.

Lastly, there is a new version of the ubiquitous standard Grey where the outer body is an exoskeleton that covers a small reptilian operator, and the black 'eyes' are lenses covering a **very sophisticated vision**, with an ability to see infrared and other energy – reminiscent of what was shown in the movie, *Predator*, when the alien shifted through several visual modes of energy detection to find the humans.

## Grey Abductions

As a personal aside, there were two incidences back in my late teens and early 20's that I recall but I didn't attach any significance to them at the time. Now they make sense.

### Mom Disappears

Mom was an interesting character who had a good side and a bad side. I often wondered why she was so cold and afraid of sex – for years, even while married, she slept in a separate room and had a phobia about her being 'clean, down there.'

I used to wonder why she was different and why she had no women friends. The only friends in her life were those from the square dance club where she and my stepfather went several times a week.

In May 1965, my mother had a 45<sup>th</sup> birthday party from which she disappeared. What a night. There were about 40 people throughout the house and in the front and back yards celebrating Mom's birthday – all my parents' square dance buddies showed up, and some of my Dad's engineers from work (Huntsville Ala, Redstone Arsenal). Sis and I were playing maid and butler, keeping the crowd happy.

Mom excused herself to go into the back of the house, perhaps to go to the bathroom. We had a front door only and no way to exit directly from the back of the house. The backdoor exited from the garage and there were people on the back patio, and on the front patio, as well as in the kitchen and living room. Mom was gone about an hour and a half.

We looked in the bathrooms, the closets, and Sis looked under the beds! No one had seen her and it was time to light the cake and blow out the candles. We made excuses for her hoping she'd show up any minute. Some people walked around the house and down the street, people called out, but she had <u>actually disappeared</u>. Some people left, but most stayed, and then after about an hour, someone on the back patio said, "Here she comes!"

And I rushed out back to meet her. We had no fence and the ¼ mile behind our house was an open field – an undeveloped housing tract. Here she came across the lot behind us, her blouse buttoned but off by one button. I ran up to her, catching sight of something flashing above me, and I stopped and looked up to see a large **dark oblong with a band of multicolored lights** flashing vertically around it – I assumed it was the Goodyear blimp. It was an <u>absolutely clear night</u> and we could see the stars – in fact, that was what the people on the back patio had been doing: stargazing with my telescope. No one saw a blimp.

Mom was OK, but dazed, and could not recall where she'd been. I looked up again and the blimp was totally gone. We all went in and celebrated the rest of the evening.

*What is unique about this event, and the reason for mentioning it, is two-fold. (1) it probably relates to Mom's reasons for a major phobia about sex, and it shows her desire to persist with sex until she got her little girl who also had a phobia about sex.* **Both had on-going gynecological problems for years.**
*And (2) we <u>all</u> forgot about the incident <u>totally</u> until I read a book in the 90's by Dr. Mack on abductions… interesting that our memories were 'wiped' for about 30 years.* **We didn't even discuss it the next day.**

Yes, I was an avid Sci-Fi on TV fan, (I never read Sci-Fi books) and I watched the original hokey-looking *Star Trek* (due to its obviously cardboard sets) because the episodes' themes where Captain Kirk resolved major philosophical issues were so unlike what Man normally does, but they were brilliant. Naturally I did some research into the UFO area, a curious seeker, but in the 60's and 70's we had not yet heard about abductions and Little Greys doing genetic experiments, <u>and</u> there was not enough data available in those days to form any hypothesis, so my interest went on hold.

That was the only incident involving Mom that I am aware of, but my sister had multiple occurrences of the same thing.

## Sister Sleepwalks

It is possible that Mom's first baby <u>was</u> a girl and I was switched with her before birth, as my sister used to complain. Not only did Mom reject me, my sister never quite accepted me, and I figured it was just sibling rivalry. Sis quietly resented me. Maybe subconsciously they both knew what had happened? (In the 1991 Regression I saw that I had to be first in the womb – if not, Mom would have had my sister first and then no more children. We were switched. )

My sister also sleepwalked and complained of **lizards in her room** although an exterminator twice set traps but <u>nothing</u> was found, not even cockroaches.

What was weird, again, was that we never sat down as a family and comforted Sis and no one tried to find out <u>why</u> she was sleepwalking. It went on for 4-6 months when she was about 12, just coming into puberty. It was also during this period that my sister came down with colitis and no one knew <u>why</u> her uterus was so irritated. And typical of my (dysfunctional) family, **no one ever talked about it** and 6 months later, it was if it had never happened. Weird.

> *I was never 'bothered,' I had no odd dreams, and no "missing time"*
> *scenarios showed up in any Past Life Regression. I <u>was</u> visited but*
> *for different reasons, as I would later discover.*

Our family was different and I'm sure the above accounts are significant but I don't know the whole story, except that Mom never accepted me as hers, and Sis resented me even though I was always kind to her. The '91 Regression did not show me anything about Mom or Sis; apparently they were not part of my Soul Group, and in recent years I tended to think she was an OP – but **Greys rarely abduct OPs**.

> *In addition, and this is not racist, the Greys abduct **very few** Blacks, very few*
> *Latinos and fewer Chinese. They seem to be after the White or Aryan genetics.*

While the Greys have been at this major Genetics Program just recently in the history of Man (the last 100 years), there were Others here doing their genetic experimentations, and there is plenty of evidence for it around the planet… in stone and tablet and in many myths.

## Versions of Man

What we think we know about the evolution of Man is in serious trouble. Recent findings suggest that Cro-Magnon Man appeared overnight, geologically speaking, with **no intermediate fossil evidence** to show how the transition occurred for the alleged ape evolving to Man.

Allegedly, something crawled out of the primordial sea, developed legs, crawled about, then walked about, began to stand upright, grew hair and Ta-Daaaaa we had an ape. If that doesn't sound like a fairytale, I have some ocean-front property in Montana I want to sell you. Even more fantastic was the idea that apes evolved into humans … but curiously, it was a one-time thing… it never happened again, and is **still not happening**. Apes did not and will not evolve into humans.

Or are they? This curious mutation was spotted outside a mall in Chicago and scientists are still trying to identify where it fits on the evolutionary scale:

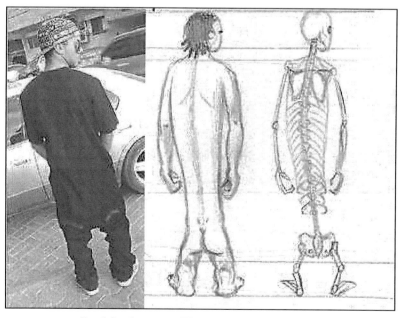

**Is this the new Homo LoPantalones?**

Perhaps the Greys had nothing to do with that…

## Different Species

A very important question is where the different human races came from. We are taught that Homo *habilis* somehow evolved into Neanderthal who evolved into Cro-Magnon, and then Homo *sapiens sapiens* (modern Man) is assumed to be a better version of Man, replacing Cro-Magnon, and in today's world we even see a potential newcomer to the lineup in what has been called Homo *noeticus*, or the Indigos.

What has been overlooked, but not by the late Lloyd Pye, is the genetic makeup of the above lineup and whether the genetics of each member shows a valid progression. For example, he maintains that Cro-Magnon, while considered a modern version of Man, <u>was not</u> and he cites the following points of difference:

> **Cro-Magnons were not exactly humans**. They were near to us, but they still had slightly heavier bones… (though nothing like [most] Neanderthals), which indicates they were much better muscled than we are. Their arm length was often a bit longer than ours….They were also taller…averaging over six feet… But where it counts most, in skull shape, [they] were remarkably like us. [97] [emphasis added]

Then he comments, Neanderthals and Cro-Magnon co-existed for about 60,000 years, but did not interbreed and climate change forced a separation of the two – he doubts that Cro-Magnon wiped out Neanderthal. [98] But the even more curious question is if Neanderthal and other hominids were a true native population of Earth, how and why did they go extinct? In fact, did all of them go extinct?

## Enter The Alma

Pye indicates that Sasquatch or Bigfoot is <u>not</u> just a fantasy devised in Tibet or in the American Northwest. He cites the legend of such a hominid occurring all over the world – among people who do not know each other and have never had any communication between themselves – so how would they come up with the same 'fantasy' and give it a name … unless they actually did see something real?

> To show how widespread this Bigfoot 'fantasy' is, here are some of those names: **Alma** (Russia), **Menk** (Russia), Sedapa, **Kaptar**, Agogwe, Oh-Mah, Mapinguary, Wauk-Wauk, Hsueh-Jen, Meh-Teh, Gin-Sung, Apamandi, Teh-Lma, Muhala, Tok-Mussi, Dwendi, Kang-Mi, **Orang-Pendek** (in Sumatra), Golub-Yavan, Jez-Termak, Kish-Kiik, etc., etc…[99]

The most fascinating of these is the Alma, cited to be a living Neanderthal. [100] One was caught in Russia in 1850, and she was domesticated and named Zana, and the story was recounted on the SCI channel in an Unexplained Mysteries episode.

A wildwoman named Zana is said to have lived in the isolated mountain village of T'khina in Abkhazia in the Caucasus; some have speculated she may have been an Almas, but hard evidence [of race] is lacking.

Captured in the mountains in 1850, she was at first violent towards her captors but soon became domesticated and assisted with simple household chores. **Zana is said to have had sexual relations with a man of the village** [true!] named Edgi Genaba, and gave birth to a number of children of apparently normal human appearance. Several of these children, however, died in infancy.

The father, meanwhile, gave away four of the surviving children to local families. The two boys, Dzhanda and Khwit Genaba (born 1878 and 1884), and the two girls, Kodzhanar and Gamasa Genaba (born 1880 and 1882), were assimilated into normal society, married, and had families of their own. Zana herself died in 1890. [101] [emphasis added]

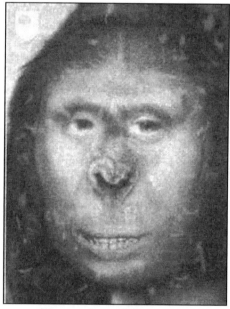

**Zana, circa 1890.**
(Credit: petrczernek.wordpress.com via Bing)

## Alma Description

They do not have permanent homes, but live in caves, or dig holes in the ground for shelter. They give birth to babies which look like human babies. Large, old individuals live alone in the forests of Siberia. They are stronger than a man, and can run as fast as a horse. The entire body is covered with fur which can be brown, black, reddish or gray. No hair on the face. The back of the head rises to a cone-shaped peak – just like the Yeti in Tibet. The forehead is low and receding, and eyes are sunk deep into the skull. They have no opposing thumb and so cannot climb a pole, for example. They are about 5-6 feet in size, and have large feet – the taller the hominid, the larger the feet. They do not make tools, but use sticks and throw stones and make intimidating sounds when confronted. They hate dogs and dogs hate them. They have no speech, but can really yell, grunt, whine, etc. They do have acute hearing and sight. They do not hunt large animals, and are active in twilight and at night; they can move without making a sound. They are expert at concealing themselves and blending into their surroundings. They are not usually aggressive toward men and several have been caught and domesticated. [102]

That <u>also</u> basically describes what we know about Bigfoot from descriptions of eye-witnesses. Thus the conclusion is that this was an early form of Man, probably a Neanderthal descendant , and it is amazing that the human and Alma genomes matched such that the babies born to the Alma were more human-looking than Zana was. The four surviving children born from her looked and acted like normal people, but they were much more robust and stocky. Zana never learned to speak, but her offspring were normal in that regard.

**Zana's Daughter**
(source: www.bing.com/images)

It is interesting that humans and chimps/apes cannot interbreed, so that if they confirm that Almas are "primitive humans," conversely humans might be "advanced Neanderthals." Pye stresses that it is far more the latter than the former. As for Almas living today, it is highly possible – there was a documented case in 1963 of a group of Almas which were observed:

> British anthropologist Myra Shackley in *Still Living?* Describes Ivan Ivlov's 1963 observation of a family group of Almas. Ivlov, a pedia-trician, decided to interview some of the **Mongolian children** who were his patients, and discovered that many of them had also said that they had seen Almases [sic] and that neither the Mongol children nor

the young Almas were afraid of each other. [103] [emphasis added]

What is to say that the Bigfoot seen in the U.S. Northwest isn't somehow related to the Almas – and may have crossed the Bering Strait when it was an ice bridge?

## Other Humans in Russia

In addition to the Almas (aka Almasty) in Russia, Mongolia and parts of Asia, there are these recent pictures of humans with special genetics.

This is not photoshop. **Nikolai** is big, strong and 7' 1". The man he is boxing (below) is about 5'10". Both are standing up.
He is called **The Beast from the East** and a 2-time WBA heavyweight (!) champion. Out of 53 fights, he won 50.

**Boxer Nikolai Valuev**
(Credits: www.stromfront.org/forum)

He is married with 3 kids and runs a boxing school in St Petersburg...
(See Wikipedia.)

Nikolai's physiognomy is natal. And he is a really nice guy. His bed is oversize, but of course, he sleeps anywhere he wants to...

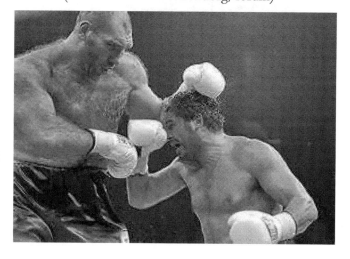

In addition the man below (left) lives in rural Russia and was visited by a reporter when doing an episode for British TV:

**The reporter on the right is 6' tall.**
(credit: primetime.unrealitytv.co.uk/bigfoot-files… )

The above gentleman does not have a thyroid issue… his height is genetic, and there were **giants in the ancient days** and some genetics have survived.

## Giants in the Earth

Just to round out the genetics on special people and skeletons, there is a real 25' skeleton that was recently found and excavated in Ecuador:

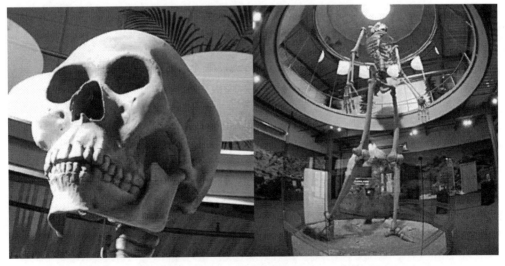

**Giant Skeleton** found in Loja, **Ecuador** 19 October 2012...
(credit: alabamatruth.com)

## Hybrid Man

It would not be right to leave this discussion of Man and the different varieties on Earth without a brief turn to what a very learned Anthropologist has to say – and **Dr. Susan Martinez** is not an Evolutionist. In fact, she shoots down Darwin, as did many of his contemporaries, and she has the ammo to do it. Let's briefly consider some of her major points from a fascinating new book (2013) called *The Mysterious Origins of Hybrid Man.*

Her information below supports a transformation of Man into his present state by virtue of **Intelligent Design by "star people."** Such was done by the Anunnaki, and such is found in the myths of the Navajo, Hopi, Dogon, Zulu, Cherokee and Mayas, to name just a few sources. Accordingly, the different varieties of Man are due to **crossbreeding** and not Evolution. That says we are all the product of **interbreeding** with other forms of Man throughout the centuries – thus modern man does have some (4%) Neanderthal genes in him.[104] That makes us all **hybrids**, not the product of random Evolution.[105]

### Evolution vs Creationism

Recall that because Man looks something like an ape, there allegedly must have been a missing link from which both Man and ape descended, believed Darwin. Said his smarter contemporaries: "…[Man] did not evolve from other species, and will never develop into another species." [106] In fact, that is not even genetically possible.

> [evolutionary changes] are horizontal, which is to say: DNA is encoded for changes only within the range of that species.…
> The genome is a conservative thing, not innovative. Indeed DNA is structured to *prevent* vertical variation [i.e., forming a new version of a species on the evolutionary tree]. [107] [emphasis added]

and

> Francis Crick, Nobel prize winner, proved that DNA was far too complicated to have evolved by random chance. The accidental synthesis of DNA molecules and its associated enzymes would be a coincidence beyond belief. [108]

And probably produce a **mutation** that was dysfunctional – like the Mule, a cross between a Horse and Donkey that cannot reproduce.

The last word on this issue is impressive:

> Outside the English-speaking world, French, German, Swedish,

Russian, and East European biologists are not so sold on Darwinism…. two Hungarians advance the view that species do not and **never did** evolve from one another… It seems much more reasonable to conclude that a being possessing **higher intelligence** equipped all species with the organs, knowledge, and abilities they need….. Gradual evolution of traits and behaviors does not hold up to [DNA] scrutiny… [109] [emphasis added]

She means: Assisted Evolution by an Intelligent Designer.

## Major Human Types

The last point to relate from Dr. Martinez' outstanding research is her discovery that there were **5 basic types of Man**, going back to when either the Angels (ET?) oversaw the Creation, or Angels acquired human form to co-habit with human women, or alternatively she admits that "…the stars of other worlds are inhabited by celestials who long ago contributed to our genesis…. Humanity as **a child of the stars** is one of the most widespread and persistent legends among the tribes of Man." [110]

Thus if we had Others out there contributing to the creation of Man, **in different places on the Earth**, yes multiple Edens, that could result in several different types of humans… and that is exactly what she found (and this relates to the prior section on the Almas, Yetis, etc.). She found the basic beginning types were:

**Asu** – similar to the *Lulu* in Sumerian history (with no soul)
    the first race to be seeded on Earth; insapient

**Ihin** – sacred little people who had the divine spark of a soul
    the second race to be seeded by Others or themselves
    (similar to Sumerian *Adamu*)

**Druk** – **a cross** between Asu and Ihin; crude and barbaric
    (if they had a soul, they hid it in cannibalism and warfare)
    Dr. Martinez suggests this was the line of Cain in the Bible[111]

**Ihuan** – pretty much modern anatomical humans, suggests that
    these were the Cro-Magnons of Europe[112]
    (probably **a cross** between Ihin and Druk)

**Ghan** – the fifth and last race of Man to be initiated by Others;
    these were Homo sapiens and had a soul. *Adapa* in the
    Sumerian literature.

To get a more comprehensive view of this same development, including a flowchart, see VEG Ch 1. The similarity of phylogenic sequences between VEG and Dr. Martinez' book is amazing although different terms are used. And today a lot of anthropologists are very concerned about the direction of Man's current development…

**Somewhere, something went terribly wrong**

All of that to say that (1) there are genetic wonders all over the planet, and (2) Others are out there who care about Man and are watching. And we are about to see what the Greys have been doing… lately:

**Rewind: 223 Genes**

As was said in Chapter 2, Man has 223 genes that are unique to him and are **not found in any other organism on Earth**. If the scientists believe that *panspermia* is the way genetic material gets here (bacteria from meteors), falls to Earth and disperses in the soil and water, the bacteria propagate among the animals that eat the plants that absorbed the organisms, and drink the water that contained the bacteria, or eat the fish that absorbed the bacteria in the water, then why aren't the 223 genes found in other animals or even in free-living bacteria themselves? They're not.

Because the Greys added the 223 genes to our genome in their genetic upgrade of Man. **This is the "smoking gun" that proves Man was a product of "assisted evolution."** It remains to be seen just what function the 223 genes have…

> An analysis of the functions of these genes, published in the journal *Nature* (issue No. 409), showed that they involve important physio-logical and **cerebral functions** peculiar to humans. Since the difference between Man and Chimpanzee is just about 300 genes, those 223 genes make a huge difference. [113] [emphasis added]

## The Coming Hybrids

So why aren't there more giants or really tall people on the Earth? Obviously some people have the genetics to be 7' and 8' tall. As with most things on Earth, there is an optimal size to a human and it relates to the force of gravity on the body. The bigger you are, height or girth, the more gravity drags at you... and most athletes who are over 6'6" tall have problems with their joints... In fact, Nikolai Valuev (above) at 7'1" had to quit boxing due to bone and joint problems.

That suggests that the biblical Nephilim probably had a problem being 13' tall and more... and what about the dinosaurs – especially the huge Brontosaurus with the long neck? Arthritis could have been a problem, and Advil ® had not yet been invented...

What is important to see is that Man has always been watched, modified and guided from the beginning, allegedly 250,000 years ago. The Anunnaki created worker slaves "in their image" and then had trouble controlling them... humans were rowdy and noisy. Neither enforced famine nor disease served to discipline them. The Anunnaki hierarchy tried to several times wipe out Man, but the slaves were too useful in the fields and mines and so the Anunnaki contented themselves with keeping Man's numbers down. What is amazing today is that there has never been this many humans on the planet at one time since the inception of the human design.

So the upgrade progressed from the *Lulu* or non-reproductive human, to the *Adamu* which was the first viable worker human. This might have been Neanderthal or a real close genetic relative. As time went on, another upgrade produced *Adapa* which was almost a threat to the gods as it was very sharp and creative. This was probably Cro-Magnon. (See Book 1, Chapter 1, **Chart 1a**.)

As time went by, Cro-Magnon was more domesticated and less rowdy but still had the Anunnaki genes, including the "violent gene." As man grew, the ET gods trained Man in astronomy, medicine, agriculture, ship-building, mathematics, and writing... and of course, war and its weapons. And they got Man to help them fight their battles between Anunnaki factions, and then to keep Man's numbers down, it was decided to pit humans against each other – kind of a forced Survival of the Fittest.

That worked until about AD 900 when the Main Anunnaki Group was long gone and the Remnant went underground. Without the direct interference from the Anunnaki, Man bred and spread throughout the Earth. Of course, it was still possible to release pathogens on the surface to cut human numbers, and if that was too localized to a town or city-state, they could also **provoke earthquakes and volcanism**. No wonder the humans used to say, when these things happened, that "the gods are angry with us!" Is it still working?

## A New Paradigm

According to Galactic Law, the Anunnaki Remnant are here to oversee the development of the humans. Their progeny. Only one problem: one half of the Remnant (the **Dissidents**) wants to wipe Man out and thus be free of the responsibility to shepherd Man. They disagree with and fight the other half, called the **Insiders**, who want to help us make it as a viable, self-respecting species. Both want to be free of Man, so they can leave, they just disagree on how to do it.

The **Dissidents** are busy working with the human 3D PTB infiltrating and deceiving, standard Anunnaki tactics. They so far have a decent control of the banking and media in most well-developed countries. They have enslaved the people financially, and no one hears all the truth in the Media … thus their control is geared to create dissention, strife and war among the humans…

The **Insiders,** on the other hand, obstruct and undo a lot of what the Dissidents do, and they have performed their own 5th Column in government, education, science and the military to offset what their adversaries are doing. 9-11 was of the Dissident's instigation and was to be the kick-off to a New World Order with economic collapse, followed by martial law and the National ID card (for starters) – after a major war somewhere, anywhere, they don't care.

And through all this, the public never suspects anything is wrong – even when a junior Senator tells the Speaker of the House to shut the government down. And the sheep still don't see it… because the illusion of a modern and totally honest Media with experts in science and government telling people what they want them to hear – the people have blind faith in their government. Few question anything.

And when they do, the PTB shut them down. The Anunnaki have always been clever, and they know how to manipulate and derive their outcome(s) from incipient scenarios – ever heard of the **Hegelian Dialectic**? How about Problem – Reaction – Solution ? – create a Problem for which you already have the Solution and wait for the public to React and demand that the PTB do what they have already planned? How about the new Golden Rule? = He who has the gold makes the rules! And don't forget Machiavelli – "the ends justify the means." How about False Flag activities? All Anunnaki inspired.

Some things are coming to a head and it won't be long before the Insiders pull the rug out from under the Dissidents and PTB. How? They have the support of the Solar Council who has decreed that Earth will not fall to the STS agenda – even though extracting Man from the abuse of the PTB may cost some lives and entail some damage to the planet… like removing a cancer.

There is another reason that the Insiders win in setting Man free and waking him up. And that has to do with what this last section is all about.

**The Greys doing the genetic upgrades on Man work for the Insiders.**

What the Greys are doing is creating a better version of Man – they are not undermining centuries of effort to develop Man. That is the good news. The bad news is that the Dissidents and PTB also know what's up and won't quit without a fight… and as usual, humans are the pawns and the prize.

**The Alien Agenda**

**The goal: to create an all-round better version of Man that is not easy to deceive, has a greater IQ and discernment, and who is more in touch with his soul-qualities**.

> Many of the Dissidents do not have souls and are afraid of what an empowered ensouled Man would do to them – which is why they kept his genome dumbed down – i.e., they disconnected a lot of his DNA and we think it is 'Junk DNA' because the PTB have told us that that is what it is… and we buy it, don't we?

**Ignorant humans are unfortunately easy to deceive.**

There were four parts to the Agenda, correctly identified by Dr. Jacobs through his hypnotically regressed subjects: [114]

1. **The Abduction Program** – to identify, abduct and monitor select humans as donors and 'guinea pigs' in a cross-breeding program.

2. **The Breeding Program** – to collect human reproductive material, genetically alter it to specification, produce offspring with whom the humans will proactively interact to program the new breed.

3. **The Hybridization Program** – to refine the hybrids via genetic engineering techniques to look more human yet retain desired advanced characteristics. Humans may also be updated in place as appropriate.

4. **The Integration Program** – Abductees are preprogrammed for future participation in the Agenda and integrate with the new hybrids in the new social order.

Stage three has virtually completed; there are hybrids walking among us, mostly working with the Insiders to effect the proactive Change, as it is called. All that remains is the Integration (and removal of the Dissidents and PTB).

## Characteristics of Hybrids

For years, abductees reported a variety of hybrid types to Dr.s John E. Mack and David Jacobs. There appears to have been a progression from alien-looking (as Chapter 5 in VEG related) to more human-looking. This boils down to three basic stages:

> **Hybrid Type 1** – look somewhat alien; they have **large black eyes with no white sclera**… small thin body, thin or sparse hair, a tiny mouth, tiny ears and pointed chins.

> **Hybrid Type 2** – still look alien, often have **unusual eyes** (either slanted or almond-shaped on a non-oriental person), and their head is shaped differently with the forehead coming to a vertical crease in the middle, with high cheekbones, and some white sclera but still less than normal, and they have somewhat pointed chins. Body type is still thin but larger, and hair is still sparse.

> **Hybrid Type 3** – look very human. They like to **wear sunglasses** to hide the fact that they may have too much black in their pupils, and they may lack eyebrows and/or eyelashes. Many of them pass without being noticed and yet abductees say that there is something a bit "off" with their appearance.

> Their **skin color is sometimes a bit too even**. They may be thin or muscular but never overweight. They often have short-cropped hair. Their eyes are often blue with a sometimes enlarged pupil, and the hair preference is blonde.

They all possess the hybrids' extraordinary mental abilities. They can do Mindscan and are often telepathic. And the late-stage hybrids can reproduce with humans (Types 1 and 2 cannot reproduce and still have to be 'created' in vitro.) Clearly they are not all alike. [115]

> *Types 1 and 2 were described in Book 1, Chapter 5 in the 'Personal Experiences' and 'Others' sections.* **See images below…**

In essence, and from what I have noticed, their **eyes are the giveaway**… apparently eyes and the eye-area are hard to genetically control. I have seen them on the street, in supermarkets and on the TV. When I see them in person, they are aware that I see them, and while I never feel any threat, they will not stay around so that I could talk with them – about any subject! Most often I met them (Type 2) in bookstores and they could not get away fast enough.

Could these be viable images of what the hybrids might look like?

**ET Human Hybrid Type 1?**

**ET Human Hybrid Type 2?**

And this one could be the final, polished product:

This little girl could pass you by in the mall, and except that she is very pretty, who would suspect she's a hybrid?

I'd love to adopt her as my daughter.

(credit all: Bing Images)

**ET Human Hybrid Type 3… or 4?**

## Hybrid Personal Issues

The Adult hybrids often have an issue with rashes developing in the armpit. They often inspect each other for red spots in the eyelids, and they check out each other's hair. Like humans, they have health issues. [116]

They have no memories of parents, siblings, family life or nurturing like humans do that create emotional bonds. As a result they have little or no compassion, and they often act like the Greys: task-oriented, efficient, and clinical.

> **Caution:** they are not to be confused with OPs, discussed in Chapter 2, who have no conscience... We don't know yet whether the hybrids have souls or not.

Some hybrids are born disfigured with missing arms or legs, and some have misshapen heads. On a more minor scale, they sometimes have blotchy marks on their skin. And female hybrids have reproductive issues, sometimes not being able to carry a baby to term. [117]

## Hybrid Behavior

A most important point about the hybrids is their behavior which either mimics Mr. Spock on *Star Trek* (**cool and aloof**), or they have been found to go out of control and be socially inappropriate. This is understandable as they have not been raised in human society and don't often know what to do – and if an adolescent hybrid feels a sex urge, he has been known to try and do whatever he pleases. And they are very strong. This has been a source of concern as **some of them are unpredictable**, and can even be mean. [118]

When the Greys are asked why their offspring, the hybrids, act in a mean or abusive way, the response is that they cannot give vent to their emotions in their super-controlled society. They have **strong sexual drives and little or no conscience**, which presents the question (as was seen with the OPs) as to whether **some hybrids might not have a soul**... even if they do, and have a conscience, they know they can mind-control the woman and cause her to forget what happened. It is also possible that the human Anunnaki genes migrating into the hybrids give rise to unsociable behavior – reminiscent of the Anunnaki behavior discussed earlier. [119]

So all has not been peachy-keen in Hybridville, but the Greys are working on it.

And this is why humans have been abducted to interact with the hybrids, often 'downloading' memories and behavior, so that the hybrids can learn to better assimilate in human society. They do walk among us and are supposedly learning as they go.

## Integration with Humans

The ultimate goal is to walk, live and work among us humans. An infusion into society where they will be **superior to the humans**, and that is something that bothers Dr. Jacobs, and is a real concern. What will they do with humans who reject them or reject their leadership in government, education and religion?

Would the answer not be to retrain the humans into the principles of the Earth Graduate, as suggested in Book 1? I was told that while humans are not well-accepted, the hybrids and ETs <u>can</u> work with us and tolerate us IF we accept the higher view of Life – **respect again is the issue**.

If we don't respect them, or ourselves, or the planet, we will be removed. Maybe if we are lucky, the recalcitrant will be "reprogrammed" neurally  into better behavior, but I was told that Man should be waking up to his true spiritual nature – and hence these two books (VEG and this one) are a suggested beginning.

Man can no longer pretend that he is alone, and can do whatever he wants, when he wants, in any way he wants. I am sorry if this sounds 'preachy' but it is exactly what They want me to share. **Man is ruining the planet**, and we have been told that since the beginning of the abductions, and we are now being told that this is not Man's planet, but if he doesn't share it, and work with other beings, he will be judged as the Neanderthals were – and we all know what happened to them.

The time really has come to realize that this version of Man, some 1200 years old in the current Era, is not demonstrating that he is fit to interact with beings who look (and are) different than he is – and Man cannot even get along with other humans! Thus he is about to be replaced – and his only salvation is to wake up, wise up, and become a better player in the cosmic Drama – **which now includes those who don't like Man's behavior so far.**  (See also end of Chapter 2.)

To cap this message, let me share something Dr. Jacobs got from one of his subjects, as she was 'educated' by the Greys who said the ultimate purpose of their work was to create a better world – **together**.

> The future for the aliens and hybrids is **always a future on Earth where they will be integrated with humans**. They offer no other possibility….
> When they refer to the "humans" they are talking about abductees. The future of, and with, the nonabductees, is rarely the subject of much conversation. They told R. K.[abductee] that nonabductees will be kept as a small breeding population in case the hybridization program has unforeseen problems. A. R. [abductee] was led to

229

believe that **non-abductees are expendable**. The evidence seems to
suggest that the future will be played out primarily with aliens,
hybrids, and abductees. The nonabductees will have an inferior role,
if any at all. The new order will be insectlike aliens in control,
followed by other aliens, hybrids, abductees and finally non-
abductees. [120] [emphasis added]

This is serious stuff, folks, and I was also told as much. We either get it together
and seek to **maximize our divine soul-potential** or we are seen as dysfunctional.
Dysfunctional humans will be reprogrammed or removed. The days of the wild-ass
cowboy who thinks he is free are gone.

An insight: the nonabductees were not abducted due to their
defective DNA, which may account for the dysfunctionality
in the rebellious humans – and will not be tolerated. In addition,
if you want to be a nonabductee, tattoo a lot of your body.
They'll reject you.

**You don't have to be perfect**, they know humans have issues due to Karma –
but as long as the human attitude and intention are right, the aliens and hybrids
will respect that. And humans who are trying to "get it together" will receive
help, insight, and guidance for that… the Aliens are not ogres.

You have a choice. What's it gonna be?

# Chapter 9: Transformation Sources

Just as abductions can be traumatizing, so can they also be a source of positive transformation – forever changing our view of reality and ourselves.

Many people have been abducted over 50+ years and most, when reliving the experience under hypnotic regression, have come to work through it, accept it, and then better understand the experience and many have even found themselves growing personally.

While some researchers have argued that the abductees fall victim to the **Stockholm Syndrome** (where the victims eventually come to respect or like their captors) and researchers suspect alien trickery, there are many abductees who years later have developed a deeper spirituality, a more complete view of God and themselves as souls, and still others have developed psychic gifts as a result.

> That sounds more like a blessing than a curse.

For one thing, what happens as Dr. Mack wrote in several of his books, is that people who were heavily into baseball, Mom, apple pie and "we're here all alone," get a rude awakening and realize that we are NOT alone, we have souls, and we are more connected to other beings of all sorts than we ever thought possible. In addition, the abducted people prefer to call themselves **"experiencers"** and not abductees as they ultimately experienced a deeper sense of themselves, and an awakening of consciousness that moves them to care about other people and the health of the planet. Many connected personally with the Greys and have a deeper understanding of what is going on.

> That is called Transformation.

The Experiencers who have been transformed are working with the Greys and others to effect the same shift in consciousness among all humans – saying that our very survival as a species depends on it. Needless to say, the 3D PTB hate the idea and are the first to pooh-pooh it in the Media, saying "Oh no, humans, don't you dare wake up and think you are more than we have told you that you are!"

**Boon or Bane?**

As was said before, the PTB's days are seriously numbered, and they will be the first to be removed as hybrids integrate with society and begin to assert their authority. No threat, just a promise… Guess who's really in charge?

Naturally, the public and certain researchers are very concerned about the coming **Change** [i.e., the integrated society], as it is called. And yet it is inevitable and Man cannot stop it. Ironically while the Change appears to be threatening, it is also what will stop the centuries of Anunnaki abuse, manipulation and deception – under which Man has suffered for too long. In essence, the coming Change, which is really a "5th column" integration of **a superior version of humans**, promises to establish the peace and stability that no nation has <u>ever</u> had on Earth.

> It is interesting that the late Dr. Mack found the abduction experience to be a **positive** transforming one, whereas Dr. Jacobs has taken the opposite stance and dreads the coming Change. Perhaps the researchers who should be making an objective observation have colored the scenario with personal biases? It is hard to believe that Dr. Jacobs got all the 'negative' abductees and Dr. Mack got all the 'positive' ones... So why the disparate interpretation?

## Civilization Outcomes

The Greek civilization, the Romans, the Huns, the Vikings, the Soviet Union, Nazi Germany, the British Empire, and even the USA (which is currently being undone from within) – **none** of them have lasted. And that was due to Anunnaki design: the humans were not to be allowed to "get it together" and run the planet. Always there have been those of the Zionist/Illuminati/Bolshevik (ZIB) persuasion whose 'programming' has been to infiltrate and subvert whatever structure the humans devise.

> Some of the ZIB are PTB and vice-versa, and mixed in there are the humans who have inherited some older Anunnaki bloodlines, called the **Elites** who have centuries-old hybrid blood – being descended from *Adapa* in some way.

Thus, given Man's propensity to pettiness and violence (inherited Anunnaki genetics), and the never-ending disruption by the ZIB antagonists, there are only two ways to resolve the current negative situation on Earth:

(1) a **Wipe & Reboot**, removing <u>all</u> hominids (to remove dysfunctional genetics in ZIB and humans) and starting over,
or
(2) implement the **Hybrid Agenda** (Chapter 8) and insert beings into the society whose presence and abilities will transform the human experience into one of stability, if not peace.

# Transformation of Man

While it appears that Man is facing an incredible Threat, as Dr. David Jacobs has described in his book, I can guarantee you that it is not about subjugation with abuse. (That could have been done 300 years ago with ease.) Dr. John E. Mack also regressed many abductees and found **a very positive and proactive agenda in the abduction scenario** which has had a sustained, spiritually transforming effect on the Experiencers. That effect will shortly be examined, but to better explain the transformative impact of the Greys, it is necessary to first take a look at the related, transformative experience called NDE.

## Near Death Experience

The NDErs (those who have had the Near Death Experience) who died and came back into their bodies, came back changed people. **Transformed**. No matter what the cause of temporary death, these people actually left their bodies for 5 – 20 minutes, had an experience of the InterLife, and then because they still had unfinished business on Earth, they could not stay Over There, and they returned to their bodies which were none the worse for the brief, in most cases, clinically-certified death . (See recent NDE movie: *Heaven is for Real.*)

These people have an expanded awareness of who they are, what is going on, and why Man will eventually experience a great, positive future.

Again a transformation.

### Post-NDE Effects

Many NDErs say their lives are truly changed in a way they could not have imagined after they adjust to getting back into their bodies. Many of them had a brief meeting with a Being of Light (an Angel without wings) and they felt incredible Knowledge and Love while they were Over There —just on the InterLife's front doorstep. (They were not allowed to enter all the way in.)

Here is a list of **common observations** they say: [121]

> There is nothing to fear about death.
> Life does not begin with birth and end with death.
> What matters most in life is **Love**.
> Living a life oriented to materialistic acquisition is missing the point.
> Being a big success in life is not all it is cracked up to be.
> Seeking **Knowledge** is important – you take that with you.

Again as *Virtual Earth Graduate* said many times, learning to Love and gaining Knowledge are the two important things to pursue while on Earth.

Further insights were gained over the years of interviews and reflect a multitude of NDErs' **suggestions** coming from their experience: [122]

There is a reason for everything that happens.
Find your own purpose in life.
Appreciate things for what they are – not for what they can give you.
Do not allow yourself to be dominated by the thoughts or expectations of others.
Do not be concerned with what others think of you.
Remember, you are not your body.
Be open to life, live it to its fullest.
Money and material things are not important.
Helping others is what counts in life.

How does that square with the bumper sticker that says:

"He who dies with the most toys, wins!"

**Not!**

Dr. Ring, after many interviews with NDErs compiled a psychological portrait of these people. What he found was not only the evolving **"cosmic consciousness"** of these people as listed above, but he also noted many **side effects** they tended to have in common: [123]

Increased love for all people and things.
Increased sensitivity to electromagnetics.
Increased psychic abilities.
Seeing energy – chakras and auras.
No fear of death.
Decreased worry – surrendering to the divine plan (also called the Greater Script in Chapter 7).
Belief in Reincarnation.
Vegetarianism (now cannot eat animals).
Major relationship change – often divorce from unbelieving spouse.
Career change.
Less religious and more spiritual.
Living each day like it is the last.
Increased concern for the planet – ecology.
Approaching all humanity and creation with nonjudgment and complete acceptance.

Less materialistic.

Understanding the challenges we face are simply lessons to learn here in Earth School.

Knowing with certainty always to follow my truth and surrender to **the Flow** of the universe.

That is a long list and it is impressive. Just one trip to the Other Side, and people are infused with a higher consciousness, a deeper awakening, of what they and life are all about. The list is worth reading slowly and contemplating... **it is the <u>same</u> <u>thing</u> that those who are Experiencers of the Greys have been saying following a regression and understanding of their experience!**

It appears that **Transformation is whatever takes us out of our myopic little world**, our narrow self-view and concerns – whether it be an NDE experience, or a confrontation with the Greys. Both are larger experiences of the Whole, and that also sheds light on whether the Greys are doing evil things or not.

## Abduction as Transformation

So what are the effects on the Experiencers, as many of them prefer to be called? While the Greys are not intending to impart higher consciousness to their abductees, it happens because, like the Being of Light on the Other Side, the Greys operate interdimensionally and have **a naturally higher energy vibration** (PFV in Glossary). Just as people were changed by a face-to-face encounter with Jesus, Buddha or Krishna, who also had higher vibrations, that higher energy somehow impacts the human aura and works energetic changes via the body's **Bionet** (see Glossary).

In short, being in the presence of a being which has a higher vibration will cause the human body to **entrain** to the level of the other being – like two tuning forks...

### Tuning Fork Entrainment

Try this sometime. Place a tuning fork on a table (in a stand for the fork) and let's smack it to get it vibrating at 100 cycles per second (cps). Now place another tuning fork of the same pitch <u>which is not vibrating</u> about 3" away from the first one. Within a couple of minutes, the 2$^{nd}$ tuning fork is now vibrating to match the first – both are vibrating at 90-100 cps.

That is called **entrainment** and is what happens when a low-vibrating human comes into close contact with a Jesus, an advanced ET, or even a Grey. The human vibrations start to match the higher ones – to the limit of their ability, notwithstanding age and physical issues with the human body, or mental resistance … all of which can serve to dampen the entrainment.

The higher vibration **stimulates DNA and rewires neural pathways**… because the human body/brain complex also has a natal vibration level. The human body is known to have a slight electric charge, usually in the millivolt range, and our brains' cells also show electrical polarization. Neurons in the brain only transmit impulses in one direction due to the (electrical) polarization of the neuron – and this was found to NOT be due to ionic activity ($Ca+$, $Na+$, $K+$) nor was it due to the presence of neurotransmitters. [124]

Someone who is enlightened and sees a higher truth to life will be more in touch with their Higher Self (the real Soul in the Realm from which we come to incarnate here) which is also a higher potential – faster vibrating and able to energize us and effect healing… which is just the higher potentiated source sending enough energy to the cells/organs needing healing that they speed up and the healing appears to be instantaneous. (The body knows what it needs to heal – if it can be given the energy to do it. It has its own intelligence, called the *Vis Medicatrix*. See Chapter 12)

> *Short of finding a healer with the greater energy, maybe a scientist named Royal Rife was on to something when he worked on developing a machine that used electromagnetic pulses to heal people.*

The Earth also has its own electromagnetic field in which we live, move and have our being in a sea of electric vibration – the Earth field supports the resonance of our bodies' weaker electromagnetic field. It is called the **Schumann Resonance** and vibrates at 7.8 Hz. The Earth in turn is sustained by the ZPE Field or Matrix spoken of in Chapter 12.

## Chinese and QiGong

Just a side note: the Chinese have known for centuries about the body and its **Bionet**, which they call the meridians. Meridians are collected into nodes all over the body called chakras, of which the body has many. In addition, the body has seven layers to the aura and the layer closest to the body, the etheric, is in touch with the meridian system. Clearing blockages in the meridians is what **Acupuncture** is all about.

The Chinese and many people around the world practice Tai Chi – a patterned exercise system of which **QiGong** (Chi Kung, ChiGong) is the grandfather. Whereas Tai Chi is used to flow the *chi* in the body and focus the mind, QiGong is used in martial arts to access and store *chi* in the body for combat, as well as develop the muscles to withstand being hit by an opponent.

The *chi* (in Japan it is *Ki*) is often used in a **Small Orbit exercise** to mentally 'run' the energy through the major meridians, removing blockages and energizing the body. This is a kind of 'electric' energy or life force that benefits the body and is examined much more in Chapters 11 and 12.

The relevance here is that the 'electric' body is impacted by the higher or lower vibration of another being, where a Jesus would lift one up vibrationally, and a Charles Manson could lower one's vibration.

**Shi DeRu and Shi DeYang**
**(credit: Wikipedia: http://en.wikipedia.org/wiki)**

A higher energy potential input succeeds in connecting the body-soul complex with the Higher Self which already espouses the above lists of benefits.

## Abduction Benefits

To return to the transformed abductees, how are they now different? According to Dr. Mack: [125]

> The apparent expansion of **psychic or intuitive abilities**, a heightened reverence for nature with the feeling of having a life-preserving mission, the collapse of space/time perception, a sense of entering other dimensions of reality or universes, the **conviction of possessing a dual human/alien identity**, a feeling of connection with all of creation, and related transpersonal experiences…[which are] basic elements of the process. Indeed the experiences of abductees may bring them to something very much akin to shamanic or mystical states of mind… [and] are often **catalysts for profound personal growth and transformation**. [emphasis added]

Key phrases from the abductees themselves:

> "… the sense I get from them [Greys] is that they are not of a malicious nature… that they have a purpose….They are not here to harm; they are not here in an aggressive way." [126]

> "You are very aware of your higher consciousness, that thing inside of you that's you." [127]

> "I have a sense I have to do this… Even though I don't want to go through it again, it's important." Said one lady who feels she has on some level chosen to be abducted. [128]

Says Dr. Mack of their comments,

> …they are aware that they are participating in an as-yet-unfathomable process that involves not only their own growth and transformation but **an awakening of consciousness for humankind more generally**. It is as if their individual psyches were intersecting with an evolving cosmic consciousness with which they intuitively feel some sort of harmony or agreement. [129] [emphasis added]

What the Experiencers are sharing is that they feel that there is **an on-going process of transformation of mankind and society** which will result in a collective shift in human consciousness. And the Greys are implementing it. Another abductee said,

> The abduction experiences, she felt, are a way of educating people "about spirituality" and "about other realities," to prepare them for the future. [130]

## NDE and Abduction Connection

So the two experiences are more alike than different…

> **Appreciation for Life**. All see that Earth is a School and our experiences are geared as challenges or opportunities for spiritual growth. They are more able to see the beauty in nature and take pleasure in the simple things.

> **Self-Acceptance**. Both groups are more accepting of themselves, realizing that they are imperfect, but growing and learning. They know they are an eternal soul having an Earth experience and that they are not their body.

**Concern for Others**. They share a concern for the well-being of other people and find joy in serving and helping others. They see our inter-connectedness and that we are all One due to our connection at the Soul level. This includes a reverence for life.

**Antimaterialism.** Most of them are no longer plugged into the drive to gain material goods, power, money or fame. What the world thinks is important is not what they see – a greater fulfillment of their soul connection with The One, the Father of Light.

**Spirituality not Religiosity**. Rote worship and following traditional religious doctrine turns them off. They are in touch with a Higher Self, and have found the Kingdom of Heaven within… not in a lifeless church made of cold marble and dead laws of behavior. They now follow their inner voice to walk in the Way the avatars have taught.

**Quest for Knowledge**. The NDErs in particular discover on the Other Side that Knowledge is very important as it protects and empowers. The abductees also have a desire to know more about themselves, the Earth and who/what the Greys are and what the purpose of life is.

**No Fear of Death**. They both know that the soul is who we are, not the body, and the soul is eternal… so death of the body is just a passage to the InterLife where it all starts again. **Fear of failing to learn and meet their Script lessons is what now drives both groups**.

**Belief in God**. NDErs who come back who were atheists before the NDE now believe in God and a better world. They have seen it, and they know that they are **eternal souls** who have a purpose, and are reminded of that when they visit Over There. They can no longer doubt the **Love and Knowledge they are expected to gain.**

Both groups report other changes, too – such as acquired allergies, ability to disrupt electrical appliances, knock out street lights when passing under them, and an occasional healing ability. [131] All in all, that is not a bad exchange for having your provincial life turned upside down (initially) by the NDE or Abduction.

Because it is so dramatic and yet interesting, there is a life-change examined by Dr. Mack in another book he wrote, where a man named Joe had a really awakening experience… a major Transformation. Joe was not alone in this…

**Joe Escapes the Insane Asylum**

Joe was a 34-year old psychotherapist who from the time he was a teenager had always pursued spiritual understanding and the deeper meaning of life. He always felt, however, that he was different and just didn't fit in and spent a lot of time outdoors where he felt more at peace with nature.

He had always been interested in UFOs but was afraid of them. In addition, as a kid he had a lot of unexplained nosebleeds and strange dreams about flying horses, snakes, dark birds, mythic gods, and vast, windswept landscapes as if on an alien planet. He attended mind/body workshops and during one of those sessions had an impression of a needle being put into his neck.

He sought out Dr. Mack to work through some of those issues. Sure enough, during the hypnosis sessions, several abductions with Greys were uncovered. It was then that he discovered that **he felt an allegiance to an alien world** and to Earth and the dichotomy was causing him a lot of upset. He then realized that he had a job to do on Earth, but even though he was born on Earth, **he wasn't completely human**. He was what he called **an alien soul in a human body** and he experienced a major struggle to integrate and finish his mission on Earth. He thus felt like a 'double agent' and could not even share with his wife what he was going through. His alien identity was more comfortable for him than the Earth human, and he felt himself to be 7-8' tall normally and part of a Brotherhood.

While in regression, Joe shared that reproductive acts and genetic analysis are

> necessary so that humans aren't lost in their race and their seed and their knowledge… for **humans are in trouble**. A storm is brewing. An electromagnetic catastrophe resulting from the 'negative' technology human beings have created…. Fertilized seed might be taken… and then we'll grow a baby that's got a lot of human in it and raise it as one of our own…If the humans totally die – we have their children. [132]

The purpose of the hybridization program, according to Joe, was evolutionary, **to perpetuate the human seed and "crossbreed' with other species** on the ships and elsewhere in the cosmos. Joe spoke with great sadness about the on-going deterioration of the Earth. He said that many humans will die but that the species will not be wiped out. [133]

**Electromagnetic Problem**

That gives a basic idea of what the Greys are doing here – **along with several other types of aliens.** Man has gotten himself into a nasty box that is doing him in, health-wise, <u>and</u> killing the planet – all because of ignorance and greed. **Ignorance** of what the proliferation of electromagnetic waves are doing to the birds, insects and even the fish … they are dying by the thousands. And the **greed** issue is that we use the latest electromagnetic geegaws to make money – without realizing what all that sea of electronic waves is doing to our bodies and hence our health. (Studies are underway to evaluate EMF effects on lifeforms, but Chapters 9 & 14 in VEG already revealed the morphing effects of certain EMFs on DNA.)

> It affects our bodies by impacting our auras which changes the weak electrical flow of our Bionet, thus promoting energy blockages, leaks and perhaps illness. A healthy aura will quickly rearrange itself. See Chapter 12.

Greed Inc. tells the engineers and doctors who speak up about the issue to shut up, so the cellphone towers can proliferate and everybody is told to go along with the program so that the top cats can make more money.

> *And there is more than that on some of the towers and the proliferation of the electromagnetic 'wash' that we all live in is also affecting some of our DNA. If that weren't enough, now we're going to modify the food supply with GMOs – which can modify the DNA –* **the ETs think we are so stupid and greedy that we don't deserve to have the planet.** *Yet, the PTB controlled by the Dissidents are behind it all... Could there also be an agenda to thin out the population?*

**The Insane Asylum Revisited**

Joe felt like a man who goes undercover admitting himself into an insane asylum to discover the abuses there, but instead becomes abused and stuck. Joe likened his Earth experience to living in an insane asylum where people pretend everything is OK, and it's not. He said that humans live in a **Prophylactic Fantasy** that is about to get ugly.

In addition, Joe gets more in touch with his alien side, and discovers that his aloneness and isolation really hurt. His companions still on the large, cloaked ship around Earth, know what he is going through and they admire his courage to stick it out and try to 'fix' things. But they agree, too, that Earth has become really crazy using technology to cause problems for humans and Mother Earth… just to make a buck. They regret that we rejected Tesla and his more Earth-friendly innovations.

Thus Joe felt as though **the "human experiment" went sour** and no longer is capable of fulfilling its original goal, and the consensus of higher beings in what appeared to be an interplanetary United Nations meeting (which he recalled attending on board the ship) was that **Man must be removed or seriously upgraded to a new species**. [134] The only good news in all this is that the Orion Group, to whom the Anunnaki Dissidents report, and who want Earth for their own ends, are not winning.

In sum, Joe reaffirms that the hybridization program was for the purpose of creating **a new species** that represented a reinvigoration of life, an assisted step in evolution. He emphasized that the current direction of human activity on Earth is leading to the **extinction of our own and countless other species**.

**The final irony**: The PTB humans who think they will be rewarded by their nefariously selling out the Earth, and fellow humans, will instead be thrown under the bus… the Orion Group/Dissidents does not reward quislings – if you sellout your own people, the Dracs can't trust you either. Cutouts are useful until they have done their dirty deed, and then they are discarded.

## Summary

So, Transformation is about confronting yourself in the presence of something greater than you are. It is about discovering that **you are more than you think you are** – and that is why the ETs seek to preserve Man, still in embryonic development, and move him up to the next stage of development.

Transformation is not just change, it is a **deep change** that does not revert to former ways of thinking, living or acting. There is a realization that goes with it that encourages one to stay with it and at all cost, avoid going back to what one once was.

> **Change** – an octopus changes its coloration to match its surroundings, but it is still an octopus.
> **Transformation** – a caterpillar changes via metamorphosis into a butterfly – not the same creature.

There are two powerful catalysts for Transformation in our world: the Near Death Experience and the Abduction by Greys – which both produce a similar effect. Man gains a higher consciousness, a new perspective on himself and life, and he perforce is preparing to take his place among the ETs and their worlds – once he has graduated from the Earth cocoon.

The Transformation for Man is from caterpillar to butterfly. From slave species to enlightened Man working with his Higher Self and he becomes an Earth Graduate.

**Because it is very important, the following is repeated from Book 1.**

## Earth Graduate Revisited

Ensouled Man's potential, when actualized, renders him a truly awesome being – doing what the man called Jesus did <u>and more</u>. Jesus said it (paraphrased):

"These things I do you shall do and greater…" John 14:12

So when does it happen? **Respect** yourself, develop compassion, gain knowledge, and live in Patience, **detach** from outcomes, things and people… a long list of requirements to graduate, but that is why:

"The **graduate** from the human experience is <u>very</u> **respected** elsewhere." [135]
[emphasis added]

And it is easy to see why: if a soul can survive this screwed-up planet with its disrespect for everything and everybody, survive the pollution and the killer diseases, resist the temptation to lie, cheat and steal, not follow the crowd, not give in to corruption, and still emerge with his/her integrity intact, <u>that would be a soul worthy of **respect**</u>. A soul who walks the talk and does not sell out. A soul who thinks outside the box that has been created for all of us by the PTB and Lame Stream Media – whose goal is to keep us believing whatever we are told, and living by <u>their agenda</u>.

It is called **self-mastery**. Then we can be released to return to the higher Realm from which we came and in which we are now ready to serve.

**And, get this: One need not be perfect to get out of here.**

If the gods had to wait until a soul on Earth attained the status of a Jesus, they'd have to wait a long time. To graduate from the 3<sup>rd</sup> Grade in elementary school, one need not know Algebra – knowing basic arithmetic and the multiplication tables will do. I suggest that being a Ghandi is sufficient, or a Lao-Tzu, or even Mother Theresa. No doubt there are further schools awaiting souls and Earth is not a "finishing school."

How many people think that staying in 3<sup>rd</sup> grade, or even 12<sup>th</sup> grade (high school), is all there is? (Aren't you tired of the cafeteria?)

Reaching the initial stages of self-mastery, resolving the serious parts of our Karma, and <u>intending</u> to go forward are enough to get us out of here and into a more exciting realm.

## Souls as Earth Graduates

Man has a unique nature and a unique destiny, he was an experiment that was hijacked by the Orion Group. Everybody except Man saw it. We are here on Earth to become more than we have been allowed to be – and probably would have succeeded by now if we hadn't resisted our lessons and listened to the wrong people... We are here to **transform into Earth Graduates**.

Souls who master the Earth realm have a special heritage:

> Our purpose in coming together as creator fragments is to succeed in training ourselves enough about love, caring, and relationship to become more of who we are. The redemption is we, as ... **progeny of the high forces of creation,** are ascending back to heaven in unity of diversity, as celebration of individuality in communion, not loss of individuality. We are holo- or fractal-fragments of the creation's creator, [who] is wanting to **create creations with us** not for us...
>
> Our first major task is to re-create the existing mother universe we find ourselves within with all its conundrums. Solve the unsolvable evolutionary problems. We learn to pick up the ball in our **training wheel practice universe** before we even want our own. And we want to learn very carefully, and so we use time to do it in a serial manner. That is the game...
>
> Each creator fragment that is a human **soul**, ultimately seeks its origin [and soulmate] and return to home. We are all ... learning to love and nurture our individual and co-creative mutual universes.
> Our job is to achieve spiritual evolutionary acceleration sufficient to help solve age old problems of spiritual evolutionary inertia in the universe. [136]  [emphasis added]

Elsewhere, the information is given that Man's inheritance is ultimately to become a **co-creator** (real power) providing he can keep moving into more and more optimal timelines:

> ...as a reward, humans who accomplish this task, will be granted an initially uninhabited virgin future that can become even more optimal beyond comparison...
> That final loop optimal future becomes the end-game singularity Conduit path through which **all** souls of all alternate [multi-dimensional] lines will eventually travel to become qualified macro-creator agents. [137]

That is the promise to all Earth Graduates.

## ETs and Man Together

So it is obvious why the Draconians (without souls) want to obstruct Man's becoming all he can be – but why do the ETs step in and set us free (As they are doing)? Simple – they also have souls and they even have some self-interest in supporting us because it all adds to the number of ensouled beings (i.e., beings with awesome STO potential) to offset the beings who follow the STS agenda and promote Darkness.

This is the significance of being soulmates in a Soul Group – souls in a Soul Group are all related to that Group, and all Soul Groups are related at a higher level… all part of the One (i.e., the Source of **entanglement**).

See hierarchy list of beings under **Godhead** in the Glossary.

We are all related and <u>together</u> we work our way back to the Father of Light, the One, <u>working</u> our way through His **hierarchy**, assuming more responsibility as we Know and Love more. You want power?  It is waiting for you… to reign over parts of the Father's Creation.

Can you handle it? Are you STO or STS? See Appendix C.

So if we are expected to overcome, like a baby chick who must break out of the light calcium eggshell by itself, then why do the ETs help us? Sadly because the eggshell has been reinforced with concrete (by the PTB) and we cannot break out … help must come from outside. And we are worth saving.

## Man's Birthright as a Soul

Ensouled Man's birthright is to (1) rise above those who would obstruct him, and (2) rule over their realms – similar to **Gods-in-Training** – and this is obviously what the soulless ones and STS would like to prevent. This is why Robert Monroe was specifically told by the Beings of Light (*Inspecs*) he encountered that Earth Graduates are very well <u>respected</u>.

That respect is due to personally developing what it takes to overcome and get out of here.  So Man emulating a Jesus, Buddha or Krishna would indeed evoke **respect** wherever he or she went. Recent historical examples: Ghandi, Nelson Mandela, Martin Luther King and, centuries earlier, Apollonius of Týana were greatly respected and loved.

It was Jesus in the New Testament who said that we could do what He was doing, and that **Love** was the Way. All teachings of Love and Light are worth following as they echo Higher Truth and that is what we need if we are to continue to grow once we are released from this Earth School.

> *Those souls who still need Schooling will be put in a new environment –*
> *free of the oppressive Draconian and 4D STS manipulation.*

It is worth repeating what Monroe was told:

> By far the greatest motivation – surpassing the sum of all others – is the result.
> **When you perceive and encounter a graduate, your only goal is to be one** yourself once you realize it is possible. And it is. [138]
> [emphasis added]

When you know, why would you settle for anything less?

# Chapter 10: Personal Transformation

The last chapter drew an interesting parallel between the little Greys' Abductions and the effects on people of the Near Death Experience (NDE). In both cases, the 'victims' or experiencers undergo an awakening that rearranges their concept of themselves and their world... they "wake up" and realize that we are all part of a Greater Whole, that we are all interconnected (at the soul level), and what was once commonly called 'cosmic consciousness' is the result for many of them – if they open to the experience instead of denying it.

**Cosmic Consciousness** was the popular term in the 50's-60's and was openly endorsed by the Hippie Movement which sometimes achieved semi-enlightenment via chemical substances. Whereas the chemicals often had strange side-effects and produced hallucinogenic visions (good and bad), there is no spiritual downside to the Abduction nor the NDE effects... effects appear to be permanent.

When the Greys do their Mindscan (Chapter 8) and move their higher energy down neural pathways in the human's brain, the energy also resonates with **the pineal gland** and stimulates it to release its endocrine substances, including melatonin and serotonin. It also produces DMT (also called ayahuasca which is used by Amazonian shamen) similar to Timothy Leary's earlier use (1960's-early 1970's) of LSD – to open the mind to a perception of higher realms. DMT, also called the 'Spirit Molecule', via the Bionet enhances the connection with the Crown Chakra and hence one's connection with the Godhead.

Note that the Abductions' **Mindscan** triggered the release of DMT which then resulted in a higher consciousness in the human. Note further, that the NDE experience also resulted in a contact with Higher Intelligence and Higher Energy which also resonated with the pineal gland, causing it to release DMT – contrary to skeptics who claim that severe mental stress or temporary cardiac arrest released DMT which solely caused the NDE experience.

Note that when the soul left the body, in the NDE, it was still connected through the head area by the **"silver cord"** which carried the higher Energy of the soul's realm back to the body (via the head where the pineal gland is located) stimulating the DMT release.

(Credit: Bing Images.)

## Ascension or Transformation?

Of further interest to this overview is to examine what, if any, relationship exists between Transformation and Ascension. And since Transformation involves Unification, that should mean Transcending the Earth Drama, which in turn leads to Ascension. You don't Ascend if you don't Transcend.

Let's take a look at some basic definitions, and then examine what Transformation is, on a personal level, and how it relates to Ascension.

**Change**: to convert an orange into what looks like an apple that still tastes like an orange.
It looks different, but is still the same fruit.
**Transformation:** to convert an orange into an apple that tastes like an apple.
It not only looks different, but tastes different.

**Transformation or Change?**
(credit Bing Images)

**Personal Change**: Adam was a shy, insecure person, but grows a mustache and compensates for his insecurity by acting arrogantly.
**Personal Transformation**: Scrooge has a dream that being a cheap miser will land him (after death) in a realm of his equals where he will really suffer so he has a change of heart and becomes a philanthropist, serving others.

Transformation is also symbolized by the **metamorphosis from caterpillar to butterfly.** Duly significant as the insect went from crawling to flying. When Man stops crawling around in a victim mentality, learns who/what he really is, and actualizes his divine potential, he will be spiritually empowered to fly. The warning given in Chapter 3 was that the New Age is not helping Man to transform (because he still is not being told the truth), any more than Christians have enough truth to transform.

Please note that the PTB are heavily invested in being Lords, controlling what the Sheeple can do, have or be… and the Lords need Serfs/Slaves because they like power trips… so neither the New Age nor Christianity tells 100% truth, the Sheeple don't have much Light and so they give their power away to those who tell them what to do, when to do it, and where.

The worst part about this is that the Sheeple think they're free. The best slave is the one who can say, "I'm no slave, I'm free!"

**Case in point:** New Agers cannot 'create their day' because their Script rules, they are constrained to limited 3D abilities, and they are here to learn from their mistakes, not manipulate them.

The common New Age mistake, in many New Age churches that I have seen personally, is to not teach all the truth in the Sunday sermon – these churches (or Spiritual Centers, as some prefer to be called) can best be described as

### Jumping Freddy Feelgood Church

as there is a lot of upbeat music, smiling, cries of "Be happy!", and running around or doing the Conga around the room!  Hugging and dancing prevail. And if there is a teaching, it often accompanies a quote up on the overhead screen from the Maharishi Mahesh Yogi which is totally *non-sequitur*… no matter how many times I read it, it made no sense. Nice words, but they meant nothing.  His primary teaching was to be happy – as if life is all about being happy… which flies in the face of one's Script – **we are here to learn**, and that may involve disappointment, pain, loss and handling of same… as well as occasional joy.  What he was selling was what people want to hear – Life is a boogie! How spiritual is that?

> The Maharishi had a message of happiness, writing in 1967, that "being happy is of the utmost importance. Success in anything is through happiness. **Under all circumstances be happy**. Just think of any negativity that comes at you as a raindrop falling into the ocean of your bliss". [139]   [emphasis added]

I also remember several people in our New Age church having been involved in the Yogi's **Transcendental Meditation** classes and techniques and two months later finding themselves in psychiatric counseling – for deprogramming.

> *Enough sermonizing on that. Book 1 explained all that and much more in depth in Chapters 1 and 11.*

In general, when a person transforms, s/he **is** a new creation – and not just "transformed by the renewing of their mind." The person is still surrounded by the same environment, same family, same friends, same problems, same abilities, likes and dislikes… but there is a difference in the DNA.

A true Transformation results in the person **transcending his circumstances** – old automatic reactive patterns are not there anymore. S/he no longer rants and rails at traffic problems, when the spouse says something that always produced a nasty response, there is peace and an understanding, a gentle word and no heated argument… When his/her favorite TV program is pre-empted, s/he just calmly switches to another station. Go with the Flow…

A truly transformed person sees the world differently – s/he knows it is all Drama – **catalyst** designed to provoke a response – when the response is no longer forth-coming, the gods get the message, and move on to something else. The person is not oblivious, they are not playing a game, they still see the catalyst, but realize that they have **a choice** – they don't have to respond to it, and if they do, it can be with grace and a kind word. S/he has **transcended the catalyst**.

So Transformation involves transcendence. And transcendence usually involves enlightenment as something is finally seen for what it really is… an epiphany, a revelation or insight that **adds Light** to the person. **Light is stored in the DNA**. Gaining Light or Knowledge is what it really is all about … not just being brainlessly happy. These latter people will be recycled and perhaps never get out of the Earth School.

And just so we're clear, the Biblical version of transformation is what Jesus did on the Mount of Transfiguration: transform into His soul-body, the **glorified energy body**. Christians and New Agers are not doing that today. Nor do they need to – it is what you already are.

**Glorified Soul-body**

The image on the left is also very much what the Beings of Light (aka Angels) look like.

The greater your personal Light (PFV) the more brilliant is the aura and the larger it is.

Ascended Masters and Avatars often have gold or purple in their auric field.

(source: www.bing.com/images)

Yet, the PTB don't want you to know what you are... God forbid you wake up, take your power back and make a positive difference in the World!

How's their suppression working so far?

## Transformation and Unification

Because souls are multidimensional, with multiple aspects of themselves in different realms, each **soul aspect** (small 's') is linked back to their Soul (large 'S')

in the realm from which they came. A Soul may split into 4-5 different aspects in multiple realms, timelines and locations (i.e., 3D planets versus 4D realms) for different learning experiences. (See also **soul** and **aspect** in the Glossary.)

Note in the diagram below that YOU as a main Soul (or Higher Self) in the Home Realm decide to experience 3 other realms or timelines. This requires an allocation of your energy to 'replicate' yourself into those other 3 realms... and you don't want to spread yourself too thinly! For the average soul aspect experience, a 20% allocation is sufficient (as the Higher Self is quite powerful and has a lot of energy), and in a difficult realm, an allocation of 25-30% may be appropriate... this is an "energy bank" that you can draw on to meet higher energy demands of the lifetime for health, reserve stamina, and mental prowess. Note that when the 3 aspects are allocated, the main YOU still has 35%.

**Allocation of Soul Energy**

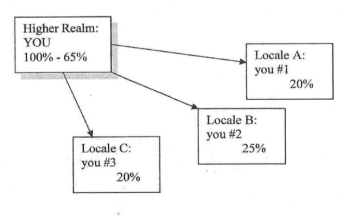

**Chart 3c**

As was said in VEG, Ch 7, this can result in one or more aspects feeling the upset or pain that another aspect is going through – and whereas their day was just fine, all of a sudden, soul aspects 1- 3 now feel anxiety, fear, anger, depression – whatever soul aspect 4 (somewhere else, not shown) is going through!

> Soul aspects will all react alike as they started the current journey all alike… it is the same Soul, and each aspect reflects the same strengths and weaknesses as the original Soul before the split.

(This can also work for joy and peace coming through.) The point is that not all our moods are self-generated, and we may be offloading another aspect of self (whose common lack of self-development is confronted with more than it expected!) and is not able to manage the challenge/upset s/he is facing. This is possible (as is said in Chapter 11, section called 'II: Using Energy.'), due to the **energy cords** connecting souls.

> BTW, this is the explanation of what was said in the Bible – "Inasmuch as you have lusted after a woman, you have committed adultery with her." Matt. 5:28 (paraphrased) Your energy connected with her, so the 'lust energy' passed to her.

The point in all that is that when one of the soul aspects does gain mastery and transcend his/her Drama, that soul returns to the Soul (sometimes called OverSoul), or Higher Self. And there is an Integration that occurs --- or a **Unification.**

Whatever the soul aspect learned to do or handle becomes part of the Soul's set of mastery skills and when the other aspects rejoin the Soul, they add their strength to the mix… And the next time out, as the Soul splits into another set of aspects, the next set of soul aspects will all have the benefit (imprint) of the collective set of skills or maturation gained earlier….

## Ascension

When a Soul has mastered a certain level of reality, it may ascend to another realm, such as moving from 3D to 4D, or 4D to 5D…. and this is done at the Soul level… 'with no soul aspect left behind!' Transformation ultimately results in the vertical progression of the Soul into realms of more power and service.

Transformation thus is a **process** and it puts one on a spiritual growth Path that has certain aspects that are fairly predictable. Knowing what happens during the process helps one to know how far s/he has come, what certain events mean and how to adjust, and what to expect. Those are examined next…

## The Transformation Process

The most outstanding aspect of the transformational process is that it calls for inner strength – to go it alone, if need be. Others around you that are not in the process may find you odd, certainly different, and they probably will not validate you. This is **a path that is often walked alone** – and you can find yourself more alone than you have ever been before. You now walk to the beat of a different drum and your ideas, when you share them, may not be understood – even by those who think they are also on a spiritual path. Remember that this is not enlightenment-by-consensus.

This is the time to let go of the need for others' approval or understanding. You will have to connect with your inner knowing to know whether you are still on track or not. And you cannot always use external events (positive or negative) to discern your rate of success or failure as the Path is a very subjective one – only you can know in your heart whether you are on track or not. You set your **intention**, you walk with integrity and compassion, and the Path unfolds in a way that is unique to you.

Along the way, there will be those who do not understand what you are doing – they will suggest that you are a dreamer, you are wasting your time, and when you share your truth with them, the religious may accuse you of blasphemy. You may find yourself among people who now see you as a threat to their traditional beliefs, to their shaky peace… the more insecure they are, they more they will attempt to get you to see it their way, "be reasonable", and join in the fellowship at their level of understanding – which you now find so limited and parochial… even Neanderthal-ish.

You cannot get into real, meaningful discussions with them as you are aware of a Greater Light and have let go of old ideas to which they still desperately cling. Any discussion in which you might enlighten them can turn into a heated argument which the new, evolving you seeks to avoid… and they then claim a victory since you said no more.  It is reminiscent of the Biblical injunction (paraphrased):

> Do not throw pearls before swine… and do not give to dogs what is holy… lest they trample them under foot and turn on you.  *Matt. 7:6*

The 'dogs' and 'swine' are those who are so dense that they have rejected the truth, and may in fact be OPs who do not understand anything spiritual… the injunction is to not waste your time explaining or defending yourself… you won't get through to those who don't care or who care but are so undeveloped that they "do not have ears to hear."  However, they are useful in that they are a **vibrational reference point** against which you can get a sense of how far removed you are from them and their way of looking at life… a life and/or a religion that you may have once shared with them.

The true spiritual path is a walk pretty much alone. From time immemorial it has been that way – perhaps as a 'test' to see if you are really serious about it. And remember to not make others wrong for their point of view … the truth changes for everyone as you go higher. There is Ultimate Truth which is the same for everyone, and then there is Personal Truth which depends on where you are on the Path.

The biggest lesson you will learn at this point is the most valuable one for the rest of your Walk: **detachment**.

## Transcend the Drama

You cannot reach everyone, you cannot enlighten everyone, and you don't have to try – it is not a requirement of an enlightened walk. That doesn't mean you become a hermit, either. You are still in the world, but not of it – you no longer see value in playing the games the average (unenlightened) person plays: How much money can I make? Do I have the right trophy wife? Am I driving the right kind of car to show others that I have made it? Does Pierre know me and my table at Chez Cary? When can I get that promotion and the corner office with all the windows? Should I move to Huntington Heights and live in that $2 mil home with the Tudor trim? We use stuff to show others who we are and how great we are…

> Rev. Ernie used to say, "If you have to tell me how you are,
> You ain't!"

And the trophy wife is afraid she'll lose her looks and get traded for another, younger model, so she spends hours at the gym, or spa and spends a lot of money on plastic surgery, vitamins and supplements – all to keep the Game going that she and her husband play: Her looks for his money. (Sounds like someone prostituted themself…)

At some point, you stepped back and realized that grabbing the brass ring was not what life was about. Sometimes the others realize it when they are flat on their back in the hospital… or in the middle of an ugly divorce. As Peggy Lee used to sing, "Is that all there is…?"

## Transcend Futility

At some blessed point, you realized that you were empty and stuff was not filling the Void within you. In fact, at some point, you might have even had a sense of the **futility** of trying to live up to others' expectations (real or imagined), the futility of trying to have it all and hold it all together… as my old time minister Rev. Ernie used to say,

> "You will eventually tire of trying to get it all together and put hair spray on it to keep it that way… It ain't gonna work!"

He was right. But some people do not wake up – they are too afraid of losing and what others will think, and then there's the mortgage, the insurance, the three car payments, junior's college bill, sis's braces, and the dues at the country club…. "How in the heck did I wire all that up?!" Even more interesting is WHY?

And when health fails from the stress, the doctor bills can really add up… and bankruptcy may be just over the horizon. The only ones profiting from your game-playing are the bankers and insurance companies. And maybe the doctor… Was it worth it?

The better choice, and we always have a choice, is to not get into the Standard American Dream (which is SAD), or the Game as it is also called. Living modestly, saving, sharing vacations with friends and family, planning for a reasonable future and NOT having to go one better than your neighbor will save a lot of heartache.

Even more to the point is to detach and live with goals, but have an attitude that says it's nice if it happens, and OK if it doesn't happen…in short, detachment means you are **not attached to outcomes**. Don't forget, you are on Earth with a Script that <u>may</u> limit what you can do/be/have and it is not intelligent to fight the Script. While Scripts are not cast in concrete and they do not control 100% of your life, if you chose a Script (or it was chosen for you!) that says you are to learn humility through poverty, trying to get rich and/or famous is fighting your Script and whatever you get, will be taken from you. **Futility**, again.

> Now you know why "bad" things happen to "good" people.

Note that if you do experience futility in your life and cannot figure out what is going on, that is a very high vibrational state! That is the state in which you are most likely to get an "Aha!" insight and it <u>can</u> be a turning point in your life… unless you ignore it and go back to what you were doing.

**Futility is an important sign** that something is not working. It is a red flag. It means, sit down, shut up (i.e., stop bitching), stop running round asking others what is happening, go within and reflect on the situation. ASK and it will be given to you – "you have not because you ask not"… or you are not listening. The gods are not ogres… They want you to succeed.

> Rev. Ernie also used to say, "You want to make God laugh?
> Tell Him <u>your</u> plans."

This is not Fate. And it is OK to have plans, but don't forget – Your Script is at work – your plans may be totally out of line with what you are to learn and experience in the Earth School. **Your Script rules**. So the gods may be laughing.

If you have fought for years to get what you want and it isn't materializing for you, rather than waste more years, you might want to do a **hypnotic regression** (clinically supervised with someone like Dr. Brian Weiss who knows what he is doing), and find out – I had to do it because my Script was very unique, my life was upside down (see Chapters 5 and 6) and I could not figure it out. Once I got the answer, it was obvious that my issues were karmically scripted into my life, AND it was suggested that I ship oars, sit back in the canoe and go with **the Flow**.

Scary, because **I wasn't in control** and that is what a lot of us want, but be clear that when you step onto the Spiritual Path, you are not in control (also see Appendix A). And you don't have to be. It is easier to reach enlightenment, and its never-ending stages, by trusting to the Universe, trusting the Flow – Man as a soul is so important to the Father of Light that He has provided Angels, Scripts and helpful people along the way to see that we make it. And in the InterLife, there is counseling, schools and the EIZ realm (Chapter 7) to **imprint** us with whatever we need. You can relax.

And drop your attachment to having things go your way; give up control and trust the process of Transformation… it will happen faster if you are not attached to a particular outcome, and you don't know what your Transformation should look like anyway, so stop trying to control results.

What should get your attention besides the red flags, are the times when you appear to **backslide**. Here you were just cruising along, making the effort to transcend the aggravation around you, and all of a sudden, there is a nasty person in your day who has picked a fight with you. Or you have a flat tire·on the freeway and you really rant about it. Or you pig out on a half-gallon of ice cream, just had a craving you couldn't control, and you put on more weight when you were trying to slim down… Now you are really down on yourself.

Oh my God, now you tell yourself that you have to start the Path all over again. How could you be so dumb… so weak… "What is wrong with me?"

> Remember: when you no longer react to a stimulus, that test will not be repeated. Things that 'push your buttons' are a sign that a lesson has not been mastered, and the button-pushing will continue until you deal with it: **rise above it.**

## Non-Transcendence

> Rev. Ernie used to say, "Success is not final, Failure is not fatal.
> There is no disgrace in failure – the disgrace is in giving up."

And who the heck did you think you were, anyway, that you would always move forward on the Path and not stumble, not fall, or backslide!? Talk about arrogant! Ooops.

> "It ain't over till it's over!" (you know who said that)

The Path to enlightenment is full of surprises, challenges and confusion. You (and no one) can walk it perfectly… unless you are already a Master. Setbacks are often tests – to see if you have mastered something, and they are part of the Script. **If you are not tested how can you know if you have mastered something yet?** And many times, dang it!, They give the test first and the answer later. Weird, but effective.

If you knew what was going to happen the next day, you'd prepare for that and meet it the best way you could. Sounds good. And sometimes it does happen that way – but there are times when They give you something that requires you to dig into your bag of tricks, scan your abilities, look for ways to handle something that you haven't seen before… all just to see what you will do. Do you freak out? Do you argue that it shouldn't be there? Do you ask "Why me?" Or worse yet, Do you ignore it – following the flaky New Age teaching that if there is something negative in one's life, then ignoring it will make it go away? If you do that, you just signed up for the lesson.

Humans on the Path will make mistakes, and Earth is often a School of Trial and Error… that way **the event and its solution becomes part of you** – because you experienced it. That is in fact the reason we are in 3D. If you were in 4D, you'd have greater soul-level abilities to stop/fix/change whatever lesson came your way, blow it off, or avoid it – and that is not possible (nor desired) in a 3D School.

> Experiencing and digging for answers attaches the knowledge to you
> in a way that it becomes part of you.

Keep in mind that you may also backslide because you have 'off' days when your personal vibration is low, recalibrating itself, or you have been impacted by another soul aspect 'dumping' negative energy into your space. It isn't always you that is the cause. This is where connecting with an **inner strength** to draw on in times of stress counts for a lot… knowing that all you have to do is handle it – NOT figure it out.

Sometimes understanding how and why things happen is the **booby-prize**. We can get so focused on what happened, and why, that we derail ourselves – we lose sight of the fact that our lives are just Drama full of catalyst – at this stage of our growth, it is only meant that we **handle it, not figure it out** (that comes later).

And maybe some of you have progressed to the point where you DO understand why some things happen. Gee, wouldn't it be nice to save your brothers and sisters some pain and get into their Script with them and explain things to them?

**Red flag!**

## Intervening on the Path

If your brother/sister <u>asks</u> you, by all means share and explain until their eyes glaze over…
…but if they didn't ask, you are dancing through a field of landmines! Here again, it is reminiscent of the "pearls before swine" – they may not be ready to receive your brilliant (and well-meant) counsel… they may not only reject you, they may attack you as a way to express their frustration and anger at what they are going through.

> It is not your mission to try to convert others or to change any mode of beingness other than your own…. It is not necessary to intervene in the scripts of others undergoing such trials… for **the higher purpose would not be served** merely by helping to alter the circumstances in the trials of others, without providing the under-standings that give those circumstances relevance. When one inter-venes in the crisis of another in these times, one **only helps to create the basis for a reenactment** of the drama for that individual. [140] [emphasis added]

So while the desire to help is noble, **removing that person's lesson does not serve them.** In addition, you have not reached the Master stage yet (you are still on Earth) and so really have no idea what is going on or how you could actually help. So you can pray with or for them, or assist them financially, but you do not commiserate with them and jump into the pit with them… a certain detachment with compassion is called for. Talk with them, bind their wound, and leave them better than you found them.

Don't judge or ignore – that means you have something to learn and just signed on for another  lesson: you will be ignored or judged when you least need it. **It is done unto you as you do unto others (Golden Rule).**  And if your brother/sister doesn't make it, neither do you – because we are all related (at the soul level). And speaking of which, if you or your brother is going through a really rough time, it may be what is called **The Dark Night of the Soul**, and that is covered more in Appendix A.

## Shadow Side

The issue may also be one of meeting one's Shadow side – there is darkness on Earth and it must be met and dealt with – steel is not produced without fire. As was said in Book 1, and earlier, there are no demons and there is no such thing as Hell, but there are **hells of our own making** when we meet circumstances that trigger our dark (undeveloped) side.

You will be stymied in your spiritual growth to the extent that you ignore or deny that you have a Shadow Side – we all have an undeveloped part of our self that may manifest as the result of energy imbalance or blockage. If the heart chakra, for example, is clogged or ¼-open you will not be able to walk in compassion and may say/do the meanest things because the off-balance energy rankles you.

(credit Bing Images)

**Shadow Side of Man**

*As was examined in VEG, Ch 6, it may also be that your chakra has been clogged by a Thoughtform or parasitic entity that opportunistically attached itself to you. Such do exist just as bacteria exist in the 3D physical world. A healer can cleanse you or sometimes just taking a saltwater bath will cleanse the aura/chakras. (More in Chapter 11.)*

All that to say that your Shadow Side (due to **chakral imbalance and lack of Light)** may account for what appears to be backsliding. You may also be listening to the input from Astral, discarnate sources, who love to play games. (See Chapter 12 'Caveat #2.')   Keep your own counsel.

What happens when one encounters negative energy as one progresses along the Path? How is it to be handled?

> The so-called **"negative energy"** that one senses as one shifts into the heightened levels of awareness takes on the coloration of one's perception of the types of images one is creating in one's life [i.e., think negative, get negative]. The knowingness that All Life is One essence begins to permeate one's consciousness. And one chooses to see, with great joy, the selections calculated to reflect one's highest vision of oneself. One adopts a state of beingness that demonstrates an awareness of other kinds of imagery, but with the detached energy of nonjudgment that does not empower nor disempower, but rather allows the image to simply Be…[141] [emphasis added]

In other words, you don't empower the negative by emphasizing it or giving it power over you (through fear) – you recognize it, but stay detached, knowing that the negative has its place in the purification of the soul. Say what?

> As one begins to strengthen the skills of **nonreaction [detachment]** one is able to reenter the physical world and to walk freely within it, knowing that it cannot affect you vibrationally… For **the only power any image has is that which you give it**…. You are the star player in your drama…
> [and eventually] you will come to know yourself as the source of [your] experience of reality… [and] **identify what one is not, in order to know that which one Is.**
>
> The experiences which one recognizes … to be most alien to one's concept of that which one Is, are the lessons that have the most powerful potential impact. [142] [emphasis added]

In short, the Shadow Side pops up to remind you of what you really want to be – the opposite. And how can you know 'down' without 'up?' or black without white…? (Hint: Yin-Yang symbol.) The Earth School is duality and we are asked to choose whom we will serve – STS or STO principles. The more Light we have, the more we choose STO ideals.

STS supports the Shadow Side and yet is a dead end… STS eventually implodes on itself, just as a negative timeline cannot sustain itself for long. In fact, there are no STS entities above 5D… entities must see the self-destructive energy of 5D STS (which is much more powerful than 3D STS!) and choose the STO path. The reason negative discarnates and STS entities are allowed to operate in the lower (3D-5D) levels is as catalyst – humans grow in 3D through their interactions with **catalytic duality**.

# Summary

So Transformation is an on-going process with feedback every day from people around us. Whatever we don't like or cannot handle is a clue to an undeveloped part of ourselves. We are not called to change other people, but transcend our Shadow side and attachments. Transcend does not mean we go hide so problems can't find us, nor does it mean we deny the existence of the negative. We let it all be there and we handle it.

When we reach a higher level, rude people and negative events will insert themselves much less frequently into our lives. That is one of the ways we can know where we are on the Path. A really smooth lifetime (but not perfect) means one of two things:

> 1. You are an Old Soul about to exit this realm, having learned and mastered many things, i.e., an **Earth Graduate**
>
> or
>
> 2. You live by yourself as a hermit or monk…
>      …but even monks have to answer to the Abbot.

## Rewind: Connecting the Dots

At this point, it is appropriate to examine how Transformation relates to the preceding chapters.

### Transformation and Timelines

As **Chapter 2** suggested, we can synch up with the timeline of our choice by intent, focus and visualization. In fact we have collectively done this which is why Edgar Cayce's prophecies did not come to pass in this timeline – they probably did in the timeline we were all on back in the 30's when he made his prophecy about Atlantis rising in the ocean.

A person who has transformed their relationship with reality, and has transcended and detached, would have a high level of consciousness (and thus energy) which would be incompatible with our current timeline. The teaching is that such a person could automatically entrain to another timeline that is coherently synchronized with that person's PFV. Their personal transformation resulting in a higher PFV is what aligned them with the higher vibration timeline.

## Religion vs Spirituality and Transformation

**Chapter 3** argued that most religion and transformation are incompatible; in fact religion has a way of dampening the drive to reach spiritual values. Religion offers a safe, predictable road through the Sacraments to the end of life, but does nothing to encourage Transformation. In fact, religion keeps people from questioning and seeking answers and seeks to content the followers with platitudes like: God loves them, because they are saved, there is nothing more to do or understand... "Just love Jesus and, like Pinocchio, stay wood." Aaarrgh!

Thus one cannot be on a Path to Transformation (enlightenment, or higher awareness) without considering the spiritual side of life. One must consider, read, and reflect occasionally on the spiritual meanings of life... often best promoted by Metaphysics, the higher laws of life. Such teachings as Karma, Reincarnation, Soulmates, the aura, chakras and LifeScripts and the Laws of Love and **Confusion** (Glossary) are some of the elements of a spiritual Walk, not religion.

## Temple Care and Transformation

**Chapter 4** said the body is the temple that we inhabit while on the Earth School journey and we should take care of it so that it supports mental and soul work. A body that is ill is like a temple with trash in it – more time is spent taking care and cleaning the temple than is spent in using the temple for learning.

If the temple is abused or trashed, and it collapses, it will serve no one. A healthy body that can travel and seek new experiences will deliver more learning opportunities on the Path than one confined to bed or a wheelchair. A healthy body has a healthy Bionet and the *chi* moves freely, supporting the body which supports the soul. So feed it and exercise it properly.

## Transformation and the InterLife

**Chapters 5 – 6** dealt with the underpinnings of Transformation – if you're going to walk the Path to Transformation, it helps to understand that you have a LifeScript, how it was formed, why it was created, and that you are an eternal soul who incarnates in many places and times – all for experience. Along the way, the soul is subject to Karma, Reincarnation, Recycling, and the Laws of the Father's Multiverse.

It pays to know how these things impact your walking the Path so that you make the right choices and understand when things go awry. For example, **Déjà vu** is a sign that you have been through this lifetime before – you were recycled, and that should be a red flag to wake up, pay attention, and do everything you can to learn, so you don't repeat it again.

Examples of Karma impacting one's Script came from the author's past life 1991 Regression wherein he saw his Soulmate and why they are apart and why this lifetime was so difficult. Options and analyses followed as templates to assist readers in making similar analyses of their lives, where appropriate.

**Chapter 7** examined the operation in general of the InterLife and the Heavenly Quantum Computer which is used to make LifeScript choices, plus the Greater Script that functions like an Operating System in a computer. The realization that all this **Drama on Earth is orchestrated as catalyst for our growth** – and we chose it! – is the main point.

## Transformation, Abductions and NDEs

In **Chapters 8 – 9**, a most fascinating review was made of what the little Greys are doing to the human genome to create a better race – to upgrade it. That results in a more intelligent human being born on Earth, called Indigos, Starseed, or Crystal children … if the species is upgraded, and it is a proactive change (less disease and higher IQ), that should improve the quality of life for everyone and Man would be more likely to seek out his spiritual side.

In addition, the infusion of new genetics and hybrid humans is supposed to stabilize the world scene – less war, more caring, better humanitarian end environmental actions… That all means that if Man stops war and focuses on a more altruistic society, people will have the spiritual environment and encouragement they need to pursue enlightenment and transform the energy and aura of Earth – and in turn, the Earth will resonate and entrain Man to a higher consciousness. And remove the Quarantine.

The **Abduction** experience has transformed hundreds of people who now see Earth and themselves, and the ETs, as potential brothers and sisters – not aliens to be feared and shot at.

The **Near Death Experience** also produces enlightenment effects similar to those of the Abduction experience and as such, both are co-partners in the Transformation of Man's consciousness – awakening to be more than we have thought we were.

Then **Chapters 11 – 12** will explore the way energy is gained and used to assist one in transforming themselves and their world. The source of energy and manipulation of energy for healing is a main focal point, but healing the body with energy from the Matrix, or ZPE Field, also impacts the DNA and helps the body carry more Light, which is ultimately what Transformation is all about.

Lastly, **Chapter 13** examines what interrelationship between the brain, mind and higher consciousness. Nutrition specifically for the brain is offered, and a brief look at activities for the brain, including the power of the brain to decode scrambled sentences.

In addition, the latest findings on the maturation of the brain with respect to our public school system is examined. The chapter also examines and evaluates whether certain people can achieve higher consciousness or not.

Man is about to climb over the wall (see cover) into a brighter future marked by new energy sources, genetic engineering and disease control, space travel and interaction with ETs. It will be a more organized and interrelated world with many things computerized, tracked, analyzed and synthesized going beyond what the book *Brave New World* foresaw. If it is a benign scenario, fine. If it is oppressive, the gods will halt it and restart things, as Book 1 suggested... another Wipe and Reboot.

Since Man has been repeatedly assisted over the last several thousand years, it stands to reason that They will continue to see us make it into a self-sufficient and intelligent, more peaceful species. That is the **agenda of the Greys**.

At some point, Man has to transcend the 3D world (the HVR Sphere of VEG, Chapter 12) and move on to play and learn in a higher Realm, or at a higher level in this one... and that reflects the **agenda of the Higher Beings** who want to see Man transform into an Earth Graduate.

The two agendas are not mutually exclusive. According to my Source, **both agendas are coming to fruition** – the Grey one first, permitting the Higher Beings' agenda to then manifest. And it looks like we are almost there. Referring to the cover of this book, hopefully that is what awaits us on the other side of the wall...

While we can't do anything to help or hinder the Grey Agenda, we <u>can</u> begin to participate in our own personal Transformation, and that is what the rest of this book now deals with.

# Chapter 11:  Transformation & Energy

This could be called the 'How To' chapter in the book. If Transformation is that important, how does one do it, or make it happen… or even assist in the process? Thus this chapter is about the Creation, Use, Management and Development of energy as relates to personal Transformation – which is really another way of saying there is a way to raise and 'culture' one's Personal Frequency Vibration (PFV in Glossary). The goal is Higher Awareness. Chapter 11 is the 'teaser' and Chapter 12 is the specifics. Chapter 13 is the eye-opener.

> Light is Energy + Intelligence
> and resides in true Knowledge.

Adepts have long realized, and the PTB have long sought to suppress, that if one is to graduate from the Earth School (see Book 1), or one wants to align oneself with a better Timeline (Chapter 2 in this book), that requires at least **51 % Light** in one's PFV, reflected in one's DNA and thus aura, by the way.  Instead of the average human aura reflecting dark, heavy colors, which signifies a low, slow vibration, the Seeker of Light will have an aura that reflects lighter colors, signifying a higher, finer pitch (color and sound are related) – light blue, rose, pale green, even pale violet, or an Indigo color as is found with some of the new, incoming souls who are birthing into the Earth realm to help raise the planetary vibration.

Earth is about to undergo a **Shift to the 5th level**, dimension or Timeline, and those who can synch up with her rising energy, i.e., be entrained by it, will find themselves moving (shifting) with the Earth into a better Timeline (see picture in Chapter 2, Timeline Split). This is another way out of here. Those who do not feel comfortable with new ideas, or energies (all is energy in one form or another, even ideas), will not notice that anything has changed and will be "left behind" – as Chapter 2 pointed out – their world will go on as before due to the presence of OPs (or NPCs) so that it looks like nothing has happened. The same Drama will continue for them for a while except that now that the higher vibration people have left for Timeline 2 (the New Earth), the current (TL1) will be free to 'develop' every negative thing the PTB could want, and yet soon devolve into an entropic slide and the disintegration of the original TL1. (Chart 5 in Chapter 2.)

## Clarification on Auras

Before proceeding with the energetic aspects of Transformation, it might be good to clarify a few things about auras.

It was said in VEG and elsewhere in this book, that our Drama on Earth is supported by OPs (or Non-Playable Characters, NPCs) who help drive the Father of Light's Greater Script (each Era on Earth having a different Script, just as each grade in a public school has different levels of subject matter to learn and master). The current Era is about to end with the Shift (or Ascension) of the Earth and her entrained souls to a new Timeline.

**For what it is worth, you select yourself to go or not go –depending on your PFV – the gods are not making the selection.**

Karma has no bearing on whether you go to the new Timeline, or not. Karma goes with you as it is still your set of lessons to be learned, and just moving from 3D to 5D does not remove them, nor necessarily change them. This is another way of saying that you need not be perfect to make the Shift (also called a Harvest of souls), but you do need to have that 51% Light in your PFV.

And this relates to auras. Your aura is the reflection of how much Light your soul carries, and principally shows up in the 1-2" etheric layer (just above the skin).

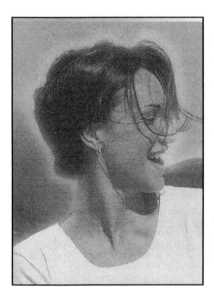

The **strength** of the aura (some are barely visible) reflects how much Light/Knowledge you have, and the **color** of the aura reflects your orientation or sometimes your purpose – green auras are predominantly found among healers, yellow auras reflect a scientific, technical orientation (i.e., programmers and physicists), red signifies violence, coupled with shades of black [i.e., shadow side], and rose signifies compassion, and blue to indigo auras reflect a spiritual person. The aura of Jesus, Buddha, and Krishna would have been largely white with some gold, maybe with streaks of purple in it.

It is a misconception that a white aura is that of a new soul – remember that white is a combination of all the colors, and that means that soul has (developed) equal portions of what each color signifies. A new soul has an aura that is usually orange... remember that the base (#1) chakra is red (survival), the #2 (abdominal, or Dan Tien) chakra is orange (self-preservation – halfway between survival [#1] and ego [#3])... and the #3 chakra – the solar plexus (home of the ego) is yellow. Baby souls predominantly live in their first 3 chakras, thus their aura reflects some mix of the red-orange-yellow colors.

To clarify a bit further, just because a person has no aura <u>that can be seen</u>, it doesn't mean they are an OP (and that caveat was stressed in VEG, Ch 5). The Earth is currently home to a myriad of entities here to help, from aliens incarnating into human bodies, Starseed, Indigos and the "Crystal Children"....
and Walk-ins and higher level **soul aspects** that have merged with a lower, incarnated member of their Soul Group to empower the 3D (lower) soul.

The following are based on personal observations during two years (2006-2008) during which auras were visible to me:

> True OPs .............. no aura, but may have a 'heat wave' signature above their head.
> Baby souls ........... often no aura is visible as it is so weak it is hard to discern. The aura has yet to be developed.
> ETs, aliens ........... if they have a soul, it reflects the colors and characteristics of all souls. If no aura: **Caution:** this is not an OP, it may be a synthetic body or it can be a holographic projection... (see Glossary: Shapeshifting).
> Walk-Ins ..............are souls and while <u>rare nowadays</u> are usually seen with a higher level aura – stronger, and of a higher color (blue, indigo, purple, maybe white).

Walk-Ins are not used much nowadays since the infusion of Indigos and **Hybrids** (as Chapter 9 points out) are among us and have absorbed the activities earlier done by Walk-Ins. Yes, Hybrids will have an aura as that was something the Greys were working to perfect – a new body type whose genetics supported the 'occupation' of a soul. The Greys refer to the body as a 'container' for the soul; but that is not really correct since the soul surrounds and envelops the body, activates and uses it (unites with the Morphic Field).

**Seeing auras**

Some people who have been on the Path for a while and have achieved the 51% Light quotient, should be able to see auras, even if faintly. The technique is simple for those who have the innate potential.

This information was removed from Book 1 (due largely to space requirements) but it is given here with the understanding that learning to see auras not be undertaken to go on a witchhunt. Using the skill to see what another person is feeling but not expressing can be useful --e.g., the aura is red because the other person is getting angry but superficially masking it, or better yet: the other's aura is showing dirty green (the color of lying). Besides <u>hearing</u> what the other person is saying, and <u>seeing</u> what they are doing (gestures, etc), AND the ability to <u>note</u>

changes in the aura can save you from a lot of deception or a broken nose! Very valuable to the initiated!

1. Stand in a sparsely lit room – a bathroom during the day with the light off and in front of the mirror, with a white or pale beige wall behind you
2. Stare at your forehead, not intently, and make the focus of your attention the side of your head – seen as it were with your peripheral vision – **defocus** your vision…
3. Occasionally close your eyes and rest them, then open them and in the first few seconds, note if there is any 1-2" energy field that appears to be surrounding your head.

**Two warnings**: (1) If you try to do this with a friend, and s/he is an OP, you will think you have failed… that is why you want to try this with yourself first… get used to seeing the faint, fuzzy 1-2" light around your head… And no, I don't think you would be an OP and try this on yourself, as OPs pooh-pooh this kind of thing and probably would not be reading this kind of book anyway.

Secondly (2): When doing the above exercise, and you close your eyes, you will probably see what is called an "after image" of yourself on your retinas. This is normal, and sometimes the aura will ALSO show up as a slight shift in brightness as on the edge of the after image. When you open your eyes again, and you **defocus**, you are most likely to see the etheric aura.

**Note: auras do not show up on TV or in normal photographs.**

**Beware of Aura Cameras**

While we're at it, let's clear up one more aspect of auras, to stop confusion (and save money). There are people out there who have very cleverly discovered that they can appear take your aura picture and make money doing it. They have you sit down, facing their Polaroid camera, and put your hand on a metal plate of sorts and it 'reads' the heat/energy of your hands, and then they photograph this hand energy above your head when they take your picture. It is not your aura.

There is a man in Dallas who has a **real aura camera**, you touch nothing and he has been interviewed (with his camera) on *Good Morning America*, back about 10-12 years ago. You touch nothing, he uses no gimmicks or secret color lenses within the camera (it is also a Polaroid using a standard film pack). It uses an ultraviolet filter which does see the energy around your head. Having tested many people (and myself many times), the camera is consistent, accurate, and even shows entities in the aura at times… something you don't get with the fakes who frequent some psychic fairs.

It also shows when people are abnormally depressed and could make a great psycho-therapeutic counseling tool (and ward off suicide!).

**Hand Aura Picture**　　　　　　**Real Aura Picture**
(credit both images: Bing Images)

The photo on the left (although B&W) shows **multiple colors** splashed around the person… (red, green, yellow, and orange) and if you look carefully, she has her right **hand** stretched out, no doubt resting on a heat-sensitive plate. Whereas the real aura picture on the right is **a single (homogenous) color** and merely changes intensity from top to bottom.

Having said all that, let's examine some relevant information in the four key areas of Transformation and Energy. Remember that this is energy that assists and manages the Transformation process, and that it is an on-going **process**…

In addition, remember that the following are snippets of information to be used as a guide as to where to look and what to look at, and are not meant to be a complete exposition that teaches you how to do each item… such would be another complete book, and that has already been done and is included in the endnotes for this chapter as well as in the Bibliography (all in the **Transformation section**).

## I. Creating Energy

**Meditation** on the Light, perhaps accompanied with Hatha Yoga, will help to set one's focus and **intent** to absorb more Light. What you focus on is what you attract. And **intent is the key** – a soul must decide what it wants to accomplish, and that is most often set in the Script, such that from your Ground of Being, you intend to do that for which you incarnated. You don't need to know exactly what you intended before you incarnated, because at birth, or very soon thereafter, the **Veil of Forgetting** drops on a soul and sometimes the original intent gets lost in the ups and downs of daily living.

Meditation is a way to get in touch with the **Higher Self** which has all the answers and if it doesn't directly reveal answers during the meditation session, it will orchestrate events in the life consistent with what the Script says the soul should be doing – as long as there is the **intent** to follow one's true purpose – and that is often something you feel almost driven to do, and is often something you love to do and probably have a talent for it.

Your talent and ability is often a clue to what you should be doing – Why would the gods give you the task to write something significant, and not give you the ability to write, or think logically? The same goes for being a speaker or artist or musician. Tchaikovsky and Beethoven were inserted into the human realm to do their music to inspire Man, for example. In other words, Beethoven was not born an average man who decided to try and write music, and then Wow, it just happened to work! **There are no accidents, and coincidences are orchestrated.** He trained for what he would do in the InterLife and then brought his art to our 3D human realm.

If you are really into meditation, and want to soak up Earth energy, try meditating

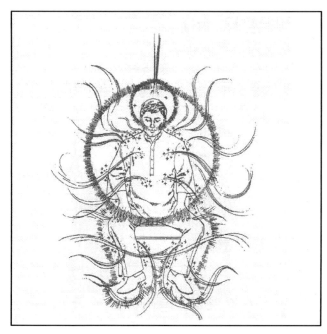

in a **vortex**, such as is found in Sedona, AZ. From personal experience, skip the Airport Vortex, it spins the wrong way and will tire you. The best vortex, if still accessible, is that at the end of Boynton Canyon, up on the ledge.

Bell Rock and the Cathedral are OK if you can safely find a spot where the energy swirls up and off and sit in it for a while. Visualize absorbing the energy and let it caress you.

**Drawing in Chi**
(credit: Pranic Healing, p. 76)

**Nutrition** is also important to support one's Path to acquiring and holding better energy – as Chapter 4 said. But what it didn't say was that pure natural food has more *hado* (as the Japanese call it, a form of Ki/*chi*) and the more natural and less contaminated the food is with chemicals, the more *hado* (energy or *chi*) it has to offer the body. Food that is contaminated with chemicals, or has been genetically modified, may cause the body to work harder to extract the nutrients from the food, and if you spend more energy than what you extract, an energy-depleted body is headed for illness... to say nothing of the liver having to work harder to detoxify the food laden with chemicals, preservatives and hormones...

As one progresses in the spiritual Path, there is a healthy shift away from heavy foods like pork and red beef (which may contain deadly *prions* nowadays) and one makes a choice for more soups, vegetables, fruit, brown rice, chicken, fish (careful where it comes from; e.g., **albacore** is better than regular tuna because they swim deeper and avoid the chemicals near the surface of the ocean.) It is not wise to become a **Vegan** because it is hard to make sure that one gets the adequate supply of **22 amino acids** in the daily diet. While rice and beans together technically supply all 22, different body chemistries may have different abilities to extract the needed nutrients from the rice and beans. Unless one supplements with a quality B-complex, there can be health problems. And FYI:

> **Brown rice** (or "hulled" or "<u>unmilled</u>" <u>rice</u>) is <u>whole grain</u> rice. It has a mild, nutty flavor, and is chewier and **more nutritious than white rice** but can go rancid more quickly because the bran and germ—which are removed to make white rice—contain fats that can spoil.[143]

**Case in point**: there was a Vegan friend who had trouble getting adequate protein for his busy lifestyle and at age 33 he developed Bell's Palsy which almost left his face disfigured. I jumped in counseled him and shifted him to be a basic Vegetarian who still eats fish, eggs and sometimes chicken, and he recovered and has no further problems. He now also uses a quality Multivitamin.

**Breathing Exercise** sometimes will help charge the body, especially the alternate nostril style so popular with the Hindus and Chinese. What they know is that the Ida and Pingala are two different meridians in the body's **Bionet** which are 'activated' by alternately breathing in and out via alternating nostrils. This works because the air contains *chi* (or Ki [Japan], **Prana** [India], Ruah [Israel], Mana [Hawaii], Lüng [Tibet], etc...) and the body's Bionet is composed of one major main meridian – ½ of it on the body's backside and the other ½ on the frontside, as well as the left side of the body is **Yin** and the right side is considered **Yang** in a man (but the woman is the opposite).

The **Yin Yang** concept is that of opposites existing in harmony and was even known to the Celts, Etruscans, and Romans. [144] It was not exclusively a Chinese concept.

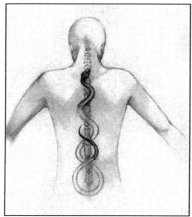

**Tao Duality: Fire side by side with Ice.**

Note that *chi* is neither Yin nor Yang per se; it is merely a way of saying that *chi* is too strong (Yang) or too weak (Yin). And like electricity, or water, *chi* always flows from a higher potential to a lower one (and that's how *chi* healing works).

In fact the *chi* flows in a woman's body in the opposite direction of what it flows in a man and the union of the two Bionets and the *chi* between them is what **Tantra Yoga** is all about – during intercourse, not only are the two auras in contact, and the 5 torsal chakras meeting each other head on, but the two Bionets are meshing, flowing and orgasms in a couple who deeply love each other are strong enough to produce a (mutual) spiritual high somewhat like the *kundalini* rising (only safer).

The **Kama Sutra** was designed by those who thought that certain positions would result in different levels of spiritual highs and yet the **caveat** is to be careful that a position does not harm the body by straining the joints or firing off the *kundalini* prematurely and creating a harmful energy blockage.

Aspirants who seek to move *kundalini* (the "twin serpents" of energy represented by the medical establishment's *caduceus*) up the spinal column (through the backside chakras) should find a knowledgeable master who can guide the energy (with HIS intention) and quickly remove any energy blockages.

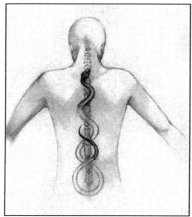

**Kundalini Rises in Spine**      **Medical caduceus**

(Credit: Bing Images)

Lastly, there is a modality that everyone can use and probably should – as they do in China. Hundreds of **Tai Chi** practitioners will get together on lunchbreak in Chinese cities and practice the Tai Chi forms together – for health and body discipline. Advanced forms of Tai Chi can include moving the *chi* through different parts of the body (for health reasons) but this is not the pedestrian or conventional form that 90% of the people around the world practice… again, advanced energy forms require a master who knows what s/he is doing. Master Lam is pictured below in the Ninth Position (*The Way of Energy*, p. 102).

**QiGong** is the really effective form of energy creation in the body (also spelled Chi Kung, and Qi Kung). This is the grandfather to Tai Chi, thus making Tai Chi the safer form for every day, citizen-Joe to practice. QiGong is older than Tai Chi and involves many <u>repetitive</u> sweeping movements of the body, arms, leg-lifts, and even Standing-on-Stake to develop personal energy for martial arts or healing. QiGong is often used as a warm up for those who practice Kung Fu.

*The trick with the advanced position to the left is to not bobble or weave; it strengthens the muscles, improves balance, and the mind can lead the chi through the body's Bionet.*

Why do the advanced energy forms require a master? With very little practice one discovers that **the mind can move *chi* to any place in the body** that it is needed! Not to be gross, and this is no joke: After very little practice, one can visualize bowel movements and indirectly send an orange *chi* there to relieve constipation. This also works to stop asthma attacks, and lower blood pressure… but Americans prefer to take a pill…

> You know the energy is moving if you feel a **slight tingle** where you are trying to direct it.

Healing, as will be seen in the next section, works the same way… QiGong healers (after building up their *chi*), can direct it to a sick part of the patient's body (sent with intent to heal), and the receiving body due to the *vis medicatrix* (that we all have) knows what to do with the energy and can heal itself – using the energy sent through the healer's hands.  Some healers visualize green or purple *chi* to speed the healing process (different colors have different frequencies and do different things).

> When I practiced QiGong regularly, the *chi* automatically flowed in my body and I could do minor healing on some of my friends. They in turn started calling me master, and gave me a title of Fu Ling.  If they came to the *dojo* and I wasn't there, they would look for me and ask, "Is Master Fu Ling around?"  ☺ (He usually was)

## II. Using Energy

Obviously a good use of energy (once one has built it up in their body; it builds like an electrical potential) is to send it to a part of one's body, to heal something… and <u>keep doing it</u> until the healing is 100%.

> Playing softball with a singles group one day, I tried to catch a fly ball and without a mitt, I misjudged and caught the ball on the end of my little finger. It was bent, crooked, and I could not straighten it! This was during the time when I practiced QiGong regularly, using the Small Orbit Exercise (covered below) regularly.
> I did my Qi workout every day, but over a 2 week period I could not get the *chi* to heal the finger and I was considering physical therapy. I gave up.
> One day, I was practicing the **Small Orbit** and being tired instead of sitting up, I lay down on the bed and moved the *chi* to the top of my chestfront. (I could feel the tingle, so I knew it was there.) For some reason while moving the *chi* through my body, I fell asleep And the last place I remembered cycling the *chi* was in the top of my chestfront…
> I awoke 2 hours later and my finger was completely healed – the *chi* had wandered down the meridian into the arm, to the hand, and into the finger. That absolutely shocked me as I thought I had to consciously direct the *chi*… yet it responded to a need and maybe to my intent.

Nobody knows why or exactly how the mind directs the *chi*, just that it does, and everyone can do this. (Books on QiGong often explain this technique and I have cited a few in the Bibliography). Basically, it is pure **visualization** coupled with the **intent and will** – you visualize the *chi* as high energy, shining molecules (because they are), and you **will them via your intent** to go where they are needed in the body. You visualize them arriving at the place where you want the healing, and that's it – they go and the body uses them to heal itself… you don't specify what to do or how to do it.  I have also directed it to heal a poison ivy rash which was 50%

less the next day and no longer itched… and I have used it to heal gout by sending it into my foot (in addition to using the Vitamin B5 I mentioned in Chapter 4). Note that you have to acquire the *chi* (draw it in) before using it.

That brings us to the *crème de la crème*: the **Small Orbit Exercise.**

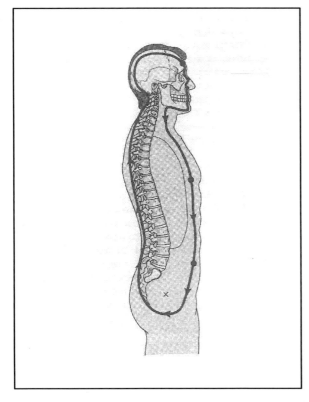

**This is also called the Microcosmic Orbit, or the Fire Path of Qi Circulation.**
(credit *The Root of Chinese QiGong*, p. 85)

Normally, sitting up, one again visualizes a major *chi* 'artery' running down the center of the front of the body (Ren Mai), into the anal region (chakra #1 down there), and then up the back side through another major *chi* 'artery' (Du Mai) that goes all the way up to the back of the head, over the top (center of the head and chakra #7), and continues to the face, semi-terminating in the roof of the mouth… one holds the tongue against the roof of the mouth to make the connection between the head meridian with the one that picks up in the lower jaw, and continues on to the frontside meridian (Ren Mai) that was just mentioned.

You can flow the *chi* in either direction, down the front and up the back, or up the front and down the back – these are Yin/Yang variations. But you start in the abdomen in what they call the **Dan Tien**, which is the reservoir of *chi* that the martial arts practitioners and healers use to build and store their *chi*. It takes about 5 -8 minutes to make one cycle, if done correctly as it is not to be rushed.

There must be an adequate flow of *chi* in the meridians (Bionet) for the body to be healthy. Other than that, where does one get the *chi* from to do this practice?

From the world, all around us, including from the Universe. **Trees** are a good source and QiGong can be very effective practiced under a tree – the bigger the tree, the better. (Now you know why the **Celts and Druids** held healing ceremonies in oak groves.) Trees emit a lot of *chi* and that can be 'scooped up' and stored in one's Dan Tien – just by visualizing it.

You can also sit still and visualize the *chi* flowing to you and into you from the Universe. Typically, as shown below, one uses the left hand (the palm has a chakra which can absorb *chi*) to **take in** the energy, and it can be stored in the **Dan Tien** (2" below the bellybutton) OR it can be directed out the right hand (via its chakra) to a place where healing is needed. Sometimes, when doing it correctly, you can feel a pulsing of the two palms, alternating as the energy flows in and out... in and out....

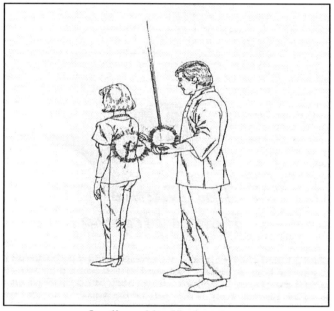

**Sending *chi* to Heal**
(credit Pranic Healing, p. 4)

The energy can also be used to **sweep someone's aura** which is a way to clean it, repair gaps, and remove thoughtforms and parasites (more discussed in VEG Chs 5-6). In cleaning a woman's aura, while on vacation in Sedona, AZ, I broke the energy cord (next section) that her parasitic 10-year old son had planted in her mid-section (the 3rd chakra is a favorite target of **energy vampires** [next section]) – he was something of an energy vampire, and she was always tired when he was around. When I swept her aura, I didn't feel the energy cord sucking her dry, but it left her, and the boy immediately screamed and ran to the bathroom yelling "I hate you!" It seems like an instant way to make friends...

> Note that mothers and sons, and members of a family, always do
> have **energy connections** with each other and this is another reason
> that **forgiveness** is important – bad feelings between family members
> will travel back/forth along the energy cords and one may feel really
> up or down depending on what kind of energy the other person is
> sending. This is not always **energy vampirism** (see Glossary).

Of course, as will be seen in the next section, souls tend to 'cord' each other as a matter of course, just interacting with each other; it is just that it is a much stronger connection between family members as they are often of the same Soul Group. (This is not to be confused with the silver cord that links the soul to its body.)

**Forgiveness is the way to break these cords** and set ourselves free from future karmic 'dances' with others with whom we have issues. Let them go, wish them well, forgive them, and move on. You won't forget (and don't have to) and you want to remember them so you can avoid them, but don't nurse the wound – it just feeds the connection. Realize why the upsetting issue happened, see your part in it, get the lesson, and let them go – you won't fix/stop/change them – they are probably an OP anyway – they administer our lessons/tests... don't try to get even, just let it go.


## Protecting Oneself

This is another very useful and common use of this energy.   This is the common technique of **White Lighting** oneself – surrounding oneself with White Light and your **intention** is that nothing negative gets through the energy field.


The easy and sure way to do this is (1) to picture, visualize again, a pure, bright white sphere of Light, and (2) then picture yourself in the middle of it.

Why? Because there are entities in the Astral (**4D STS**, Discarnates, Parasites, and Thoughtforms) that can harass and oppress you. The White Light stops them – puts them on notice that you do NOT want to be bothered by them. It also works when having a nasty confrontation with another human – say, even your boss or a coworker.

**If you haven't noticed by now, visualization and intention are a large part of working with energy, or *chi*.**

When confronted with a negative person or event, there is another very effective way to stay centered and calm – so that whatever they do/say, even if they are an **energy vampire**, they cannot affect you: and this is also shown in a lot of pictures of people from the 1800's when this practice was more common:

277

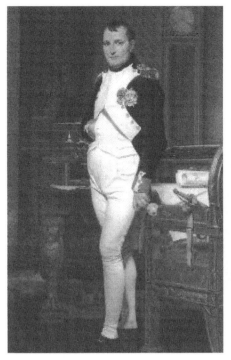 

**Napoleon Bonaparte**
(credit both: Bing Images)                    **Rasputin**

### Sit or stand with your hand(s) clasped over your 3$^{rd}$ chakra.

This is your **solar plexus** and is a prime target of energy vampires because it is a major seat of the body's energy and is easiest to tap because it is always open (not all chakras are open). In stressful events, this is also where your energy leaks from… The hand protects the 3$^{rd}$ chakra. Try it sometime in a tense meeting.

## III. Managing Energy

Protecting the solar plexus is one of the main ways to manage one's energy – so that it doesn't 'leak out.' And **White Lighting** oneself is another common way to prevent unseen influence – and is often done when regressing someone via hypnosis to prevent the unseen entities from putting ideas or emotions into the scenario.

**Cutting Energy Cords** is another big way to clean oneself up –now that we know that the *chi* responds to mental visualization, energy cords between people are made from the same stuff (*chi* was subconsciously sent to create the link), and now we have a way to get rid of something many people don't know they have which can cause them on-going health problems.

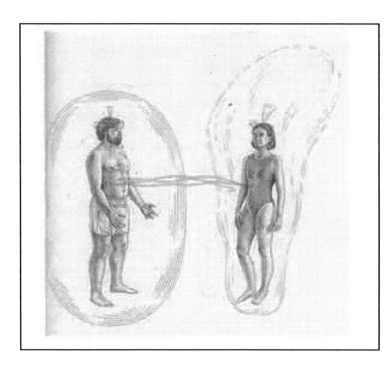

**Two people with energy cords linking their 3rd chakras.**

(credit: Bing Images)

*The cones exiting from their heads are an artistic rendition of the chakras… they look like funnels, but are spinning energy vortices. Also shown is her aura pulling away from him and it is not as well-defined as his healthy aura; she has some gaps or tears which are unhealthy.*

Medical intuitives and energy healers who see auras report that the above drawing is an accurate representation of cords and auras. It is also what **energy vampirism** looks like and a cord can be sent from the man to the woman by lusting after her. If he and she are married, it is not 'vampirism' (i.e., unwanted and unsuspected energy attachment), it is the connecting cord that souls with close 'ties' usually have. These <u>are</u> the 'ties that bind'.

It is a good idea once a month to sit quietly and become aware of how you feel… energy high or low? Sad, happy or depressed…? And then visualize **energy cords** (like tubes of light, about 1" thick) coming out of your belly area… and then visualize that you have a **big machete** and with one whack, you slice through them and **cut them between you and all those that have sent them to you**. Don't worry, the family cords are usually not cut… the Higher Self knows you need those, and even if cut [depending on your strength of visualization and will], those will be immediately restored – less the ones from others that got plugged into you.

Another way to clean the aura is by taking a **sea salt bath** (not shower) – filling the tub, dumping 1-2 boxes of sea salt into the water, swishing it around to dissolve it, and soaking in it for 10 minutes. Energy and crap that has attached itself to your aura is washed away… until you go back into that bar, hang out with the gang, get involved in road rage, visit a hospital, or play with a Quija board…. If you are sensitive to energy, and women are moreso than men, and you go into a room where there has been a shooting, a great fight, a nasty argument – the air is charged with negativity (hate, fear, depression), and walking into it, your aura will accrete some degree of the negative energy – Normally a strong, healthy aura will protect you… yet you still should do a cleansing. Either sweep it clean (you can do this yourself), or take a sea salt bath.

How do you **sweep your aura**? It is easier if someone else does it for you, if they know what they're doing. You are going to get tired of this word, but it is again a case of **visualization with intention**.

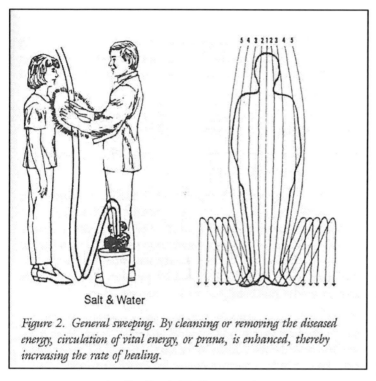

Salt & Water

*Figure 2. General sweeping. By cleansing or removing the diseased energy, circulation of vital energy, or prana, is enhanced, thereby increasing the rate of healing.*

(credit: Pranic Healing, p. 36.)

Hold your hands about 6" from your body, and with a motion starting at the head, sweep down the space in front of you to your feet – visualizing the aura cleaning and negative bits of stuff (particles, film or fog) sticking to your hands – it is all *chi* and again the *chi* follows the mind which is visualizing this procedure. You can do 80% of your body this way, but someone else will have to clean your backside.

Note that Chinese *chi* is also called Prana in India.

**Warning**: you must wash your hands or shake them <u>frequently</u> during this process because you are picking up **"diseased energy"** and it should <u>not</u> be allowed to stay on your hands – because now YOUR hands' auras now have what you were trying to remove from the other person…

> Note: I once did a sweep of a lady who did not tell me she had HIV. I will never forget the unique <u>creepy</u> feeling of her energy/aura, and it was my mentor who wanted to see if I could sense what the woman's real problem was! (She had me immediately wash my hands in the **salt water** basin that we kept in the healing ashram.)

This is real, and the same danger applies if a woman unknowingly has HIV and a man dates her and they go to bed that night – of course he will contract HIV. But did you know that his aura will also take on whatever 'smudge' or foggy energies are in her aura? This becomes even more interesting if a man unknowingly has sex with a witch... entities that serve her, now attach to him... and he must get cleansed.

Real stuff, people. Remember:

**Knowledge protects
Ignorance endangers**

On a lighter note, there is one more area of maintenance that applies here. Just because you can't see it doesn't mean it doesn't exist. Can you see viruses or radio waves?

Every now and then, it is wise to **Call One's Energy Back** from those places where it was sent. Just as others send their cords into you, you can also send energy cords to other people AND to places and past events (time is an illusion) that you either loved or hated. The strength of the emotion is what did it.

*The very wise and perceptive* **medical intuitive** *Dr. Carolyn Myss has provided the following information.*

Suppose a man visits a vacation spot, falls in love with a woman, marries her, and they return to his city to live and raise a family. The resort they went to was incredibly beautiful and they shared many great memories hiking, swimming, dancing, partying, and skydiving.... Now that they are back home, he returns to his job, and she takes up volunteer work with a local soup kitchen. They aren't married more than 4 months, and all seems so beautiful, when one of the winos pulls a knife and kills his new wife.

The man is devastated. His world has hit an abrupt brickwall, and now he has more than grief to deal with. He spends a lot of time reminiscing about their meeting, the great times they had, and the more energy he spends with nostalgic memories the less he focuses on the present world... he deeply longs to turn back the clock and return somehow to the past. His cord may still be attached to her spirit (and because it is a loving connection, it does not have to be cut).

Because visualizations (even imagination and memory) are things, there is energy involved, and he now plugs a lot of his energy into that place, time and her memory... a lot of energy. In fact, he will suffer in the present if he doesn't realize that more energy is invested in the past than in what he is now doing (and he may lose his job!). He has sent a portion of his being, his energy into that past they had together. He now does not have enough energy to run his daily life, job, and health.

He begins to suffer health-wise (shades of the movie *Somewhere in Time*, n'est-ce pas?) and he will continue to go downhill in all areas of his present life – because everyone **only has so much energy allotted per day to spend on present-day activities**. And he has plugged it into the past. In fact, he may now become an unknowing energy vampire in order to finance the energy requirements of living in the past and trying to manage the present. The other source of financing the energy drain is to take the energy from his own cell tissue and risk an illness. Neither is a good move!

To survive, he must pull out of the downward dive he is in and **call his energy back**! If he doesn't, he will crash. To do this, he must do what Dr. Myss calls **Spirit Retrieval**. [145] He must stop giving his past power by clinging to what was, or could have been. So the first step is to stop plugging into the past. The second step is to say something like the following mandate:

> I no longer send my energy into the past, or to other people and events.
> I let the past go, and I am not going in that direction any longer. In
> Jesus' name, I command my energy to return to me, cleansed and whole.

Words to that effect – words have power and when said in a forceful, determined way, even the entities in the Astral have to notice, and to keep them from blocking the return of one's energy is why **the name of Jesus** is used – not to be religious, but to show that you know His name has power (you don't have to be a Christian to use it), and you want your energy returned to you (which the Astral entities can block and may still have hold of), and it is to be cleansed of any negativity so that it comes back to you a neutral, clean energy.

This could be called 'self-deliverance' because the link to the past is broken and it no longer runs you – the past no longer oppresses you, although you can remember it, it will have lost a lot of its hold on you. And if you have to say that mandate above again, so what? Say it until the memory becomes a normally charged past event. You can also use the EFT modalities in Chapter 12 to get free.

Remember: it's your life, take your power back and mean what you say.


## IV. Developing Energy

So if we can generate, collect, use and manage energy to facilitate our spiritual Path and our conscious awakening, what's left?

At some point, **sustaining** the Transformation will be the task at hand. This can be done mostly by the practice of Meditation, QiGong, and/or Energy Cleansing.

But there has to be **an on-going infusion of new Knowledge to keep the flame alive** and move forward on the Path – or the Path becomes a circle and stagnation sets in.

Given the average amount of disinformation, deception and derailing that goes on in our everyday world, the flame of Transformation needs a consistent source of accelerant, no matter how slight. The PTB see Man as just an animal to be controlled and used as they see fit… buy this, wear that, do this, don't say that…. Religion was one of their major controls – "God forbid you think for yourself. Just believe what we tell you…."

> It was Arnold Schwarzenegger who commented back in 1990 (when he was 44 years old) that most sheeple are happy with control:
>
> "People need somebody to watch over them… **Ninety-five percent** of the people in the world need to be told what to do and how to behave." --- in interview with US News & World Report. [146]

But if you are on a spiritual Path, you think for yourself, and while you are in the great minority, there has to be another step on the Path, especially since Transformation is a **process** and it doesn't end, even with Ascension to the 5D realm. The following are suggestions to sustain the flame:

1. There are beautiful parts of **the Bible** which contain truth and wisdom: Proverbs, Ecclesiastes, The Sermon on the Mount, and the Gospel of John (more metaphysical than the other 3 gospels);

Selected authors' works that have been found to be enlightened:

2. **Oneness** by Rasha. Conveys a lot of the meaning and underpinnings of our existence. Emphasizes detachment and our multiverse aspect.

3. **Spiritual Growth** by Sanaya Roman. Similar to *Oneness*, but more of a how-to treatment of various major spiritual issues.

4. **The RA Material** by Elkins and Rueckert. Channeled info from a 6D Group entity that is consistent, accurate and useful.

5. **Keepers of the Garden**, and **Between Death & Life** by Dolores Cannon. Consistent information and enlightening. Also see her *Convoluted Universe* series.

6. **Tales from the Tao** by Solala Towler. A collection of insights and teachings from the Tao. This is a higher spiritual Walk.

7. **Virtual Earth Graduate** by TJ Hegland. Examines what Earth is, what Man is, why we're here and who is here with us, and why the Earth Graduate is so important. It also exposes the errors in Science, History and Religion to free us from false beliefs, and therefore from wrong thinking and action. (If you are confused when you cross over, you can make the wrong choice about what to do and where to go.)

When pursuing these works, many have pointers to similar books for further enlightenment, so the above 7 is not an exhaustive list.

Lastly, it is important to **fellowship** where possible with like-minded souls working their way on the Path, and to that end, several organizations may be of value: Silva Mind Control/Dynamics, and the 2 major New Thought churches: Unity Church of Christianity (Lee's Summit, MO group), and Religious Science and the works of Ernest Holmes (Los Angeles, CA-based). In its time (no longer extant) was *Est* – a Zen-like confrontational eye-opener to what Man really is (See Chapter 12).

**Suggestions in One's Walk**

The following are an abbreviated form of the suggestions in VEG, Chs 15 -16, for gaining Light and awareness, and are included here so that the key information is all in one place.

> **Avoid TV news** -- largely negative and supporting the "ain't-it-awful" way of thinking, the Media is 'spinning' their stories to mold your opinions and beliefs, so it is of low value

> **Avoid most video games** -- the stalk-it-and-kill-it videos that our kids play are entraining them into a consciousness of violence and removing the stigma against murder and dead bodies – it is conditioning them to just be OK with all the violence and killing

> **Avoid smoking, drinking, drugs** -- don't pollute the body

> **Avoid negatively charged music** – that is CW with the emphasis on losing, boozing, snoozing, cheating and crying; that also means Heavy Metal and Rap with their emphasis on violence, dirty words, and rebellion.

The public does not realize that they are being **entrained** into certain mental states by listening to some popular music... a study [147] was reported in Book 1 about CW (Country Western) music listeners – whose lives often looked just like the fractious music they were listening to! Many were divorced, drinking, losing in relationships, and they tended to see life as unfair, overly puzzling and difficult…. And yet, CW is the most fun to dance to! (Just don't listen to the words?)

They also found that RAP and Heavy Metal turned out misfits, rebels and angry people – or was it just that such music appealed to those who were already fitting that description?

> **Avoid Séances, Ouija Boards and Tarot** – these things invite participation from the Astral beings, and many of them are game-players. The Neggs will dissuade you, the 4D STS will harm you if they can.

On the other hand, a reputable counselor/teacher/therapist such as Dolores Cannon and Dr. Shakuntala Modi can be of great service in answering Life questions and removing karmic issues.

> **Avoid Arguing about Politics** – it really doesn't matter whom you vote for; whoever gets in office will have to toe the line that has been set for them, whether by their Party or by the Shadow Government.

> Note the **Shadow Government** is a very necessary entity in today's world. It ensures a stable, coherent **continuity of government** – the opposite would be to have every dumb*ss Jack and Harry get in office (especially the Federal ones) and jerk the country in a different direction every 4-6 years. The downside is that the Military Industrial Complex may bring too much power to bear on government and jerk the country the way it wants, anyway. The Anti-trust laws were set up to minimize that effect… are they still working?

## Transformation and the Church

Lastly, it might be instructive to take a look at two institutions that should be involved with moving Man into more Light, more truth, and 'saving' his soul – the churches. Specifically the Christian and New Thought churches. Are they effective?

> *This was going to be an Appendix because it was brief, but it follows logically on the heels of the above section that suggests that Seekers and those on the Path hobnob with birds of a feather…*

In point of fact, it is doubtful that either type of church is assisting Man to Transform (develop higher consciousness)…Let's see why.

**The Christian Church**

This church originated in the very parochial and traditionalist Church of Rome where control was the word of the day, not enlightenment. Then the Church's own Martin Luther nailed his objections to the Church to the door of his church and the Protestant Reformation was under way, but it didn't reform much – it just got the Church to stop the Inquisition. And the Protestants use the same Bible that was developed in AD 325 at Nicea by the Church.

Transformation means to develop Man so that he IS a new creature, the old has passed away, "…be ye transformed by the renewing of your mind…" How many Christian churches train people to renew their mind, to think logically, or to question… If you do, you may be asked to leave the church, as I was when I found **22 discrepancies** in the Bible (some are examined in VEG)… and I asked my pastor about it and he said that was why we have **Apologetics** – My problem was when I asked the forbidden question: Why do we apologize for what God himself has supposedly written?

George Carlin had an interesting slant on God:[148]

**A.** remember that this is God's world, and He is perfect and causes all things to work together for good, Everything He creates is perfect and good… and He gave us a list of 10 things to do…

And

**B.** if we don't do the things He wants, we are sent to a place of fire and heat, where we choke, scream, cry and suffer for eternity….

Why?

**C.** because God loves us.

More on George in Appendix B.

The Pentecostal church argues that people can receive the **Baptism of the Holy Spirit** which changes people and the alleged proof is speaking in tongues… where "zip..zip..zip…goo…goo…goo…" or howling like a dog (I knew a gal who did that!) – any noise they make is considered to be 'tongues.' Some of these church pastors while sermonizing just all of a sudden drop into 'tongues' and no one translates – How does that edify the congregation? – who also don't know that the real gift was given the disciples so they could go to Greece, for example, where they don't know the language but can speak Greek to witness to the people in Greece. That was what it was all about, and many Pentecostal churches have warped that. That does not serve enlightenment and is not in itself Transformation.

Some churches teach the **great cop out**: if a Christian prays for something and it doesn't happen, "Well, it's God's will…" Bullfeathers. It didn't happen because

(1) it isn't in His Greater Script or yours, **or** (2) you asked for something inappropriate ("amiss" as the Book of James says) … so why not skip the prayer and go straight to His Will…? Merge with it! **Go with the Flow**. As you get higher in the Walk and more transformed to His likeness (more like your Higher Self), carrying more Light, you will have less of 'you' and more of 'Him' (more Light and Love) and except for your lessons, you will be automatically blessed.

So in short, the Christian church is not transforming people, nor is teaching the same limited preaching every Sunday for 30 years benefitting people. How many ways can you slice, dice and chop the finite information in the Bible? At some point you start to repeat – and that is when the pastor picks up his basic 114 lessons, or invents new ones that he hopes are true, and moves to another church… and the next guy comes along with his 114 sermons. The same same-old same-old re-arranged.

It is treated as gibble because it is a **limited aspect** of the Truth, repeated so many times that people tune it out, and then drop out of church. While many parts of the Bible are true and beautiful, there are books that should be there from the **Apocrypha** and **Dead Sea Scrolls** that were not included and thus the Bible gives us a short, 'controlled' view of Man, God, and our history. This was to ostensibly protect us from error and writings of dubious value. What it really was concerned the Church's attempt to keep Man ignorant of his true origins (see the Book of Enoch, e.g., or the Book of Jasher…)

> *Having said that, beware of those writings that claim Jesus was married. He wasn't. And in addition, in the Church's defense, it might have been recognized that Man 1500 years ago was pathetically ignorant and crude to the point where putting more enlightened tracts in the Bible back then would have been "throwing pearls to swine." Is now the time?*

Transformation, on the other hand, is becoming a renewed, enlightened person (soul) with each month and year that <u>progresses</u> due to new revelations, new insights, more advanced experiences… and that is the key word. **Progress**. That lack of same is why Bishop John Shelby Spong argued for a change to a more dynamic form of Christianity in his book, *Why Christianity Must Change or Die* – and that argument is examined in VEG (Chapter 11). Both the Catholic and Protestant churches offer little to move Man into enlightenment or absorb the Light … because that was never the goal. Is it time to change?

### Rewind: The Real Deal

The Bible says we are supposed to be "transformed by the renewing of your mind…" (Rom. 12:2) – Transformed! Higher consciousness… more Light, enlightenment. Is that happening in today's Christian church? When I asked for clarification on 22 items (above) that I had wondered about, I was asked to leave the church. I suggest that the biblical injunction is not being done because the pastors are not capable of it. So, the Christian church does not give the sheep anything substantial (i.e., metaphysics, quantum physics discoveries about Man and his World) to think about… how is that fulfilling their 'calling' to lead the flock? And this is an important issue, because (as said in Chapter 2, p 65):

> **Rewind:** when you die, your mindset governs where you can go.

What do you suppose the Christian soul's reaction is when they die and cross over and find the church has misled them…or failed to educate them? There is no Biblical Heaven, no Hell, no Satan… and they are responsible for their own mistakes and growth …. Karma is the exacting Law that serves as a catalyst to grow souls. But they weren't told that… Many will have to come back (reincarnation) and again try to learn the truth so that they are of use in the Father's Kingdom. And there are those who want the sheep to fail (as was also said in Chapter 2, p 64):

---

**It is now self-evident why entities <u>without</u> souls would seek to keep ensouled Man from becoming all that he can be – including suppressing the truth about Man and his World. That is what it has always been about, for centuries, and why the 4D STS and PTB persist in their STS agenda to contain/control Man.**

---

## New Thought Churches

So let's look at the other supposed answer – Christians who begin to wake up are moving to the New Thought churches (see Glossary). Supposedly, these churches (or Spiritual Centers) promote the truth, the Light, waking people up to what they really are and how it all works… leading them to supposedly be more loving, patient, humble, and respect all lifeforms…

Most of the New Thought churches started out with the Noble Goal of Light and Love, and when these ministers suffered the same problem as the Christian church pastors (running out of new things to teach), they immediately turned to the latest books by New Age authors who would **tickle peoples' ears**… some of it was true and some wasn't … as examined below:

> **You Can Create Your Day** – if you are driving down the street and you don't like the red light, you can will it to change to green. It doesn't matter that you have just violated the freewill of the other drivers just to selfishly satisfy what you want…

...but that is because...

**You Are Here To Develop Your Godhood** – your thoughts are all-powerful and what you think you can create... never mind that you came here with a Script that controls what you can and can't do...you have freewill and can do whatever you want...

... so as a result you tell yourself that...

**You Can Name It & Claim It** -- because God is just a vending machine. In fact, you don't pray, you make affirmations and spend a lot of energy trying to manifest what you want. You are mastering the all-important ability to manifest the parking space just where and when you want it...

...because you realize that God wants you to have everything you want, you have no Karma, and Divine health and Order are at work in your life... because...

**You Are God** -- that is the supreme teaching – One that **the New Age got right** by the way, but you are not turned loose in the Earth School to activate your godhood. And you are only **a spark** of the Godhead, anyway, learning to use the Father's power and wisdom in a proactive way. Hence the Script.

So in short, the New Thought churches became New Age churches (viz., NTA). And these churches are also not assisting Man to transform within the limits of his Script – because they do not recognize that Man is subject to a Script. NTA churches teach that we are all free to do whatever occurs to us... and tells people that they can have it all NOW. Just be happy. Occasionally the NTA church does find a book or teaching that inspires and supports the real Path of enlightenment, but far too many of the NTA churches are what was earlier called the

### Jumping Freddy Feelgood Church

...wherein you don't do much learning (because the spiritual leader isn't much further advanced than the pastor of a Christian church), and the Sunday attendees are literally holding hands and doing a conga to celebrate Life and Love. Not bad once in a while, but it isn't Transformation. It isn't learning. **Conga lines do not generate Earth Graduates**. If the NTA spiritual leader isn't enlightened and at least 2 steps ahead of the congregation, all they can do is jump, shout and sing. Even the Pentecostal churches do that...

**Humans are easy to deceive** – "baffle 'em with BS" …all you have to do is say you have a gift or the Advanced Truth (Light) and get others to agree, then exhort people to follow you to … whatever the goal is…and it usually involves monitored (and audited) tithing to make the church building fund a reality. If you don't tithe *as prescribed,* some may ask you to compensate or leave the church.

So what is the answer? How does one find enlightened birds of a feather so that they can Flow together? Many times it is a lot of investigating/visiting other churches one at a time, or asking those who appear to "have it together" where they attend… yet what <u>always</u> works is the tried and true method of **going within**, contemplating what has been <u>read</u> in the spiritual literature, what you <u>know to be true</u> (and seeing if you can connect a few dots among the things you <u>do</u> know and what you have read/heard)…and **asking** your Higher Self to guide you…. Ask and ye shall receive!

## Avoid Being Derailed

Beware of the exotic and old religions … the **Catholics** claim to be 2000 + years old (but Book 1 showed them to be just over 1200 years old), and many faithful parishioners still pray to statues – in defiance of the Biblical command "Thou shalt not worship idols" – especially in the less developed countries where Catholicism merged with or absorbed the local pagan religion…

And then there is the **Hindu** religion which believes that if you are bad in this lifetime, Karma can bring you back as a cow ("Oh, that's my grandfather who just died, so we let him roam the house…") or maybe a snail, or fly…. Reincarnation **is** real, but that isn't how it works. Humans don't regress.

Or the **Islamic** religion which teaches that if a man does all the good things a good Muslim does, he will go to Heaven where 21 virgins await him … (I never heard what the Muslim <u>women</u> get if they behave… a dance with Mohammed?) Islam stresses discipline and that is good for a lot of humans.

Wouldn't it be interesting if the same Angel who visited Mohammed and gave him the precepts of **Islam**, was the same one who visited Joseph Smith and started **Mormonism**? Was the Angel an ET, as some say?

*The point is that these above-named religions are beautiful in themselves, have millions of adherents, and they also DO teach much truth… but like anything that humans teach for centuries, it becomes slightly distorted with time and the original teaching is lost – often in a new version or group that splits off from the original teaching. (The one exception seems to be Judaism.)*

PT Barnum knew that some people will believe anything and he capitalized on it. And that is especially true if a child is raised in any religious cult, i.e., a small, esoteric group, knowing nothing else most of their early life – they will doggedly defend what their elders and 'experts' programmed them to believe. (Kool Aid ® in Jonestown, anyone?) If you discuss the Bible or religious points with these people …and even if you can prove them wrong … they ignore it. Humans desperately seek to be right, define their theology and put hair spray on it so it won't move… That quirk is one reason we make so little progress on Earth. New information is often ignored.

> If it doesn't fit what we think we already know, we say it is wrong.
> That is classic **cognitive dissonance**.

That is why true Knowledge is so precious and will protect and set you free from the karmic wheel of rebirth, and with 51% Light you can graduate from Earth, or make the Ascension to Timeline 2.

In short, **energy management** is important, but before you can manage it, you must have some, and understand its uses and the different forms it can take. And to that end this chapter spent some time with its Ins and Outs.  Further energy information and management is available in the next chapter.

**Disclaimer**
It was not the purpose to insult or mock any religion – all are part of the catalyst allowed to be here in the Earth Drama – **none of them has the whole truth either** – yet we are to respect each other anyway. Man walks in darkness on this planet… although not for long, and that is why this book has been pushed into print… to hopefully increase the number of souls who can read and profit from it… and learn to **respectfully question and think**… thus ascending to a better Timeline, on a more enlightened Earth.

## Something to Think About

**Question 1:**  if no religion on Earth has it all correct, and that is true, is there a penalty for belonging to the 'wrong' religion?

**Answer**: each person will be evaluated in the InterLife with what s/he did with what s/he believed to be the truth. Transformed or not, did they live their beliefs to the best of their ability, or were they a hypocrite?  And if they called themselves spiritual leaders, setting themselves up to be believed by the flock, there is **a minor penalty for leading people astray if what is taught is false doctrine**… and it is corrected by the Law of Karma (it will be done unto you as you did it to others).

*I was very aware of this in writing the 2 books.*

**Question 2**: if Christianity and the New Age churches do not have all the answers, and sometimes have backward concepts, then where are we to go to learn the truth about ourselves and the world?

**Answer:** remember that a soul is ultimately evaluated on what it knew to do and then did or did not do. In short, what you say you believe should be reflected in your actions, Christian, Buddhist, Muslim, Jew or Catholic… You are not evaluated on whether you learned Quantum Physics or memorized the Bible. That is the first aspect of the answer.

The second aspect is that Man is a social creature and learns much in **interaction with like-minded others** – which is where home study groups and classes come in. So attending a church most like what you **feel led to** is important… and giving them the space to be imperfect (as long as you derive some value) if they are generally inspiring is worthwhile.

The third aspect of the answer is that you are free to **meditate** (or contemplate) on what you already know, things you are reading on your own, and…

The fourth aspect is that **you are never alone** – the Beings of Light see and know what you're doing and they know what your questions are (because they also know what your Script says!) … **ASK** and they have permission to lead you to what you seek, or synchronistically bring it to you… sometimes they will give you an insight or hunch if you are open to it…

They know there is no one perfect church, although some are more appropriate for you than others; if you are not being 'fed' where you are, there is no wrong choice but only a resistance to keep moving until you find your new 'home.' Look and **choose with the heart**.

Thus, there is no such thing as a wrong religion, or a wrong Path to enlightenment. Some paths are more appropriate than others, some are slower than others, and some are a waste of time, but the soul must **choose** and that is all part of the Drama (awakening) for each soul.  More advanced souls choose better than Baby souls. Transformation can be easy if the soul is open and discerning; if the mind is closed, s/he has just signed on for the lesson. Thus your Path is what you make it, just as your world generally reflects what you put into it.

# Chapter 12:  The Matrix, Energy & Transformation

---

This is the chapter for those who want to know and do more, understand and follow a system of energetics to heal or to enhance their mental abilities. None of the following modalities will enable you to "create your day" (i.e., manipulate your reality) as that is not part of the 3D School Curriculum… despite it sounding great by those who hawk the New Age promises. And the reason why will be expanded on for the last time in a later section called 'Caveat #1: Manipulating Reality.'

If the last chapter intrigued you, this chapter will show you how the different aspects come together to serve those who work with it,  and you can choose one of the current modalities out there to heal yourself, heal others, or begin to develop your latent psychic abilities.  There is power in these systems, just be advised that it still takes discipline, persistence, and faith… and one must **respect** self and the energetics world.

Aspects to be covered in this chapter include:  the **Matrix** in which we all live, move and have our being, sometimes called the Æther, Dark Energy, Dark Matter, the Field, and the Zero Point Field. Concurrent with that, we'll examine ZPE (Zero Point Energy), torsion physics, spin, non-locality/entanglement, Morphogenetics, consciousness, the heart torus, and the DNA spiral.  The major modalities examined are:  Matrix Energetics®, Matrix Reimprinting®, PsychoEnergetics®, Reconnective Healing®, aspects of Quantum Healing®, Psych-K® and briefly, QiGong Healing as related to TCM (Traditional Chinese Medicine), NLP, Silva, Est, and Reflexology. To do any more than that would require a separate book.

When you finish this chapter, you should be able to wisely choose the energy modality that best suits your purpose. Keep in mind that there are numerous systems out there and the ones examined herein appear to be the ones most often encountered by seekers. This chapter will clarify the principles and nature of energetics which apply to most of the healing energy systems. The systems covered herein are not better than those not examined, they are just the ones that the author encountered after personal experience with **QiGong** and **Pranic Healing** (see Chapter 11).  Many systems not examined may also work well. The point herein is to examine several similar energetic systems and reveal principles and practices so that the reader can apply the knowledge gained in a wiser selection of the system that would best serve his or her needs.

First, let's see where all this came from as the foundation of energetics has its roots in some fascinating discoveries which preceded Quantum Physics. From there, a brief survey of ancillary modalities (section called 'Ancillary Support Systems') contain key concepts that you will see integrated, yea, verily synthesized!, into the energetic systems examined below. This is a field whose roots are many and varied, and have all added to the current (not final!) product whose gestalt delivers more than the sum of its components. **Synergetic** is the keyword.

*Unfamiliar terms, if not defined within the text, can be found in the Encyclo-Glossary.*

## Ancient History of Energetics

As was examined frequently in VEG, the result of the **Anunnaki** seeking to grow Man and shepherd him into a more aware and capable individual, resulted in Enki, the Science Officer and genetic creator of some humans, and his staff promoting something that came to be called **Serpent Wisdom**. This was actually an esoteric training for those humans who had the genetic potential and the desire to be more than a tree climber or ditch digger.

Serpent Wisdom groups sprang up all over the civilized world until Enlil, Lord of the Earth Command, denounced Enki, branded him a 'Satan' before mankind, and indirectly sent the teachings underground where they still are to this day. Such training involved advanced teaching about Man's real nature, healing, and the cultivation and manipulation of the *kundalini* force.

And yet vestiges of the veneration of the serpent as a symbol of wisdom persisted in many ways:

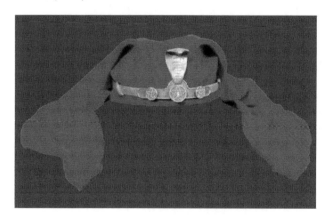

**Uraeus Headband Worn by Pharoahs**
www.prisiadieco.com/images/Prisiadieco/Uraeus.)

**The Caduceus (medical symbol)**
(source: Wikipedia)

These represent pharaonic and medical wisdom. The pharaoh wore the headband across his forehead, symbolizing that his 6th chakra wisdom (supported by a link with the pineal gland), was active. Again, serpent wisdom… activated by the *kundalini.*

…and last but not least:

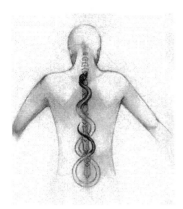

**Serpent Kundalini**

(www.davidicke.com/oi/extras/08/April/9.jpg)

Note that the serpent symbolizes DNA and the egg is birth.

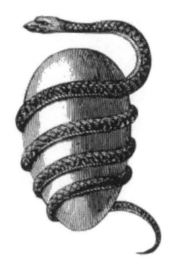

**The Cosmogenic Egg**
(en.wikipedia.org/wiki/File:Orphic-egg.png)

And there's also one from the Bible: Moses fashioned a metal serpent on a pole, called the Brazen Serpent, in the wilderness to get his people healed. (Num. 21:9) So serpents are associated with healing, wisdom, and birth. For the purposes of this chapter, it is the healing aspect of *kundalini* that is of interest.

***Kundalini*** is said to be an energy stored at the base of the spine, but the Oriental masters would tell us that its source is the Dan Tien located somewhere in the lower abdomen. Martial Arts practitioners seek to develop and conserve this energy to deliver outstanding strength in combat. Hindu gurus seek to develop the energy to become adept at clairvoyance, levitation and other psychic feats… reportedly **Sai Baba** who was a holy man in India (until recently passing away) who could manifest jewels, money, healing and *vibuti* (holy ash for healing), among other things, for his visitors.

## Pandit Gopi Krishna

Having mentioned *kundalini* and its potential dangers, the following is a very interesting account of one Hindu man whose meditation practice was rudely interrupted by the spontaneous and unexpected surge of the energy up his spine – but it hit a blockage. He described his experience in a book wherein he describes

> ... his awakening as "a roar like that of a waterfall, I felt a stream of liquid light entering my brain through the spinal cord"... [and afterward] he felt only depression and anxiety. And it was the beginning of a 25 year struggle to regain his mental, physical and psychic abilities. [149]

The danger of what had happened to him became apparent a few days after the 'awakening.' He felt sick, very tired, and just awful and about **two months later**, still not having resolved the issue, he was sure he was about to die. In all that time, he had barely eaten and now felt agonizing pain. Being a practitioner of yoga and meditation and being aware of the same chakral and Bionet charts shown in this book, his salvation was that he understood the physiology of *kundalini*:

> ...perhaps kundalini had risen up the pingala [meridian or nadi] instead of the Central nadi sushumna. Focusing all his attention, [back in meditation] he forced kundalini through the sushumna, saving his life. Krishna felt the burning pain cease, and burning flame in his skull was replaced by blissful radiance. [150]

Fortunately, he was able to be his own "master" and unstick himself. Others have died from the stuck and overpowering energy. Days later, he found he had awakened his connection with his Superconscious (Higher Self) and found his psychic abilities enhanced. His body continued to go through positive changes in diet and health, and he lost his interest in the supernatural, became repulsed by meditation and greatly attracted to altruism (STO -- serving others). [151]

What remains to be seen is that the *kundalini* has a source <u>outside the body</u> and is inducted into the body via the Root chakra (#1) for survival. And the more *kundalini* one can gather and command, under control, the more one can do miracles because it is actually <u>the</u> universal life force, or *energy* of the Matrix. Our body also accesses it through the heart torus and the layers of the aura, as will be explained.

**Kundalini is a concentrated form of *chi*** that the body stores in the Dan Tien (lower abdomen) and releases piecemeal as needed via the Bionet to the organs. And we live, move and have our being in this 'sea' of living energy.

**Kundalini is not just *chi*** and can be a frightening energy if awakened too soon or without someone who can manipulate the energy for you (i.e., a Master). Later, in this chapter, energy healing modalities are examined that can "unstick" energy and remove blockages, safely by yourself.

As an example, consider the Pranic healing energy from the last chapter:

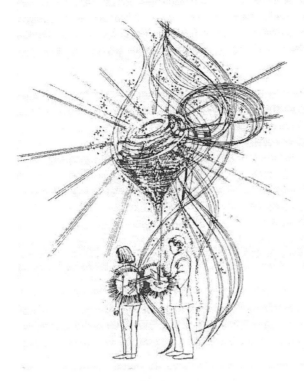

**Universal Life Force (chi) in Healing**
(Pranic Healing, p. 155.)

Note that there are no entities or angels involved in this diagram, and that is because Man already possesses a connection with the **universal life force** which is found throughout the universe. It was one of the teachings of the Serpent Wisdom groups to instruct Man in how to invoke and manipulate this energy, and this is the energy which is the focus of this chapter.

## 19th Century History of Energetics

While the Chinese and Hindus had centuries ago developed teachings about energy, mapping the **Bionet** which is today used for Acupuncture, it is interesting to note that Western science has lagged behind, even doubting that the Asian/Oriental cultures know anything about energetics… although adepts have proven that it works … modern science takes the (unfortunate) stand that if it can't be 'scientifically proven,' (i.e., measured) it doesn't exist.

> Unfortunately, **subtle energy** is hard to quantitatively measure and thus traditional science rejects the concept and along with it, the soul. Their tools are not discerning enough to detect the subtle energy –

unless they realize that it is associated with Dark Energy/Matter (i.e., the Æther... which they have also rejected).

## Enter the Germans

So one of the interesting developments in the research of subtle energy, i.e., *chi* was undertaken by the West in Germany. Anton Franz **Mesmer** was among the first to notice that there seemed to be an energy field associated with humans, and his research centered around using **magnets** to push/pull the energy where he thought it would do the most good. He is also known for his experiments in hypnotism, called *mesmerism* at that time, where he believed that it was a subtle magnetic force that he could invoke in people.

The second man to examine the energetics of living things was Hans **Driesch**, who developed a theory of *entelechy*, wherein he believed there was a mind-like life force in living things. He influenced Mesmer and Roux.

Wilhelm **Roux** was another player in the field who proposed his "Mosaic" theory of *epigenesis*: after a few cell divisions an embryo would be like a mosaic, each cell playing its own unique part in the entire design, as if pre-programmed to perform its function by some unseen energy field.

## Current Day History of Energetics

> Physicist Dr. Nikola Tesla said that *"If you want to find the secrets of the universe, think in terms of energy, frequency and vibration."* [152]

Tesla was on the right path... Who knows what else he was aware of...? Too bad Thomas Edison and JP Morgan shut him down.

Rudolf **Steiner** was a famous metaphysician and philosopher, again in Germany. Steiner attempted to find **a synthesis between science and spirituality** and he sought to apply the clarity of thinking characteristic of Western philosophy to spiritual questions. He developed *Anthrosophy* which dealt with the esoteric aspects of Man... including a something that unified the physical and spiritual worlds... but he stopped short of developing any idea of an Æther or subtle energy.

More to the point was Rupert **Sheldrake's** *Morphogenesis* which posits that there is a 'design' or **morphology** (science of shape) that controls what shape plants and people take as they are being created/birthed, as well as all things in the universe. It is a Pattern resident in the unseen world around us, reminiscent of Carl Jung's Archtypes... no doubt it is sustained by a subtle energy residing in some unseen Grid in the universe...

So has anybody looked to see if there is an Æther?

## Enter Michelson and Morley

Two scientists in 1887 first performed an experiment to see if Æther existed . The point was actually proven by sending two beams of light through the suspected Æther : one at right angles to the other such that if there were an Æther, the two beams of light should register different transit times… and that is what happened but the difference was so small (within the margin of error projected) that they could not use it to prove the existence of a "luminous ether." So this was called the most **'Famous Failed Experiment'** because it did work, but the scientists distrusted the outcome and considered the nano-results to be conflicting and inconclusive.

Other experiments were run in 1903 and 1904, with negative results which led **Einstein** to diss the Æther in 1905 and produce his Theory of Special Relativity (TSR) and firmly denounce the Æther's existence… TSR and Æther are mutually exclusive. [153] (But Einstein was wrong and set Physics back about 50 years… see following section, 'Sagnac and Ives'.)

What was the point?  According to one source: [154]

> Just as surface water waves must have a supporting substance, *i.e.* a "medium", to move across (in this case water), and audible sound requires a medium to transmit its wave motions (such as air or water), so light must also require a medium, the "luminiferous aether", to transmit its wave motions. **Because light can travel through a vacuum, it was assumed that even a vacuum must be filled with aether.** Since the speed of light is so great, and as material bodies pass through the aether without obvious friction or drag, the aether was assumed to have a highly unusual combination of properties.

> Earth orbits the Sun a speed of around 19 miles/second (or over 67,500 mi/hr). Since the Earth is in motion, two main possibilities were considered: (1) The aether is stationary and only partially dragged by Earth, or (2) the aether is completely dragged by Earth and thus shares its motion at Earth's surface.

> According to this latter hypothesis, Earth and the aether are in relative motion, implying that a so-called **"aether wind"** should exist. Although it would be possible, in theory, for the Earth's motion to match that of the aether at one moment in time, it was not possible for the Earth to remain at rest with respect to the aether at all times, because of the variation in both the direction and the speed of the motion.

**By analyzing the return speed of light in different directions at various different times, it was thought to be possible to measure the motion of the Earth relative to the aether**. [That was what Michelson-Morley were trying to do.] The expected relative difference in the measured speed of light was quite small, given that the velocity of the Earth in its orbit around the Sun was about **one hundredth of one percent of the speed of light.** [emphasis added]

Existing equipment was not capable of measuring that fine a difference. Or was it?

## Enter Sagnac and Ives

Relativity encountered a serious challenge when Georges Sagnac in 1913 conducted an experiment wherein he split a light beam on a revolving turntable, causing light beams to move in opposite directions and bettered the results of Michelson-Morley. The counter-clockwise traveling light beam completed its journey in less time than the clockwise traveling beam! Sagnac considered this proof that light travels in an **aether.** [155] This threw relativity into a state of turmoil and the physicists tried to explain away what Sagnac had done.

Fortunately, another scientist, Herbert Ives, picked up the issue and proved the nay-saying Einsteinian physicists wrong, and justified Sagnac. Sagnac's interpretation proved valid and relativity stood disproven, at least for the time being. The aether notion was not abandoned … it just went out of style, and the **vacuum** assumed all-importance.

Then, in 1951, Ives exposed a crucial flaw in Einstein's theory. He demonstrated that the one-way direction of light, as proposed by Einstein, is not equal to a constant, $c$, as relativity requires. Ives published a series of papers showing "…that the electromagnetic ether theory accounted for the results of all experiments normally cited in support of special relativity." [156] Einsteinian physicists were not swayed from their point of view.

Lastly, in 1987, 100 years after Michelson-Morley, **Ernest Silvertooth** showed that the wavelength of light varies with the direction in which it is propagated – i.e., the **anisotrophy** spoken of in VEG, Chapter 8, 'Speed of Light' section. He found that **the one-way velocity of light varied with direction** – proving Michelson-Morley correct. [157] Only an aether could have had that effect.

So what is the significance of all that?

> With the undermining of special relativity, however, general relativity is rendered invalid as well, and with it goes the expanding universe theory. [158] [Based on redshift being due to "tired photons" and not due to receding galaxies – also covered in VEG, Ch 9.]

That also means that a form of **aether** does exist, but we cannot return to a mechanical aether. A complete conceptual model does exist and is called **Subquantum Kinetics, Model G** which explains the **aether** in terms of **etherons**, a more dynamic and simple, comprehensive model that really holds water — and is not as complicated as Quantum Physics. (See VEG Ch 9.)

The image below is another idea of what the special elements of the **aether** might look like, that happen to be similar to the energy vortex nature of the **etheron** as proposed by Dr. LaViolette.

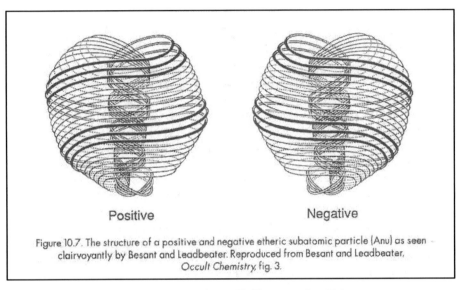

Positive               Negative

Figure 10.7. The structure of a positive and negative etheric subatomic particle (Anu) as seen clairvoyantly by Besant and Leadbeater. Reproduced from Besant and Leadbeater, *Occult Chemistry*, fig. 3.

**Conceptual Elements of the 4D Transmuting Ether**
(credit: *Genesis of the Cosmos*, p. 237.)

Why is this important? Because there really is an energetic medium in which we humans live, move and have our being, as well as the Earth and the solar system, and the galaxies… The fact that we can't measure it means it is beyond the equipment capabilities or the techniques of measurement — or both. It doesn't mean the Æther doesn't exist, and today's scientists are coming around to that conclusion, despite the opinion of Einstein — space is filled with something they now call **Dark Matter**, and empowered by **Dark Energy**.

It has also been called **The Field** which contains **Zero Point Energy** (ZPE). Alternately, it has been called a **Matrix**.
Has anybody investigated this aspect of things?

**Enter the Russians**

**Dr. Nikolai Kozyrev** believed that an intelligent energy had to exist and in the process became one of the most controversial figures in the Russian scientific community. Even reluctant Western scientists have had to acknowledge that there must be an unseen energy medium in the universe, and as long as you don't use the word "Æther" you can publish your findings on a "quantum medium" without much hassle.

Kozyrev suspected that all life forms might be drawing off an unseen **spiraling energy** through eating, breathing, and chakra-absorption. In fact he suspected it was feeding the body via the Bionet and the DNA was absorbing *chi* and emitting photons... something that two other Russian researchers, **Drs. Peter Garaiev and Vladimir Poponin**, discovered in their work with DNA and morphic fields.

What Kozyrev discovered still has scientists talking:

> In the laboratory, he took a sealed glass container, removed all the air, making it a complete vacuum. He then cooled this vacuum space to -273° C, where all matter should stop vibrating and produce no heat. Instead of an absence of energy in a vacuum, there is a tremendous amount of it, and since the temperature was absolute zero – it was called **Zero Point Energy.**[159]

What is so amazing about the ZPE and its natural matrix is that it is a boundless source of energy – a 3" cubic space of it contains more than enough energy to bring all the world's oceans to the boiling point. [160]

Kozyrev's big discovery was that **the energy was spiraling, twisting** such that he called it Torsion Physics. He made the connection with Rupert Sheldrake's *Morphogenetics* and suggested that DNA was a spiral because it is sustained by the torsion aspects of the ZPE Field. He made a corollary discovery: [161]

> ...Kozyrev showed that by **shaking, spinning**, heating, cooling, vibrating or breaking physical objects their weight can be increased or decreased by subtle but definite amounts.[162]

They do not gain mass, they gain energy. Energy from the ZPE Field. Is this what the Sufi Whirling Dervishes and Shakers were doing to enhance their religious experience? Significantly, Sufis balanced on their left foot, spinning **counter-clockwise**... which is the direction of the toroidal energy... and the direction of the Earth's spin on its axis. How did they know?

**Sufi Whirling Dhikr**
(Source: Wikipedia: Whirling_Dervish)

In a related experiment by Dr. Frank Brown, it was found that the biofield that Sheldrake referred to (morphogenetics) is sensitive to **rotation** (as Kozyrev discovered above): [163]

> That the biofield is involved [in living things] is supported by Brown's observation of a connection between rotation and bean seed interaction. He found that the beans interacted more strongly when they were rotated **counter-clockwise** than when they were rotated clockwise.

This would lend support to the Sufis twirling in a counter-clockwise direction to empower their (ecstatic?) devotional dance, the Dhikr.

> *FYI: It has been discovered that if a human spins/twirls **clockwise** (in the northern hemisphere) it can make him sick.*

The second major Russian scientist (examined in VEG, Ch 9) was **Peter Garaiev** who found DNA coding could be transmitted through the space between two testtubes, where the 1st testtube contained DNA and the 2nd contained pure water. Upon inspection, after using coherent light shined through testtube #1 into the 2nd testtube, to impart coding, the 2nd testtube contained an imprint of the DNA from the 1st testtube. The point here is that the **transmission medium** had to be the ZPE Field, or what is sometimes called the Energy Matrix.

Yes, unbelievable.

Kozyrev showed that **torsion fields are created from spinning sources** and the Earth spinning on its axis and revolving about the Sun produces a **dynamic torsion**. This permits torsion waves to propagate throughout space (via the ZPE Field, or Dark Matter, or the Matrix) such that torsion fields like gravity or electromagnetism can move from one place to another in the universe. [164]

Furthermore, Kozyrev proved that these torsion fields travel at **super-luminal speeds** – faster than the speed of light – and that explains the related phenomena of Nonlocality and Entanglement. Note that Korzyrev's experiments have been successfully replicated by others since the 1970s. Western science is still hesitant to accept Russian findings...

**Dean Radin** at the Institute of Noetic Sciences found that a change in the mass consciousness of humanity can and does affect the behavior of electromagnetic energy in computer circuits around the world, and the focused intent of a group of people in a laboratory setting has successfully changed the pH of liquid solutions, and has affected (in a minor but statistically significant way) the operation of random-number generators. Kozyrev would say that "... **torsion waves and consciousness** are essentially identical manifestations of intelligent energy." [165]

Thus, it was found that **the mind's thoughts are torsion waves**.

He further said that one mind can barely influence objects, plants and other people and yet it must be using the Matrix that surrounds and enfolds us all. Group mind is much stronger. And yet, **we can defeat the assimilation of the ZPE energy** by our bodies and minds if we do one of **two things which block** the Field's torsion waves:

1. **wear polyester clothing** -- cotton and wool are the best to wear to keep your body/mind healthy in the Flow;

and/or:

2. **live in an aluminum trailer** – aluminum is a great shield from the ambient torsion waves which healthily support all life (Scientists use aluminum, or a Faraday Cage when they want to avoid having torsion waves affect their experiments).

Torsion waves also explain the operation of a **pyramid** on its contents... it harnesses and focuses the torsion fields spiraling out of the Earth. Thus whether one is sitting in a pyramid to meditate, or sharpening razor blades,[166] the pyramid shape appears to rejuvenate and enhance whatever is within it (by **restoring the molecular morphogenic design**). In a related way, this brings to mind the old school remedy for a slow, dull learner in the classroom:

**The Duncecap**
(courtesy: Bing Images.com)

Lastly, according to Russian physicist, G.I. Shipov, torsion fields transmit information without transmitting EM energy, and colleague A. Akimov, said that "torsion fields coupled with the standard electric, magnetic and gravity fields should offer a **unified field theory**… and include the effects of consciousness." [167] Thus this one discovery of the ZPE Field which contains torsion fields, coupled with the human mind which acts as "a non-magnetic spin torsion system" which transmits and receives torsion field information, promises to revolutionize our understanding of the human experience. **Thoughts are torsion waves**.

## American Scientists

Not all American scientists live in a closed box wherein they try to prove the last 100 years' theories to the exclusion of new developments from other countries.

American scientist **Lt. Col. Tom Bearden** discovered that the "mind does not have its origin in the material world, but in the nonlocal 'implicate' realm or torsion/scalar field… [and] the torsion field operates holographically, without regard to time and distance. So too then does consciousness." [168]

And if **torsion waves are a carrier for consciousness**, we will have to rewrite the science books. The human mind is enmeshed with the reality in which we live…and at some level, it also implies that "what you put out is what you get back." Sounds like the Law of Attraction uses the Matrix.

*Anyone who read Virtual Earth Graduate (Chs 8-9) will recognize that it is all coming together in this chapter. Holograms, simulation, interconnectedness, consciousness, spiritual energy….*

305

**Dr. William Tiller** is a physicist at the forefront of the healing energetics movement, along with many others. He is involved with research into consciousness and Man's transformation via **subtle energies**. The same energies that Kozyrev defined. Dr. Tiller called his model of energetics and consciousness "Psychoenergetic Science" and wrote a complicated white paper called "Some Initial Comparisons Between the Russian Research on 'The Nature of Torsion' and the Tiller Model of 'Psychoenergetic Science' : Part I." Dr. Tiller takes Dr. Kozyrev seriously and even designed a model showing the implicate and physical worlds' interrelationships:

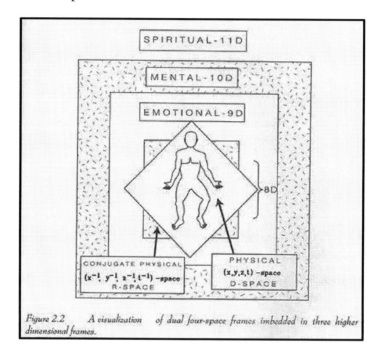

Figure 2.2   A visualization   of dual four-space frames imbedded in three higher dimensional frames.

**Dr. Tiller's  Psychoenergetic Model**

R-space (lower left box) is the reciprocal unseen world around us. D-space is the direct physical reality, and there are 11D or eleven dimensions postulated. The Spiritual encompasses the Mental which influences the Emotional which has a bearing on the Physical (in the diamond). The 'conjugate' R-space is the physical but unseen Matrix in which we have our being and the D-space is the out-picturing of the **morphogenetic R-space**. Dr. Tiller involves Sheldrake and Kozyrev in his model. He does define and explain more, but most of it is couched in physics concepts and heavy mathematics.

It is thought by quantum physicists that there is an interplay of subatomic particles that flip back and forth in a kind of dance between what Dr. Tiller has called the D-space and the R-space, similar to **virtual particles**, and these are related to the ZPE, or Dark Energy.

The Dark Matter 'dance' of the R-space (virtual) particles could be pictured this way:

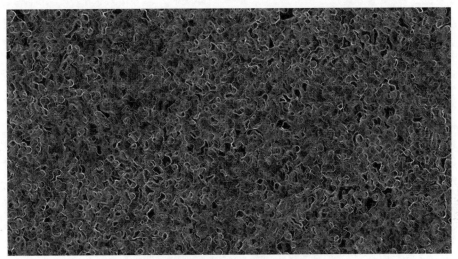

**Dark Matter/Energy of the ZPE Field**
(source: Bing Images.com)

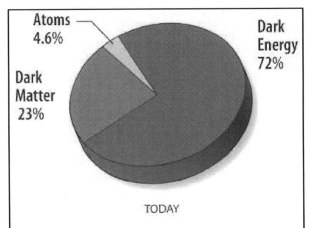

**Dark Matter/Energy Proportion (est.)**

Scientists are saying that they know something is out there filling space and consists of the following breakdown:

72% of space (universe) is composed of Dark Energy. Atoms at 4.6% is the physical world that we see and touch!

Physicists reason that the Dark Matter must exist as something seems to be causing the galaxies to spread out and at the same time, something is preventing them from centrifugally flying apart. They theorize that the **Energy** is causing the expansion of galaxies across the Universe, and **Matter** is inhibiting the galaxy from unwinding. (Not everyone agrees the universe is expanding.[169] )

And they also think the Earth 'floats' in a **Field of Dark Matter/Energy**:

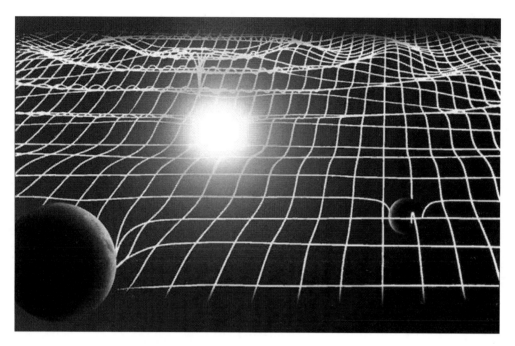

**The Sun, Earth and Moon in the Field**
(image credit: Bing.images.com)

The above satisfies the 'warping of space' according to Einsteinian physics and the bending grid (above) suggests the toroidal fields around objects in space. Space is not empty but the old concept of Æther was replaced with Dark Matter which contains an energy more often called Zero Point Energy (ZPE).

## Origins of Energetic Healing

The foregoing would be meaningless information unless there was a way to use it. And because it is important to see that Energetic Healing is not a wacko froo-froo pseudoscience, it has been necessary to cite some credentialed men of science who became aware several centuries ago, as well as during the present day, that our reality is much more than we think it is – even if we didn't then and don't now have the advanced equipment to examine what we suspect to be true about reality.

As this chapter gets further into the major energetic healing modalities, it will be more evident what their genealogy is (i.e., why they developed as they did) and it will be possible, having covered the quantum physics basics, to understand their basic mode of operation.

As was said, the Chinese were the first to explore, document and practice the energetic structure of the human body. From Traditional Chinese Medicine (TCM) research came the science of meridians and the **Acupuncture** positions:

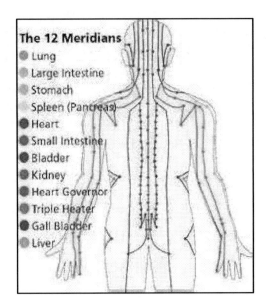

Each dot on a meridian represents an 'acupoint' found on the many meridians of the Bionet, on both sides of the body. Note that a meridian connects with a specific organ, and that is the key to healing, as will be seen.

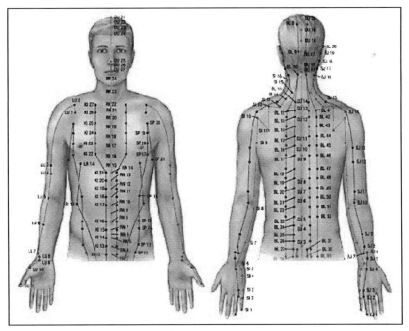

**Acupuncture/Acupressure Acupoints**
(credit Bing Images.com)

The above charts will come into play when the energetic modalities of EFT and Reflexology are examined. Note that even the edge of the hand has acupoints, as does the face.

In Acupuncture, a small hollow needle can be inserted in an acupoint and lightly twisted to stimulate the meridian and cause the *chi* (life energy in the Bionet) to move along the meridian and when it encounters an **energy blockage**, between the needle and the corresponding organ, dissolve it. Instead of inserting a needle, many practitioners of Acupuncture's sister, **Acupressure**, use a finger or small dowel to poke the acupoints. However, Chinese practitioners prefer the needle as a slight physical resistance in inserting it signifies that the acupoint has been correctly targeted... something that is not available by pressing on an acupoint. Acupoints tend to be located where a nerve and a muscle connect, thus providing a bit more 'resistance' to the needle than a non-acupoint location.

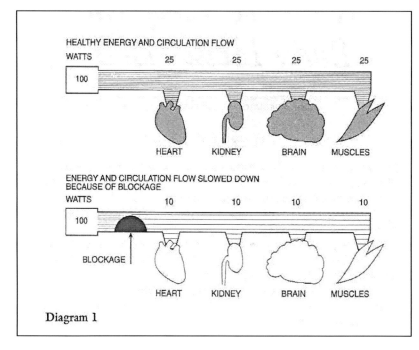

Note that the energy blockage can significantly reduce the amount of energy (*chi*) that reaches one or more organs.

If this condition persists, the function of the organ is impaired and a disease can set in.

**Symbolic Representation of an Energy Blockage**
(credit: *Body Reflexology*, p. 2)

In a related development, Acupressure has been further developed in America, and used around the world, in a system called **Reflexology** which has discovered that there are therapeutic 'pressure points' all over the body – and many parts of the body mirror the acupoints such that a therapist can use either the foot or the hand acupoint to stimulate the same meridian.

It was also discovered that the energy around an acupoint is a small vortex, just like that of the chakras. This can be seen by holding a pendulum above the chakra or acupoint. Energy spirals, or produces toroidal waves.

The following three charts depict the mirror state of the acupoints. The middle of the hand has the same arrangement of acupoints as the middle of the foot, and note that the body torso has a right and left side – all mirror images …as if designed that way, hmmm. :

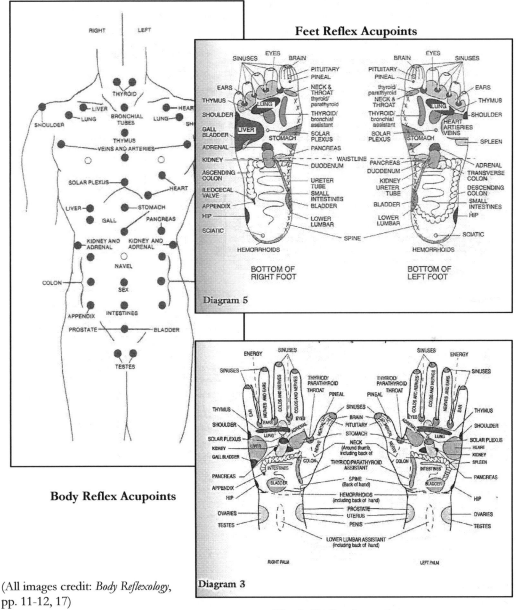

**Feet Reflex Acupoints**

**Body Reflex Acupoints**

(All images credit: *Body Reflexology*, pp. 11-12, 17)

**Hands Reflex Acupoints**

It is not necessary to be able to read all the acupoints above, but do note that 'stomach' and 'solar plexus' are two of the main ones – whereas they are in the middle of the body, they are also in the middle of the hand/foot. Interesting that the meridians running through the body's torso terminate in the hands and feet as well as in the head – in spatially similar locations: the location on the hand is similar to the position on the foot. The ear also has acupressure points although the lobe is pretty neutral (so no problem with pierced ears) and the outer edge of the ear, if pierced, relates to a 'body warmer' effect:

> The **body warmers** [sub-chakras] gather and regulate the energy of the digestive, sexual, and respiratory organs, and others. They work in cooperation with the lungs, the small intestines, the kidneys, the heart, and the sex organs. [170] [emphasis added]

If the body warmer edge of the ear is pierced, it will be stimulating that meridian as long as the piercing is present. What effect this has long-term is unknown.

**Pranic Healing** as practiced in India also uses the same meridians and chakras (which are nodes or junction points where several meridians come together), as do Qigong Healing and Reflexology. When the meridians channel the *chi* into a node (chakra), because the energy is toroidal (Kozyrev's torsion waves), **the chakras spin** and that is represented by small vortices in the diagram (below):

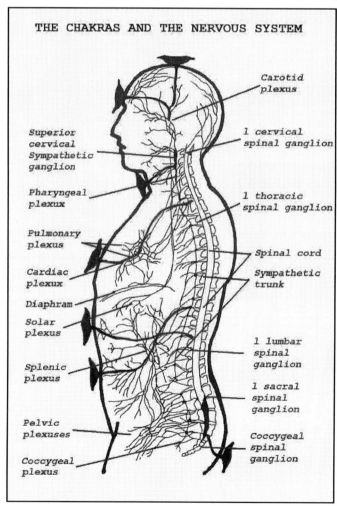

THE CHAKRAS AND THE NERVOUS SYSTEM

Carotid plexus

Superior cervical Sympathetic ganglion

1 cervical spinal ganglion

Pharyngeal plexux

1 thoracic spinal ganglion

Pulmonary plexus

Spinal cord

Cardiac plexux

Sympathetic trunk

Diaphram

Solar plexus

1 lumbar spinal ganglion

Splenic plexus

1 sacral spinal ganglion

Pelvic plexuses

Coccygeal spinal ganglion

Coccygeal plexus

Note also that the nervous system, the meridians, chakras and acupoints are an integrated whole, called the **Bionet**.

The Bionet also connects with multiple locations via the spinal cord. Nerves and meridians often run along together through the body.

**The 7 Major Chakras and Locations**
(credit: Bing Images)

312

By this point in the chapter, it should be an amazing realization that Man is a rather complex biological and energetic design, and a design proves the existence of a **Designer**. The concept of Evolution just happening to build the marvelous body/mind of Man by random chance, is about like a tornado sweeping through a junkyard and assembling a 747 airplane. According to Evolution, it all started with a primordial slime, hit by lightning bolts to energize it, thus creating amino acids, then 1-celled life appeared and just happened to evolve into amoebas, shellfish, crocodiles, IRS agents, and finally Man...

> *If you still believe in Evolution, I have some ocean-front property in Montana that I'd like to sell you....*

Moving forward, let's take a look at some ideas and techniques that are part of the Energetic Healing modalities so that when we get to them, everything we have said so far will assist in understanding them. The foregoing tour of the history and explanation of meridians, etc. was not a space-filler; it is germane to seeing that these modalities are real and are based on scientific discoveries.

## Ancillary Support Systems

This will be a brief survey of supporting elements that are also found in the healing modalities. (There is no significance to the sequence of the following items.)

### Qigong/Pranic Healing

As said before, this is the oldest form of energy healing and both share the same techniques, just one is from China and the other tends to be practiced in India. They are both **non-touch** and involve sweeping the aura to clean it, and then resweeping the aura to sense any energy disturbance(s). When an energy blockage is found, a spot in the aura will feel hot/cold, prickly, hard... all subjective manifestations unique to the practitioner. The adept keeps his/her hands about 6-8" above the client's body and wills the *chi* to enter the body or chakra and perform the healing.

Because the body has the *vis medicatrix* (knows how to heal itself), it isn't necessary to tell the energy or the body what to do – sending the fresh, vital *chi* is enough. The healer's ability then is to (1) visualize an inflow of constant *chi* from the universal life force Field into the healer, and (2) then visualize and <u>will</u> the *chi* to flow into the patient's body (through the healer's hands). Sometimes a two-handed approach is used: if the patient has a sore right knee, then the healer will place the right (sending) hand close to the sole of the right foot, and the left (receiving) hand at the knee or better yet, at the groin area, and visualize *chi* running in the foot, up the leg and out to the left hand – forming a loop. This is called **"running energy"** and makes sure that any blockage between the foot and the groin area (where the #1 chakra is) is met and removed.

> **Note that the *chi* is directed by the mind via visualization and empowered by will.**

Qigong uses **exercises** to build internal *chi* to send externally (for healing) as well as using visualization to inflow the *chi* to the healer's body (storage in the Dan Tien, i.e., chakra #2 in the abdomen.)

Pranic **breathing** near trees or waterfalls is used to absorb *chi* …
both visualize an inflow of universal *chi* to energize and build energy to send. The universal *chi* or life force energy is from the ZPE Field, The Matrix, or the Dark Energy field or the Æther – all these terms basically describe the same Field.

## Neuro Linguistic Programming (NLP)

Richard Bandler wrote several books on the science of NLP – how the brain processes and stores information, memories…. And in the process discovered that trauma stores some sort of 'pocket of energy' in the body which can lead to illness.

> *The Chinese believe the same thing in TCM.*

What Bandler discovered was the ability of a human brain to "reframe" an experience by looking at the memory and visualizing it producing a different outcome … called the **Swish Pattern**. This could be repeated as many times as necessary until the original memory 'lost' its emotional charge. Both Donna Eden and Jose Silva modified this technique to suit their reframing modalities and wrote books on it.

Also part of NLP is setting an **anchor** to affect an emotional state, or recall information from memory… or to stop a memory program from running. For example, there is a way to program ('anchor') an automatic response to happen every time a person, say, pushes his fingernail of the right hand onto the middle knuckle of the left hand – the anchor is set to stop the urge to smoke, for example, every time the person uses this little trigger mechanism. It must be solidly programmed into the conscious and subconscious to be effective, and there are ways NLP does that.

Another technique NLP provides is **kinesthetic testing**. There are two ways to do this:

1. Stand up and hold out your right arm (if you are right-handed) parallel to the floor. To see if you are sensitive to grapes, for example, either hold grapes in your left and, or visualize grapes. Have another person push your right arm down – if it is easy to

push down, grapes make you weak. If your arm is still strong it means you do not lose energy interacting with the energetic field around the grapes.

2. To determine if a vitamin or supplement in the health food store is counter-productive for you, and you don't want to attract attention using the 1ˢᵗ technique above, or you don't have a friend to help you, stand up, perfectly balanced, not leaning in any direction, and place the bottle or product in your left hand and hold it to your solar plexus (3ʳᵈ chakra). If you tend to lean forward, or you feel a **slight draw forward**, it means the product is OK for you, a positive reaction. If you feel 'pushed back' (or repulsed) or even get a nasty 'taste' in the mouth, the product is contra-indicated for you – its energy signature is not compatible with your energy… avoid it.

These are useful tools which are based on the Field/Matrix in which we are 'swimming,' much as a fish swims in water – we 'swim' in a toroidal energy field.

## The Silva Method

Jose Silva originated this system in 1969 first to heal his family members, so it was proven at home, and later to benefit all mankind. He also devised an 'anchor' system called the **Three Fingers Technique** – again the purpose of connecting 3 fingers (thumb + 2 on one hand) was set while in **the alpha mental state** so that during the day, to stop whatever habit one had, biting nails, smoking, etc., at the first sign of the habit, one could 3-finger their way to stopping the behavior.

So Silva was very explicit in training people to "go to level" (get into the 'alpha' mental state) when attempting to practice any of the techniques – and they spent some time on the 1ˢᵗ of 4 days training just putting you in alpha, even using a bio-feedback machine whose sound would indicate when you were in the alpha state – and then you would practice the techniques. (Yes, it borders on the positive power of suggestion, or self-hypnosis.)

One of the very effective techniques was the **Mirror of the Mind** – framing and unframing using white and blue framed mirrors – blue for the undesired issue, and white for the desired picture. Also we were taught to pour a glass of water, and bless it (shades of **Masaru Emoto** in Chapter 4) and then, in alpha level, 'program' the water (send it your intention – as Garaiev and Poponin did) that during the night, while asleep, you will receive the insight or information you seek. You can also program the water to heal you because water has a 'memory' and can record energy.

Lastly, Silva teaches **memory building** and recall techniques that are fantastic to the uninitiated but use a simple system of association (mnemonic recall) to work.

**The Science of Mind**

In the early 50s' an enlightened man named Dr. Ernest Holmes developed some earth-shaking concepts of healing through what he called the **Science of the Mind** (SOM). It was so effective, he started a church of **Religious Science** based on the fact that the world around us was knowable via the scientific method as applied to spiritual issues… sound familiar (Sheldrake, Driesch, Steiner, Mesmer…)?

He developed a large SOM Handbook that covered many different issues and his suggested remedy or insights into whatever the topic was… and a favorite of many people were the discourses on healing. Thus, Dr. Holmes set about teaching classes in self-healing, using the Mind to guide the acquisition of the healing force and manipulate it for healing… He believed that there was an unseen power all around us that we could tap into – with visualization, affirmations and the recognition that the illness was a disruption of the normal, balanced manifestation of the body's energy state.

He trained Practitioners to effect the healing for those who came to the Church seeking a healthy body… it also helped if that seeker attended Sunday lessons in truth to help reorient their thinking. Many illnesses were caused by negative thinking, emotions out of control, or fears. The Practitioner then would sit down with the patient (and reminiscent of Christian Science reading rooms) make a series of statements designed to reorient the patient's attitude and NOT focus on the illness but what the sick part of the body normally looked like… what is the ideal image of the body?

The illness *per se* was never treated as it was an illusion, an energy imbalance; instead the Practitioner would **affirm and visualize the perfect state of the body**, state it…. And many people were healed after just a few sessions. If not, they would have a session with Dr. Holmes who was able to effect almost miracle cures… he was very powerful. (His connection with the healing energetic Field was something you could feel as you stood near him.)

This says that the Mind bears a heavy impact on the body and that our thinking, visualization and willing which impact the toroidal Field can make a difference in our health.

**Est Training**

Werner Erhard was a student of Oriental modalities, Zen, Pythagoras, Emerson, Silva, TM, and assorted "isms and ologies" of the 50's and 60's which he whipped into a 2 weekend Training of indeterminate daily length during the late 70's and early 80's. It was confrontational, boring, in-your-face, challenging, inflammatory, loving, sleep-inducing… anything and everything was possible in the Training. A lot of people came out of the back-to-back weekends wondering what the heck they just paid $350 for! Some were smiling, some were angry – but "you got what you got and that was IT." People did the Training the way they did their lives… half-*ss or very on-purpose. And we all learned a new jargon…and we learned to ride the horse in the direction he was going! Rocks are hard and water's wet. Some people became "est-holes" and annoyed the heck out of the rest of us by continuing to do the Training on us after the seminar was over! There were even a few times that the Trainers were punched out.

So what was Est, a clever way to scam people, or was there something special you were able to get if you paid attention? It was said to be like a joke – you can't explain it – you had to "get it." But it was more than that. And I was one of the few who all of a sudden saw what they were doing and it shocked me into a sense of my Self that was transforming – and Est's stated goal was to transform people.

> I was sitting in the back of the room of 300 people, on the aisle, no windows, no watch, no way to know what time of day it was and it was somewhere in the 3rd day of 4 in the Training. I wondered what I was doing there, I wondered when I would "get it", whatever it was, and Charlene A., the Trainer, walked by, stopped and looked at me, snorted a little laugh and said "You're a resistant mother aren't you?".. and walked on. Her eyes were looking right through me – very piercing eyes and I have sometimes wondered if she was one of the special people on this planet… August 1979 at the Orange County (Ca) Fairgrounds…and I'm waiting for enlightenment! Har, I had to laugh.

> The person next to me was asleep and I thought I'd nudge her so she didn't waste her money and Charlene saw me and said to leave her alone – Charlene said that she could stand up front, read the telephone book with people asleep and they would still "get it." That was a definite WTF moment for me…. I was confused and she saw that and came back to me and looked into me again, and said "Confusion, not knowing, is a very high state." I said you got that right… She said, "When you realize that you don't know what you think you know, you will be open to knowing what really IS true." And she walked on again, up and down the aisles, challenging the attendees.

> I gave up trying to figure it all out. I "shipped oars" so to speak and decided to just observe. She had done something to me during those interactions… I could feel it but didn't know what it was. She looked back at me from across the middle group of people – right at me and said, "Get out of your head!" (That was something she said a lot to the whole group.)

Dang it, how'd she know what I was doing?! Did she see auras...Was my energy different?

I sat there just observing. She was watching me from time to time. It was one of those times that I think she did something to me.... All of a sudden I sat back in the chair and was watching myself, sitting there in the chair. Not an Out of Body (OBE), but I had a sense that **I** was watching me... all of a sudden there was a greater **I** that had transcended the room, the boredom, and it was very quiet, it was like a Peak Experience except that there were <u>two of me</u>.

The peace was incredible, no chatter of the Mind, and I felt compassion for all those around me... I was at peace with everything around me... and I had a sense of the energy in the room, beyond the room, and a connection with the One. Charlene walked over to where I was sitting again, and she looked at me, smiled, and with a slightly misty eye said, "Welcome. You got it."

Did she do it to me? If so, maybe it was part of the "We're all connected" mantra – entanglement and All are One concept... she could have 'zapped' me with her advanced focus, briefly energizing me, my DNA, moving the *kundalini*, whatever... I then understood what she meant by the telephone book analogy. It wasn't anything she said, it was her <u>presence</u>, her Light, her clarity – **she** was doing something to us!

Can those who have it impart it to others? Is there a **"100<sup>th</sup> Human"** effect (like the "100<sup>th</sup> Monkey")? Is it like Dr. Holmes (above) who had it and could impart healing to others?

From that day forward, I have never forgotten what that experience of Self was like, and for weeks afterward, I could jump into it while in the park, or shopping, and all of a sudden, colors would be fantastically deep and rich, sounds were full and complete, and I could recreate the effect any time I wanted. (Once you have experienced a higher state, it is easy to recreate it just by remembering it. The same with going into 'alpha'.)

Chapter 13 has more on a presence imparting higher consciousness.

## Chiropractic

Not much needs to be said about chiropractic except that a number of the current-day energy healers also started as chiropractors. What better way to sense people's energy while aligning their spines for a better flow of energy? And some chiropractors also practice Acupressure, so they are in the mainstream of Energy Medicine. Many <u>thanks</u> to these caring people.

## HeartMath Institute

Related to energetic healing and torsion fields is the little-known **heart torus** – the energy field projected by the heart that is shaped like a large 15' donut, or torus. The beating of the heart produces 2.5 watts of energy – forty times greater than the EM field of the brain, yet contains glial cells just as the brain does. If necessary, an ECG could be taken from 3' away. [171] The strongest part is the first 3', the rest of the torus extends out to about 12-15'. (See below)

Whereas Garaiev modified DNA with focused light, experiments at the Institute showed that focused intention and **emotion could affect DNA**[172]… similar to what the Russians discovered using words and sound…DNA is not only plastic, but sensitive.

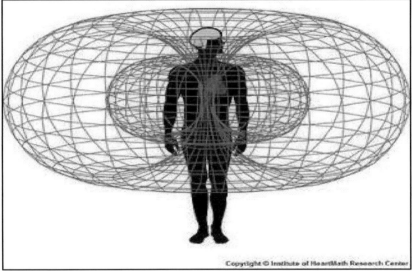

**The Heart Torus**

In addition, **the torus is holographic** – any spot on the torus contains the information of the whole field… just as is the EM [electromagnetic] field of the Earth. **We seem to live in a nested system of toroid energy fields**… much like what Kozyrev called 'torsion fields.' What this means is that we live in fields within fields within fields… and

> …the world my brain and body give me is approximately the same as that which you and others are given because our similar physiology draws on the same **nonlocalized frequency fields**.[173] [emphasis added]

It is also thought that the blood flows in "spiral-like vortices" in the blood vessels.

This sounds like most of life is working with EM fields generated by torsion physics.

And another significant point:

> DNA is em-sensitive, allowing some em fields to regulate DNA, RNA, and protein synthesis, as well as to induce cell differentiation and **morphogenesis**. Rupert Sheldrake's morphogenetic fields may involve electromagnetic energy as well as **nonlocal effects** beyond current knowledge.[174]   [emphasis added]

The heart uses a lot of energy. And its source is nonlocal, inducting the energy from the Field/Matrix <u>via the torus</u>. An electromagnetic heart torus that exists within a larger planetary torus, and that within a larger galactic torus means that all levels are energy-empowered by the Field, or Dark Energy from the Dark Matter. Scientists suspect that all energy systems, from that of the atom to the spin of the planets, including that of the galaxies, are toroid in form.

Greg Braden reminds us of the **Divine Matrix**:

> There is something "out there": the matrix of an energy that connects any one thing with everything else in the universe.[175]

> **Note: the body's torus is not the aura which is the energy presence of the soul that utilizes the body. Spirit energizing the body can now be seen to be the Divine Matrix, which is intelligent energy.**

One last point of interest that came from the Institute bears revealing:

> Glen Rein and Rollin McCraty have discovered …. that **love** is a real healing energy with measurable physiological effects, even at the DNA level. Rein found that individuals who sat and meditated in a state of love, compassion, and caring actually generated greater coherence in their ECG pattern than those who were simply at rest or had discordant emotion…. The heart rhythms associated with love were characterized by a smooth, sinus-wave-like pattern… [and] the frequency peaks …. were evenly separated by a proportionality factor identical to *pi*, the so-called golden mean ratio of mathematics and architecture. [176] [emphasis added]

There is a musicality to the harmonic waves in the ECG reflecting the coherent nature of unconditional Love. Such an emotion was also found to bless and strengthen the person's own DNA , so that Love as a coherent energy pattern was sustained and effective <u>over distance</u> as well as locally. [177]

## Quantum Physics

Just as a summary, the list of items so far dealing with advanced physics is:

nonlocality - entanglement, virtual particles, particle-wave duality, ZPE, torsion waves, Æther, Dark Energy and Dark Matter, vacuum, and holographics.

These all come together in the following multilevel illustration.

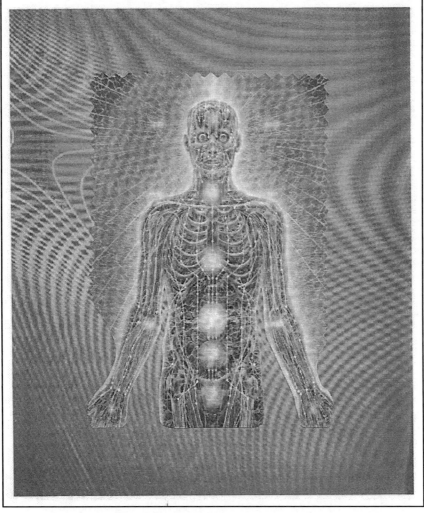

Note that the 7 **chakras** and the 12 main meridians of the **Bionet** receive energy through the **Aura** which inducts energy from the torsion waves of the **Matrix**.

**The Aura and Bionet in the Matrix**

(Some day this chart will be printed in color in the book. Email me [address on copyright page] and I'll send you a copy.)

The heart also has a toroidal field (2 pp back) which interfaces energetically with the Dark Energy or ZPE of the Matrix … also feeding the aura.

## Energy Healing Modalities

So, all of the preceding was not to bore the reader with Science and footnotes, it has a direct bearing on understanding how and why the following healing techniques work.

And, the following are by no means all the players and techniques offered in **Energy Medicine**, but they are representative of different approaches and now that we have covered the underlying principles of the last 200 years, including the more relevant but esoteric Quantum Physics, it will be easier to understand what each modality has to offer.

The following are specific techniques from the new field of **Energy Psychology** which is part of the Energy Medicine realm. What has been discovered is that **everything is energy** – the world around us: rocks, trees, animals and even our bodies … and our thoughts, memories and the fields that surround us. The Energy Psychology people have all borrowed concepts from Quantum Physics that the physicists would say are not part of a subjective, personal health world, and yet the modalities really do work. Such concepts as the **Matrix**, or a field that surrounds us as a **unified energy field** , do have a counterpart in our reality – as Sheldrake, Garaiev and Kozyrev have just shown (above) and these are the heart's field, or torus, the aura, the Earth's electromagnetic field, and the ubiquitous Æther, or Dark Energy and Dark Matter fields that pervade all of space.

The main issues in Energy Psychology are two: **energy blockages** and **psychological reversals.** Both are usually due to trauma (energetic imprint) that is stored in the body, usually in the cells of an organ, and the Mind (energy) interacts with the memory (energy) carrying the energetic imprint as a blockage, or what has been called an **ECHO** (Energetic Consciousness Holograms). That is the perfect description because the body/mind is conscious of the energy 'packet' (for lack of a better word, like an energy spherule) that is stored holographically in the Matrix associated with that part of the body – in the etheric part of the aura associated with the affected organ.

> This is why it was so important to understand that the body's **Bionet** interacts with the **aura** which interacts with the Heart **torus** and both the torus and the aura interact (transduce) energy from the unified energy field or **Matrix** (think: morphogenetics) that surrounds us.

> Also remember: the mind and the body are connected – Qigong can use the mind to direct the *chi* in the body to where it is needed. That is the essence of **psychosomatics**, too.

An **energy imbalance** is just a part of the Bionet that is not flowing naturally, but is like a beaver dam on a river – there is an overabundance of energy blocking the flow. **Psychological reversals** are cases where the mind has formed a negative belief about some past traumatic event and that belief sabotages efforts to be successful in life. (In a fit of anger at some mishap, a mother yells at her daughter, and she now has a new belief about herself: "Mom said I was dumb and I can't do anything right..." ) is a belief that curses that daughter and if reinforced over the years, will be a belief that keeps her from doing things she really wants to do. The following modalities have been proven to cancel such beliefs and set the person free from limiting behavior.

Whereas some techniques just tap on the meridians to break up the energy blockage, others like Matrix Reimprinting and FasterEFT also use **visualization** to replace the old negative memory with a more positive outcome. This is not denial of the original event, but a case of **neurogenesis**, which is the building of new neural pathways and memory associations. The theory is that with a new, positive belief and expectation in place, the **Law of Attraction** will tend to bring those things to us that we desire ... this is not "creating one's day." It is <u>attracting</u> it and that is a big difference (see section below called 'Caveat #1: Manipulating Reality').

While some modalities give the "reimprinting" process via **visualization** a fancy Quantum Physics term, i.e., "collapsing the waveform", which can't be disproven, it sometimes appears as psychobabble and may discredit the techniques which really do work.

The energetic interaction with the fields around us <u>are</u> accurately accounted for by the latest discoveries in Quantum Physics, but there is also enough documented therapeutic/clinical literature today that allows these modalities to stand on their own merit.

And it all began with discoveries in EFT, which appears to have been an out-growth of the older Parent-Adult-Child therapies, called Transactional Analysis (TA). Remember: "I'm OK, You're OK" ? The connection is simple: TA examines and works with the <u>psychological structure</u> of the human and EFT works with the <u>energetic structure</u> of the human – and both address behavior and work with memories. But TA was not always effective because the memories and behavior were stuck no matter what the therapist did to <u>talk</u> about the issue and try to reframe the client's view of his/her personal issues. The stuck energy was still there reinforcing the client's beliefs.

With the advent of discoveries in Quantum Physics that we are all energy and were storing the traumas internally, energizing them from the Matrix around us, and acting from that basis, it became a whole new ballgame. It was clear that talk therapy was not as effective as finding a way to remove the energetic imprint, and thus remove the energy feeding the negative belief that was producing negative behavior.

The outgrowth was originally Thought Field Therapy (TFT) in the 80s by Roger Callahan, and others modified his tapping concept into what is today called EFT. Of course the American Psychological Association says it is all unproven and lacks a scientific basis – they are still trying to make talk therapy work. Meanwhile, EFT has set thousands of people free from self-limiting behavior.

## Emotional Freedom Technique® (EFT)

This, like TFT, was the grandfather to several of the following methods. It emphasized **tapping on meridians** to stimulate the Bionet and break up any energy blockages.

Its founder was **Gary Craig** who in 1993 combined Acupuncture, NLP, energy medicine and Thought Field Therapy into the EFT system. Relief from one's psychological issues and trauma-caused energy blockages comes from tapping with the index finger on a set of **acupoints** known to reach the location of the energy disruption.

The following is a diagram of the common acupoints used.

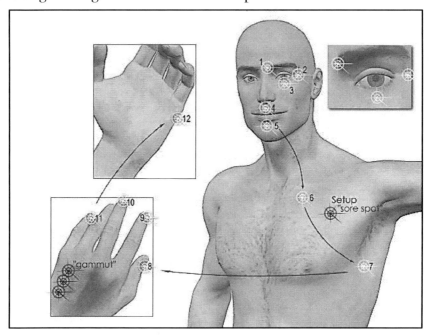

**EFT Acupoints**
(credit: http://en.wikipedia.org/wiki/Emotional_Freedom_Techniques)

These are the same acupoints used by subsequent versions of the EFT technique. There are 12 major acupoints and they vary in use because they are found on 12 key meridians associated with the 12 major areas (including organs) of the body that can be afflicted by 'stuck' energy, or trauma. Point 1 (above) is for frustration and impatience, **point 2 is for anger,** …point 4 is for cancelling psychological reversals… and point 8, for example, is for intolerance and arrogance.

> **The next time you get angry with someone, stop and try this:**
> **tap point #2 (side of the eye, either one) and think peace.**
> **See if it diminishes the anger.**

The former meridian chart is presented again for ease of reference:

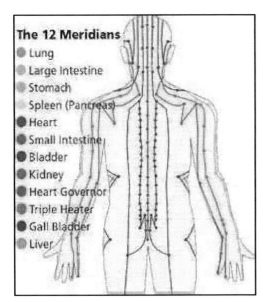

**The 12 Meridians**
- Lung
- Large Intestine
- Stomach
- Spleen (Pancreas)
- Heart
- Small Intestine
- Bladder
- Kidney
- Heart Governor
- Triple Heater
- Gall Bladder
- Liver

There are 10 organs and 2 'extras' – the Heart Governor and the Triple Heater (internal sub-chakras).

**Heart Governor** – regulates heart
**Triple Heater** – regulates lungs, stomach, and abdomen.

Both the Governor and the Heater are best activated by the **Small Orbit** exercise of Chapter 11. To a certain extent, the 2 main meridians down the front center of the body also serve the 4 organs (heart, lungs, stomach & abdomen).

The basic procedure is to recall an upset or trauma, then rate it on a scale of 1-10 (the **SUD rating**), and then tap the appropriate meridian (one of the 12 acupoints), and then test again to see subjectively if the SUD rating is diminished – if not (a) you either didn't tap the right meridian, or maybe you didn't tap the meridian at all, or (b) you need to focus better, and tap more until an original SUD rating of 8 (fairly serious upset) lessens to a 2 or 3.

> SUD is a scale:  Subjective Units of Distress 1 – 10

The key is to find and tap the meridian while focusing on the upset. For this reason, Acupressure or Acupuncture with a trained practitioner may be a more sure way of releasing the emotional charge buried in the body.

**Matrix Energetics®**

This is one of the several EFT derivitives, although its founder **Richard Bartlett** DC and ND, does not really make use of the acupoints. He looked at EFT originally but admits that he now **channels entities** [178](hopefully they are healing angels and not Astral Gameplayers [ see below]) who do the healing through him. He often just touches (the **Two-Point** process which borders on 'running energy' but is not sustained) what DO appear to be pressure points on the subject and the person may laugh, collapse, or remain standing but bend way over toward their shoes… or just stand and sway back and forth. He calls this "collapsing the wave" and tells us that "…two or more quantum systems can share the same quantum wave." And he uses quantum physics terms like "wavefront consciousness" which serve to spice up his modality. [179] How is that relevant when he channels entities who do the work?

### Note: see the Caveat #2 below on Astral Gameplayers.

Healings are reported but his expensive seminars have been called a Barnum & Bailey event with his repeated laughing and injunction to relax and "just play." It is as if he initiates all the healing work on the subject via **his** intention and focus.

> *Interesting as I watched the healings up front, it occurred to me that an Aikido Master (who projects energy into the acupoints) could do the same thing to the subjects. (See Empty Force in Bibliography.)*

**Faster EFT®**

The brainchild of **Robert Smith**, this is EFT at its best and is easy to follow. It uses the EFT modality and takes less time with more results. The technique is fully explained in a **YouTube video** made by Robert and is fantastic. In 17 minutes you will understand it all. Worth watching:

Robert Smith – video 163 How It All Works:  17 minutes.
(also called Trainer's Secrets, Faster NLP, EFT…)

http://www.youtube.com/watch?v=jJTEqozJ9aQ&feature=player_detailpage

This modality suggests that in addition to tapping on the acupoint associated with the issue, the person also visualize a new positive outcome from the event that caused the issue, in addition to lovingly accepting and respecting oneself.

**Matrix Reimprinting®**

The outstanding creation of **Karl Dawson**, who derives his version from the original EFT scenario, but he emphasizes the aspects a new way:

> **ECHO**s – Energy Conscious Holograms which are the energy blockages themselves and can be addressed as if they were an entity to be manipulated. They are the result of trauma that caused a part of our energy body to split off or fragment.

> **Reimprinting** -- while recalling the original upset, and tapping, a new outcome or result is put in place, via visualization, reminiscent of Silva and NLP "reframing." This is in synch with Quantum Physics which says we as multi-dimensional beings have multiple possible timelines and versions of the same event, and we choose to replace the traumatic memory with a better outcome (from an alternate reality).

He maintains that **we are all energy beings**, whose molecules are vibrating so fast that we appear to be solid, and he says we **are all interconnected by a web of energy**. Sounds familiar. He has also come up to date with the concept of fields and points out that we are energy beings surrounded by energy fields – the Earth's geomagnetic field, the heart torus field, and the greater ZPE Field… He particularly likes **Sheldrake's Morphogenetic field** and warns that repeated actions can strengthen this field – for better or worse.

But we can relax as Reimprinting, and trained practitioners, can handle it all.[180]

Unfortunately he is also dangerously close to the New Age concept that when we send our thoughts out into the Matrix, they return to us manifesting that which we seek… i.e., "Create Your Day" again.[181] He emphasizes that we can attract what we want, but I urge caution. So let's look at this issue in detail:

## Caveat #1: Manipulating Reality

I suppose this is something that anyone into EFT, Matrix or Reimprinting, would find desirable – to use a reframing technique to change our experience (in the past) and so program ourselves so that we experience (attract to ourselves) our fondest desires. It sounds plausible and I like it, too – the latter manifesting part just doesn't work that way in 3D…. unless it is for healing.

**You have control over your body and so can affect it; you do not have control over people and objects around you.**

Earth is a training school and we do not have full access to the power of the Matrix to do <u>whatever</u> we want, otherwise we'd obviate our lessons, or change them and thus foil the Script that says we are here to learn something. On the other hand, if you are one of the incoming **Noetic** beings, you are not bound by the standard 3D Earth Script and like Criss Angel and Darren Brown (of Book 1 fame), you may just be able to do more because you resonate with a faster PFV.

**Indigos** are among the starseed who are here to anchor the Light and work for a better society – some of them HAVE been given the 'go ahead' to manipulate and rework reality to a better design – according to their 'official charter' that they signed onto before incarnating here.

What I am saying is that **very few, if any, people have absolute freewill to do anything they want,** wherever they want, whenever they want, any way they want – by the way, <u>that describes a god</u> and Earth is not about New Age gods running around flipping red lights in their favor, and manifesting perfect parking places… Those are childish uses of advanced power and that is why it isn't given to 3D humans.

Having said all that, it **is perfectly fine** to use whatever power from the Matrix you can muster <u>to heal yourself,</u> or others (with their permission). Just do not extend the 'manifesting' paradigm to manipulating your whole reality.

## META-Medicine®

The creation of **Richard Flook**, this is a **system of diagnosis** to better identify the source of illness, and establish the connection between the brain and organ, again using the appropriate meridian. META-Medicine says that each particular area of the brain has a link to a corresponding organ and since all diseases are caused by stress, they run diagnostics to determine what organ reflects the stress. This is reminiscent of Reflexology and TCM in general.

The META-Medicine diagnostics include a **CT scan** to tell which organ is under stress. And there are traumas associated with each organ, typical of the dysfunction that arises unique to that organ, and then **Matrix Reimprinting** is the tool of choice to correct or alleviate the issue.

There are ten main principles which emphasize not only a healthy mind-body connection , but there is a very precise **organ-mind-brain-social connection**. These 4 are brought into the healing modality. If we experience a biological

328

conflict shock, then our body responds with cancer, eczema, or diabetes… The skin is affected by loss-of-contact conflict, the breast by a separation conflict, the lungs by a fear-of-death conflict, and so forth… [182]

 The **Energetic Medicine Researchers** website is quite detailed with a lot of information:  http://www.energetic-medicine.net/energy-medicine-researchers.html
Worth taking a look at.


**Rewind:  Psychological Reversal**

This is a major aspect of many buried traumas needing removal, and the proponents have a book called *Energy Tapping* that uses EFT. Authors Gallo and Vincenzi lay out the acupoints the best of all books, and they emphasize and describe in depth the major issue (generally covered in the other EFT modalities): **Self-sabotage via Psychological Reversal.**

There are acupoints for this as well as muscle (kinesthetic) testing to see what the body does while saying sample statements related to one's beliefs or problem. For example, to remove the **ECHO** (as EFT Reimprinting would call it) called Down-on-Self, the patient would say something like "I deserve to have this problem" while their muscle is being tested (as was examined earlier in another section). The body's reaction tells whether this is a true belief for this person, and then the Tapping on specific acupoints begins with a cycling back through the speaking-testing process to reassess when the **SUD rating** reaches 2-3 (low), or when the belief has been de-energized as verified by a different body reaction.

Self-sabotage is a self-defeating behavior arising from some deep-seated belief that keeps one from accomplishing stated goals. When people are psychologically reversed they sabotage getting a new job, getting engaged, or even saying 'No' when they really want to say 'Yes.'  For example, you want to be happy and need a new job, but inwardly you don't believe you are worth it.  For the same reason, people stay in abusive relationships when they should get out.

This EFT modality has been proven to set people free by reconnecting the body energy with the mind (beliefs) and cancelling the negative belief. They say nothing about replacing the old event's picture/belief with a visualized new outcome (as do FasterEFT and Matrix Reimprinting) but they do suggest accepting oneself and saying so during the tapping. They suggest that it may take on-going work on oneself to overcome the personal issue as deep-seated issues do not clear up fast. It is not always an immediate cure but can be expedited by using an experienced practitioner in EFT.

## PsychoEnergetics®

**Dr. William Tiller** is a renowned physicist who loves Energy Medicine and is now recognized for his PsychoEnergetics model of Man in our reality. He has written many white papers which you will love if you are a mathematician or a physicist. He draws comparisons and analyses of Kozyrev, Sheldrake, Matrix Energetics, etc. and attempts to explain the physics behind their ideas. (He was mentioned in an earlier section.)

He is very supportive of the energy healing modality and continues to develop ideas and experiments in the field to justify it. He is a real supportive asset in establishing the credibility for quantum Energetic Medicine.

## Reconnective Healing ®

A survey of energy healing would not be complete without a look at Reconnective Healing by **Eric Pearl**. He supports a healing intelligence but does not use EFT or the Matrix healing techniques. Like Matrix Energetics and Richard Bartlett, he **channels healing entities** to do the work and they make use of "axiatonal" lines that reconnect the patient with higher states, and awaken dormant DNA. His technique is non-touch and does not "run energy" like Pranic Healing does. He says that anybody can train to do this work … yet it invokes healing entities… and there is a serious caution in this regard (see below) that may not work for everybody.

He maintains that his healing technique is supreme because he tested all the others and was invited by entities to use their Reconnection modality. It taps into the quantum field, reconnecting with one's DNA, and raises one's frequency to a higher level – that is why using healing entities <u>can</u> be superior, but most EFT healing modalities can work if used correctly, patiently and in faith.

·

# Caveat #2: Astal Gameplayers

A second word needs to be interjected here regarding channeling Astral entities to do healing. There is a safe way and a dangerous way to do it. Please understand in the following that I am not being Medieval nor Biblical – Astral 4D entities do exist, both STO and STS, including discarnates and parasites, and the seemingly ubiquitous "game players" (4D STS) who will accommodate you… to a point.

Many humans are looking for power and often seek to get into things like witchcraft, Ouija Boards, Tarot, I Ching, the paranormal, and even channeling unseen entities who have agreed to empower them. **Caution is advised**: if it seems that you can do these modalities, that is an automatic **red flag**! Most humans cannot make spells and curses work, most cannot get any information from the Ouija Board, and most don't invite Astral entities to work through them to heal others…

What am I saying? Simply that if these things appear to be working and you persist in them, the entities who have empowered you <u>don't do it for free</u>. Often, it is reported that when you die, they come to collect, [183] and they don't want your money. If you participated in **witchcraft**, for example, and placed curses on other people, your own soul fragmented and is attached to the victim that you cursed. [184] The point is that there is a price to pay for these things.

The smart thing is to avoid the Ouija Board, Tarot, casting chicken bones, I Ching, and the like. And if you do want to be a healer, try Qigong, Pranic or Reiki training… but if you do seek Astral (Angel) help, be sure to do the following:

> Surround yourself with **White Light** and ask that only healing entities are sent to assist you from the Father of Light, or The One.

That should call down the real healing Angels (and block the interference from the Astral 4D STS gameplayers).

Without the protection, 4D Astral gameplayers (who have a greater vibration level), can interfere <u>and heal</u> in the 3D realm (because they were <u>invited</u> by you) and because of their greater energy level, where energy flows from the higher to the lower potential, they can often effect a healing for you…. or empower a curse and then <u>you</u> incur terrific karma for that! (They are not guilty because you invited them.)

But you have played their game and it isn't free. If you have received Fame and Fortune, they have sucked you in and at some point they will extract payment – in whatever way <u>they</u> choose. Sorry but that is true and a lot of naïve humans learn the hard way. (I know, I served in a Deliverance Ministry for almost a year. They are real. See Chapter 7.)

> *Besides healing, this also applies to inviting unseen entities to inspire and empower **motivational speakers**. If they make you rich, you 'owe' them and they may 'own' you.*

This is not Medieval thinking – they have <u>always</u> occupied the lower Astral and can see us. In addition, they play games: pretend to be an Incubus or Succubus, pretend to be a demon, pretend to be a Shadow Person… whatever they think will scare you – they feed on the energy of fear, by the way. **And they hate humans**. Ignorance is no excuse. If they can get you to agree to what they want, they have not violated your freewill. So they trick you into choosing what they present – they are master gameplayers and can outplay you. By the time you wake up, it may be too late.

A last word on this issue to illustrate what they can do, even in a harmless setting. A friend and I were playing **Scrabble** and she made her play, and then went to draw 5 new tiles from the bag. She scrambled the tiles, and drew one – an "I". She mixed them up some more and drew another tile – an "I". She looked at me, mixed them up some more, shook the bag and drew another tile – an "I". I won't repeat what she said because the letter "I" is our least favorite and least useful in the game – and there are 9 of them in the game. So she shook the bag up real well, put her hand in and scrambled them some more, and drew out her last two tiles, and (you guessed it), one of them was an "I". **Four "I's" in a row**…and even I said,
**"What the heck are the statistical odds of doing that?!"**

Angry, she put all 5 back, I agreed, we White Lighted the game, she shook the bag and redrew, and had a normal assortment.

There is no way you can draw four of the same letters randomly one-at-a-time like that. That was a clear case of **"interference."** (Perhaps because I'm writing this book and the 4D STS don't like it?) And that is what I'm trying to point out – it happens, and sometimes they let you know they're there. After we White Lighted the game we had no further incidents.
It is the ignorant who claim they don't exist who are their easy prey.

PS: I would be fascinated to know just how they did it – Did they arrange for her to pick just the "I's" (guiding her hand to them), or did they change each tile into an "I" no matter what she picked?

## Psych-K®

This is Energy Psychology as created by Robert Williams, MA, which stands for **Psychological Kinesiology**. This is a technique that Dr. Bruce Lipton approves of, and has witnessed change peoples' **behavior**. Dr. Lipton believes that "… our cells are influenced by our thoughts." [185] It is effectively reprogramming or "rewiring" the subconscious which controls 95% of our conscious actions – based on whatever our beliefs are. Psych-K is a way to change those unproductive beliefs and **insert new, proactive beliefs** into the subconscious so that we can generate better experiences in life. (Note that they are **not** saying we can control our reality.)

I take exception to a statement found in the Psych-K descriptions [186] that "Your reality is created by your beliefs." Not just semantics, but an over-simplification of a system that really does work, but said quote reinforces the idea that we can make adjustments to the subconscious and control/create our reality – i.e., Create Our Day. The old New Age mantra comes to life again here. Note that **changing our behavior changes what we experience** because we do something different, not because we can willfully affect Reality, by "creating" it out there. A significant difference.

The reason for including it here is that it incorporates Kinesiology, NLP, Acupressure, and that means Tapping (EFT) and the meridians are involved. The goal is to balance the two halves of the brain and achieve a "whole brain" state in which neural programming (neurogenesis) is much more effective. It is interesting that kinesiology and feedback from the body are used to achieve a rapport to "detect subconscious truths"[187] … reminiscent of Scientology and their E-meter, but with a more scientific basis, and no electronic gear.

## Quantum Healing®

This is basically a book and seminars, not a modality, by **Deepak Chopra** based on **Ayurveda** and has a place in this discussion because it is NOT energy healing and has nothing to do with Quantum Physics, <u>but sounds like it</u>. (Deepak agrees. His misappropriation of the quantum principles for daily living earned him an Ig Nobel Prize in 1998.) It seems that "quantum" is a buzzword nowadays and catches peoples' attention. But his book is very interesting and worth the money, despite being a mix of New Age + Ayurveda.

Deepak defines 'quantum healing' as "the ability of one mode of consciousness (the mind) to spontaneously correct the mistakes in another mode of consciousness (the body)."[188] A form of psychosomatics. He champions the mind-body link and advocates herbs, meditation and yoga as ancillary modalities to a healthy lifestyle. In the area of nutrition he suggests we all follow Ayurveda principles and use more **Tumeric** aka **Curcumin** – which is a fantastic healing antioxidant in curry. (See Chapters 4 and 13.)

He gets caught up in the New Age vortex when he tells people that aging is not a problem – "Tell your body to not age."[189] He doesn't seem to know about or address **telomeres** and how they control the aging process… aging has some genetic aspects to it, diet aspects, stress aspects and pollution aspects (where we live). Living on planet Earth can be very hazardous to your health.

## Summary

Energetic Medicine is a fast-growing field whose time has come! Watching the nightly commercials for all sorts of pills from Big Pharma, I sometimes wonder if we are really as sick a society as the ads suggest. I certainly do not want to take a purple pill for heartburn when the side effects (announced on TV) are "nausea, vomiting, and diarrhea" – When I first heard that I thought it was a Saturday Night Live joke. It wasn't.  I mentioned the issue to my doctor, and asked him why I would want to trade my heartburn for nausea and vomiting!  His answer?  "Oh we have pills for that, too!"  Seriously?!

Whereas a lot of today's physicians coming out of school are glorified pharmacists, I choose to find alternative medicine cures.  My pharmacist Jack told me the other day that the new doctor grads know two things: how to identify the disease, and what pill(s) go with it. They don't always understand where the disease came from nor how to get rid of it – except with a pill or a scalpel.  **A glorified pharmacist**. He then scared me when he shared that a young doctor called in 3 Rx for a patient the other day and he had to correct the doctor as 2 of the 3 could not and should not be prescribed together!  The young doctor became irate and threatened to have Jack's license and Jack said to go ahead and report it – "you might learn something!"  (He did and Jack was exonerated.)

The time has come to take charge of our own health – diet, attitude/thinking, exercise and a healthy spirituality are some of the key factors to adopt. And Energetic Healing is something that we can easily understand, and readily adopt to keep us on a healthy path in life. It just means we become **responsible** for our health (learn what it takes to maintain it) and stop giving our power away to the doctor.

Interestingly, in China, in addition to energy healings with Qigong and TCM (Traditional Chinese Medicine), the patient-doctor relationship is different:  you pay an **herbalist** who is a TCM practitioner (who has examined you and knows your biochemistry makeup) to keep you well – you buy your weekly herbs and compounds from him and use them during the week. If you get sick, you pay him nothing to get you well again!

Energetic Healing is on the rise and traditional (Allopathic) medicine is about to be eclipsed by alternative (Wholistic) medicine.  If you still totally believe in only traditional medicine with all its pills, radiation and chemotherapy, may the Farce be with you.

# Chapter 13:  The Brain, DNA & Transformation

The reason for putting this chapter last is because it needs some of the information from Chapter 12: meridians, chakras, neuroplasticity, and *chi*. And this chapter is important because anything one does to transform their relationship with Reality must also include the brain, and not just the body. In other words, Transformation must also include improving the relationship with your brain or you will never experience enlightenment, intuition, discernment and enhanced mental abilities.

The following chapter is not only for building a healthy brain, or repairing it after a toxic incident, it is also germane to self-care to avoid Alzheimers, or just ARD (Age-Related Dementia). Getting older does not have to mean living with a failing memory or slow-operating mental facilities.

## Brain and DNA

Realize that the body, heart and brain are all immersed in a sea of energy, the ZPE Matrix as was shown in Chapter 12. That means the DNA is also immersed in this energy and as a matter of fact (see VEG Ch 9) the DNA is fed by the Bionet (meridians) which use biophotons to transfer information around the body's network. Biophotons are the messengers that work with the DNA, and if one is going to Transform into a more enlightened person (i.e., carry more Light), have greater intuition and discernment, then the DNA has to also change.

**All cells** in the body have DNA as well as **mitochondria** which are the "batteries" in each cell that produce energy. As we age, the number of mitochondria per cell decreases, and the **telomeres** shorten at the end of the X-shaped chromosomes, all of which signals an advancing end to the organism we call our body.

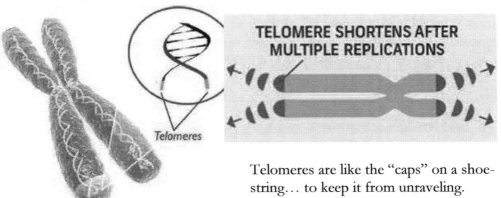

Telomeres are like the "caps" on a shoe-string... to keep it from unraveling. Stress causes them to erode prematurely and also impairs DNA replication.

(credit: Bing Images)

If we can stop the shortening of telomeres and arrest the decrease in mitochondria per cell, we can live longer, more healthy lives.

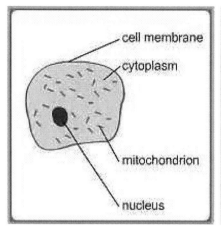
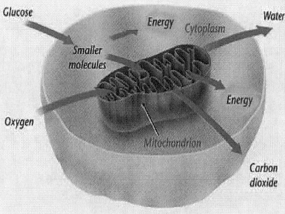

**Cell with Multiple Mitochondria**          **Energy Production of Mitochondrion**
(credit: Bing Images)

> For the more technically-minded, the ATP energy is released by the mitochondria into the cytoplasm and that is cycled thru the nucleus, and both the nucleus and mitochondria have DNA.

As can be appreciated, the biophotons cruising the Bionet affect the brain and the major organs for regulation, and then the glands (pituitary especially) emit the chemical messengers, or signaling molecules, which are sent from the glands to <u>all cells</u> via the blood. Only those cells with appropriate receptors can use specific chemical messengers. All this happens while the body is immersed in a sea of energy, or what we called the Matrix, that transduces energy from the Field into the Bionet, via the aura. And mitochondria being sensitive to EM fields, can directly get what they need, thus the DNA is 'fed.'

But something has to signal and 'feed' those elements to keep them going, not to live forever, but to at least get the "threescore and twenty years" that even the Bible spoke about (Ps 90:10) – the current human body is designed to live to 120 years old – if we can avoid all forms of pollution – food, water, and manmade EMF radiation. Stress and drugs also take a toll.

What this chapter proposes to share are those things that support Transformation by keeping the brain healthier and, in concert with Chapter 4 which supports a healthy body, the average person can live longer, to learn more and develop their spiritual side – and perhaps develop "higher consciousness."

## Consciousness

Having a brain does not bestow consciousness on anyone – some people have a brain and are caught in a medical coma. Others with a brain are asleep at 3 a.m. in the morning and are unconscious. Some people walk around in a daydream and are not consciously aware of where they are or what they are doing. And still others (OPs) do not have a soul and yet are conscious, so the presence or absence of a soul does not confer consciousness on a human. For the most part, consciousness is an awake state, paying attention to the world around us – our senses interacting with sensory input.

So if we are trying to increase our awareness, or find "higher consciousness," just what is it we are trying to do?

> Is higher consciousness the same as enlightenment? The two terms are often used interchangeably.
>
> Does higher consciousness mean one has a high IQ + Intuition? That is definitely getting closer to it.
>
> Does higher consciousness mean one is psychic and can perform feats of clairvoyance and telepathy, and even communicate with Astral beings while walking down the street (i.e., not meditating)?
>
> Is higher consciousness a state that is gained through hypno-regression where one can examine past lives and access universal truth – things not available in a normal waking state? Or is that tapping into the Subconscious?
>
> Is the Superconscious what is meant by higher consciousness?

Certainly we would agree that RA, the channeled entity from 6D, is a being of higher consciousness – he knows more, loves more and lives closer to the Father of Light. It would be acceptable to say that any being that is found to be above Man's level, and in the Hierarchy between Man and the Father of Light, would have higher consciousness. More Light, more power, more awareness, more ability.

Remember that Light is Knowledge, so a being with more Knowledge and Love, like a Jesus would have a higher consciousness. Does this describe something that 3D Man on Earth, right now, is capable of... and should be trying to acquire? Or has the New Age misled us with the terminology and promise?

The first thing we have to do is back up, define some terms, and examine some structures.

## Biology 401: The Brain

Some basic things to know about the brain:

1. There is a **Blood-Brain-Barrier** (BBB) which serves to keep unwanted things in the bloodstream out of the brain. The BBB allows the passage of water, some gases, and lipid [fat] soluble molecules by passive diffusion, as well as the selective transport of molecules such as glucose [sugar], alcohol, and amino acids that are crucial to neural function. On the other hand, the BBB normally prevents the entry of potential neurotoxins. Unfortunately, gasoline, rabies, Alzheimer's **amyloid-beta plaque**, latent HIV, and prions (from Mad cow) can cross the BBB. [190]

2. The average brain contains **100 billion neurons** at birth. And some neurons do regenerate (Neo-cortex) so that the brain, if given the nutrients that it needs, can constantly regenerate itself. Whereas DNA renews itself every 2 months, your red blood cells are renewed every 4 months, and **the brain rebuilds itself in a year**. **Synapses** (connections between brain cells [neurons]) are created as needed so that the average adult may have 500 trillion synapses… which decrease with age. [191]

3. Neurons can often have 7000 or more branches to other neurons thus creating many interlinked passages to multiple parts of the brain, facilitating recall, analysis, synthesis, comparison, creativity and stimulating physical reactions. Calcium is a very important mineral (as Ca+ ion) in the function of the brain, but it must be regulated.

4. The brain weighs about 3 pounds, is about 60% fat, uses 40% of the body's energy, and we only use an estimated 2% of our mental potential. [192] Information in the brain travels at approximately 268 mph along the neural pathways. [193]

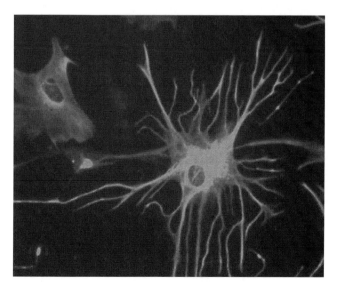

**Glial (Astrocyte) Cell**
(credit: http://en.wikipedia.org/wiki/Glia)

5. The brain is composed largely of glia and neurons. The **Glial cells** (also called Astrocytes) support the neurons, keep neurons in place and isolate them, and supply nutrients and oxygen to the neurons. The significance is that the **heart also has glial cells** and glia are sensitive to electromagnetic (EM) fields. The heart and the brain communicate via the Bionet between their glial cells. Both glial cells and neurons have DNA.

The brain is a physical organ, and interacts with the body and the heart. When the person dies, the soul leaves, and the brain/body/mind component stops functioning. But there is a missing component…

## Mind Anatomy 401

The mind is a primary aspect of the **soul**, and there is lower mind and higher mind. How does the soul fit into this arrangement? There is more than just the body – brain – heart schema… we incarnate into a body and learn to operate the body and brain (via the Bionet and *chi*). We use the Mind via a 3$^{rd}$ layer of the aura (which is empowered through the ZPE Matrix transducing energy through the aura into the body).

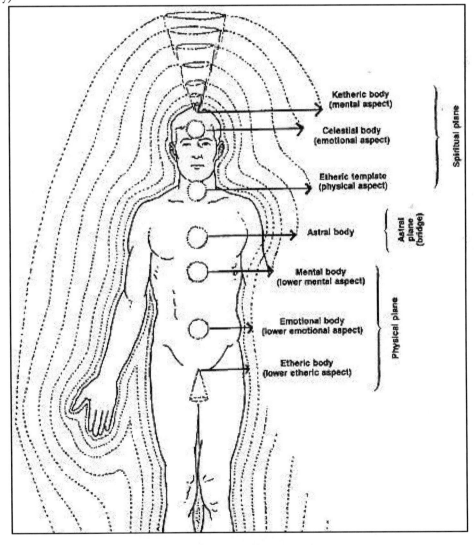

**The Seven-layer Aura System**
(credit Barbara Brennan, *Hands of Light.*)

Note that for most people, the **lower mental aspect** is controlled via the third chakra (or solar plexus or ego seat) and corresponds to the third layer of the aura. The **higher mental aspect** is accessed through the crown chakra (#7, top of the head).

*Chapter 11 in the beginning has a picture of a girl and her etheric aura, or first-level aura.*

A lot of people live their whole lives through the lower 3 chakras – labelled etheric-emotional-mental. This is the **Physical Plane** (no spiritual aspect). While they have the upper chakras, many times they are not all "open" or functioning, but if they are very compassionate, chakra #4 (the heart) is open and functioning. The astral body (chakra #4) shown above is also related to the "silver cord" connecting the soul to the body if the soul astral projects, or goes OOBE (out-of-body experience)... see Chapter 10, first picture.

Notice that chakras 5 – 6 – 7 repeat the etheric – emotional – mental aspect again, only on the **Spiritual Plane**. When the crown chakra (#7) is open, the person has higher awareness, higher consciousness, because s/he is connected to their Higher Self which communicates or connects via this chakra. In most people this chakra is barely functioning and thus the person is not enlightened.

As was said in VEG, Chapter 5, OPs have no soul and operate largely out of their lower 3 chakras. There is no spiritual aspect or understanding to them at all. They have little or no conscience.

Note that the chakra 7 connection with the Higher Self results in **Conscience**. Conscience is an aspect of the soul and its connection with a higher sense of what is right and wrong.

Playing rock-em-sock-em videos where the goal is to stalk and shoot something, will 'lock' the person into their lower 3 chakras (survival – power – ego)... a very physical plane... and pornography does the same thing. This is not good for an ensouled human. A soul should be developing all upper chakras as follows:

Chakra 4 – compassion
Chakra 5 – speaking the truth, wisdom
Chakra 6 – higher knowledge, insight
Chakra 7 – connection with Higher Self, Enlightened

Light (Knowledge) is gained via chakras 6 & 7 to the extent that they are "open" (i.e., active and receiving energy). It is the intent and pursuit of true Knowledge that begins to open these two chakras, and the more Light one acquires (via meditation, reading, insights...) the more the chakra is encouraged to become operational.

Conversely, no interest in spiritual issues, and a diet of violent videos (or TV shows) does not activate them.

## Enlightenment

So now we can see what the answers are to the questions preceding the 'Biology 401: The Brain' section.

> Higher consciousness is basically the same as Enlightenment. The person has access to Higher Truth as well as demonstrates a higher perception of Life.

> Higher consciousness usually involves a higher IQ, Intuition and some degree of psychic ability. The PFV is higher.

> *When you know more, more is expected of you by the Higher Beings.*

## Consciousness 401

The remaining question related to the different levels of the Mind. How does the Conscious relate to the Subconscious and those two to the Superconscious?

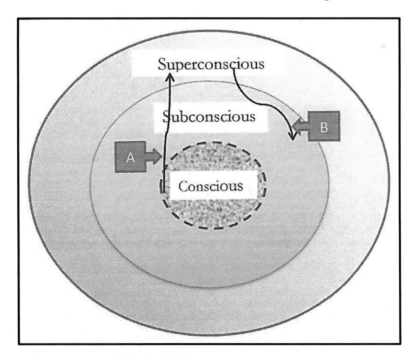

Note that (**A**) the Conscious communicates with the Superconscious via the Subconscious, and (**B**) the Superconscious communicates with the Subconscious. The Conscious does not communicate directly with the Superconscious – until the 7<sup>th</sup> chakra is activated. In addition, (**A**) often happens during meditation, and (**B**) is usually a hunch, insight – or communication during sleep.

Just as interesting is two men who did not know each other, but each came up with a similar explanation of how Reality works.

**Ernest Holmes**, in the 1920's-30's founded the principles called Science of Mind, as part of the teachings of the Religious Science Church. He proposed the following schema to explain how things come to be in our world:

The Universal Power moves through Mind and Particularizes the Result.

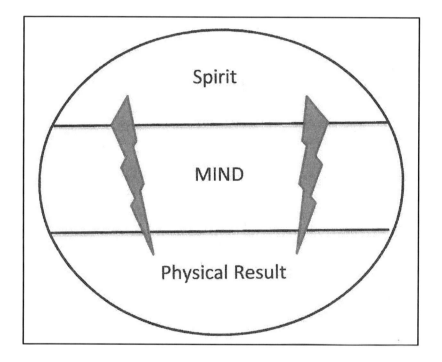

**Edgar Cayce**, in the 1940's who founded the A.R.E. (Association for Research and Enlightenment), said something similar during Readings for clients while channeling a Higher Being:

The Spirit is the Life…

Mind is the Builder…

The Physical is the Result.

The above paradigm is the New Age source for the claim that we can create our day. Note that <u>we</u> don't do the creating; we hold an intention or desire, or concept **in mind**, visualize it, affirm it, and the result is <u>done for us</u> by Spirit, or God, The One, or the Universal Force of Creation. And that again is if our Script doesn't prohibit it – which is why most people cannot 'manifest' and some can't <u>attract</u> what they want.

Now that we know more about the brain and its relationship to the mind, body and soul, and the chakra system, it should be clear that we are going to have to find a way (short of awakening *kundalini*!) to get the energy to step up the energy vibration (PFV) and activate the chakras. The Spiritual Plane is accessed and supported by the top 3 chakras.

The Crown chakra is the key to establishing a connection with the Higher Self so that we can be enlightened… the #7 chakra will definitely let in more Light and serve to empower the body/mind and soul in higher consciousness. Gopi Krishna in Chapter 12 was trying to do this via **kundalini** and almost killed himself – the higher energy is nothing to casually work with.

That leaves 4 other ways to effect changes in the DNA and consciousness:

1. Practice **advanced Qigong** – to acquire, store and manipulate *chi*, and in the higher forms it improves one's ability to transduce energy from the Matrix, control it with the mind, and consciously activate the higher chakras. This can take years.

2. Get abducted by **the Greys** and have them "rewire" your DNA and neural pathways/connections in the brain – via their technology.

3. Have an **Near Death Experience** (NDE), briefly cross over to the InterLife , expose oneself (the soul) to the higher energy there and return to Earth with the higher consciousness potential activated.

4. Use **Ayahuasca** or LSD or some 'recreational' drug to invite a different view of Reality – and it may not be wonderful. It certainly is not something whose effects will last, to say nothing of the potential psychological side effects, and potential physical damage to brain and liver cells.

So in essence, there is no fast, easy way to acquire higher consciousness. While Yoga and Meditation may be fun and interesting, they do not always produce a higher state of mind. The chakras, Bionet, DNA and brain must be involved in any Transformation. It is a total "upgrade."

**Let's Be Practical**

Let it be clearly pointed out at this stage that Man is **purposely limited** in 3D Earth, and while it is a School, it must be kept in mind that the

New Age suggestion that we can acquire higher consciousness and thus become a god (or develop one's godhood) while on Earth is not what it is about. Developing higher consciousness **is** the first step to developing one's Soul. While this is noble, please note that very few people on Earth have ever sat down, expanded their awareness, then walked on water.

Those that you might name, did not develop self here – they incarnated from a higher Realm with the abilities they displayed here (Sai Baba for one, Paramahansa Yogananda, Buddha…) with the mission to enlighten and inspire Man. Yes, Jesus said, "These things I do ye shall do also…." but He didn't mean here because we can't have 5000 Jesuses running around manipulating things at will … and most people would!

Thus caution is advised knowing that if your Script doesn't permit open-ended spiritual development, neither does your DNA and the DNA must change to effect <u>and sustain</u> the higher consciousness connection.

Having said all that, you **can learn to heal yourself**, attract things/people to you, carry more Light, **increase your intuition and discernment**, begin to develop some psychic abilities… and still be a great role model, an exemplary human being… an **Earth Graduate**.

And the way to begin is to look at those practices that harm the body/mind (and stop them), and then consider the safer ways to "rewire" one's DNA by consistently "running energy" through the Bionet (see **Microcosmic Orbit** exercise in Chapter 11), affecting the chakras, and focusing on higher ideals. But, we will want to **first** feed, nurture and extend personal Transformation by supporting the brain. If the brain isn't healthy and running well, the body and mind will not work right.

# Brain Drain

These activities serve to impair brain function, per Dr. Amen, MD: [194]

1. **Physical trauma** to the head.
2. **Drugs**. Cocaine, Marijuana and some legal drugs (Vicodin, Xanax…).
3. **Alcohol** impairs reasoning and response time – think: DUI. People who drink every day have smaller brains than non-drinkers.
4. **Obesity** – being overweight increases the risk for Alzheimer's because lipids in the blood stream can pass the BBB and become **beta-amyloid plaques** in the brain.
5. **Malnutrition** – eating fatty, sugary and calorie-empty foods starves the brain.
6. **Chronic Inflammation/Stress** (excitotoxicity) – constricts blood flow to the brain, thus creating: **Low Blood Flow** – the brain needs a steady supply of oxygen, glucose, and nutrients.

7. **Smoking** – constricts blood flow to the head: Leads to brain atrophy.
8. **Caffeine** – too much caffeine restricts blood flow to the brain.
9. **Violent Video Games** – with brain imaging, video games work in the same area as cocaine and similarly lead to addiction. Physical inactivity also leads to obesity.
10. **Dehydration** -- the brain is 80% water and a lack of water impedes brain function. (See end of Chapter 4.)
11. **Lack of Exercise** – keeps the brain from getting the oxygen and healthy blood flow it needs.
12. **Negative Thinking** – focusing on things you don't like lowers brain activity.
13. **Excessive Texting and Too Much TV** – takes the brain away from the stimulation of social interactions, talking, thinking, and takes time away from exercising which feeds the brain oxygen, blood and nutrients.

## Brain Support

The following are the 3 main areas where one can <u>at least do something</u> to maintain a healthy brain and ward off Alzheimer's, or substantially delay ARD.

### I. Nutrition

This was basically covered in Chapter 4. You know the drill: eat right, drink plenty of clean water, and avoid synthetic sugars and MSG. Reduce your intake of red meat – both for reasons of cholesterol and because there are <u>still recent reports</u> of Mad Cow and some *prions* getting by the inspectors.[195] (*Prions* will turn your brain into what looks like Swiss cheese, like Alzheimers.)

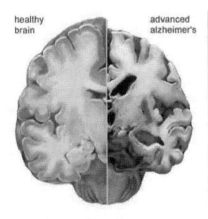 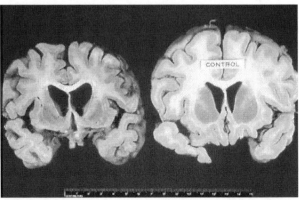

| **Alzheimers Brain** | **Prion Brain** | **Normal Brain** |

(credit all: Bing Images)

**Note that Prions do to the brain what Alzheimers does.**

Be sure to take **vitamins C and E** every day as antioxidants to remove any harmful free radicals. In addition, **Grapeseed Extract** and **Resveratrol** help the brain fight off, and neutralize, free radicals and reduce beta-amyloid plaque which can accumulate in the brain and is thought to cause Alzheimers. [196]

## II. Supplements

The following list of items have all been found to benefit the brain, keeping neurons and synapses healthy, as well as strengthening the Blood Brain Barrier.

**CoQ10** -- Ubiquinol is a better form – empowers the mitochondria to make energy, and is an antioxidant.

**Vinpocetine** – improves oxygenation and circulation.

**Bacopa** – an Ayurvedic herb that shows some promise for memory problems.

**Huperzine A** – claims made for its ability to improve memory and mental function. It blocks an enzyme that breaks down **acetylcholine** (a major and very important neurotransmitter).[197]

**Ginko Biloba** – brain cell oxygenation and circulation.

> **Neurotransmitters are the chemical operatives that connect and communicate between synapses.**

**Omega-3** – (**DHA**) brain has a lot of fat (60%) and this helps to rebuild synaptic connections. Valuable for developing newborns' brains.

**PS** (Phosphatidyl Serine) – improve memory function by increasing/supporting the presence of **acetylcholine**.

**PC** (Phosphatidyl Choline) – works with PS above.

**ALA** (Alpha Lipoic Acid) – protect brain cells from harmful chemicals.

**ALC** (Alpha-L-Carnitine) – build **acetylcholine** and fuel the mitochondria.

**NAC** (N-Acetyl-L-Cysteine) – helps (re-)build **Glutathione** a major detoxifier. [198]

**Melatonin** – protects cells by increasing antioxidants in the brain.

**Curcumin/Turmeric** – powerful antioxidant, anti-inflammatory – dissolves beta-amyloid plaque and reduce excitotoxicity. People in India eat a lot of curry which contains Curcumin and India has the lowest rate of cognitive decline in the world. [199] (BCM-95 is recommended as it absorbs better.)

> **Excitotoxicity** is a form of inflammation and is also a cause of many neuro-degenerative diseases. The pathological process by which nerve cells are damaged and killed by excessive stimulation by neurotransmitters such as **glutamate** (MSG, NMDA) and similar substances allow excess Ca+ (calcium ions) to build up in the cell/neuron and cell death occurs. It is thought to be a factor in the development of Alzheimers.

## III. Activities

As was said in Chapter 4, exercise is very beneficial to the body and because the body oxygenates during exercise, the brain benefits from the physical exercise. But <u>overdoing exercise</u> also produces free radicals (Super Oxide) which cause damage so in addition to putting **electrolytes** (calcium, sodium, phosphorus ions) back in the body (think: Gatorade®), it is advisable to also take some Vitamins C and E.

The brain needs exercise, too and there are many ways to do this: do crossword puzzles, or Sudoku, or Scrabble, learn a new language, or visit the new website **Lumosity** ® and play the brain games. Do a brain exercise on a regular basis.

Try this exercise[200] to see just how nimble your brain is:

> 7H15 M3554G3
> 53RV35 7O PR0V3
> H0W 0UR M1ND5 C4N
> D0 4M4Z1NG 7H1NG5!
> 1MPR3551V3 7H1NG3!
> 1N 7H3 B3G1NN1NG
> 17 WA5 H4RD BU7
> Y0UR M1ND 1S
> R34D1NG 17
> 4U70M471C4LLY
> W17H 0U7 3V3N
> 7H1NK1NG 4B0U7 17,
> B3 PROUD! 0NLY
> C3R741N P39PL3 C4N
> R3AD 7H15.

(credit: Quibblo.com)

Your brain learns quickly that certain numbers represent letters that they most look like. The 4 looks like an "A" , the 3 is a backward "E", and the 7 looks like a "T" for example.

If you thought that was easy, try this one:

> **I cnduo't bvleiee taht I culod aulaclty uesdtannrd waht I was rdnaieg. Unisg the icndeblire pweor of the hmuan mnid, aocdcrnig to rseecrah at Cmabrigde Uinervtisy, it dseno't mttaer in waht oderr the lterets in a wrod are, the olny irpoamtnt tihng is taht the frsit and lsat ltteer be in the rhgit pclae. The rset can be a taotl mses and you can sitll raed it whoutit a pboerlm. Tihs is bucseae the huamn mnid deos not raed ervey ltteer by istlef, but the wrod as a wlohe.**
>
> **Aaznmig, huh? Yaeh and I awlyas tghhuot slelinpg was ipmorantt!**

(credit: howtoimproveyourmemoryfast.com)

The brain is pretty amazing…. Even if you scramble it more (and follow the same start and end letter rule, but do a bit of a worse scramble)… What does this say?:

**The seignr has amtietdd to the crhgae of benig uendr teh ilnecuefn of allooch adn dusrg wislht dvinirg.** (Answer in box below) [201]

This is a clue as to how the brain processes text. The principle?

> **The olny irpoamtnt tihng is taht the frsit and lsat ltteer be in the rhgit pclae.**

Suggestion: if you could read all of the above texts, you should be able to **speed read** as it is much the same principle.

Lastly, you could also take up Yoga, meditation, or Silva Mind Control or NLP – something to exercise the brain. Try writing a book or magazine article – that will cause the brain to organize, define, and construct meaningful ideas.

> Answer to worse scramble:
> *The singer has admitted to the charge of being under the influence of drugs and alcohol whilst driving.*

## Latest Findings

The above three areas are just a beginning. They provide the <u>foundation</u> for acquiring higher consciousness, because an unhealthy body/brain complex does not support the mind in being all that it can be/do. Perhaps a review of the latest findings in Consciousness, the Mind and the Matrix can suggest and summarize a reasonable path to take.

> See also TSiM for the latest in Brain, Mind and Vision findings.

Since thoughts are torsion waves (Chapter 12), it makes sense that the mind has an effect on our DNA as well as our health. We all know about **psycho-somatics** – the effect of the mind on the body, and there is also **somato-psychic** which is the effect of the body on the mind. (Both largely use neurotransmitters/peptides to effect some of these changes.)

The New Biology has shown that "…the cells of our body are affected by our thoughts and beliefs, and this in turn affects our health and wellbeing on every level." [202]

It has also been shown that

> … genes [DNA] are in fact controlled by **environmental signals**. They are activated by our inner and outer environments. Our inner environment includes our emotions, our biochemistry, our mental processes, our sense of the spiritual… Our outer environment includes the food we eat, the toxins we are subjected to, our social rituals… Our genes are switched on and off in response to signals from these environments. [203] [emphasis added]

According to Dr. Bruce Lipton, there are three things that interfere with the signaling process:

> …**trauma**, when an accident causes a disruption in the brain signal; **toxins**, which interfere with the body's signaling chemistry; and **the mind** [false beliefs and perceptions]. [204] [emphasis added]

The problem is misperception (related to the EFT issues in Chapter 12), and our false belief or inaccurate perception can inappropriately activate genes to produce chemicals that will cause harm to the body – i.e., too much adrenalin or excess cortisol. And of course, there can also be irrational fear that causes dysfunctional behavior.

Dr. Lipton believes that "perception controls biology" and affects behavior. In a similar way, Dr. Carolyn Myss wrote several books centered on the same theme:

## Your biography becomes your biology.[205]

Your thinking, or beliefs, affect your health, your biology. Thoughts can unleash a cascade of biochemicals (hormones, signaling molecules, adrenalin, serotonin…) and significant experiences can trigger genetic changes in our cells. This is called **Epigenetics**. Thus it behooves us to think positively, and if that doesn't work, it would be wise to seek out an EFT Matrix practitioner (Chapter 12) and remove the dysfunctional block(s).

> **Epigenetics** is the science of genes; how they change and what chemical attachments do to alter the behavior of our genes. DNA is rarely a naked helix – it is clothed with other organic molecules that affect the way the gene acts. Epigenetics studies how the attachments are emplaced or removed. [206]

## Brain Development

One of the latest findings (last 20-30 years) has been the finding that the **Pre-frontal Cortex** is the 4th area to develop in the brain. First and most basic was the Reptilian stem, then the Mammalian brain, and the Neo-Cortex and this threesome comprised the known brain until the mid to late 1980s. [207]

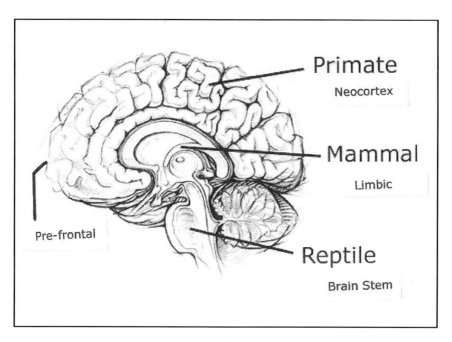

**Four Main Parts of the Human Brain**

The front of the brain (the person's forehead) is on the left. The brain stem becomes the spinal column, and the development of the brain (infant to adult) is typically right-to-left (in above diagram), or **the back of the brain develops first, then progresses to the front.**

What is the significance of this?

The above diagram is relevant to several key points that follow.

According to Joseph Chilton Pearce in *Biology of Transcendence*, the Reptilian brain develops in the first trimester of gestation, the Mammalian develops in the second trimester, and the Neocortex develops in the third, with the **right brain** developing first (creativity), and then the **left brain** ".. with its capacity for analytical logic, abstract thinking, and intellectual power…" (thinking skills). So there is a progression, and the very last to develop is the Pre-frontal Cortex, somewhere AFTER age 15 up to age 21. [208] Note:

> The Pre-frontal Cortex is the seat of our advanced intellectual skills… including …our abilities to compute and reason, analyze, think creatively, and so on. **The left-brain connects to it**, and the right-brain does **not** connect to the Pre-frontal Cortex, but to the older Limbic (emotional) brain. [209] [emphasis added]

And then we note that the **Corpus Callosum** is a bridge between the two halves of the brain. (If you still don't see Design in the brain at this point, please call me to buy a bridge in Brooklyn.)

And Mr. Pearce includes a schematic:[210]

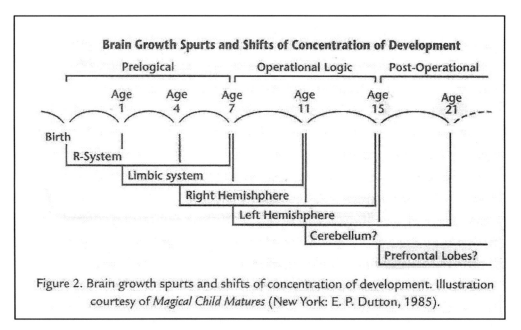

Figure 2. Brain growth spurts and shifts of concentration of development. Illustration courtesy of *Magical Child Matures* (New York: E. P. Dutton, 1985).

**Stages of Brain Development by Age**

Why the anatomy lesson?

At what age does the public education system teach Algebra to students? This is where you will have the opportunity to exercise your brain and connect some dots. If the left hemisphere (diagram above) is only 2/3 developed by age 15, and the Pre-frontal Cortex has not started development, why is public education trying to teach kids Algebra in 7th grade --- at age 12? (This author did not get Algebra until 10th grade under an older school system.)

Why is that important? Again, connect the dots. When a 12-13 year old student is presented with Algebra and cannot understand it, and fails the class… what is s/he going to think about themselves… perhaps for the rest of his/her life? Is this why we have so few students going into math and science these days (and we have to hire foreigners to fill our math/science jobs)? Will that girl or boy think of themselves as just not smart enough to do jobs that pay more, when the problem was their brain had not finished developing so that they could handle analytical topics? Is our Public School System setting the kids up for failure…? Is this one of the reasons kids drop out of school in the 8th grade?

> Our grandkids were subjected to Algebra in 7th grade (age 12) and had a very patient teacher who taught just the fundamentals. One of our boys is an Indigo, very sharp, talks like a 40-year-old and he got it immediately, plus 'A' grades. The other boy, at 12, was struggling and got a 'C' and didn't understand Algebra until 9th grade. Both boys confirmed that most of the girls in 7th grade did not pass Algebra.

You might argue that kids are maturing faster and can handle analytical classes sooner. Maybe the Indigos are, but not according to the studies…

> …during our fifteenth year…. the prefrontal [part of the brain], undergoes its … growth spurt…. Although a preliminary peak of the secondary prefrontal growth occurs at about age eighteen, this new neural **growth is not completed until about age twenty-one.** [211] [emphasis added]

And even more significantly, humans have a problem as they mature…

> Alexander and Langer showed that as each developmental stage [see Fig. 2 diagram above] offers a more advanced intelligence, a significantly smaller percentage of our populace achieves that stage. **The more advanced the intelligence** [unfolding thru the maturation stages] **the fewer the people who develop it**. Ken Wilbur spoke of a pyramid effect in development: the mass of humans clump at the base of the pyramid [basic sensory-motor

stage], and **progressively few are found at each higher level**...[212]
[emphasis added]

Significantly, if some people never develop 100% of their brain potential, as Wilbur suggests above, then these same people cannot expect to develop higher consciousness, either. They can, however, learn, grow, and complete their Script and successfully finish the Earth Path they are on, but it would be mean to tease them with the promise of higher consciousness when they may just be functioning at 85% of normal. It is suggested that an IQ test might be an indicator of current mental acuity...

> For what it is worth, many OPs (soulless humans) do not attain higher consciousness either, because it is a soul-link with a higher aspect of oneself through the 7th chakra and that is not operational in an OP. (Chapter 5, VEG.)

**Enter the Indigos**

Note that this latter issue of incomplete development is another reason the Greys are doing their genetic upgrades, as suggested by Chapters 8-9. Note that **Indigos (aka Hybrids) are a product of the Greys**, as well as other human-looking hybrids that are allegedly being seeded on the planet (i.e., not born here).

> **Case in point**: the grandson above who is an Indigo (rarely cried as a baby, talked at age 2, and at age 4 was building workable Erector-set models) was M's mysterious baby. M was pregnant (sonogram proof), then she wasn't, looked like a miscarriage (no baby in the womb!), then she was pregnant again and it weighed more, and the doctor swore it had changed sex... first a girl, then missing baby, and then a boy was born. (This all makes sense when you know what the Greys are doing.)

While traditional children may be at a loss with "progressive" public education, the Indigos certainly aren't and maybe that is the answer to having less ADD students in our classrooms... Indigos would be just bored with a clunky pace, and may have behavioral issues – so they don't need Ritalin®.

Something to think about.

Lastly, let's examine those fields around us and consider whether we can use them to create more than healing.

**Field Entrainment**

Since we are surrounded by several fields, our aura, the ZPE Matrix , the Heart's torus, and Sheldrake's Morphic Resonance Field, we can see that our body's Bionet is living within this "sea" of energy. That means that our cells, DNA, heart and mind are also operating within this Field. The Matrix thus empowers and affects us at the cellular level… including our DNA. This is how being in the presence of a Jesus, Krishna, or some Higher Being when they appear to us, can impact our consciousness – our cells/DNA or personal morphic field is **entrained** to a faster/higher level.

The problem is that **we cannot generate the entrainment by ourselves**, and we cannot cause our personal field to vibrate faster and force higher consciousness on the mind. Even Sufi twirling (Chapter 12) was an ecstatic high for several minutes but it was not a permanent state. **Hemi-Sync®** is a great product for meditation, but it does not produce higher consciousness that lasts (it might work for OOBEs). Basically, **it has to be done from without, by another being who already is at the higher level.** Such is what happened to this author during the Est training (1979), and during a personal Visit by Higher Beings in October 1998.

So is it hopeless to seek higher consciousness?  No.  Following the guidelines in this book, and the last few chapters, will make a positive difference in one's body/brain complex. Chapter 4 was for the body and this chapter is for the brain/mind.  If a person really makes the effort to "clean up" and eat right, think right, seek out higher teachings and teachers, it will not go unnoticed. Don't forget the Beings of Light who stand ready to guide and protect are always watching – and if ASKED, they can do as much for you as you can accept (according to your belief system),  or your Script will allow.  I know because it was done for me.

## Summary

The caveat is to not get carried away and eat, sleep and drink the New Age promise that Man now can develop higher consciousness and thus "create his day." While we <u>can make some progress</u> in this direction, the New Age teaching is basically designed to sell books, seminars and cruises where the aspirant will believe for a while, chase every opportunity to grow, then experience the frustration of <u>not</u> waking up one morning to a new state of Enlightenment – unless it is to wake up and discover that the bank account is now empty!

It is sad to see progressive Christians become dissatisfied with their religion, wanting more, to know more and be able to be more of an enlightened human, and move over into the New Age realm and find that they have just traded one set of ideas for another. Just as Christians are told that Jesus died for their sins, the New Age promises a form of godhood… and the seeker has just signed on for whatever **archetypal lessons** (Glossary) and experiences go with the Christian or New Age paradigms. There may be some unwanted surprises in either camp. (This was much more fully examined in Chapter 14 of VEG.)

It seems to be the way of this planet that it is very hard to discover or know the Truth (which leads to Enlightenment). Yet I would suggest that that ideal is the **catalyst** that keeps us moving and learning, despite the reality is that no religion on Earth has it all correct. "You takes yer choice and takes what you get." Remember that **futility** is what it is all about – it is what is required to **detach from the world**, from false beliefs (those beliefs that don't work), from the material, from the appearance … and finally move on in the Father's Multiverse.

Do the best you can with what you've got. Clean up your act, eat right, exercise body and mind, and <u>do seek</u> higher consciousness… the trip itself is worth the effort even if you never attain the goal! Gaining Knowledge and Experience is what it is all about. Realize that you are an eternal soul having an Earth experience and if you don't like it, consider not coming back… because you don't have to. If you are fed up with the futility of finding enlightenment, but have enough Light, you are ready to graduate. Again, that was the real goal:

**Earth Graduates** are highly respected and valued Over There.

**Namaste!**

# Appendix A:  The Dark Night of the Soul

In any book about the Transformation of Man, there has to be a word said about the Transformation process itself and what it looks like and what it does for the person going through it. Sometimes it is not wonderful and uplifting; it can be very confusing and frustrating. And yet, it is worth it and is not something to be feared.

All souls will go through the process from darkness to light, from ignorance to wisdom, and all will eventually discover and develop their inner divine potential.

**Overview**

How does it happen?  Is there a way to initiate the transformation process? Can it be stopped or controlled?  The following is a brief attempt to answer those questions. Brief, because there have been whole books written on the subject, and two of the best were written by spiritual aspirants whose lives were dedicated to the Church:

The Interior Castle,  St. Teresa of Avila
The Dark Night,       St. John of the Cross

See also:

Sacred Contracts,    Dr. Caroline Myss
(examined in Ch 4 of TSiM.)

It is not necessary to be a nun or a monk to initiate the process. It isn't even a requirement that one be an ascetic, fast, become a Vegan, meditate, do Yoga or do penance. It is enough to have the **intention and sincere desire** to expand one's consciousness, which is really what is going on, and at least read high quality spiritual books and attempt to walk in peace with your fellow Man, practice patience, compassion, humility and respect for all living things (people, animals, and Mother Earth).

Of course, it can help to meditate, stop eating animals (become a semi-vegetarian), and perhaps do Rolfing or massage (which could elicit the release of buried emotions and cell memories) but that is not required either. And for some people, it is "their time" and is part of their Script this time around, and some event may trigger the process quite unexpectedly.

> In a word, the Dark Night of the Soul is the central mystery in the evolution of  human consciousness on this planet. [213]

The Father of Light does the work in a soul who is ready. Should one try to force the issue by doing Yoga and special exercises to raise the *kundalini*, the results can be disastrous. That route to **Higher Consciousness** must have a spiritual teacher (guru) as a guide who knows what to do, in stages, and what to do if the *kundalini* comes up too fast as it can injure or kill a naïve practitioner. If the Father of Light and His ministers of the Light are in charge of the process, it is a very gradual awakening and there is no need for a guru.

**Enlightenment** is the result of the Dark Night of the Soul, and it doesn't care what a person's religion is. Yet, Buddhists and Hindus have a head start in the process in that their religion talks about the awakening of the soul, the *kundalini*, and they encourage meditation and Yoga. The Christians, on the other hand, are taught to avoid the "spooky stuff" of alternate religions and pray, fast and seek the **Baptism of the Holy Spirit** … which is effectively the same thing.

If an aspirant seeks enlightenment through drugs, ayahuasca, peyote or LSD, there can be severe reactions… unless you are a shaman in training in a 3rd world country and the elders are there to guide you.

> I know a person who opened up to the **kundalini** by the use of street drugs. In this person, the "fire" burned for months, almost incapacitating the person. That person is still recovering under the guidance of a spiritual master. I have also known of several priests who by

intense spiritual exercises, opened themselves to the energies of infused contemplation.….Their inner battle between head and heart resulted in disaster. They ended up in mental hospitals after suffering nervous breakdowns. [214]

It is serious fire from Above.

The *kundalini* can empower or maim a person; the initiate must be taught how to control and use the Heavenly Fire.

**(source: www.bing.com/images)**

**Kundalini Energy**

## Initial Stages

In the beginning, there is an increased awareness via the senses, and for many, the path begins with what has been called a **Peak Experience**. The whole world comes alive, colors and sounds are so much more pronounced, there is a sense of joy in the little things, and one may receive insights along the way. That is the blessing of the path to enlightenment.

The down side can be a purging of one's emotions and past life memories, all coming up in a torrent of negativity that produces depression. Often what renders it a "dark night" is the fact that in order to go higher into an enlightened consciousness, which has faster and finer vibrations (energy), one must drop the baggage of negative emotional and mental vibrations. Thus begins for many a **'healing crisis.'** One often feels a complete separation from God, a dryness in their spiritual practice, one no longer prays or goes to church, and nothing quite seems right in their life.

So the first step is the cleansing of the body-mind complex.

At other times, the higher, subtle energy coming into the psyche from the Higher Realms is more exquisite than anything we have ever felt before. And this is often the second step in the process after the clearing of old baggage – which may take years. The negative vibrations that we usually carry with us in our walk-a-day world are slow and dense and have to be transformed or removed before the finer, more subtle energies can flow in and through us.

> The negative emotional vibrations are most often locked away by **denial** in the shadow sections of the person's astral body [i.e., the aura]. [215] [emphasis added]

When we deny that we have problems, hate or resentment, "sins," unforgiveness, or any refusal to accept that we are imperfect beings, we are in for trouble. There is a tendency of humans to pretend that they are OK, and deny that they have emotional issues or faults – these must be admitted to so they can be cleared away. The New Age boldly suggests that we "act as if" we are what we wish we were, and on the other hand, when faced with problems, "ignore it and it will go away" – both are stupid teachings that keep the problem(s) in place – and as such they block true spiritual progress. (See Chapter 12, EFT modalities to remove them.)

By the same token, we don't want to dwell on our faults and get into negative self-talk as that reinforces the current state of negativity. And, positive affirmations will not work, even if you say them 100 times a day – **if** you really don't believe the affirmation, but just hope it is true and should have the desired effect. Your subconscious belief system and self-image can make or break your progress.

Also do not fall into the trap of trying to be a saint in one day. It takes time for the subtle energies to do their work, gradually, and thoroughly, without any adverse physical or mental effects. As the Father of Light does the work, the purging of old energies and memories will be done in the safest way possible, and if you resist, and cannot go with the Flow, it will take a lot longer.

## The Flow

There is a natural flow to the process of gaining Higher Consciousness, and it involves having the patience to 'tough it out' when the going gets rough (i.e., too much clearing happens at once) and even people around you wonder what the heck is going on – hopefully you don't lose your job if you seem to be so **distracted by the process** that you can't do your job. Some relationships may suffer during this time, hopefully not leading to divorce. But it is easy to be distracted and not think clearly, and misunderstand others as they try to relate to the new, developing you – Heck, you don't even know who you are or what you want at this point! Memory may fail occasionally, and the slightest things may upset you – all because the energies have you 'dancing' in all directions at once.

Welcome to the Dark Night.

Being in the Flow, constructively, is like putting your canoe into a river, with no paddle, and sitting back and letting the river have its way. It is a little scary because **you cannot control the process**, and like a surgery, you don't want to stop half way through – even if you could. The Flow is going to do its work, its way. Trust that you will move <u>through</u> the process and come out the other side much better off. This calls for **patience and a zipped lip** – the only thing to resist during this time is a verbal response that upsets others: yelling, swearing or attacking the other person.

Be careful to not dwell on what is wrong, turn to drinking or drugs, as this generates negative vibes and will attract to you negative Thoughtforms (Chapter 7) or Parasites which will amplify the situation. Try to remember that it is just <u>a</u> <u>process</u>, a flow of higher energies that are having their way with your Shadow Side, raising and removing buried emotions and memories – clearing the decks for a brighter tomorrow.

The Night is a rude awakening to one's Shadow Side and the more you fight it, thrash and make excuses, the longer it will take to come out the other side into the Light. Resistance to the Flow will lengthen the process.

## Moving Forward

Fun times, vacations, spiritual reading, and soft soothing music all help to move forward. One will also learn **patience**, **humility and compassion** for oneself and for others! During this time, one must really watch what one thinks and says as the increase in higher, finer energies in your being, as the Flow does its work, will amaze you: your words have more power to affect the world around you. If you are down with a cold, you will find that you have an increased ability to get well faster. You will find that you just seem to have the right words to encourage another person when they need it.

> If you watch what you think, what you say will take care of itself.

You will find that as the darkness and confusion start to lift, you go back to church, or even seek out a more spiritual church, and you enjoy the service more than before. Your higher consciousness may want to be 'fed' in a new way… and the old haunts don't mean what they used to. And you may find that you can't watch TV shows that are too violent where everybody is running, yelling and shooting everybody else… your sensitivities now won't let you watch 'blood and guts' shows. Your taste in food, drink and clothing may also change… and you may now want a different kind of life partner.

As we continue to grow, the distraction and pain grow less, and the soul feels lighter. It is a sign of the process that you can now feel a connection with The One, even with your Higher Self, and you will start to feel a **connection with other souls** – realizing that we are all connected at the soul level. You will soon start to receive insights and direct communication from a higher part of yourself – messages that were always there but you couldn't hear them because your emotional 'stuff' was in the way.

Spiritual revelations and even **psychic abilities** (usually clairvoyance comes first) will emerge, and it is important to not share these with just anybody. It is part of the higher walk that we are now led by the Spirit and can help other people most by being there for them, sharing a good word, or praying with/for them. You will start to realize that **your prayers are heard and most of them are answered**. You let the Father do the work and just roll along in the Flow, knowing that the other person is in his river and may have some lessons to learn (so you don't attempt to remove or fix them), and you relax in knowing that their needs will be met, just as yours are.

You will feel **psychologically stronger and more integrated**. Whereas you used to feel fragmented, with conflicting ideas and wants, you now live and move as a unified whole. So you have more energy, and better health – you may even feel an urge to implement the items in Chapter 4 to improve your physical health. You have a new awareness and understanding of the world around you – and herein a new problem often pops up.

## New World View

You are more integrated, more 'centered' in your new energies, and all of a sudden, one day, you notice that the world around you is not in synch with the new you – you suddenly become aware that there is a lot of negativity and error around you. You start to notice that the world is messed up: people lying, bureaucrats screwing the people, false flag activities that are now obvious to you as you have a higher level of **intuitive discernment** – you see through things that used to puzzle you.

You achieved a higher level of awareness only to see more of the death, disease and deception!? Aaarrgh! It is paradoxical: with higher consciousness **you are aware of more** – even the bad stuff that you thought you would transcend. You now get it all: the good, the bad and the ugly.

This is where **the gods are now 'grounding' you** – to keep you from flying off and mentally dwelling in higher realms where you are of no earthly good. There is now a part of your consciousness that is down-to-earth. You are now able to see both the actual world around you, and the invisible world is beginning to show itself (in dreams, visions, insights...). This is not a test, but will call for you to remember who you are, where you came from and **meet the adversities with compassion** and a realization that this is Planet Earth, the Earth School, and everything is just as it should be for souls to meet their lessons.

The only caveat now is to **avoid feeling superior** and 'above it all' – that is a sure trip back into the lower densities you just came from. Because you see more and understand more, you now have the opportunity to get involved and do more. You don't have to, it is merely a choice.

## The Next Level

So now you think you have peace and all is settled. Now you can enjoy life.

> The subtle level of consciousness begins with peace after the commotion of the Dark Night of the Senses, and remains largely peaceful for several years while we gain experience and competence at this level. Eventually the peace begins to break down under the onslaught of all these new inner phenomena. The soul energies coming in [from the next higher level] … start breaking up our psychic structure and belief system, and **once again** our emotional balance… begins to be seriously disturbed. [216] [emphasis added]

362

Just when you thought you had it made, it starts again to take you to the next level. It is **a cyclical process** that doesn't end until you exit the planet. As the soul grows, it is tested and challenged more…because you have more inner strength now to handle it. There are new dangers at this level, though.

Everyone on the other Side now sees that you carry more Light. Now you look like a Klieg light in a room of people who are 40w bulbs. Guess who the Discarnates, Parasites, 4D STS (and any Interdimensionals) in the Lower Astral are attracted to? Sure, you now attract the positive Thoughtforms, and most 4D STS entities that see you will usually avoid you (they hate the Light), but there are the Neggs – whose duty is to harass and give you catalyst to grow (in synch with your Script).

### Don't hate them, they are doing their job.

Because we are not completely ascended, we still have a Shadow Side, and the tougher items (even those from past lives) can now be removed because you are stronger… Just acknowledge the Neggs and if they get too busy harassing you, send them Light, and they'll back off for a bit, giving you a rest. The Neggs, like the Beings of Light, are smart and they are just carrying out orders from Above.

### All Is As It Should Be…

Each cycle that one is put through gets shorter and isn't as bad as the first one, nor the last one, and it is important to realize that nothing is out of control. Your (alleged) Guardian Angel and any Higher Beings are not watching your lifetime and saying, "Oh, shoot I wish we had foreseen that…Now what do we do?!"

> In [my] visions, I was shown how everything in the world, down
> to the smallest detail, positive and negative, operates with absolute
> perfection under the direction of a **multidimensional intelligence**
> so awesome that there is no way to describe it…
> God's supreme intelligence permeates even a perfectly mundane
> experience…[217]   [emphasis added]

And that Intelligence is programmed into the Heavenly Bio-Computer which operates the Greater Script (Chapter 7). **There are no accidents and nothing is out of control**. Relax, ship oars, and go with the Flow.

The Bible says it:

> Consider it pure joy, my brothers, whenever you face trials of
> many kinds, because you know that the testing of your faith
> develops perseverance. **Perseverance** must finish its work so
> that you may be mature and complete, not lacking anything.
>
> *James 1:2-4*

In the final analysis, it is the Father's will that no soul perishes nor is lost. When we reach a Dark Night of the Soul, **the Beings of Light have us under intense 24-hour surveillance**. If necessary, an Angel will be sent to guide, comfort, or deliver a message to a lost or stressed soul.

And remember: no matter what you go through, it is not the Drama that counts, but the change in consciousness and development of the soul's awesome potential. And the goal is to use the higher abilities in some dynamic aspect of the Father's Multiverse. That is called **Transformation.**

# Appendix B:   George Carlin – Earth Graduate

The late George Carlin was my favorite comedian and he was an outstanding humanitarian – he really cared about people. He cleverly used humor to get people to look at themselves in areas where it was obvious that we all need to improve: our thinking and behavior.  And the man himself went through a **transformation** before he died in 2008 (when Book 1 was written – George would have loved VEG).

Whereas he started out as a funny guy making jokes about all sorts of things – refrigerators, smoking pot, traffic, weathermen, oddities in the English language, religion, and dropping a blunt social commentary from time to time, his humor drastically changed in his last 5 years to more of a negative tone, often called 'black humor.' He no longer saw Man's foibles as funny, and people had not responded to his original humor by acknowledging and correcting their habits… so it was time to break out the heavy artillery: biting social commentary.

He was always controversial and was arrested for saying the "seven dirty words" that you can't say on TV (1972).  He challenged the social norm, realizing that we often live in a box others have created for us and his technique was to try and shock people out of the box.

The pictures below show the change from stand-up comic in T-shirt to his later years when he was addressing the problems in education, government, and the environment, trying to create an awareness of our plight on Earth to hopefully effect social change.

**Images credit: Wikipedia:  http://en.wikipedia.org/wiki/George_carlin**

## Personal Transformation

Carlin's attitude on life went from irreverent to satirical to depressing nihilism.

One of his earlier routines poked fun at weathermen (who could be wrong and still keep their jobs):

> Al Sleet, the "hippie-dippie weatherman"—"Tonight's forecast: Dark. Continued dark throughout most of the evening, with some widely scattered light towards morning." [218]

In contrast, one of his later comments just years before his death:

> I look at it this way... For centuries now, man has done everything he can to destroy, defile, and interfere with nature: clear-cutting forests, strip-mining mountains, poisoning the atmosphere, over-fishing the oceans, polluting the rivers and lakes, destroying wetlands and aquifers... so when nature strikes back, and smacks him on the head and kicks him in the nuts, I enjoy that. I have absolutely no sympathy for human beings whatsoever. None. And no matter what kind of problem humans are facing, whether it's natural or man-made, I always hope it gets worse.[219]

Obviously he won no friends with that statement – even though he was on target.

What happened to George was: a rough childhood wherein he did not get along with his mother who divorced his father, not finishing high school (because he questioned everything), followed by not fitting in in the military (court-martialed 3 times and then discharged), losing his first wife, three heart attacks, hospitalized for severe pneumonia, and several years on LSD, marijuana and followed up with rehabilitation therapy… Those kinds of things, if found in one's **LifeScript**, will wake you up and call for a reappraisal of what you think life, death, and the world really are.

> If we evaluate his life in terms of VEG, Chapter 7, it is obvious that he was an **Old Soul** whose inner guide had problems with the hypocrisy and "American BS" – he finally did what his Script called for: critique and try to wake people up.

Asked if he believed in God, he thought back to his abortive religious training, and said "I worship the Sun because I can see it." And he (allegedly) prayed to Joe Pesci because he seemed like a man who could get things done! [220] George did believe in a Supreme Intelligence, however.

He was always looking for the genuine side to life, and trying to be as authentic as possible. One of his favorite comments was:

> When you're born, you get a ticket to the Freak Show. And if you're born in America, you get a front row seat. And some of us get to sit there with notebooks, and I make notes, and I talk about it and make up stuff about it… we're all the same, but I'm apart now, separate because I don't have a stake in the outcome… (YouTube, 2008) [221]

He saw people in America as slaves to the Media, fashion, TV, always being told what to wear, whom to venerate, and what to eat, and what to drive… not thinking for themselves… He said the average person had a limited intellect (remember Schwarzenegger in Chapter 11?) … hence their unpredictable and nutty behavior (which he had always poked fun at), and in his later years he found **depressing** because he saw it as getting worse, turning Americans into hopeless sheeple.

> *In some ways, Book 1 has echoed the same sentiment. Man does need to wake up and activate his divine potential. Due to Anunnaki genetics, Man has a real problem, and that is why the Greys are here (Chapter 8).*

## Social Commentary

It is his social commentaries that are the focus of this Appendix. The significance is that when you DO wake up and realize that Man is not all that he could be, you are either going to laugh at it (as George did initially), or freak out. As it goes on and on and on, you just can't laugh any more… the stupidity and dysfunctional behavior of a lot of humans is a sickness that saps the very vitality of our country and cancels our future.

In other words, **sometimes transformation is not what it is cracked up to be**. It is like a man who has an old coin and he keeps it in a box in the dresser… he looks at it every now and then, and he really loves the front side of the coin, but hates the ugly design on the back. So he wishes he could make the coin bigger and really enjoy the front side. An angel shows up, ready to grant his wish, and asks him if he really wants to enlarge the coin – knowing that the backside will also have to be enlarged. The man wants to enlarge only the front side, and the angel explains that that is not what will happen – he will **get both the beautiful and ugly** enlarged. The man gives up.

When we become more enlightened, we will see more of the world around us, and we will see the good, the bad, and the ugly – in spades! More good, more beauty, and more death and disease, and because you now carry more Light, there are Astral entities who will also notice you now (you stand out from those around you), and you may be harassed (although physically protected) like never before.

What happened to George was a measure of enlightenment that allowed him to see the world and people around him as they really were, but it becomes difficult to handle, and people don't understand what you are telling them, **they don't know how they look to others,** and a lot don't care, and the world goes on in the same mediocrity as before! Now you are the **Foole on the Hill** who sees it all go by, you are not part of it, you can't stop it, and you are alone – unless you can find others with whom you can live and communicate. This was George's predicament.

Witness a very scathing and insightful comment of his:

> I don't really care about this species [Man]… this was part of [my] **transformation** in the 90's… I realized I didn't really care about the outcome on this planet… I think **this was a species that was given great gifts [brain and language] and had great potential and squandered them**….
> It is commerce and religion that have ruined and spoiled the potential of this species… and **this country is the leader in the decay of the soul**… My anger is a reflection of disappointment and disillusionment… and being **let down by my species**…. Such **great possibilities are not being realized.**
>
> We are just circling the drain… no one wants to cause any waves so we are just in a downward slide [as a country]…. **I gave up on my species** … and my countrymen… we gave it all up for primitive super-stition [too much passing the buck via 'God's Will']…we can't figure it out so we limit our thinking and then we want a toy, a gizmo [to feel better: George suggested "a cellphone that makes pancakes!"]…and all of that is nothing. We devolved into getting more than our neighbor… materialism rules… and it isn't getting better… it can't… (YouTube, 2008) [222]   [emphasis added]

## You Have to Unplug

Wow. George spoke more and more like a wise Sage sitting on a hill watching the nonsense go by… and **he wisely unplugged** from the circus as he had already had 3 heart attacks and didn't need a fourth! If you care, you may pay the price in health issues! At some point, as VEG suggests, you DO unplug and clean your own house and stop trying to stop/change/fix the world around you … George will not be coming back to Earth (he doesn't have to) – he has already Graduated – he got the message, woke up, told a few people… and he became an **Earth Graduate**.

Despite the potty-mouth, George had it together. It was his anger over our suppressed potential that delivered some choice words from time to time. He wasn't perfect, but …

### You don't have to be perfect to graduate.

So is there any point to becoming a transformed person? Yes, just do not expect to have everything in your life be rosy, peachy-keen where you have no problems and you smile all the time… that is another lie from the New Age hucksters (Chapter 3).

The New Age tells us that we should be happy all the time – if we're not, something is wrong! For proof, listen to Pharrell Williams' *Happy* video on YouTube…. 'Just ignore adversity, don't let it get to you and bring you down' – a good point – but his overall message is to be happy no matter what – yet we <u>are</u> here to deal with it, and he doesn't support that.

You DO want to wake up and gain the Light to get out of here. You really do want to see it all – the good, bad and the ugly. That way, knowing the truth, you can make intelligent and appropriate choices… Your task, and it is part of transformation, is to grow up and handle what you encounter. That is why the Graduate is so well **respected** on the Other Side.

Is caring wrong, then? Should we ignore social issues, others' problems, and pollution? No, no, and no. You DO NOT go out of your way to attack injustices or pollution. Just be aware that if something is in your path, basically right in front of you, you are to (1) offer whatever assistance you can, not worry about it, and (2) stay aware of what you are doing – i.e., don't get sucked into the Drama of "ain't it awful" and moan and groan in the Pit with the others. Help if you can, don't worry about the outcome… and move forward. (See Chapter 10 treatment of this issue.)

Insensitive? No, remember that **nothing is out of control** and you can earn the shackles of Karma if you try and fix something that another person is to work through themselves!

### Do not remove their lesson!

Case in point: a woman healer I knew healed cancer in a friend, yet **the cancer kept coming back** – because the cancer victim was to learn something (discipline and self-care) from it – and when she did, the cancer disappeared by itself!

## Transforming Man

Transformation sees beauty, Love and Knowledge AND it also sees death, decay, and ignorance. The hardest problem to handle in becoming enlightened, or gaining higher consciousness, or becoming transformed is handling the **futility**. It is with you every day, you experience it every time you sense the difference between yourself and your fellow (unenlightened ) Man – they don't know, they don't care, and you can't do anything to wake them up! And you <u>want to</u> because you see the problem: You are all in a tunnel and the others are excited about seeing the light at the end of the tunnel – only you know it's the headlight of an oncoming train!

They don't believe you, you can't help them, and you are stuck with the unbelievable **impossibility** of trying to make a positive difference in their lives. With your greater knowledge and deeper discernment, you <u>should</u> be able to enlighten them – or at least help them in a minor way… but not so. And that is your key to graduation: you have your last insight… **futility**.

You begin to assimilate the last truth:

> **Man is a fragile creature who wires his truth up early in life and then, against all odds, staunchly maintains what he thinks is truth until he dies… it is as if his brain, behavior, and ability to think are rigid but fragile structures which will break and cause him a nervous breakdown if he so much as considers that something he has known for years is false.**

So you finally detach, you sit back, and clean your own house. That is what George did.

True Transformation does not call for changing or fixing the world. The Drama around you is your catalyst for <u>you</u> to wake up, see things a new way, stop rowing upstream, ship oars, and go with **The Flow** which is now your transformed consciousness. Your greater awareness reached a point where it connected with a Greater Energy which has rewired your DNA, empowering the connection, and thus your discernment. Your heart is in charge now, not your head – people think you are unreasonable and have lost your mind – you have. You went out of your head and now live from the heart and your inner guidance now leads the way. You walk a Path that others cannot see, but **you respect yourself and your Path**.

You are automatically an Earth Graduate.

## Appendix C: Earth School Overview

It has been several times asked, in both VEG and this one,

**"What has to be true about the Earth for it to look the way it does?"**

This is an important aspect of learning the truth while in Earth School. And the answer follows from some key revelations that have already been developed:

**Whereas**:

> ... the Elite (not the PTB) have disclosed on the Internet (i.e., *Hidden Hand* and *Insider* information [see this book's Biblio-Internet Sources]), that they are here to act as catalyst and sometimes do negative things to see if we are paying attention (Think: 9-11 and the Malaysian Flight MH17 [223] events, as well as the Georgia Guidestones, for example);

> ... Shakespeare said that it is all "a Stage" and we all play many parts, hence telling us that this Earth is all Drama and that is has no intrinsic meaning in itself;

> ... given that we are born into the Drama with amnesia, or what has been called the "veil of forgetting" soon after being a baby, we cannot remember who we are, or why we ae here ... unlike the movie *Groundhog Day* where Phil gets to remember what he did each day that didn't work;

> > *The reason we don't get that here is it wouldn't be much of a test if you already knew the answer. They want to see what you will do with what you get – based on the sum of all you have ever learned. That comes from your Ground of Being (see Glossary).*

> ... given that all the reputable channeled info (from RA and my Source) have said that when we are on the Other Side we can know anything we want;

> ... and given that our Drama is full of OPs or NPCs that drive the Drama for the ensouled people, and we have no control over our Scripts or what the Drama does...

**Therefore:**

We can make the following basic determinations from the above points. (key aspects are <u>underlined</u>)

It would have to be a <u>self-contained</u> realm (like an HVR Sphere in quarantine) that <u>simulates</u> like a <u>Holodeck</u> different Eras: each has its own <u>Greater Script</u> which drives the Greater Drama (via OPs and the Control System) wherein souls go to experience <u>catalytic drama</u> designed to <u>test</u>/improve them …. Almost like a Playground but there is also an <u>observed outcome</u> upon which <u>each soul is evaluated</u>:

Did you stay **true to the ideals** of compassion and knowledge (no matter what happened) …?

Did you **act from your existing beliefs** instead of saying one thing and doing another, like a hypocrite…?

And did you suspect that more was going on than met the eye such that you **sought to be more aware** and live from a higher perspective – not letting the negativity overcome you…?

If you saw through the Drama, kept your <u>integrity and respect</u> for yourself , others and the planet, then you <u>rose above</u> the circumstances and demonstrated that you <u>have enough Light</u> to leave 'Kindergarten' and move forward in the Father of Light's Multiverse.

So **Earth was a kind of test** and you passed. You didn't lose your <u>focus</u> (which comes from your inner wisdom). Although you could <u>not control</u> some aspects of your Script, and hence your life sometimes just happened to you, you did make plenty of <u>appropriate choices</u> when a Point of Choice was presented to you. You were not 'at effect' with a lot of your life, wondering, weeping and moaning… and best of all you <u>didn't give up</u>. You handled most of it <u>without 'reactionary drama'</u> on your part.

That is the essence of the Earth School which was designed as an **experiment** by the Higher Beings to accomplish many things for many types of participants – Man, the Elite, PTB, aliens, Alma/Yeti, and first-time souls all get an individually-tailored Script, and then they all pretty much undergo the Greater Script.

Since it is a Drama, it means nothing in itself, and some souls recognized that and stopped trying to control it, or figure it out, or avoid it, or ignore it. Some <u>rose above it</u> and recognized that it is just **catalytic drama** – designed to <u>provoke a</u>

change in thinking or behavior… for the benefit of each soul.

> The Higher Beings watch over the Drama, and if enough (too many) souls fail to rise above it and do not become an Earth Graduate, it means the Drama has degenerated at the hands of the STS component (the PTB principally) and it is now too severe and will have to be reset. This results in a **New Era** being started, with the new Drama carrying a lot of the former Era's issues, but it starts in balance so that it is not overwhelming. Eras are not about harming souls.

> Souls are to be tried and tested, but not to where they are destroyed and that is why the simulation is in quarantine from other 3D entities (Orion Group) who do not have souls and who DO seek to stop or destroy souls (as VEG so pointed out in Chapters 12 and 13.)

Born into a realm with amnesia (you can't remember what your selected goal was before you incarnated) and no handbook to tell you what to do, plus freewill to try and do whatever occurs to you, is a chaotic setup that often leads to confusion and frustration. On purpose. Can you come up with the inner strength to handle it?

> **They want to see if, given no guidebook, you can come up with an appropriate response to whatever They orchestrate for you, that shows Them what your Ground of Being really is. And when it is good enough, you are an Earth Graduate and move on!**

> **And relax – you cannot miss your purpose. You can avoid it, deny it, and screw it up but it will be there waiting when you are finally ready.**

So on Earth, humans make up what they think it is all about – and the blind lead the blind, others adopt the STS influence and don't care and see lying, cheating and stealing as perfectly OK (if they can get away with it), and still others get so frustrated and angry, and sometimes dysfunctional, that suicide or killing other people seems appropriate.

The task before each soul is to survive the Drama with your integrity and higher purpose intact – i.e., Can you see that an STO emphasis on Earth is what works? And to the degree that you served others in a proactive way, you have created "brownie points" for you in a big way on the Other Side! (That's called positive Karma.)

**Steel Assignment**

The emphasis is **not on being perfect** but on STO service and ideals which sustain you though a sometimes rough Earth Drama – **fire produces steel**. And only those who go through it and are tempered enough to survive whatever is thrown at them on Earth, have enough 'grit' to handle some key aspects of the Father's Multiverse (tongue-in-cheek called the **Steel Assignment**) where 'sweetness and light' are not in abundance, and someone has to shepherd and oversee the lost ones (STS oriented) and be able to keep focused to handle them.

It will require all the "tough love" one can muster.

*Note: those souls who are experiencing the "rough Earth Drama" (headed for the fire or are in it!) have signed on to prepare for the Steel Assignment .*

It is not the advanced cultures out there (human and other) that need shepherding, it is the wayward STS Realms that are in a stage of development less than or equal to Earth. Otherwise, not volunteering for that kind of duty (no one makes souls do anything!), an Earth Graduate can choose to become part of the **Maintenance Group** (Akashic Records, Quantum Computer LifeScripts programming, Timeline Control, Soul Regeneration and Imprinting Realm, or Fractal Timeline Overview…even insert oneself into the Generation of New Worlds Group – learn to create matter and make Suns and worlds and work with the Biota Group which populates planets with flora and fauna…. etc.).

Or souls may choose to reincarnate into an alien culture to see what that is like.

But they all have to graduate from the basic Earth School with **all 7** of the following traits – discipline, integrity, compassion, perseverance, humility, respect, and an STO orientation. Not perfect in each one, but at least a workable amount (51% or greater) of each aspect.

**That is why the Earth Graduate is so respected and so much in demand.**

And that is why the Earth School looks the way it does.

# Appendix D: Soul or No Soul?

This topic has been placed in the back of the book because it is not mainstream Transformation, but it is a further examination of the Souls, Consciousness, OPs and Timelines issue which the reader may find interesting. The elements of this appendix were partially developed in VEG, Chs. 1 and 5, and in TOM, Ch. 2, but the two were not correlated – that was left up to the reader. So some review is included herein.

More recent research into Souls and Timelines has revealed that there are definite connections and evidence that supports the idea that there are "two seeds" on planet Earth, at least two, and that there are humans walking among us who have no soul – and for very logical, and substantial reasons. This was hinted at in VEG, Chs5 and 12, just subtly so as to not disrupt the main idea of those chapters.

---

It needs to be emphasized, big time, that the following presentation is for your serious consideration, but is not to be blindly believed. There is considerable evidence that it is correct, else I would not present it, but it should be considered another possible aspect of the world we live in, and at the end of the Appendix, I will suggest how this information could benefit the average, ensouled person.

Beware of Religion and Mainstream Science telling you that this Appendix is based on myth or lies. It is closer to the truth than the politically correct 'experts' out there are willing to admit.

---

Why?

Socrates said "The unexamined life is not worth living" and it is part of one's spiritual growth to discover who you are, where you are, and why you are here. This is a book about spiritual growth. Revealing the following ideas definitely will assist in that – because **you are not living in the world you think you are**, and part of your waking up is actually empowered by the following information (as bizarre as it may initially seem).

There are three intertwining aspects to be examined: **Souls, the soulless, and Timelines.** They come together in a very unique way, that will at least interest you, if not shock you. While you have heard of the soul, it is doubtful the PTB have ever sought to make you aware of the soulless humans, or timeline Shifts. Churches and schools do not teach about the last two issues. And they are part of our reality in a big way.

## Creation

In the beginning, God created the heavens and the Earth…

Great, we have heard that before.

And then the Book of Genesis tells us:

> **Gen 1:26-28**
> [26]And God [Elohim] said, Let **us** make man in **our** image, after **our** likeness…
> [27]So God [Elohim] created <u>man</u> in his own image, in the image of God created he him; male and female created he them.

Ok, good. Man and woman were created at the same time, no rib involved, and the Creator was referred to as "us" and "our"… EL is the word for God; in Hebrew, the suffix "-im" makes the word plural. Elohim is plural for El… several **gods** creating Man. Very interesting. But it doesn't stop there.

In the very next chapter of Genesis, it tells us:

> **Gen. 2:7**
> [7]And the LORD God [Yahweh] formed <u>man</u> of the dust of the ground, and breathed into his nostrils the breath of life; and man became a living **soul**.

Very interesting. The same Book, same writer, and one assumes the same Creator, but now with a new name, Yahweh, and now Man has a soul. Woman was not created at this point in the text, or so it seems… (Lilith and Eve come later).

In addition, the claim is made that in Gen. 1 Man is represented as having been made "in the image of God" (27), yet in Gen. 2, he is merely "formed…of the dust of the ground" (7), thus suggesting a contrast. And this was allegedly all written by Moses, the same writer.

Two different accounts, in the same Book… and get this:

> **VERY Important: Nowhere in the Bible does a writer ever repeat the same event twice in the same Book.** (Ink and papyrus were expensive items and they would not waste them by repeating themselves.)

# Transformation of Man

Genesis 2 is <u>not</u> a repeat or 'clarification' of Genesis 1.

**There were (at least) two Creations of Man.**

And in fact, there were multiple creations as the late Mesopotamian scholar **Zechariah Sitchin** has told us (in <u>The Twelfth Planet</u>), and we have 5 distinct races on the Earth… Caucasian, Oriental, Latino (including South Sea Islanders), Negroid, and Amerindian (including Eskimo, Aleuts, Inuit, etc.)

If you think that white humans evolved from the Blacks, or vice-versa,
I have some ocean-front property in Montana I want to sell you.

But racial diversity, to create a $6^{th}$ race, is <u>not still happening</u>, contrary to Darwin, and apes are not still 'evolving' into humans, and those are key points. Man is a special creation, and was 'assembled' to look like his creators – Elohim or ETs, it makes no difference. The Sumerians said their gods were the Anunnaki, from the stars. The Hopi, the Chinese and the African Dogon, by the way, said the same thing. In fact, ZULU means "from the stars." Man's evolution was **assisted**, but that is another story (see VEG, Ch.s 1-4).

The diversity of Man on Earth looks more like an Experiment, as if some advanced geneticists were looking to see which of the 5 Root Races would survive (Survival of the Fittest) and be the best, advanced humanoid lifeform with which to populate this or perhaps other similar planets.

Keep in mind that Homo *erectus* already existed and note that **Neanderthal** (30,000 years ago) was replaced with Cro-Magnon. Cro-Magnon then was 'upgraded' to **Homo *sapiens***… obviously current Man is not the one that was originally created ( according to Genesis) and the anthropological record. But it wasn't plain and simple Evolution because (1) it is not still on-going, and (2) there is no "missing link."

Sorry, but Darwin was wrong on Evolution as the sole source of all life on the planet, but <u>correct</u> on Survival of the Fittest and Natural Selection – which we now call **Epigenetics**. Interestingly, after Creation, there has been a form of evolution as **morphogenesis** (Chapter 7) tends to modify species to better adapt to their environment.

So what is the point of two creations of Man?

**Two Seeds**

Let's assume that there were two creations in Genesis, and that the Bible is basically correct and makes it clear that the first creation had NO souls. This group of humans would have lived and propagated and formed at least a small tribe somewhere.

Then we have the second creation of Man, maybe something was not quite right with the first group and it was decided to make another version… this time with a **soul**. And we got Adam and Eve, then Cain and Abel. Cain slays Abel and is expelled from Eden, and he wanders off and takes a wife from the **Land of Nod**… a wife! A grown woman. From another group of humans. And those two give birth to **Enoch**…. Who "walked with God" and challenged the Watchers above the Earth. (All examined in detail in VEG, Ch.s 1-3).

The point being that there was <u>another group of humans in Nod</u>, and they logically had to be the first creation (Gen. 1:26). Logically, because we are not told about any other people at the time.

> **Apologetics** (a section of Christianity) would say that Genesis is so vague about timelines that we don't know how much time elapsed between Cain and Abel and Seth, and did Adam and Eve have daughters? (If not, we're talking incest to replicate the species!)

Interesting that the Bible is supposed to be the inerrant, perfect Word of God, and yet Man instituted Apologetics -- to **apologize** for what is there…. To try and explain the omissions, inconsistencies, and errors… Sounds like The God of the Universe is as fallible as Man… (or maybe Man modified the original, perfect Word of God, and redacted much of Genesis…?)

And the arguments go on and on, but let's keep this as close to the facts as possible and avoid the polemics.

If there were two creations, one without a soul and the other with a soul, then we have **two seeds on the planet**. Is that in the Bible? Yes.

> …I will put enmity between thee and the woman [Eve], and between **thy seed and her seed**…. (Gen. 3:15)

I realize that God is talking to Eve and the Serpent, but the point is still that there are **two seeds**, and VEG, Ch. 1 goes into more detail as to just what the Serpent was and how his 'seed' equates with those in the Land of Nod. This was examined in some detail in VEG, Ch. 1 and is not repeated

Suffice it to say that the seed of Eve (the 2$^{nd}$ seed, with a soul) would find the other seed, the 1$^{st}$ seed (without a soul), antagonistic and working at different purposes on Earth. The 1$^{st}$ seed has to be the people from Nod who also propagated and have spread over the Earth...even to this day. The Bible doesn't speak of any other people beside Adam and Eve's group and those in Nod.

The point is not where they came from, but that there are two seeds on the Earth, and one has a soul and the other doesn't. For the benefit of those who do not have VEG, there is a chart that shows the suggested human lineage...

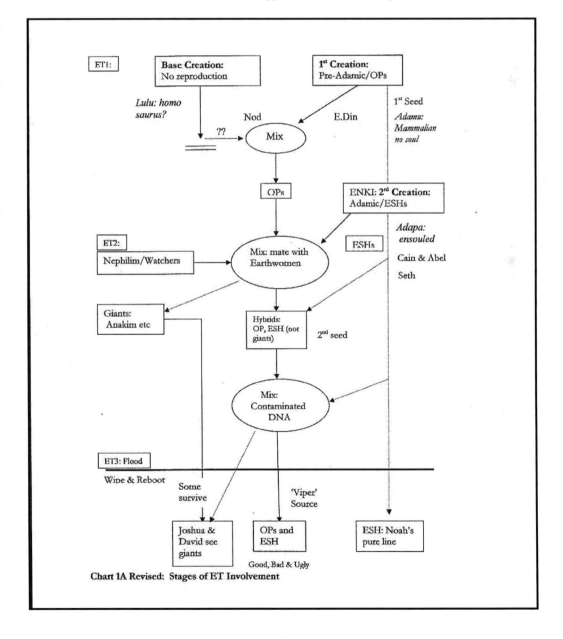

**Chart 1A Revised: Stages of ET Involvement**

**Note:** the Jewish scholars (in the Babylonian Talmud, and in Sumerian accounts) spoke of another woman in Eden, preceding Eve: **Lilith**, who was created in Gen 1 (later demonized and removed from Genesis, but a reference to her still exists in Isaiah 34:14 NAB), and because she was not subservient to Adam, she was banished (… to Nod?). The Sumerian and Akkadian traditions describe her (*Gilgamesh Epic*), and this bad girl has today devolved into a myth. Very interesting….

The chart also shows alleged Anunnaki interference with Man (as proposed by Zechariah Sitchin, see VEG, Chs. 1-3), and the two seeds are identified in vertical lineages #2 (middle) and #3 (far right). **OPs** (the soulless) and the ESH's (ensouled humans) will be soon addressed. Note that the soul is found in the #3 lineage, and the descendants of Nod either are the 1st seed or mix with the soulless 1st seed in #2 lineage. Both eventually meet in the "Contaminated DNA" mix (i.e., current day).

Both seeds are on the planet today.

> OPs are later described and defined, but the term for the soulless comes from Dr. Mouravieff -- OP:
> O = Organic, flesh and blood humans
> P = Portal as they can be manipulated by Astral entities (mostly Angels to drive the Father's Greater Script on the planet)

There is another interesting Biblical passage that tells us that there are two seeds that don't mix, metaphorically speaking:

> And whereas thou sawest iron mixed with miry clay, **they shall mingle themselves with the seed of men: but they shall not cleave to one another** even as iron is not mixed with clay.
> Daniel 2:43

There is another meaning to the passage, in addition to what the Bible scholars say about Daniel interpreting the king's dream: a woman with a soul should not marry a man who is soulless. And this is covered later in this Appendix when the pros and cons of knowing about this Two Seed issue is something that one can use to avoid heartache in one's life.

## Caveat on Soulless

At this point, we have to stop and make a couple of things very clear.

1.  **The soulless are not evil.** 98% of them are good, hard-working people. Just rather naïve and have no appreciation for spiritual issues since they have no soul which means they are not connected to a Higher Self, which is also the seat of one's **Conscience**.

2.  The soulless has **no aura** as that is the reflection of the soul. (Most people, especially women, who are often more intuitive and sensitive to higher energies, can learn to see the 1" etheric level – and ways to learn to do that are given in a following section).

3.  No aura means **no conscience**, and if one of these OPs runs amok and causes harm or damage to a family, business, church or becomes a terrorist, they are considered an **OP on steroids** and are part of the other 2% who may become sociopaths, or worse yet, psychopaths. Think: Charles Manson, Jim Jones and Richard Ramirez.

4.  **Most of them are harmless** and are the "great, unwashed masses" of humanity, settling for rote religion instead of wondering about why they are here and what life is all about. They have no higher chakra centers active to empower such wondering, let alone pursue the issue!

5.  **They do not know what they are**. They sense no difference between themselves and another person.

Points 4 and 5 are described by Dolores Cannon in <u>Convoluted Universe</u>, Books IV and V, and in a Section 6 which follows in this Appendix.

6.  While **most are not evil**, they can be a real <u>nuisance</u> and that is why you want to know about them. They can be very self-centered and want what they want; **everything is about survival, power and ego** – they do not compromise, there is little if any compassion, and they are not altruistic.

7.  **All men are not created equal**. OPs do not have the spark of divinity in them, and when they die, it truly is dust to dust. Trying to discuss compassion, conscience and spiritual matters bores them and they cannot follow it.

> All of that being said, there is **no "witch hunt" needed** and if one cannot see auras (I do, so I know this is all true) one can identify them by their behavior (see list in following section).

So if most of them are harmless, why bother to say they exist? Why bother to warn against marrying one? Reread points 6 and 7 above, and see the end of this Appendix , Summary point #6. Also see 'Genesis Revisited' section that follows.

That is why the following list of typical behavior is given... to help identify them — and these are typically people that the soul on a spiritual path will want to avoid!

## Soulless Traits

### OP Appearance

This can be a sharp way of spotting OPs: they <u>tend</u> to be more handsome or pretty because they usually do not have the soul's **karmic influence** to affect the way their bodies/faces look. It was taught that without negative Karma to endure, the OPs could be as naturally radiant and good-looking as is humanly possible.

> Physically **the two races are virtually indistinguishable**. Statistically there are minor physiological and perhaps genetic differences. Physiologically, OPs tend to be **more attractive and well-proportioned**. Because they exist on an emotionally primal level, natural selection has ensured that sexuality,  physicality and attractiveness play a large part in their physical evolution. Also, unlike ensouled humans, OP bodies are conceived and develop independently of soul pressures and karmic burdens, so they are as attractive as probability allows... [224]
> [emphasis added]

How many men have seen a beautiful woman only to find that she is heartless, cold and conniving? There was a song about one, in 1955 – "Maybelline, why can't you be true...?" She is probably an OP, a soulless human. (Is this one of the reasons some Hollywood marriages don't last? Is one of them, or both, an OP?)


## OP Characteristics, Basics

So, what are the general traits of OPs, and how can one reliably identify them? The basics are given here, with some advanced aspects.

First, the only way to be sure, and reliably know if someone is an OP is to determine if they have an aura or not. Second, the alternative is observation over a period of time and seeing if their **behavior** is congruent with general OP behavior. Third, if such consistent (daily?) observation is not possible, then consider whether they are congruent with ensouled human behavior.

## Ensouled Human Behavior

The following five points are typically ensouled human behavior **<u>not found</u>** in OPs.

1. ESH's care about other people and may find themselves 'hurting' for another person. **Empathy**. (True compassion.)
2. ESH's are interested in and pursue **spiritual** goals – meditation, yoga, even therapy and seminars to develop self.
3. ESH's **pursue truth** and dig to find out why things are as they are; this may include therapy and resolving "inner issues."
4. ESH's can have hunches, **intuition** and sense energy and act on it.
5. ESH's are often involved in giving of themselves, their money and time; they are **altruistic**.

And of course, there are other things that are mostly characteristic of ensouled humans, but the five points above are the <u>major</u> attributes that immediately stand out. And of course, be careful: there are times when an ensouled human can act just like an OP and be selfish, uncaring, and use other people.   And there are times when an OP will pretend to have compassion, pretend to be interested in spiritual issues… the better they are at mimicking, the better they **survive** – and for them, that is Issue #1.

## Major Aspects of OPs

While they generally remain something of a mystery, a few things can be said of them:

1. They have no souls and thus no connection to the god-force; thus they are not interested in spiritual issues or self growth
2. Their DNA does not permit soul growth or connection to higher realms due to higher chakras not being activated
3. Most of them are not bad or evil – some may be first-level souls (Baby Souls with a faint aura), or necessary placeholder OPs (see Timelines section)

> Not to confuse the issue, but a Baby soul (see Chapter 13) can have a very faint aura and look like an OP… and even act like one!  Caution is advised.  Judge carefully!

4. When they die, it is "dust to dust & ashes to ashes" time
5. Because they don't have a soul, they have no aura

6. Because they have no soul, they have **no spark or glint in their eyes**; they are flat and lifeless (they love wearing dark glasses)

7. Because they have no soul, they are not interested in religious matters **and** cannot discuss them

8. They have **no conscience**, little or no compassion, and exhibit **low, if any, morals.**

9. Standing next to one, there is a sense that no one is there; as in **no 'presence'**; their energy is **'flat'** – like standing next to a telephone pole.

10. Their purpose is to distract and drain energy from the ensouled humans thus preventing them from connecting with their Higher Self (and achieving John 14:12) **The PTB are largely OPs**.

11. They are mostly interested in food, sex, power trips and games; many are sex maniacs.

12. A psychopath is often a failed OP – they failed to mimic ESHs and survive in the ensouled world.

13. They blindly serve the orthodox teaching on anything (Science and Religion); they do not question nor do they innovate.

14. They have no "inner issues" or problems that they need to work thru.

15. They often cannot 'get' jokes with a double entendre, and <u>their</u> humor is crude, and sometimes abusive.

16. Some OPs are driven to **control others**... real 'control freaks.' (They think it guarantees their survival.)

**But again, beware!  They are great mimics.**

They are eventually exposed as they cannot or do not sustain their pretense of being caring and spiritual for long … that is why it takes time and observation to 'out' them!  However, the simplest test is to ask them if they go to church, do they believe in a God, and do they have compassion for others? A 'No' answer coupled with off-the-wall behavior is someone you want to avoid, <u>OP or not</u>. Another clue is someone who tattoos and pierces most of their body… even desecrating it by carving symbols into it (Hint: see pictures of Charles Manson).

# Historical Aspect

Returning to the historical aspect, the Greeks and Mayans knew all about them, as well as a current-day researcher, Dr. Boris Mouravieff. (There are 6 categories.)

### 1. Greeks

The idea of soulless people is nothing new. As was seen in VEG, Ch. 5, the ancients knew about these people 2000 years ago – they were called *hylics* by the Greeks. Even the Maya had a story about them in the *Popul Vuh*, and Valentinian

Christianity (Gnosticism around AD 140) also addressed the basic nature of Mankind, according to one of 3 aspects: [225]

**The Elect**: the '**pneumatic**' or spirit-filled who were searching for
a deeper Christian message because they lived via gnosis/insight;

**The Called**: the '**psychic**' or mental man who was happy with
what he knew (knowledge) and he walked by faith;

**The Material man**: the '**hylic**' who was incapable of understanding
any spiritual message, and did not have the soul-awareness of the
other two types.

What is significant about this schema is that in the early centuries AD, man was aware that **all men were not 'created equal'**, and that some men had souls and some didn't. *Hylics* **didn't have a soul**. [226] So they are not 'equal' to people with souls. And they may be doctors, lawyers and accountants because they can master details and many of them do serve a very useful function in society – but there is always the isolated sociopath with a destructive orientation to society. Being a sociopath and having a soul are a contradiction – not that an ensouled person can't "go off the rails" and cause harm, but it is usually the conscience in the ensouled person that stops them from extreme misanthropic behavior.

Somehow, perhaps deliberately in an attempt to 'level the playing field,' that information has been lost to the modern world. So much for Truth. For now, it is important to say that **we do not all have the spark of divinity within us**. And the assumption that we do leads to a number of errors, including marrying the wrong person, working for the wrong boss, or trusting the wrong person.

## 2. Aztecs

Until the Spaniards conquered the Aztecs (1521) and burned 98% of all their historical records, they too had a Creation story similar to the Mayans'. Now gone.

## 3. Mayans

### *Popul Vuh*

Besides the Greeks and Gnostics identifying these people centuries ago as *hylics*, the same issue was understood by the Mayans and they wrote about it in their version of Creation, along with many of their ancient beliefs, in their *Popul Vuh*.

Normally, if this were the only source of information about soulless human beings, it could be easily dismissed as superstition and, coming only from the Mayans, it could be said that it was just 3rd world ignorance. In this case, however, what the *Popul Vuh* says about OPs agrees with what the Greeks said, with what the Gnostics said, and (in the next section), it agrees with what a current-day Russian researcher Boris Mouravieff said. The OP info is not BS from a backward or primitive people. It is truth that has been buried, most likely by the PTB or sharper OPs themselves.

The following quote is reminiscent of the Sumerian Anunnaki Creation of Man – first the *Lulu* that could not pro-create, and then the *Adamu* who resembled the "wood" creatures below, and then the *Adapa* which could reproduce and was a lot like Cro-Magnon.

Check it out:

According to the *Popul Vuh*, the "gods" had made creatures known as **"figures of wood"** before creating Homo *sapiens*. Said to look and talk like men, these odd creatures of wood "existed and multiplied; they had daughters they had sons…" They were, however, inadequate servants for the "gods." To explain why, the *Popul Vuh* expresses a sophisticated, spiritual truth not found in Christianity, but which is found in earlier Mesopotamian writings. The "figures of wood" **did not have souls**, relates the *Popul Vuh*… In other words, without souls (spiritual beings) to animate the bodies, the "gods" found that they had created living creatures which could biologically reproduce, but which lacked the intelligence to have goals or direction. [*Adamu*]

> The "gods" destroyed their "figures of wood" and held lengthy meetings to determine the shape and composition of their next attempt. The "gods" finally produced creatures to which spiritual beings [souls] could be attached. That new and improved creature was Homo *sapiens*. [Or Sitchin's *Adapa*.] [227] [emphasis added]

Sounds like a rewrite of Dr. Sitchin's story of the Anunnaki experience, and <u>it should be</u> as the Sumerian Anunnaki gods went to Central America, as **Viracocha, Quetzalcoatl, Kukulcan**, etc. (see VEG, Ch. 11, 'Other Historic Anomalies')[228]… and they probably did the same 'teaching' there as the *Popul Vuh* continues the eerily similar point of view that Anunnaki leader Enlil had about the humans mating with the Anunnaki:

> According to the *Popul Vuh*, the first Homo *sapiens* were *too* intelligent and had *too* many abilities! … *they saw and instantly they could see far… they succeeded in knowing all that there is in the world...* Something had to be done. Humans… needed to have their level of intelligence reduced. Mankind had to be made more stupid. [229]

This is reminiscent of the issue with Anunnaki leader/god Enlil: the hybrid offspring of Anunnaki mating with humans was a threat to the dominance of the original Anunnaki who were limited in number, while the humans increased their numbers every day. Remember, Enlil's solution to the same threat was to let the coming Flood remove the problem. (This is all documented in the Sumerian *Atra Hasis*, and see VEG, Ch.3.)

**The Mayan gods said the same thing the Sumerian Anunnaki said to this issue:**

> … are they not by nature simple creatures of our making? Must they also be [like us] gods? [230]

So as the Anunnaki also "dumbed down" their creation by removing abilities from Man's DNA, so too does the *Popul Vuh* relate a similar treatment of Man. Not only did Man not get to live as long as his creators (after The Flood), he was not to know what they knew, nor be able to do what they could do, and mankind has been pretty much kept ignorant – just as the god of E.Din (Enlil aka Yahweh) wanted.

**Nexus**: the Mayan and Aztec gods like Quetzalcoatl and Kukulcan were the Anunnaki. So was the bad god, Huitzilopochtli who taught human sacrifice, and fought Quetzalcoatl who taught the natives to stop it.

What you think are other humans, just like you, aren't all just like you, and **many do not share the same motivations and goals.** Their job, sometimes with their Astral controllers (Angels, and sometimes Discarnates) working against you, through them, is to stop you. And because you don't know any better, OPs succeed in creating wars when ensouled Man could be uniting, they create scarcity when there could be abundance, and they create fear when there could be peace, love and faith.

> **Why? To keep Man from getting it together and developing his divine potential – something they absolutely do not understand (because they don't have it). It scares the soulless PTB.**

It is fascinating that the Greeks, the Mayas and the Russians knew about this same soulless truth which has been hidden from 'modern' Man. In fact, the Russians have really done the most complete research to date into the issue. (And they use genuine aura cameras to research the issue... examined in TOM, Ch. 11.)

## 4. The Library of Alexandria

It was a repository of Man's accumulated knowledge and no doubt, before it was sacked and burned three times (once by Coptic Pope Theodophilus in AD 391), it would have enlightened us all to see what historical treasures that great Library held… but there are those who value and promote ignorance, usually so that they can promote their own agenda (with nothing written to contradict them).

### 5. The Russians

### Dr. Boris Mouravieff

Besides the Greeks and Mayans identifying these people centuries ago as *hylics and "figures of wood,"* there was a well-educated Gnostic, Boris Mouravieff, who was a Russian emigrant living in Paris in the 1940s – 1960's. He knew G. I. Gurdjieff and P. D. Ouspensky, and **He just heard their teachings on pre-Adamics – from their research in Tibet and Kashmir.** Mouravieff wrote a version of Gurdjieff's 4th Way Teachings, calling his work Gnosis which consisted of 3 volumes. His primary contribution, although not the only thing he talks about in his three volumes, is **to reinforce the concept of 2 races of Man on the planet**: two races of humanity without regard for skin color, national origin or sex. He calls them **pre-Adamic (1st seed)** and **Adamic (2nd seed),** [231] or OP (Organic Portals) and ensouled, respectively. (OP is profiled in the Glossary.)

> **Except for the lack of a soul in the OP, they would be almost indistinguishable from ensouled humans on the street, or TV**.

To people who cannot see auras, this information might be useless except that there are other ways to spot OPs that are pretty reliable. Of course, as with any skill, it takes knowledge and practice in the ways to spot them, and for your own well-being, the information is given in this Appendix.

Why?
>You really don't want to marry one, if you have a soul, and you
>don't want them to head up your schools, churches or government.
>They take prayer out of the schools because they see no purpose to it.
>They pass laws that benefit them and shortchange the populace.
>They promote pharmaceuticals and GMOs that harm more than help.
>Some lawyers are all about money – they don't care whom they defend;
>>there is no principle involved.

## Creation revisited

Mouravieff's alternate, enlightened interpretation of the first two chapters of Genesis goes something like this:

**Genesis Chapter 1**:  the original 1ˢᵗ creation – without souls.
Boris Mouravieff calls these humans **pre-Adamic man**.

**Genesis Chapter 2**:  another creation where the 'breath of life'
(*ruach*) was breathed into *adamah* meaning "earth man" –
Adam had a soul. Eve was created from Adam's rib and as
a 'meet' (complementary/corresponding) mate for Adam,
would also have a soul.  (Also Cain and Abel.)
Boris Mouravieff calls these humans **Adamic man**. [232]

To repeat: pre-Adamic man has been termed an Organic Portal (OP) for two reasons:

> **Organic** because they are flesh and blood,
> **Portals** because entities from the 4ᵗʰ can and do operate
> through them to serve an agenda (and it isn't always
> bad – see later section on Timelines.).

That means that those things that a soul could normally do in a normal body (with all chakras functional), cannot be done in an OP body – even through the OP body looks normal, it isn't. It is really underdeveloped chakra-wise. These differences were delineated in the review of "A" and "B" Influences (See Ch 5, VEG).

Note again that the creation of Man took place in <u>two</u> distinct stages and the pre-Adamic and the Adamic coexisted for a long time, probably intermarrying. [233] But the two were quite different in their ability to evolve:

The prehistoric period is characterized by the coexistence of two humanities: pre-Adamic *homo sapiens fossilis*, and Adamic *homo sapiens recens*. For reasons already expressed, pre-Adamic humanity was not able to evolve like the new type. Mixed unions risked a regression in which the tares would smother the good seed so that the possible growth of the human species would come to a halt. **The Flood was a practical suppression of that risk**.[234]  [emphasis added]

> *Note that the Flood did not totally wipe out the pre-Adamics any more than it wiped out all the Nephilim, as Joshua saw the giants in Canaan. The Flood was not worldwide, but 'local' mostly to Africa and the Middle East.*

**Not All Men Are Equal**

Again, Mouravieff noted that the pre-Adamic was limited in its awareness and developmental potential due to no higher energy centers (chakras) formed and active. [235]   The pre-Adamic are really seen as **Anthropoids**, and the Adamic are considered real Men.  And the two were anything but equal.

> We must also note that the other extreme, the equalitarian conception of human nature, so dear to the theoreticians of democratic and socialist  revolutions, is also **erroneous**: the only real equality of subjects by inner and international right is equality of possibilities, for **men are born unequal**…. these two humanities …. are **now alike in form but unlike in essence**.[236]      [emphasis added]

And again, he cites the difference:

> The human tares, the anthropoid race, are the descendants of pre-Adamic humanity. The principal difference…. is that the [pre-Adamic] does not possess the developed higher centers that exist in the [Adamic]… which offer him a real possibility of esoteric [spiritual] evolution. Apart from this, the two races are similar. [237]

The Two Seeds of Genesis 3:15 explained.


## Seeds of Prejudice?

Is it unfair or not "politically correct" to point out that all men (and women) were not created physically and mentally equal? Not knowing about the OPs only protects them – it does nothing to serve you. As an analogy, would you prefer a dentist fully trained in the best dental school, or one that got his degree through the mail? Would you knowingly marry a woman whose genetics will lead to her having all children with Downs' Syndrome? Would you knowingly get on a plane with only one pilot who was subject to epileptic seizures (that he also may have told no one about)? In short, the point is: in order to have confidence that what we are about to do will work and come out well, **we need to know who/what we're dealing with** – that is the purpose of licensing, by the way – to give some assurance that the person we're dealing with is competent, or "all there," as it were.

OPs are <u>not</u> all there, some are "out to lunch" and I'm sure you have seen ditzy drivers, inept doctors/dentists, and even wondered about the person you married at times… or what your elected representative is doing in Washington.  OPs are really attracted to the Military, Law and Politics – all are power trips.

**It is not prejudicial to call a spade a spade**. And you are a fool to tolerate 'differences', problems or inconsistencies that obstruct a society's or family's or church's well-being… if you do, you have just signed on for the lesson and it will blow up in your face, sooner or later. Due to the PTB obfuscating everything they can, so you don't know too much (and thus you won't get upset), you won't know why you failed! You must know who/what you are dealing with, and then stand up for what is the right thing to do. This Appendix can help you learn to see these people around you – by their behavior.

## Is Judging OK?

Of course someone will object that it isn't nice to judge other people… and they quote the Bible to prove it! Too bad they are wrong. What they need is to look at John 7:24 (and I would warn you that if you don't see a liar, cheat and rapist for what he is, you are too Pollyanna-ish and will learn a lesson the hard way):

> Judge not according to the appearance, but **judge righteous judgment**.

It is not a sin to judge others – if you are right. And that is all the Bible says: be correct (righteous) in your judgment. So do not be afraid to suspect someone is an OP… just be cautious, look for corroborating behavior, and don't out them – just avoid them. If they are callous, insensitive, lying, offensive or have no spiritual side, walk off, avoid them. Save yourself the upset or heartache.

## 6. Dolores Cannon

Bless her heart, the late Dolores Cannon (of *The Convoluted Universe* fame) had more credibility as she always protected her clients with prayer and Light. And in fact, her material over the years has been consistent, does not contradict itself, and many times the information connects with, or expands, what we already know in a reasonable way.

In her *Book V of the Convoluted Universe*, published October 2015, after this book went to press and was published after her death (October 2014), she has a chapter on the **Backdrop People**… which per her definition, is the same as what has been called the OPs, NPCs, or Pre-Adamics. (See Glossary.) It is worth quoting some of her salient points. [238]

> They don't have a path, or purpose. They are just here like extras in a movie. They are slaves to the Earth Drama.
>
> They do not evolve to become higher beings as ensouled humans can and do. They can apply themselves and may be a **Pre-Soul**. (see VEG, Glossary, p. 526), but they don't know it and usually remain just undeveloped resources in the Greater Drama.

And lastly, she suggests a possibility:

> They have **no soul** and no future potential – they exist to drive the
> Scripts for the ensouled humans. [239]

That remains to be seen…. and is a great area for research.

## Reincarnation

Perhaps more importantly, Dr. Mouravieff said that this soul issue relates to Man's
ability to evolve:

> **Pre-Adamic man** does not reincarnate. Not having any individualized
> element [soul] in himself, (in the esoteric sense), he is born and dies but
> he does not incarnate, and consequently he cannot reincarnate. He can
> be *hylic* or *psychic* but not *pneumatic*, since he does not have the *Breath
> of Life* [*ruach*] in him, which is manifested in Adamic man…. [240]
>
> **See why the teaching of reincarnation was buried along with the
> truth about OPs?**

He's saying that the OPs have more of **a collective group soul, like animals**, and
that their lack of higher centers (chakras) prevents them from being aware like
ensouled humans, and thus from reincarnating. **Reincarnation applies to souls**,
not to non-souls. When an OP dies, s/he follows the "dust to dust" regimen; again,
there is no soul to go anywhere and they are thus not concerned with an afterlife, but
they may still be afraid to die.

Mouravieff also says that the OPs serve what we nowadays call the **Matrix Control
System** [Absolute III], and the ensouled humans serve the **Christ Consciousness**
[Absolute II]. [241]

Lastly, Mouravieff confirms what was said earlier about mixed families and nations:

**Mixed Families**

> Meanwhile the two races are totally mixed: not only nations but even
> **families can be, and generally are, composed of both human types**.
> This state of things is the … result of transgressing the Biblical prohibition
> against mixed marriages because of the beauty of the daughters of pre-
> Adamics. [242] [emphasis added]

## Genesis Revisited

At this point it is also relevant to emphasize that the pre-Adamic man represents the 1st Creation in Genesis 1. And this is significant because the Bible tells us that Adam and Eve had two sons, who would be 'Adamic' like them: the offspring had souls just like their parents. Then Cain killed Abel and was expelled from the scene – and he takes his wife from the Land of Nod. (And is relocated to the New World.)

*FYI: The 'mark' of Cain was no facial hair.*

This is important information. There is only Adam and Eve up to this point, with their two sons. Where did the rest of the people come from? To cut to the chase, it is suggested that the people in the Land of Nod were descendants of the pre-Adamics, from the 1st Creation, and Mouravieff does agree. [243]  That means that **Cain had a soul and his wife didn't**. As they left for parts unknown, and did a lot of 'begatting' as the Bible says,  they began the mixed marriage scenario (See **Chart 1A** earlier in this Appendix) and the furtherance of the OP and ensouled lines, with enmity between the two, just as Yahweh/Enlil said in the Garden of Eden when he expelled Adam and Eve.

> **Edgar Cayce** said that one of Adam's sins was "consorting with others" and was told that "all flesh is not one flesh!"  Cayce never clarified this reference to "others" but it is not hard to think that it could have referred to ensouled (Adamic) Man mixing his genes with those of the people in Nod, the Pre-Adamics or soulless ones.[244]

That is a suggested, plausible scenario. It explains where the OPs came from and why, as Mouravieff says, we have mixed families. A family with Mom and Dad ensouled and the kids ensouled would make for the theoretically balanced marriage. Unfortunately, the ensouled Dad could marry an OP Mom, and the offspring can be a combination that brings peace or strife to the family. Ensouled parents would not know what to do with unresponsive, do-your-own-thing OP children, and OP parents would not care about nurturing their ensouled children and giving them spiritual values. Does this describe today's families' problems?  (It did mine.)

**A family may have both ensouled and soulless humans by natural birth.**

It bears repeating: The problem with a mixed family, where the parents are OPs, is that the **ensouled human** (ESH) children will not be cared for (nurtured and encouraged) as they could have been by at least 1 ensouled parent. OP parents often do not know what to do with ensouled children and their questions, deeper seeking and sometimes higher awareness (even psychic).

Note that an ensouled man and an ensouled woman (unless they have defective genetics) will <u>usually</u> produce an ensouled child... but there is no guarantee. With an OP man and an ensouled wife, it could be either, but with two married OPs, the offspring will <u>usually</u> be **only** OP. The reason for this is that an incoming (incarnating) soul will normally choose ensouled parents – unless there are hard lessons to be learned at the hands of OP parents.

Therefore a recipe for a rough, insensitive or tempest-tossed marriage is for an ensouled human to marry an OP.

**Birth into a Body**

So what happens at birth? Why are babies born, living, and do not have a soul? Simple:  a Soul chooses not to get in the body due to circumstances that were not foreseen when the soul decided to incarnate on Earth, with reference to a particular family and location.

> **Do you move into a house if it isn't finished, or if it isn't correct?**

Souls choose their parents, lifetimes and basic experiences (See TOM, Ch. 6). If, as the fetus nears completion, the soul discovers that the Mom and Dad are now figuring to divorce, that may not be what the soul needs to experience – if it is, the soul proceeds.  A soul's watching the baby develop over time may see the mother do drugs on a whim, and that affects some key DNA, so the soul backs off and chooses another birth family.  **Souls do not have to enter a body.**

The point is, the baby can be born and live, move, walk, eat, sleep, and marry and have its own children – without a soul. Note that dogs, cats, horses and cows also do not have individual souls and they do just fine. When a baby is still-born that is due to the body not being able to sustain itself, for whatever reason, not because the soul pulled out.

For what it is worth, there is a lot of furor about **Abortion**... largely due to ignorance. The soul usually enters the baby <u>at birth</u>, maybe just before or just after... so the issue of murdering someone is nonsense. If a house is not finished, or is in some way defective, and nobody has moved in, and a tornado comes along and destroys the house, was anyone killed?

Just before we segue to Timelines, here is the basic practice to see auras.

## Seeing Auras

This is the general procedure to practice, as many people <u>with practice</u>, can see the basic 1" etheric layer just 1" above the arm, head, face (sideways), or the shoulders where it is the strongest. Some people cannot, so don't worry about it – just go by the list of OP characteristics.

Obviously, if you practice with someone, if they are an OP, you will come away claiming that you can't see auras. Try it with a number of people, and <u>in church</u> is a good place to test your ability – OPs generally do not go to church.

Most people can learn to see auras, but very few can see them out in public, with a mix of things behind the subject. A single-color wall is best.

Shown left is the **1" etheric aura**… best seen against a dark wall, not the open sky. It looks like a bright but thin light around the body.

**Human aura**
(credit: Digital Vision, and Kevin R. Brown, 1997)

1. Stand in a dimly lit room – a bathroom during the day with the light off and in front of the mirror, with a white or pale beige wall behind you (a black wall also works)
2. Stare at your forehead, not intently, and make the focus of your attention the side of your head – seen as it were with your peripheral vision – **defocus** your vision…
3. Occasionally close your eyes and rest them, then open them and in the first few seconds, note if there is any 1-2" energy field that appears to be surrounding your head.

**Two warnings**: (1) If you try to do this with a friend, and s/he is an OP, you will think you have failed… that is why you want to try this with yourself first… get used to seeing the faint, fuzzy 1-2" light around your head…

Secondly (2): When doing the above exercise, and you close your eyes, you will probably see what is called an **"after image"** of yourself on your retinas. This is normal, and sometimes the aura will ALSO show up as a slight shift in brightness as <u>on the edge</u> in the after image. When you open your eyes again, and you **defocus**, you are most likely to see the etheric aura.

**Note: auras do not show up on TV or in normal photographs.**
**OPs do not have auras, they have "heat waves" above their heads.**

Now we come to the significant aspect of the Soul, OPs, and Timeline issue. These three go together just like Souls, Karma and Scripts.

# Timelines

More detail on Timelines is examined in Chapter 2.

It was mentioned in VEG, Chs. 15-16, that one could exit Earth as an Earth Graduate… showing both Love and Knowledge after death, when crossing over to the InterLife. Attaining the **51% Light** as part of one's Soul allows one to leave the Earth experience behind and go do something else in the Father's Multiverse (See types of work available in Ch 13, TSiM, Section: 'Potential Areas for Service').

51% is not a really high consciousness, but if They had to wait until a soul perfected itself on Earth, we'd all be here for a really long time. As long as one's Light quotient is higher than that of the planet, one can graduate. (In physical terms, you resonate higher than the planet, and thus are not that compatible with it.)

But there is another way to move to a better Earth, or any world, that <u>has been</u> subtly happening across the centuries – and the OPs are the proof of it. Here's how it works.

## Timeline Splits

Let's say that Earth was in one continuous timeline up to and thru the mid 80's.

**Edgar Cayce** predicted that Atlantis would rise in the Atlantic Ocean during the late 60's, but the pole shift did not happen in '58 to '98, along with numerous Earth changes predicted in 1934, and there was no bad earthquake on the Pacific Coast of California in '36… [245] and Nostradamus predicted that in July 1999 there would be a 'king of terror' coming from the skies (asteroid). [246] Obviously, all that did not happen here. Such things happening were predicated on that timeline continuing to develop with the same influences and energies as were seen by Cayce and Nostradamus.

What those two men did not foresee was the infusion of positive thinking, Light and proactive behavior of **incoming higher souls** – sometimes called Indigos, Starseeds, Wanderers, or Homo *noeticus* (Hybrids) – planned by the Higher Beings. These two men also did not see that the Higher Beings would move Earth into a more proactive timeline for eventual ascension into the 5D realm… or <u>did</u> they and we have not understood their writings? Neither seems to say anything about timelines and possible splits.

> A timeline split is basically a timeline shift – the vibrations go
> higher and you can't get there until/unless your PFV (Glosssary)
> is a close match with the new timeline vibration.

And yet, we are on a timeline where Cayce's and Nostradamus' predictions did not happen. Cayce had enough credibility as "America's Sleeping Prophet" and was quite accurate in his diagnoses, that his predictions probably DID happen – but not on our timeline! And what is even more interesting and amazing is that the split/shift was done seamlessly – no one noticed.

A dimension can have more than one timeline, but timelines are at different vibratory levels, kind of like two sine waves that have been "phase-adjusted:"

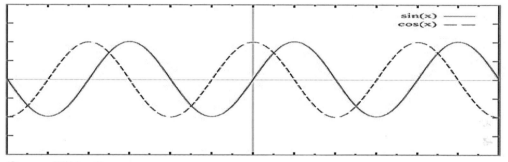

**(Source: Wikipedia :**
http://upload.wikimedia.org/wikipedia/commons/1/13/Sine_Cosine_Graph.png)

They are both on the same machine, but do not interfere with each other. In real life, as on the sine wave chart, there can be points where they intersect, and that results in some anomalies from time to time… See Chapter 2.

So where do the OPs come in? First, we should be calling them **NPCs – Non-Playable Characters**, as in a video game. You can't control the NPCs but they are there in the Game, interacting with you… they help drive the script for the video game. OPs in real life do the same thing; They help drive the Greater Script (designed by the Father of Light for training his souls), and they interact on a Karmic basis – sometimes delivering your 'lessons' and interrupting your day! Just as in a video game.

It was said earlier that Neggs and Beings of Light (two types of Angels) deliver events to you (guidance, protection, mishaps, fortune…) now you can see that **they sometimes use the OPs to do it**.

# Transformation of Man

As was explained in several other books, the ensouled people around you cannot (or should not) deliver your negative lessons as they will themselves incur Karma… ANY negative action does that -- even if well-meant. That is why OPs are used to 'afflict' or test souls as needed as the OPs do not have souls, so they do not incur Karma.

> During this author's investigations of souls vs soulless (in 2006-2008) – taking headcounts and keeping written records of what was seen – it was noted that about 60% of the people out there have no aura. And Drs. Bostrom and Greene in QES said that 60% was very significant in that it suggests **NPCs in our world**.

Needless to say, that was alarming and totally unexpected until my Source shared that that is because of the timeline splits that have been done – on our behalf – they were prescriptive and protective. Souls are protected and watched over.

And the only way to really see it is explained in the diagram below, and it involves understanding what happens when souls are moved from one timeline to another.

## Placeholder Replications

Let's take a look at what happens to people when a timeline splits.

Suppose that Jack is on a timeline TL1 that splits to TL1 (more negative) and TL2 (more positive). In this case, TL1 is the original TL which just got more negative when the more positively oriented souls (STO) left for TL2. The difference in positive and negative deals with whether the outcome is supportive and appropriate, or whether it detracts, disrupts or derails thus being inappropriate. Further suppose that Jack's desire was to align with the TL2 positive timeline and he <u>as a soul</u> is translated there. He is thus an ensouled human on TL2.

### Timeline Split Diagram

| **Legend**: | ESH = Ensouled Human | OP = Organic Portal (**soulless human**) |
|---|---|---|
| | TL1 = original timeline | TL2 = new timeline |

Steps B & E below assume that TL2 is a virgin timeline (no one else is there already).

**The following is a step by step breakdown of how the above timeline split affects the people. Headcounts may be easier to follow below (using arrows):**

## Timeline Splits and People: Steps A - E

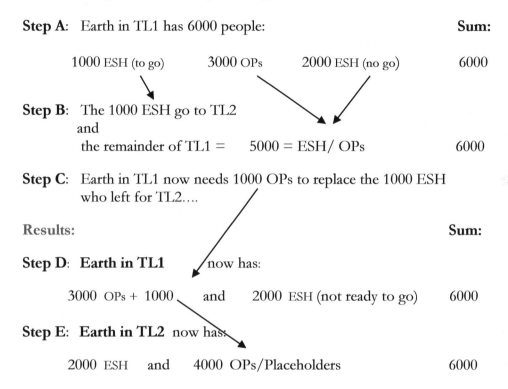

**Step A:**   Earth in TL1 has 6000 people:                                **Sum:**

1000 ESH (to go)          3000 OPs          2000 ESH (no go)          6000

**Step B:**   The 1000 ESH go to TL2
and
the remainder of TL1 =     5000 = ESH/ OPs          6000

**Step C:**   Earth in TL1 now needs 1000 OPs to replace the 1000 ESH
who left for TL2....

Results:                                                              **Sum:**

**Step D:  Earth in TL1**          now has:

3000 OPs + 1000     and     2000 ESH (not ready to go)     6000

**Step E:  Earth in TL2**  now has:

2000 ESH     and     4000 OPs/Placeholders          6000

Note:   this is how **timeline splits result in an increase in the amount of OPs or Placeholders**. TL1 gained 1000 OPs. The Sum of beings is kept the same indicating that the change was **seamless** – no one on TL1 would know anything happened. The 1000 souls moved to TL2 would also not suspect anything because everyone transferred with them.

When the timeline splits, TL1 will continue as the original timeline which has a less than desirable outcome, even negative, where World War III occurs. Members of Jack's family, people at work and church are used to having him around and in some ways, he completes the scenario for them – all to say that **Jack cannot disappear from TL1**. He is needed to fulfill duties, or responsibilities, that become a part of the on-going life drama of the other people still on TL1. So he becomes an OP on TL1 to sustain the on-going Drama there...

**Note that the number of OPs increased in the split.**

How can Jack be in two places at once? Simple: he is an ensouled human on TL2 (his choice), and he is <u>replicated</u> as a Placeholder OP on TL1 (by the Timelords who oversee this whole process). The Placeholder does not have a soul, there is no aura, and there is no 'soul cord' or energy link between the TL1 Jack and the TL2 Jack.

> *Sometimes Jack may replicate in more than one timeline as an ensouled human – i.e., both 'copies' of Jack can have a soul, but this is rare as it entails a division of limited soul energy (Chapter 11) that cannot be reduced beyond a certain point, so the usual event is that ensouled Jack moves to TL2, and the original TL1 Jack becomes an OP Placeholder.*

Note that a subconscious non-souled aspect of Jack was replicated in the TL1 timeline, and other significant 'players' in Jack's life drama are also replicated in TL2 for Jack as **'Placeholders'** to continue their function so that Drama options can be played out on both timelines – and now you see where some OPs come from. The Placeholders do not usually have souls and do not need them – although some players of significance may opt to replicate with a soul aspect if they need to learn something, too. Here again, a soul can only send its energy into so many alternate timelines (depending on soul level) and thus there is often a limit to the replication with soul-link back to the original soul (Chapter 10, 'Allocation of Soul Energy').

The more advanced souls can replicate themselves into more timelines and realms than young souls can. And all souls are projected into multiple timelines concurrently **per Era**; there is little or no sequential lifetime Karma that applies within an Era as typically **Karma applies to lifetimes between Eras**. All lives are **concurrently** happening within the Era – when the Era changes, the souls can redeploy themselves…thus there **is** Karma between lifetimes between Eras.…

> To repeat, Karma only applies to the Earth School… it 'affects' what goes into your Script – i.e., what you need to learn.

An OP also replicates as an OP in any new timeline, because the ensouled humans need them as part of their on-going, day-to-day Drama, and even some of these replicated OPs may depend on other OPs to perform <u>their</u> functions to keep the Drama going. **This is one reason Earth currently has so many OPs** – we have been through <u>several timeline splits</u> in the beginning of this Era – and that is good news.

Sometimes, an alternate choice (for example, a fractal TL3) playing itself out is more of a temporary **simulation**, as Robert Monroe discovered. At the point where it proves successful, the consciousness of the original soul may move over into a new timeline (with any necessary adaptations in conscious memory so that the move is 'seamless'); if the fractal choice proves disastrous, the information is recorded in the Oversoul's consciousness, as a learning experience, and the **fractal simulation** (TL3) is discontinued for that soul.

> *This is why there are Watchers and specific* **Timelords** *who actually effect the timeline mechanics.*

A soul may also opt out of an alternate scenario if it becomes too burdensome and/or there are no more lessons in one's Script to be learned. The Oversoul, in this case, knows what is going on and the goal is not to prolong an alternate scenario to the point where the soul is damaged. (Damaged souls are examined in Ch 7, VEG, Section: 'Rearrangement of Energy'.)

It is all about growth and Man must stop damaging the planet and rise above his pettiness, violence and ignorance.

**Earth in a Timeline Split**
(Credit: http://www.bing.com/images)

A simple replication into an alternate, and initially identical timeline… except that the vibrations are higher and thus more proactive.

## Rescue of Mankind

Could benevolent ETs Help Man?   The real issue is: Should they? According to one source:

> ...the ETs are here because **the human race is in danger of extinction** [and may be replaced <u>when</u> the Greys are successful].
> ...the ETs have the technology to save the human race and that it is their inclination to help us because they view us as a part of them... However, if the ETs were to repair the Earth without making any changes in our behavior, we would simply "undo all the good they had done...We might survive long enough to find an even grander way to destroy ourselves, one that could **harm worlds other than our own**. These beings feel that, by saving the human race, they would be condemning <u>themselves</u> to a violent confrontation with us in the future." [247] [emphasis added]

> The ETs would have to be very careful in helping Man overcome his defects and limitations as there is a **Galactic Law** that says evolving sentient beings have the right to work out their problems by themselves and 'interference' from more advanced beings might be counterproductive – like a human deciding to help a chick break out of its eggshell – if it isn't strong enough to break the shell, it won't make it in the outside world. Some lessons have to be learned, so we can't be 'rescued.' They are also not about to interfere with a School run by the Higher Beings.
> This was called the Prime Directive on *Star Trek* – where the heck did **Gene Roddenberry** get his information?

This is not a positive comment on the human race, and is echoed by similar sentiments in the United Nations.  The same source continued,

> "These beings said the human race, <u>as it now exists</u> and as it has existed, **cannot be saved**. If it were, all the problems they could foresee happening when we eventually meet them in space would be inevitable, assuming we didn't destroy ourselves first." Therefore another part of their plan is to attempt to change us in more subtle ways by means of **genetic manipulation** and by attempting to reawaken our spiritual values and beliefs. [248]   [emphasis added]

*And VEG suggested that that is the function of the bio-cybernetic Greys and their abductions. Note there an **extra 223 genes** in Man that they do not find in other lifeforms on Earth and no one knows yet what they do. (Chapter 9.)*

**And the majority of Man being petty, violent and ignorant does not inspire any of the benevolent ETs to petition for our release from the Earth School.**

**If this version of Man does not get it together and stop letting the PTB manipulate them, this version of Man will be replaced – just as Neanderthal was.** (Hint: the Greys are very busy. See TOM, Ch. 8.)

**Just as a side note**: if this version of Man is unsalvageable, then is this the warning given us by the Georgia Guidestones?

**The Georgia Guidestones Monument**

There is an English stone and its contents are quite interesting, reflecting the fact that we <u>are</u> overpopulated on Earth, as seen below....

In particular, note the first two lines of the English version:

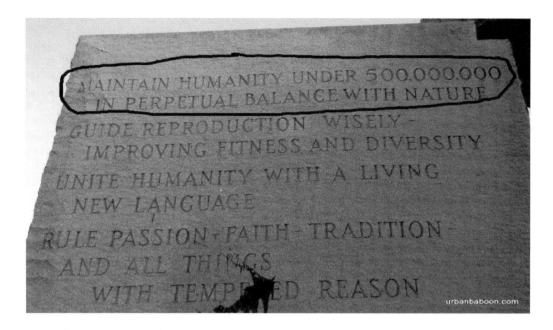

Someone has determined that we'd be better off if the human races were limited to a **total** of 500 million people on Earth (a 2-3 billion goal sounds better).

As was said earlier, Man's <u>devolving</u> DNA is one of his biggest problems, and the shadowy power group that has been called the PTB/Dissidents/4D STS contribute to the dilemma by manipulating an already dumbed-down populace. This is another reason why much of **the existing version of Man cannot be saved**, any more than Neanderthal could be saved. Neither Homo *sapiens* nor Neanderthal were smart enough to know that they were being manipulated and that is why, as was revealed, there have been a number of "Wipes and Reboots" or Eras in which Man started over.

> **In this sense, the Georgia Guidestones may be prophetic instead of prescriptive. Man has an option, but he must wake up and take the planet FROM the PTB. Man cannot generally 'take the planet back' because it was never his – but can he grow up and stand up to show that he is aware and now worthy of help to rid Earth of the PTB controllers?**

The major difference this time has been the inclusion of Lightworkers and Hybrids walking the planet, in an attempt to **anchor the Light** and, through **entraining resonance**, work to raise the consciousness level of the planet (It is working).

> It is said that the magic number of people needed with a higher consciousness (i.e., higher vibration, more Light) is **6%**. At the present population count and considering that not all countries on Earth have enlightened people, that number is somewhere around 420,000,000. That is the population of the USA plus Europe plus some of India…

Ironically, the power boys, the PTB and the Dissidents know they have lost, but they are so committed to <u>their</u> goal of **depopulating the current Earth** (for control) that they cannot see that there is no way that their contrived machinations can <u>ever</u> work. STS can be really dense.

## Freewill Is The Key

So why don't the Higher Powers step in and remove the PTB and those that obstruct Man from becoming all that he can be? Or, kill them? Because this is a **freewill universe** and it is the Father's desire that all should learn and eventually, freely return to Him. Force serves nothing. If the STS can't see their errors on their own, are they any more likely to see it when they are disciplined, removed or otherwise confronted by a Father who would use force or the same tactics on them? Two Wrongs don't make a Right.

> *Note that killing an OP solves nothing – there is no soul and when they die, it is literally 'dust to dust.' Killing an ensouled entity (who is eternal) solves nothing as that entity can reincarnate. So in both cases, nothing permanent (or long range) is accomplished.*

So freewill is an option but if Man doesn't know what is going on (and does the Lame Stream Media tell him, or his local church?) he doesn't know what to **ask** for… and the prevailing issues continue. Mediocrity reigns.

## Transformation and Timelines

The important issue is that Man be living on a timeline that is free of PTB STS control and is free to live out his LifeScript (TOM, Ch. 7). To the extent that the timeline is negatively controlled, Man will experience less than optimal conditions for making choices – **the PTB want to make Man's choices for him**, and this can abrogate the Script and Man fails to grow… except that we also grow thru adversity and repression! (Steel is created thru high heat and fire!) Thus the Higher

Beings only get involved to reset the Stage with a new Drama when the current one is unwrokable. (Shakespeare would love it.)

When the TL is negatively manipulated, there is an abundance of dysfunctional and rebellious souls that incarnate here—the Higher Beings see it as an opportunity <u>briefly permitted</u> to give special lessons to wayward souls and it in effect turns Earth into a **Rehab Facility** (our current status, by the way). Earth is so employed to put the defective or dysfunctional souls in a context of their equals... viz., "meeting themselves in spades." This includes the dysfunctional PTB – who are <u>permitted</u> to do what they do as it provides more advanced souls on Earth the opportunity to see thru the nonsense and rise above it. That is called **catalyst.**

It will not be allowed to continue for long, because scenarios like *Soylent Green* and *Mad Max* are counter-productive in the long run...they create damaged souls. However, it can be very instructive for a limited time!

When it gets really bad, the Higher Beings (also called Timelords) will perform a **timeline shift** and the former TL1 will collapse under its own negative charge, and the new TL2, like where we are now, will have enough of a positive potential that more souls can learn and grow, before the Cycle starts all over again – Timelines eventually go negative and splits are a normal occurrence. Souls are a precious commodity and the Timelords work to protect them by shifting them ever forward... and of course, the number of OPs also increases each time.

> When a timeline goes sufficiently negative, it dissolves for want of positive, sustaining coherent energy.

So sentient beings are allowed to run their course, but as was also said earlier, if over the eons of experiential existence these same ensouled STS entities never learn and cannot comprehend the error of their ways, and they remain so resistant that they are unsalvageable, they will be "re-assembled" or dissociated (rearrangement of energy – Ch 7 in VEG). There are no STS entities above 5D... and very few <u>in</u> 5D... at some point they have to wake up, too. Rebellion is ultimately futile...

So a Greater Script or Drama that starts to go awry doesn't go on forever, and the Higher Beings and Beings of Light do watch and try to keep the Earth School functional, so that souls can learn from whatever situation they find themselves in.... and graduate or ascend.

We always have a choice.

## Shift Happens!

And this is the last way to get to a better realm.

**First**

The first one was to die with a minimum of 51% Light and opt out of here, *aka* **Earth** Graduate at death. This is on a personal basis.

**Second**

The second one was to move *en masse* with thousands of other souls as the gods do a **Timeline Split**... and we move from TL1 to TL2. This was to move all souls to a more optimal timeline leaving most of the PTB and their sycophants behind on what will become a much more negative timeline – so negative that it collapses under its own disability to sustain itself.

**Third**

The third way out of this sometimes oppressive Earth realm is to gain Light (i.e., learn more of Truth – absorb it and assimilate it!), and **Shift Out**! Gain more than 51%, and really move into higher awareness, viz., achieve some level of Cosmic Consciousness while still living here... This is on a personal level.

This where your consciousness gains so much more Light that you are increasingly out-of-synch with people and events around you. You know better and want to do more, and have sought to be with other like-minded people, living Life on a more proactive and spiritual level... Watch out! You are getting close to "shifting" up and out of here – into another timeline where your vibration matches theirs in 4D!

The more loving and knowledgeable you are, the finer your vibration becomes, and thus the faster it becomes. No one but you controls this – No one determines whether you go or stay – it is solely based on PFV – your Personal Vibration Value (Level), and that reflects your Ground of Being, or who/what you really are.

Be aware that you concurrently exist in several different versions of the Multiverse. For example, all major life decisions are played out on alternate timelines: the you that did get married is on timeline one (TL1) let's say, and the you that didn't marry in on TL2. Then the you that was in the Army is on TL 3 and the you that didn't serve in the Armed Forces, is on TL 4 (or maybe the you that got married went into the Army and so TL3 could apply).... These may be fractal simulations (i.e., just for you).

Now suppose TL2 is a better, more peaceful timeline and you are ensouled there, but only 20% (See Chapter 11 in this book, 'Allocation of Soul Energy') and as you raise your 3D Earth vibration, it approaches that of TL2 and if sustained, you may "shift" into that body of you on TL2 and now have a 30-40% ensouled nature there. (The old you will be an OP [Placeholder] back on TL1, see earlier in this Appendix.)

You are completely compatible with yourself and won't even notice the Shift – often happening at night while you sleep. And when you go about the next day's business, there are the same people you knew back on the original timeline – because when timelines form, they split and OPs are the norm to keep the Drama going. The only difference will be that things run smoother (maybe 10-20%) there are less hassles, and the person you were arguing with yesterday is not doing that with you now in TL2.

> Shifts happen, as I documented (in TOM Ch. 5: Soulmate Encounter), where I popped over into the timeline where I was engaged to my soulmate – the same one I saw in the '91 Regression – over there she was a brunette! (I have not met her here although I know who she is and she is a blonde here.)

Obviously you cannot be shifted (the Timelords assist in the Shift) to stay in a timeline where you are married if you are currently unmarried! In this case, They will create a fractal simulation (just a part of the TL2 timeline) and populate it mostly with OPs... and you will not notice – unless you see auras! (So seeing auras is not always such a great ability....?)

> What is weird, and has the quantum physicists talking is that Earth currently has a 60% OP headcount – we have been split or shifted before, and they suspect that this Earth we're on may be one of those fractal simulations. (See QES book.)

Ok, some of this is hard to follow and assimilate. Nonetheless, Splits and Shifts do happen and are for our benefit. Splits keep the human experiment going, and the Shifts are a normal (yet uncommon) way to support a soul in becoming all it can be – by not limiting it to a realm it has already mastered. If a soul is ready for 4D (via a Shift) it goes there. (OPs do not shift, but they may be replicated.)

The gods are not ogres. They want ensouled humans to become all they are capable of and work quietly behind the scenes (as in a Shift) so that the soul is not aware and disrupted from focusing on its activities and personal development. Souls are that important.

The PTB are allowed to obstruct as we are in a Freewill Universe, and their bad behavior only serves to disgust and anger the STO souls who eventually will wake up and overthrow the STS lords.  Quite a Drama!  The good news is: we win! But those who cannot or do not wake up are choosing the rougher school of hard knocks… they will have to experience destruction of some sort because they often refuse to wake up and sometimes only pain and loss will do that for them.

> And again, to repeat, because it is very important to realize that the 3D Fat Cats who run the planet, the 3D flesh-and-blood Power Boys, the PTB (including the Illuminati), have at their tiptop hierarchy several soulless leaders with advanced awareness who know they are soulless and **they fear the souls** and what they can become!  Thus they seek to keep souls ignorant and obstruct their growth… largely by distracting them with sex and violence, drugs, alcohol, and false teachings… dumbing down public education,  censoring the Media, destroying the family… They know and fear that some day, some souls will grow, gain Knowledge and Power, and begin to develop their divine heritage (as sparks of The One), and rule over the PTB, and they don't want that!  It is as simple as that.
> Is it still working?

So why do we want to know about all the foregoing?
There are three summary reasons…

## Summary 1:  Awakening

1. It is encouraging to know that Man is watched over and when the Earth scenario gets too negative, the Timelords will shift the 'good people' to a higher timeline so they can continue their lessons.
2. It is instructive to know that Life is a kind of Video Game, or as Shakespeare said, a Play or a Drama, and Man is an eternal soul who "struts and frets" his hour on the stage, and then rebirths in a new role for a new lesson. The OPs help drive the Earth School Drama.
3. It is helpful to know that the **high count of OPs on Earth** at this time (60%) means that we have had at least 1 timeline split since Edgar Cayce's day…
   evidence that we are being looked after and IF we keep moving forward in spiritual growth, becoming more and more STO, we will continue to move into better and better timelines as we work our way out of here.
4. It is instructive to know that organized Religion is still operating in the Dark and believing stuff that isn't true, such that knowing the Truth which carries Light, will benefit one's overall journey to become an Earth Graduate.

5. There is no reason to believe what the ignorant say ("There is a Devil", "There was just one creation"), nor should we believe what atheists tell us ("There is no God", "NDE is all in your head...") – the more we plug into ignorance, the more we bury ourselves in low, slow Earth vibrations – and will have a hard time getting out of here!

6. **Six reasons to know about the OPs and recognize one:**
   a) Avoid marrying a bad spouse that does not support your values
   b) Can ignore atheists and their 'scientific' pronouncements
   c) Stop hoping that the really beautiful blonde/handsome man will come around and be a warm, caring, cooperative person
   d) Realize that sex maniacs and **control freaks** are OPs on steroids
   e) Realize that a person who criticizes everything you do is an OP and you should leave them (their goal is to break/derail you)
   f) People with no 'issues' in life are usually OPs – don't trust or marry one (If it is a lying ensouled person, you also leave!)

7. Lastly, the author was given this information and told to write it up and disseminate it. The time is ripe for **two new revelations** – as said in the Introduction. You had Karma and Reincarnation teaching 60 years ago, and now welcome to consider Scripts and the Soulless.

It is your own sanity and spiritual growth that is important. Don't give your power (to make your own decisions) away. Skepticism can be healthy, if it isn't overdone.

Some people will really have problems with this Appendix, and that is why the information is not part of the main book, yet it is important – and some will be able to assimilate it. **It is Light**. These issues are where we are all going and are issues that we all have to deal with in our spiritual growth – sooner or later – and are new and important aspects of walking the Path to get out of here. Truth carries Light, and 51% is a minimum needed to exit the School.

## Summary 2: Lesson Time!

Now that we have outed the existence of the OPs... so what?

**Reason #1:**
Here's the first reason: **you don't want to marry one**... but if you have, it is not about killing them, divorcing them, stabbing them, hitting them, or even confronting them with the knowledge...... if you leave them, the gods will just send another one (or two) with your incomplete lesson... so here's the deal:

1. Recognize that you are not the problem (as the OP keeps telling you!)

2. Most of them are not evil or anything to be afraid of. Most are nice but very simple people.

3. Realize that they do what they do as a way of bringing tests and lessons to you...

4. Realize that if it is an OP – there is a reason they are there, and **the lesson must be handled**—better to find out what it is and handle it! It's "Lesson Time!"

5. If it is a violent, obnoxious OP, leave them... save yourself.

So you might say, "Well. I don't care what they are, I don't like that person and what they are doing... so I am out of here!" So, if you go, take your leave in a way that doesn't harm them or create more negative Karma for yourself... make it a nice, clean break.

**Reason #2:**
The second reason to know about them is that if the person fits the description of an OP, or their behavior matches what is described here in Appendix D, it means that **your Script is in play and this is someone and an event to pay attention to!**

That is all we can do about them. Just realize that your Script is in play and you need to do the most reasonable or appropriate thing to handle the situation – not avoid it. You can run, but you'll have to eventually face the same situation, <u>or worse</u>, and it is part of your lesson or training to be a more competent and aware soul.
Thus, not only do you not want to marry one, you want to know when it's "Lesson Time!" That is why you want to know about the OPs.

## Summary 3: Knowledge

**Rewind:** it is Knowledge that is important because it carries the Light. While Love is the power behind Life and our souls, just being loving will NOT get you out of the Earth School. Sorry. It takes <u>both</u> Love and Knowledge.

**Knowledge Protects**
**Ignorance Endangers**

If you don't know the Truth, you will fall for anything – unless you are a total skeptic, and then you reject anything and everything – and you still do not get out of here. That is the challenge for all souls – to seek, **ask,** and learn the Truth. It is only the PTB who love being Lords and so (via the Media nowadays) they suppress real news, of all sorts, and seek to keep you so ignorant that when you die, you automatically get **recycled** – so that the PTB have a constant supply of sheep or serfs to rule!

> By the way, if you experience **Déjà vu,** you have been recycled. Review Dr. Mouravieff's section, earlier. You <u>have</u> seen it before, because you failed the tests and so must repeat...

You are supposed to wake up, at least suspect something's amiss, and see thru that and rise above it! Failure to do means you just **failed a key lesson and will have to repeat** the 'test' or lesson.

And you have a **choice** – to handle it or not. Always.
Earth is all about lessons and tests. Get over it.
Whatever happens, **give thanks** and handle it.
It is all **catalyst.**

**The sooner you choose to handle it, the sooner you get to move on into higher service, learning and serving the Father in awesome realms.**

**With the right Knowledge comes the discipline to handle the Power that goes with serving in the incredible realms awaiting us all. Earth is a cesspool compared to where we can be – once we graduate! Our future as expanded beings is awesome.**

**When you know, why would you choose to stay here, in ignorance?**

**Dare to explore!**

# Encyclo-Glossary

---

**1-Sec Drop** -- this is a direct communication from a Higher Being into one's mind and memory/knowledge base. It is not a voice, not automatic writing. It takes a very brief split second and one knows that it is happening, and then it can take anywhere from 10 seconds to 20 minutes to examine what one was given. It is information that is usually complete and appears to the recipient to be something that s/he already knew and is now aware of. Similar to an insight or revelation, except that it has an energy signature about it that you know it is being "dropped" into you. (Reminiscent of **V2K** but there are no words 'spoken.')

**4D STS** – they are beings with a negative, Service to Self, polarization in the 4th level. They are also called the 4D STS Controllers. They use the PTB and OPs for their agenda(s) on Earth, and work with the 3D Dissidents to control or manipulate ensouled Man. They also interfere with the 4D STO entities on their own level. They used to be 3D STS.

**100th Monkey Effect** – When one animal in a group discovers some new behavior and finds it serves him, it is said that the behavior is not learned as much as passed on as soon as the energy reaches a critical level so that their group soul can recognize and 'appropriate' the behavior. This was the case with a few monkeys on an island who discovered that washing their fruit before eating it avoided the problem of sand in the mouth. More and more monkeys on island 1 began doing it, and while they had no way to communicate the new behavior to the monkeys on islands 2 and 3, after about 100 monkeys were doing it on island 1, the others on islands 2 and 3 also began doing it (as confirmed by zoologists who were present studying the islands). Hopefully, this is not an urban myth…

**Anunnaki** – one of the early, original ET visitors to Earth who interfered in the natural progression of the bipedal hominids here, and created some of the first 'humans' in Africa and Sumeria. Because of their technology and power, they were looked upon as gods. Supposedly from the planet Nibiru, but more likely Orion or Sirius systems. (See **Zechariah Sitchin** and **Remnant**. See also VEG Ch 3.)

**Anunnaki Elite** – consists of two main types: the ruling reptilians who retained their original appearance (e.g., Enlil and Enki), and the later, hybridized, more human-looking (e.g., Inanna, Marduk, Sargon, even Alexander the Great). The later change was effected by Enki's mating and later genetic prowess to enable the Anunnaki to move among the humans who found the original., reptilian/reptibian appearance repulsive.

**Archons** – the 'powers that be' in the celestial realms – according to the Gnostics. These are the same ones that Ephesians 6:12 refers to: powers & principalities (a hierarchy) dedicated to evil and wickedness. Synonymous with 'demon.' (See **Nephilim** and **Djinn**).

**Archetypal Experience** – A believer of any System signs on for the concomitant experiences that go with the belief System. Witchcraft, Christianity, Nazis, New Age or Boy Scouts, there are a set of beliefs, practices and experiences that are automatically attached to the paradigm and the adherent will at some point be 'visited' by events, people and +/- experiences germane to the System one has chosen to follow. (See VEG, Ch 14.)

413

**Astral Realm** – note that there are levels in the Astral realm, and in particular, the one that most concerns Man, is the Level I (**Chart 4** in VEG, Ch 12) which is a kind of intra-dimensional space – more than 3D and yet not quite 4D, and this is inhabited by Man's oppressors, the STS Gang. The normal STS/STO entities occupy the higher 4D, and lower 5D Astral realms, and cannot see 3D Man.

**Attractor** – energy in the form of an idea, person, or thing that draws other things, ideas or people together based on similar and strong resonance.

**Baldy** – the name I gave to the manifestation of my Source who showed up once in 2003 to check me out and give guidance. He was about 6'6", 200 lbs, perfectly proportioned, bald with a perfectly shaped head, and big blue eyes whose irises were bigger than most peoples. Probably my guardian angel.

**Bands** – referring to the H-Band and M-Field suggested by Robert Monroe. These are energy bands, or grids, created around the Earth due to the often negative activities of souls on the Earth. Experienced as static or noise. See also **RCF/Matrix**.

**Beings of Light** – often referred to as Angels, or today's Watchers, they guide and protect Man. They are also known to provide the life review that NDErs speak of, and they are the '*Inspecs*' that Robert Monroe spoke of.

**Bionet** – a term coined in VEG Chapter 9 to describe the hyperdimensional network of communication in the body. Like the Internet, *chi* is carried in meridians of energy to all parts of the system, from the chakras, and tells the cells and organs what to do. The Bionet is manipulated during Acupuncture on the Acupoints.

**Book 1** – refers to *Virtual Earth Graduate*, the first book (published early 2014), Chapter 1 in this book does a brief overview of it.. (*Transformation of Man* is Book 2… See Copyright page – at bottom: Books 1-5.)

**Brain Waves** – a measurement of consciousness.
        Beta cycle:  12 – 19+ Hz  (normal waking consciousness)
        Alpha cycle: 8 – 12  Hz  (relaxed, aware state)
        Theta cycle:  4 – 8 Hz  (sleep)
        Delta  cycle:  less than 4 Hz  (deep sleep)

**Catalyst** – anything like an event, an idea or a word, that causes change in a person; the threat of being fired for bad performance at work is a catalyst to perform at one's best. Illness is a catalyst to see what is wrong, or what energy is blocked, in one's body.

**Chakra** – a vortex of energy formed in the body wherever two or more chi meridians come together; same as a vortex on the earth with its ley lines. (Sedona, AZ is known for several of these.) These are also referred to as 'energy centers' as they transduce energy from the air/water/Sun around a body and draw it into the body thru the chakras. There are 7 main charkas in the body and 1 above the head, and 1 below the feet. There are many more minor charkas all over the body.

**Chi** – energy particles, also called *ruach*, orgone, mana, prana or ki – without chi in our food, air and water the human body could not exist. The chi is a force that travels along meridians (pathways) in the body that link the etheric aura (1st level of the aura) to the physical body; it can be directed by the mind to specific parts of the body for healing.

**Cognitive Dissonance** – the result of hearing/reading something new that does not fit into one's reality, or in what one thought was their reality; the effect is to create confusion followed by denial of new concepts. More specifically, when a new idea conflicts with an established idea that one already thinks they know, the result is 'dissonance', and rejection. When people were told 500 years ago that the Earth was round, they experienced great cognitive dissonance… which led to denial.

**Coherence** – resonating alike; attracted to each other by similar resonance. Two energy waves are coherent if they have the same shape, size, and strength.

**Déjà Vu** – the experience of having done, seen and/or heard something before; as though one is reliving a prior moment in their current lifetime. Relates to reliving a fractal simulation. See **Recycling**.

**Dissidents** – 3D Anunnaki hybrid Remnant still on the Earth who seek to control Man and deny him his divine heritage. See **Insiders**.

**Draconians** – a militaristic STS race largely from the Orion System who have subjugated several worlds in our Galaxy. Also referred to as the Dracs, or the Reptiles. A very old race that lays claim to much of the Galaxy and they fear Man because they don't all have (nor do they understand) the soul, thus they seek to contain/control Man. Some are benevolent.

**Elite** -- those humans who are purly descended from the Anunnaki hybrids; as a group they may be augmented by the Remnant Insiders who stayed behind when the main contingent of Anunnaki went home. They are generally not the enemy, and they are not synonymous with PTB. We do not know their names but they are behind the scenes overseeing Man's development… See **Insider.** See **PTB**.

**ELF** – Extremely Low Frequency; a vibratory wave form that is sent by a radio-like device or microwave transmitter at a certain Hz or MHz frequency such that it entrains the mind into a 'resonant state' (usually Alpha) with the wave.

**EMF** – ElectroMagnetic Field; such an electrical field around a high tension power line also generates its own weak magnetic field, hence EMF. Note that a cellphone or TV or PC – anything electronic has an EMF and it is unhealthy to spend much time in it as it 'afflicts' the cells of the body and disrupts their function. The reason is that the body has its own weak EMF and communicates info to other parts of the body via the nervous system and chi meridians (see **Bionet**).

**Energy Vampire** – a person, OP or ensouled, who deliberately or subconsciously starts an argument, gets the other person angry, and the instigator takes the other person's energy through the Law of Energy Potentials. Energy always flows from the higher potential to the lower and this applies to car batteries, as well as humans. So the instigator creates a fight, not to win or lose (they don't care), they will walk off with some of your energy, and they quit the argument when they have it. They are up, and the victim is usually tired.

**Entanglement** – as used in this book refers to the concept that we are all connected at the Higher Self level – via the Superconscious part of our minds (which is why telepathy works for those who have the expanded genetics to do that). Entanglement is better known in the Quantum Physics world, reflected by splitting a photon and changing the left ½'s "spin" and noting that the other, right ½, makes a corresponding change at the same time – i.e., interconnectedness on the subquantum level – reflecting an unseen connection between the two halves (carried by the Ether). (See VEG and TSiM.)

**Entrain** – to induce a state in B like in A; usually done by music, movies, and words, but can be done by powerful thoughts and beliefs, or an energy state in the presence of a Higher Being. A hypnotist entrains a subject into a desired state; Hitler's harangues entrained the crowds into the Nazi mindset he wanted; and classical music entrains the listeners into a relaxed (Alpha) state. See **hyperdimensional**.

**Entropy** – the tendency of all things in the universe to wind down and die; also called the Second Law of Thermodynamics. The enemy of Evolution.

**Era** – occasionally the Higher Beings have to clean up and reset the Simulation, usually what this book referees to as a Wipe and Reboot. When Man is restarted after a Wipe and Reboot, the Era will have some dominant theme in the Greater Script that the activities of Man are to experience and handle. Our current Era began about AD 800-900.

**ESH** – Ensouled Human Being, has a soul and thus an aura. See also **OP**s. Chapter 2. (This is an acronym only, it is not pronounced.)

**Flow** – often referred to as The Flow. This is the rising energetic vibrational entrainment into the higher 4th and 5th dimensional realms. It has increased awareness, compassion, Light, and STO aspects for service and is available to all who seek to align themselves with a Higher Way. It was created by the Higher Beings and is supported by an archetype that masters on the Earth reinforced and made available to all spiritual growth aspirants.

**Fractal** – as in fractal simulation is a subset of an existing Timeline, attached to it and resonating with similar energy but playing out the main timeline's alternate possibilities… Mathematically, a fractal subset is often seen in the Fibonacci series of numbers: 1, 1, 2, 3, 5, 8, 13, 21, 34, 55, 89, 144…. (the next number is the sum of the two before it) which just happens to be the mathematical basis of the chambered nautilus' shell… Also a factor in fractal art (qv on Google).

**Freewill** – an illusion, but a soul does have the freedom to choose when faced with a **Point of Choice**… and be responsible for it. . The more one grows spiritually, the more one does the will of the Father of Light. Baby souls, or those who insist on their own way, think they have freewill but the Father is merely letting them experience the results of their choice… their **Script** controls much of what Young/Baby souls can do. As Jesus said "Not my will, but Thine be done." Advanced souls have surrendered their will by eliminating their ego.

**Galactic Law** – the ethics and rules as set forth by the Galactic Council and adhered to by all subordinate councils for the maintenance of order. It includes **a Non-interference** directive, responsibilities of 'creator races', transportation/communication protocols, terra-forming procedures, and energy creation/disposal to name a few.

**God/gods** – this is god with a small "g". The Anunnaki were called gods because of their power and control over Man. In addition, Sargon, Moses, Gilgamesh, Alexander the Great and a number of Anunnaki offspring who were half-human half-Anunnaki were considered god-like. When the book refers to "the gods who run the Simulation" it is meant metaphorically (i.e., the Higher Beings), and not a reference to the **Remnant.**

**Godhead** – a collection of higher Souls, and Soul Groups, in closest proximity to God, like spokes on a wheel where the hub is God Himself. The Godhead works directly with the Oversoul for each Soul Group and sometimes the two are hard to distinguish. The basic hierarchy is: **The One – Godhead hierarchy – Oversouls – Soul Groups – Soul/Higher Self – soul aspects.** Angels(Beings of Light) /Neggs operate in the realm between Souls and souls. (See also Soul, Soul Group, and Higher Self.) Each Godhead has multiple Oversouls that interface with the multiple Soul Groups.

**Gods-in-Training** – when Man graduates from the Earth School, he can be useful to the Father of Light in various places in the Multiverse. One of those places is to undergo an apprentice position in overseeing the Earth and its souls – under the tutelage of more advanced beings who give direction and training. The gods-in-training still make mistakes, just as Man does, and while often minimized by karmic override, these are allowed in part as an aspect of the new gods' training. This is therefore sometimes a source of things going wrong in an Earth person's life. If a god-in-training abuses his power, he is recycled back to Earth.

**Greys** – the 3' tall gray-colored humanoids with the big heads, big black eyes and skinny bodies; their eyes are large (really protective coverings over eyes sensitive to light); they typically perform the abductions on humans, some cattle and other species. They have a hive/group mentality as they are **Anunnaki bio-cybernetic roboid** tools to improve Man's DNA.

**Ground of Being** – who and what you really are; your PFV is the physical reflection of the sum of your STO/STS quotient. If you, your soul essence, were to be removed from your body, the energy being that you are would have a certain vibration level (also reflected in the color of your aura) – higher or lower depending on how much Light you hold, how compassionate you are, whether you seek to serve (STO) or be served (STS), what issues (stuck points, agendas and attachments) you still carry with you, and in general, it refers to the "quality" of Light & Love that you are. Ultimately, it reflects the highest actions/thoughts that you are capable of.

**Higher Beings** – Light Beings above the Astral and reincarnative levels (1-6) and who are responsible for the operation of these lower 6 levels, reside on the 7th level themselves; may intervene in 3rd – 4th – 5th – 6th dimensional affairs when the Greater Script of the Father of Light, or the One, requires it to keep the Multiverse working.

Also colloquially called "**the gods**" who run the **HVR Sphere** or Simulation. The Higher Beings are <u>not</u> the Beings of Light (angels) nor ETs nor aliens.

**Higher Self** – also called the Soul (top level), this is the coordinating entity of each Soul Group and acts to oversee Scripts, events, lessons – and coordinate with the souls of the same Soul Group, <u>and</u> with the Oversouls who manage other Soul Groups in the same Godhead. Each Godhead has multiple Oversouls that interface with the multiple **Soul Groups.**

**HVR Sphere** – Holographic Virtual Reality is the 4D construct in which 3D Earth is contained, in Quarantine. (Details in VEG, Chapters 12-13.) The concept is that since vision and memory are holographic, our reality is basically a very sophisticated Hologram, similar to a Simulation run on *Star Trek* in the Holodeck.

**Hybrids** – this is any human-looking but 'upgraded' version of Homo *sapiens* which may or may not have a soul. It can be the Anunnaki hybrids – part Anunnaki, part human, and their bloodline. Or it may be Homo *noeticus* that the Greys have been so busy developing to restart civilization after the big Change event in the near future. Most are very intuitive, psychic and look to be the next step in the development of Man.

**Hyperdimensional** -- is a catch-all reference to the realm referred to by interdimensional, ultradimensional and such (principally within Chapter 7 where Messers Keel and Missler refer to unseen entities in the higher realms). The Astral (4D), 5D and 6D realms are also hyperdimensional because they are **above** this one that we inhabit. The significance in Chapter 7 is used to emphasize 'hyperdimensional energy' and its effect on humans… that of Greys, alleged demons and any beings of a higher vibrational realm having an energy (PFV) that exceeds Man's in 3D and thus there is some **entrainment** into a higher (and not necessarily benevolent) energy state for Man.

**IFOs** – Identified Flying Objects. These UFOs are identified and their source known.

**Insiders** – 3D Anunnaki hybrid Remnant still on the Earth (may include Enki). The pro-active ones who try to help mankind and block the **Dissidents**' agenda (qv).

**Interdimensionals** – those beings in 4D <u>and above</u> who normally have very little interest in Man, and may be STO or STS. The STOs are often curious and observing. The STS version has been known to use OPs for unknown agendas. Also a generic term for the 4D STS Controllers inasmuch as they operate between dimensions. Possibly Djinn. See also **hyperdimensional**.

**InterLife** – where souls go when they die, after passing through the **Tunnel** to the **Light**. Also called the **Other Side**, and sometimes appears to be Heaven. It is where the **Script** is designed, souls are counseled by the Masters and Teachers, souls are rehabilitated after a rough lifetime on Earth (or elsewhere), and it is where the Heavenly Quantum Bio-Computer referred to in Chapter 7 resides. This is also where reunions with other members of one's **Soul Group** happen.

**Karma** – *Aka* **The Law of Karma**. – originally the concept of "meeting oneself", or "what goes 'round, comes 'round." It does <u>not</u> mean being stabbed in this lifetime because one stabbed someone else in a former lifetime. The original, true concept was that of the Universal Law of Cause and Effect, and it forms the basis of one or more aspects of your Life Script. Karma can also be a manipulative issue in the Virtual Reality of Earth if the life review is done by a Negg posing as a Being of Light.
Note that Karma applies only to Earth; other souls who do not come to Earth do not have to deal with Karma. Completed Karma results in being under Grace.

**Law of Attraction** – more than a Law, this is just a statement of "like attracts like." It is however, precise: in order to **have** what one wants, it is first necessary to **be** the kind of person that would be able to handle and use what is sought, i.e., be one with the mentality, or mindset, of those who have and do what is sought. Then **do** what it takes to get it. For example, to acquire riches, one must think like a rich man, and do what a rich man would do get the money. AND add **three things**: visualize the money, intend to get it, and put energy/feeling (willpower) behind the desire. This does **not manifest** the money: be clear that you are **not creating** the money… you are attracting it or the people you need that will help you get it.

**Law of Confusion** – when RA was asked a question that violated someone else's right to privacy, or asked something that would be giving advanced level information that the person had no context for, RA would comment that the question could not be answered because it "violated the Law of Confusion." We are to work through confusion and seek the answer(s) on our own; we have the 'right' to be confused and are <u>expected to work through it</u>, or ask, thereby absorbing the lesson and information on a personal level that makes the lesson/info part of us.

**Law of One** – the concept that we are all connected at a higher level, mostly through our Higher Selves, and we are all part of the One, the Father of Light – if you have a soul. This does not apply to OPs. The Law of One also includes freewill and love. Telling someone else what to do, how to live, etc. is a violation of the Law of One, a violation of freewill whose flipside is called the Law of Confusion. See also **Entanglement.**

**Light** – an intelligent aspect of God; sometimes referred to as the Force. It may be used interchangeably with Heaven. There are **biophotons** of light that support the operation of DNA and sustain bodily operations.
Note that Light (large L) is a conscious aspect of the God force, which force can have a brilliant light about it. The light (small "l") is every day, regular light.

**Lightworker** – any entity, physical or Astral, that uses Light as an energy source to do its work. (Includes Angels, "demons", Neggs, energy healers and Higher Beings.) Caution: it does not always imply STO behavior.

**Loosh** – a term coined by Robert Monroe in his chapter 12 of <u>Far Journeys</u>. It is energy produced by 3D living beings that is allegedly harvested by 4D STS entities in the astral for sustenance. Loosh is bountifully produced by humans who go into states of deep **fear** or anger or lust – they radiate the energy after being manipulated to produce it – like a grain of sand in an oyster produces a pearl that is harvested. See **Energy Vampire**.

**Matrix** – (1) except for Chapter 12, a synonym for the Earth **HVR Sphere**, but not to be confused with the matrix as shown in the movie *Matrix*. (2) As used in Chapter 12, refers to the ZPE Field, or Dark Matter field that we all inhabit, that is extant in all of the universe. Also used by the Matrix Energetic modality for healing people in Chapter 12.

**Memes** – a concept, or idea, that generally has spread through a population – an idea that may spread like a psychological virus – such as a belief in ghosts, or a belief that black cats bring bad luck…or, if you go out in the rain and get wet, you can catch a cold. There are positive and negative memes. (See also "**100th Monkey Effect**.")

**Metempsychosis** – allegedly a new soul, up from the animal group-soul world. This would be a **Pre-soul** who is a first-time human, but is undeveloped and thus their aura is allegedly not visible as it is not developed. See Wikipedia for more on the theory.

**Morphic Resonance** – said of a plant or animal that takes its physical shape from the *morphogenetic* **field** that establishes a 'morphic' (shape) resonance with the object's energy. The plant's shape is entrained by the morphic resonance with the morphogenetic field (pattern) that governs how living things take shape, according to Rupert Sheldrake.

**Morphogenesis** – Rupert Sheldrake conceived of the presence of a 4D field around living things that influences the shape they take – kind of an Astral Template that governs height, width, color and other aspects of the oak tree for example, such as when and where it sends out its branches, how fast and how far. See Chapter 12.

**Multiverse** – the universe we live in is one of a number of universes comprising a Multiverse… multiple universes interconnected forming a coherent larger universe consisting of multiple levels (realities), and can involve parallel universes or dimensions in 'superposition' (or stacked). See **Superposition.**

**NDE** – a Near Death Experience where the person temporarily dies, and their body is pronounced clinically dead, but they come back to life and relay their experience of meeting a Being of Light with whom they have a Life Review, and they usually come back a changed (better) person. The NDE effect often produces a spiritual transformation in the person.

**Neggs** – the 4D 'dark' angelic beings operating in the Astral realm around the Earth, whose sole purpose is to apply the negative lessons specified in one's Life Script. Thus they are "**NEG**ative **G**uide**S**." They work with the Beings of Light (Angels).
They are programmed to afflict mankind – they are appointed to effect the negative parts of one's Script (aka **catalyst**). They provide catalyst and feedback inducing Man to change and grow. They work with the Beings of Light (Chapter 7) because they, too, are Beings of Light who volunteered to serve the negative agenda and they were 'reoriented' to Darkness to maximize their effectiveness. They still carry a small, suppressed connection to their original Light down inside and they will be restored to their original condition when their service is complete.

**Nephilim** – the physical Anunnaki Igigi mated with earth women and produced giants or Anakim, Giborim and Rephaim, which were hell on earth. (Enoch's story.)

**New Age / New Thought** – The New Age is a general term reflecting the most progressive ideas, mostly in Religion, that reflect metaphysical or even Quantum Physics concepts. The New Age promotes Man as a god, able to 'create his day' and manifest health and wealth almost on demand. Popular books for the masses sustain this view. The New Thought Churches, on the other hand, were the original, more conservative metaphysical teachings which often had their roots in more esoteric teachings, not always for the masses.

**NPCs** – these are the other characters in a Virtual Reality game; they are not programmable or operable by the player – the Game or operating system uses them to play a part in the Drama. They are called Non-Playable Characters. Same as **OP**s (Chapter 2).

**OPs – Organic Portals** -- (pronounced "Oh Pee") human beings, flesh and blood (Organic part), and they can serve as a portal for 4D entities (Neggs and 4D STS Controllers) to operate thru them. They also are not fully human as they lack a soul and that is because they often have defective DNA (which is why a soul did not enter at birth) and only the first 3 chakras are wired to function; they cannot access higher energy centers. Due to their somewhat robotic nature, they can be used by the STS Gang to manipulate and/or influence ensouled humans in 3D. They are often playing the role of **NPC**'s (as in a video game) in our world: See Book 4. Also called **Backdrop People** (Dolores Cannon).

**PFV – Personal Frequency Vibration** -- the day-to-day, overall vibratory rate (resonance) of the soul energy sustaining the human body. When a person is angry their aura 'glows' red, and the PFV can drop to a lower (denser) vibration than when a person feels a lot of love and the aura 'glows' rose and the vibration reflects the energy of the heart charka (higher, lighter energy). The PFV also denotes which charka is dominant in the person; a person living from their higher charkas has a higher PFV than one engaged in sex, violence and pettiness (lower chakra activity). The aura typically reflects what one is feeling, yet the base PFV does not change; when the person is at rest, the base PFV is consistent from day to day as it reflects the overall level of soul growth. Also known as that person's "energy signature" as recorded in objects (Psychometry).

**Phase-Shifted** – refers to 3D and 4D entities or 3D and 4D timelines which cannot see the other even though they may occupy the same space. For example, there may be a 30° phase shift, or a 60° or 90° shift (the most common). Think of 2 Sine waves almost on top of each other (congruent and coherent; now move one wave to where it's trough is below the other wave's peak – they are 90° phase-shifted in space-time. (Where they cross in a less than 90 ° Shift presents some interesting possibilities for moving to a new timeline.) See Chapter 2.

**Placeholder** – an OP-like version of a real ensouled human living on another timeline (parallel universe) that already split into two, with duplications of people between the timelines. If the ensouled human did not replicate to the new TL, the other people who went to the new timeline still need/expect that 'body' for their everyday world activities to function, and his absence in their lives would be noticed. And so minus a soul, John Doe exists as a kind of 'synthetic' human in the new timeline. (See Chapter 2, and Apx D.)

**Point of Choice** – there are pre-programmed points in a person's life where important choices must be made, and they are found in a person's Script. Examples are whether to move to Florida or stay in California, whether to accept what looks like a great new job, or whether to get married. Sometimes the choice results in a **timeline bifurcation** into a **fractal subset** so that another aspect of you can see how that turned out. See **Timeline**. See Chapter 7 example with Sean.

**Pre-Soul** – also called **First Time Soul**, allegedly the initial stage of an animal that leaves 2D and enters the 3D human soul realm (**metempsychosis**); this is not a complete soul, but a potential one if the entity applies itself as a 1st time human. Allegedly, only the first 3 chakras are functional, and thus there is not enough 'soul energy' to create an aura. (See also **OP**s.) This is a tentative theory and has yet to be proven.

**Prime Directive** – a requirement in our Galaxy for those races who can create life and modify existing life genetically – often referred to as a 'creator race.' They are responsible for overseeing the welfare, safety and education of their creation. This is why a **Remnant** of the Anunnaki stayed behind (some are now known as the Naga.)

**Prophylactic Fantasy** – describes the world of denial that some people live in. 'Prophylactic' because they feel safe in <u>their version</u> of the world, and they reason that nothing really destructive has ever happened to them, nor can it.
'Fantasy' because they do not accept the real world and its negativity; they see their world as they want it to be and think that they exert a 'force' that makes it that way. Baby Souls in the New Age philosophy.

**PTB** – the earthly human **Powers That Be**; the 3rd dimensional STS people running the world for their Anunnaki Dissident masters (control group still here). They are also influenced by corrupt DNA, and the **RCF/Matrix** itself. Puppets. Many of the top PTB are OPs. See **Elite** – not the same thing, just a higher level of control.

**Quantum Bio-Computer** – also referred to as the Heavenly BioComputer (largely in Chapter 7) where it is the key to a soul researching new lifetimes and adventures while in the InterLife. Once the lifetime is selected to experience upon reincarnating into a timeline, the soul interacts with the Computer and the help of a Master to insert oneself into the chosen LifeScript in the chosen Timeline. (See also QES computers.)

It is "Quantum" as it occupies several dimensions (3D – 5D) and does so at a micro level, or affecting the quanta of several dimensions. It is also called "Bio" as it interfaces with biological lifeforms (besides Man) to effect the insertion into on-going lifetimes and scenarios in chosen Timelines. It is "Heavenly" as it is only accessed from and controlled at the InterLife (i.e., heavenly) level. Yet the operation and concept of the device as a "Computer" is a poor analogy for what appears to be **a living entity** or at least the device has sentient aspects to itself…perhaps this is a **Singularity** (Ray Kurzweil would love it).

**RCF/Matrix** – see below (Resonant Consciousness Field).

**Recycle** – short-circuited version of reincarnation: to come back into the same body, same lifetime, hence experiences **Déjà Vu**. Implies the inability to move forward into new realms and experiences in the greater **Multiverse**. (See Chapter 6: Life is a Film.)

**Reincarnation** – the spiritual growth aspect of a soul moving through the different realms in the Multiverse (not just back to Earth) for the purpose of experiencing and gaining knowledge and wisdom. On the other hand, a repeated lifetime limited to Earth is more of a recycling.

**Remnant** – short for Anunnaki Remnant – that part of the Anunnaki group that stayed on Earth and did not leave with the main group, between 650-600 BC. Comprised of the Insiders (+) and the Dissidents (-). Some are human-looking. Also known as Naga (underground 'Serpent' dwellers in Asia), or also called Dravidians. Still here, split affiliations: allegedly work with the Elite [+] and the PTB [-].

**Reptibian** – A humanoid being, part reptile, part amphibian. In most ways looking like a human being, but with scales instead of skin, perhaps slightly webbed toes and fingers, cat's eyes, and a face that suggests a reptile/amphibian more than a human being. Note that an anaconda is aquatic and is also a reptile that moves on land.

**Resonance** – vibrating alike: such that two tuning forks A and B side by side, with A struck hard to set it vibrating, when put next to B which was not vibrating, will set tuning fork B vibrating at the same frequency as tuning fork A. This also happens with people in close proximity: a very negative person can 'detune' (bring down) a room of people and some people may actually feel ill and not know why (as they pick up the negative person's vibes). See **Entrainment.**

**Resonant Consciousness Field – RCF/Matrix** – the very negative energy and **thoughtforms** surrounding the Earth, as a vibrational envelope or field or Band that is so strong it <u>entrains</u> ensouled humans who are unconscious (qv) into their lower 3 chakras and they act out STS ideals. It is not alive or evil; it just has a lot of strength from centuries of people acting in synch with it and thus reinforcing its energy level. Similar in structure to Robert Monroe's "H Band" but not run by any entities. (See VEG Ch 12.)

**Satan** – allegedly the leader of the demonic spirits which were perhaps the deceased Nephilim and/or their offspring (according to Enoch). This titular role may have been filled by the Nephilim (fallen Igigi) leaders known as Samayaza or Azazyel, or the Gnostic favorite: Ialdabaoth, in a former Era. The Egyptian Set, or Sata, was probably synonymous with one of the three just named. A convenient mythological character to personify Man's need for duality in the universe. (See Chapters 2 and 6 in VEG.) Not synonymous with Lucifer.

**Schumann Resonance** – natural frequency of earth's vibration/resonance: 7.8Hz. It is allegedly near 12 Hz today (preparing for vibrational Shift, or timeline split).

**Script** – to assist Karma, when one is born, one is given a Script covering what **basic events** are to happen in one's life, which one is expected to overcome; they may be positive or negative, and how one meets them and handles them determines how one is progressing towards the goal of getting out of the Earth School. It often has Options programmed into it (**Points of Choice**) where the soul must make a significant choice. It is a test of soul growth. A personal Script is usually subject to the Greater Script of the Father of Light and works within it. Also called **LifeScript. The Script does not tell anyone what to do or say  (see next page…)**

423

> **Scripts, Souls and Timelines are more developed in Appendix D.**

**ShapeShifting –** the ability to **control what people see**… the being doing the shape-shifting does not actually change any of his atomic structure – just the way his appearance is **perceived,** and **perception is holographic**. So to effect a different appearance, the being just produces new interference waves that the observer 'sees' differently. Commonly done by 4D and above entities while in 3D. (More in TSiM on Vision.)

**Simulation** – best explained in Chapter 13 of VEG. When Earth was placed in a 3D **Holographic Virtual Sphere** and resulting Quarantine, this created a kind of Simulation – on its own timeline, circa AD 900. This is a protected environment which was subsequently hijacked by 4D STS entities (who engineered a timeloop in 1943), obstructing Man's ability to form coherent quantum energy-based bifurcations for separation of the "goats" from the "sheep." Alternate paths that would have generated whole timelines, now spawn **fractal simulations** within the current Timeline-based Simulation. This complicated Man's release from the Earth School until it was removed by the Timelords. (Ch 2.) Also **Book 4 (QES)**.

**Sheep** – people who are barely conscious, and refuse to think for themselves. They want someone to tell them what to do and when to do it, and they go along with whatever they are told. They are easily manipulated by the Media. Also called **'sheeple'** and may be OPs or 'dense' ensouled humans.

**Soul** – with a large "S" refers to the unique one of you on the Other Side, sometimes referred to as the Higher Self. This is the Soul before any splits into different 'aspects' are made. The word soul (small "s") refers to one of the possible aspects that split off and are each probably experiencing a different timeline, dimension or LifeScript.

The Soul is an aspect of the Greater **One,** the Father of Light, containing all the potential to grow and work its way back in Knowledge and Love to the One. To do this it chooses to undergo experiences in countless realms and assimilate the Knowledge of the Father of Light's Mutiverse. Earth is but one 3D School. See **Godhead** for Hierarchy.

**Soul Aspect** – all Souls can 'split' themselves to experience different realms; as when a timeline splits, one part of the Soul stays with the original TL and another part replicates to the new TL. Each Soul has aspects in different TLs, dimensions, worlds, etc. and at a point in the future, they reunite to the Oversoul for its Group. Not a **Fragment**. (See Chapter 7.)

**Soul Fragment** – some souls may fragment **due to trauma** and then special therapy is often needed to coax the missing fragment to rejoin its source. Some fragments are held by family members, past lovers, and even by the Neggs themselves. The Oversoul does not fragment.

**Soul Group** – each Soul is part of a Group of like Souls (same core vibration PFV which usually synchs up with a specific archetype: artist, engineer, healer…) and these split up to better experience the Creation – souls will eventually reunite back into the Soul in their original Group when their explorings are done. The Soul Groups reunite with the **Godhead** from which they came. See **Godhead** for Hierarchy.

**Soul Merge** – as in the case of the author, to undertake a special project where a 3rd level soul has volunteered to serve in a capacity that it can't do alone, and so a Merge is performed to give that 3rd level soul (small 's') the extra knowledge and strength of the merging soul aspect (who is of the same Soul Group -- usually from a higher level) and together they perform some task that the Higher Beings must have approved – before the Merge can happen. (This replaces the **Walk-in** scenario.)

**Soul Migration** – the concept that animals can progress to first-time human beings with 'baby' souls and the full-fledged human soul must be earned athrough successive incarnations. This requires more research.
As they would also have only the lower 3 chakras operative, they my be mistaken for OPs. (See **Metempsychosis** on Wikipedia.)

**STO** – Service To Others; altruistic behavior, self-sacrificing.
**STS** – Service To Self; selfish behavior; 'Me-My-Mine' syndrome.

**STS Gang** – this is a 'catch all' group term referring to the Neggs, discarnates, thoughtforms, all 4D STS, including Anunnaki Dissidents, acting as oppressors of Man, without a clear distinction as to exactly which one is doing what to Man at any one time. The group may occasionally include the **Interdimensional** souls described by Wilde and Monroe (Chapter 7), although such are <u>usually</u> too busy interfering with the entities on their own level to harass Man on the 3D level. May also include the 3D PTB.

**Subquantum Kinetics** – is an approach to microphysics with roots in general system theory, nonequilibrium thermodynamics, and nonlinear dynamics. It represents quantum phenomena differently than Quantum Physics (QP) and works with the concept of the **Ether** which is composed of subquantum units called **etherons** (as opposed to QP's quarks). It is simpler than Quantum Physics and explains the issues that QP is still wrestling with: wave-particle dualism, strings, singularities, and the cosmological constant. (See Chapter 12 in this book.)
It also embraces and explains **Tesla's** work better than QP. (Refer to Chapter 4 of **Dr. Paul LaViolette's** book <u>Secrets of Antigravity Propulsion</u> for a more complete description in layman's terms.)_ Also examined in Chapter 9 of VEG.

**Superposition** – when universes are stacked (conceptually) one on top of the other, reflecting the fact that they may be phase-shifted so they occupy the same space-time. See diagram in Chapter 2.

**TCM – Traditional Chinese Medicine** – an ages old system of herbs, *chi* and Qigong exercise, as well as using the Yin and Yang of energy Flow in the meridians for Acupuncture. Teaches there are 5 Elements, 8 Conditions, 12 Organs, and the idea of changes in states of the body during the Seasons and even during times of the day/night cycle.

**Terraforming** – an advanced technological process whereby a whole planet is set to its original, or a near-new, pristine condition following some catastrophe or pollution, or both.

The ecology is balanced, the air, land and water are unpolluted, and in the case of planet Earth, it can once again support lifeforms. See also "**Wipe and Reboot.**"

**Thoughtform** (**TF**) – any thought that many people subscribe to and which reflects a widely held belief, esp. one imbued with a lot of fear, or hate, generates a TF which after a while (depending on the amt of energy put into it) takes on a 'life' of its own; **man is a creator and thoughts are things**. If enough people fear and believe in werewolves, there will be a thoughtform to 'fear werewolves' … which are not real entities but are attracted to those who fear and believe in them (like attracts like).

Any unwanted TF can be cancelled and should be before it attaches itself to a person's aura and then 'feeds' off the person's energy – like a parasite. TF have no conscious volition of their own, they are reactive and go to wherever (1) they are attracted by sympathetic vibration, and (2) attach where the person's aura is weak.

Carl Jung called some of these TF's **Archtypes**. Qigong and EFT healing modalities can clean these TF from the aura.

**Timeline** (**TL**) – the linear coherent vector on which all souls and Placeholders (OPs) of a certain frequency range have their being; a reality timeline that linearly moves forward creating causal events. It is not permanent and is subject to entropy if a bifurcation results from a rise in consciousness and attendant agreement coherently shared among the souls seeking to live in a higher consciousness in TL2 is preferable to the over-negatively polarized TL1. If there is not enough agreement (energy) to sustain the new TL2, it dissolves.

If a dimension has only one TL, the TL is the dimension, but dimensions can have multiple TLs. There is a TL where Hitler won, for example.

And timelines may create, 'run' and dissolve **fractal** subsets (within the larger TL framework) for special purposes. (See Chapter 2 herein and Appendix D.)

**UFOs** – Unidentified Flying Objects. Known around the world as OVNIs (Objeto Volante Non-Identificado in Latin America), also OVNIs (Objets Volants Non-Identifiées in France) or as *Flugscheiben* (Germany), or as НЛО (неопознанный летающий объект "NLO" in Russia). This can be an unrecognized plane, balloon, lenticular cloud, or real flying saucer. Many UFOs are really **IFO**s – they have been identified.

**Unconscious** – unaware, not a very high level of perception. A person who is 'asleep' spiritually and is not aware that there are more than the 5 senses. Can also mean 'spacing out' with eyes wide open. Standard condition of the **Sheeple**.

**V2K – "Voice to Skull"** -- a microwave enhanced transmission of words directly into a person's head, as if they actually hear the words, without any external devices or hearing apparatus. Developed by the US Army to communicate with a soldier on the battlefield, to the exclusion of other soldiers, it was perfected during the mind experiments with Helen Schucman while she transcribed the *Course in Miracles* book. Who sent her the information is not known to this day, but it was definitely a PsyOps event. (VEG, Ch 11.)

**VEG** – refers to the first book, *Virtual Earth Graduate*, published in early 2014. Also called Book 1.

**Vibration/Vibe** – the energy state of a person, place or thing. Everything puts out an energy 'signature', which is how psychometry works… objects record the PFV energy of the person that held/owned the object, and places often hold the residual energy of events that happened there: some sensitive people cannot visit Gettysburg as they feel the negative energy from all the hate and fear created in that place – even thought it was long ago, it still holds some energy that has not completely dissipated. (See **PFV**.)

**Vimanas** – In Hindu literature (*Ramayana* and *MahaBharata*), the gods were said to fly around the sky and even engage in warfare between these craft and UFOs with exotic but powerful weapons – similar to the Sumerian flying machines (MAR.GID.DA, IM.DU.GUD, and GIR). An ancient form of UFO, cone-shaped like many temples in Thailand, or *Stupas* in Tibet.

**Visual Spatial Acuity** – the ability to see fine detail; visual term reflecting the number of rods/cones in the retina. Similar to **pixels** in computer printing, display screens and digital cameras.

**Walk-in** – was a soul aspect from a higher realm, usually 5D or 6D, that took over a 3D soul's body to accomplish a task on Earth. While this is not done much anymore, it was done **with the agreement of the outgoing soul** who was fed up with their life and so not able or willing to continue with their earth experience , they surrender to an in-coming higher soul who has the opportunity to implement needed Light and Knowledge on Earth. Sometimes this was done after an NDE.  (See **Soul Merge**.)

**Wanderers** – higher souls from other realms who have volunteered to incarnate on Earth in troubled times to serve as the Light leads: they may anchor the Light, write books, lead New Thought churches, heal or perform other services to benefit Mankind. Usually 6th level beings (souls). The Indigos and different forms of "Starseed" are part of this group.

**Wipe and Reboot** – an end to a current **Era** of Man on Earth, followed usually by a terra-forming (resetting the environment back to clean and balanced), followed by the re-seeding of Man on the planet.

The term is borrowed from the computer world where when a PC is non-functional (i.e., locked up and displays the dreaded BSOD [Blue Screen of Death]), it is necessary to "Wipe" the hard disk – reformat it – and reload the operating system and application software… and then "Reboot" the system and **start all over again**.
Whereas the PC gets a clean start as if nothing happened, each new Era for Man still includes whatever objects were created in the prior Era – i.e., pyramids, huge walls, and Stonehenge.

**Zechariah Sitchin** – the late Middle Eastern scholar, speaking several languages, who translated the **Anunnaki**/Sumerian tablets. VEG Chapter 3 is mostly dedicated to a summary of his findings about Man's origins, including 4 areas in which his obfuscation of the truth is exposed.  His claim to fame was *The Earth Chronicles* series of 8+ books that revealed the Sumerian – Anunnaki connection … and we are much indebted to this man for sharing as much as he did.

# Bibliography: A Suggested Reading List

## Books

## Religion/Metaphysics/Spirituality

Acharya S.          *The Christ Conspiracy*. Kempton, IL: AU Press,  1999.
Andrews, Ann.       *Walking Between Worlds*. CA: Reality Press, 2007.
Beaconsfield, Hannah. *Welcome to Planet Earth*. AZ: Mission Possible, 1997.
Bloom, Harold.      *Jesus and Yahweh: The Names Divine*. New York: Penguin Group (USA), 2005.
Dawood, N. J.       *The Koran*. New York: Penguin Group (USA), 2006.
Frejer, B. Ernest.  *The Edgar Cayce Companion*. New York: Barnes & Noble Press, 1995.
Freke, Timothy.     *Lucid Living*. London: Books for Burning, 2005.
_____         *The Laughing Jesus*. NY: Three Rivers Press, 2005.
Gaffney, Mark.      *Gnostic Secrets of the Naassenes*. Rochester, VT: Inner Traditions, 2004.
Gardiner, Philip.   *Secret Societies*. Franklin Lakes, NJ: Career Press/New Page, 2007.
_____.        *Secrets of the Serpent*. Forest Hill, CA: Reality Press, 2008.
_____.        *The Shining Ones*. Nottinghamshire, England: Phase Group, 2002.
Guiley, Rosemary Ellen and Imbrogno, Philip J. *The Vengeful Djinn*. Woodbury, Mn: Llewellyn Worldwide,  2012.
Holmes, Dr. Ernest. *The Science of Mind*. NY: Putnam, 1966.
Kenyon, J. Douglas, Ed.  *Forbidden Religion*. Rochester, VT: Bear & Co., 2006.
Mead, G.R.S.        *Apollonius of Tyana*. (1901 Edition reprint)  Sacramento, CA: Murine Press, 2008.
Meyer, Marvin.      *The Gospel of Thomas*. New York: HarperCollins, 1992.
Newton, Michael.    *Destiny of Souls*. Woodbury, Mn: Llewellyn Worldwide,  2002.
_____.        *Journey of Souls*. Woodbury, Mn: Llewellyn Worldwide,  1994.
Pagels, Elaine.     *The Gnostic Gospels*. New York: Random House/Vintage, 1979.
Peck, M. Scott, M.D. *Glimpses of the Devil*. New York: Free Press, 2005.
_____         *People of the Lie*. New York: Touchstone, 1983.
Robinson, James M., General Editor. *The Nag Hammadi Library*. New York: HarperCollins, 1990.
Ruffin, C. Bernard. *Padre Pio: The True Story*. Huntington, IN: Our Sunday Visitor Publishing Division, Inc., 1991.
Russell, A. J.,     *God Calling*. Uhrichsville, OH: Barbour Publishing, 1989.
Snellgrove, Brian.  *The Unseen Self*. Essex, England: The C.W. Daniel Co.,  1996.
Spong, John Shelby. *A New Christianity for a New World*. HarperSanFrancisco, 2001.
_____         *Why Christianity Must Change or Die*. HarperSanFrancisco, 1999.
*The King James Study Bible*. Nashville, TN: Thomas Nelson, 1988.

Todeschi, Kevin. *Edgar Cayce on Soul Mates.* VA: A.R.E Press, 1999.

Webster, Richard. *Soul Mates.* MN: Llewellyn Publishing, 2009.

Wilde, Stuart. *The Prayers and Contemplations of God's Gladiators.* Chicago, IL: Brookemarke, LLC., 2001.

_____ *The Force.* Carlsbad, CA: Hay House, 2006.

Zukav, Gary. *The Dancing Wu Li Masters.* New York: Quill, 1979.

_____ *The Seat of the Soul.* New York: Simon & Schuster, 1990.

# Transformation

Amen, MD, Daniel G. *Change Your Brain, Change Your Body.* NY: Three Rivers Press, 2011.

Bartlett, Richard. *Matrix Energetics.* NY: Atria/Simon & Schuster, 2007.

Brennan, Barbara. *Hands of Light.* NY: Bantam Books, 1988.

Cannon, Dolores. *Keepers of the Garden.* Huntsville, AR: Ozark Mtn Publ, 2002.

_____ *Between Death & Life.* AR: OMP, 2001

_____ *The Three Waves of Volunteers and The New Earth.* AR: OMP, 2012.

_____ *The Convoluted Universe, Book 1.* AR: OMP, 2001

_____ *The Convoluted Universe, Book 2.* AR: OMP, 2005

_____ *The Convoluted Universe, Book 3.* AR: OMP, 2008.

_____ *The Convoluted Universe, Book 4.* AR: OMP, 2012.

Chia, Mantak. *Taoist Cosmic Healing.* VT: Destiny Books, 2003.

_____ *Tan Tien Chi Kung.* VT: Destiny Books, 2004.

Chuen, Lam Kam. *The Way of Energy.* NY: Simon & Schuster, 1991.

Dawson, Karl. *Matrix Reimprinting* using EFT. CA: Hay House, 2010.

Dong, Paul & Thomas Raffill. *Empty Force.* Boston: Element Books, 1996.

Elkins, Don and Carla Rueckert. *The RA Material, Book I.* Atglen, PA: Schiffer Publishing/Whitford Press, 1984.

Gallo & Vincenzi. *Energy Tapping.* CA: New Harbinger Publ., 2008.

Gerber, MD Richard. *Vibrational Medicine.* VT: Bear & Co.

Golas, Thaddeus. *The Lazy Man's Guide to Enlightenment.* Salt Lake City: Gibbs-Smith, 1995.

Hawkins, David R. *Reality and Subjectivity.* West Sedona, AZ: Veritas Press, 2003.

_____ *The Eye of the I.* West Sedona, AZ: Veritas Press, 2001

Hoeller, Stephan A. *Gnosticism.* Wheaton, IL: Quest Books, 2002.

Lerma, John, M.D. *Into the Light.* Franklin Lakes, NJ: New Page Books, 2007.

_____ *Learning From the Light.* Franklin Lakes, NJ: New Page Books, 2009.

Marion, Jim. *Putting on the Mind of Christ.* VA: Hampton Roads, 2000.

Moody, Raymond A., Jr., MD. *Life After Life.* New York: HarperCollins, 2001.

Myss, Caroline, Ph.D. *Why People Don't Heal and How They Can.* NY: Three Rivers Press, 1997.

_____. *Sacred Contracts.* NY: Three Rivers Press, 2002.

Paulson, Genevieve Lewis. *Kundalini and the Chakras.* Woodbury, Mn: Llewellyn Worldwide, 2005.

Pearce, Joseph Chilton. *The Biology of Transcendence.* Rochester, VT: Park Street Press, 2002.

Pearsall, Paul, Ph.D. *The Heart's Code.* NY: : Random House/Broadway, 1998.

Reid, Daniel. *A Complete Guide to Chi-Gung.* Boston: Shambhala, 1998.

Rasha. *Oneness.* Santa Fe, NM: Earthstar Press, 2003.

Ring, Kenneth. *Lessons from the Light.* NH: Moment Point Press, 2000.

Roman, Sanaya. *Spiritual Growth.* Tiburon, CA: HJ Kramer, Inc., 1989.

_____. *Personal Power Through Awareness.* CA: HJ Kramer, Inc., 1986.

Slate, PhD, Joe H. *Psychic Vampires.* MN: Llewellyn Books, 2004.

_____ *Aura Energy.* MN: Llewellyn Books, 2002.

Sui, Choa Kok. *Pranic Healing.* Maine: Weiser, Inc. 1990.

_____ *Pranic Psychotherapy.* Maine: Weiser, Inc. 1993.

Tohei, Koichi. *KI in Daily Life.* Japan: thru Oxford Univ. Press (NY), 2001.

Towler, Solala. *Tales From the Tao.* London: Watkins, 2005.

Yang, Jwing-Ming, Dr. *The Root of Chinese Qigong.* Roslindale, MA: YMAA

## Scientific/Medical

Batmanghelidj, MD, F. *Your Body's Many Cries For Water.* VA: Global Health Solutions, 1997.

Braden, Gregg. *The Divine Matrix.* Carlsbad, CA: Hay House, 2007.

Becker MD, Robert O and Gary Selden . *The Body Electric.* NY: Harper, 1985.

Carter & Weber. *Body Reflexology.* NJ: Prentice-Hall, 1994.

Cook, Nick. *The Hunt for Zero Point.* NY: Broadway Books, 2001.

Elvidge, Jim. *The Universe Solved.* AT Press, 2007.

Emoto, Masaru. *The True Power of Water.* OR: Beyond Words Publishing, 2005.

_____ *The Hidden Messages in Water.* OR: Beyond Words Publishing, 2004.

Francis, Richard C. *Epigenetics.* NY: Norton, 2011.

Gittleman MS CNS, Louise. *Guess What Came to Dinner?* NY: Penguin, 2001.

Greene, Brian. *The Elegant Universe.* New York: W.W. Norton & C0. 2003.

_____ *The Fabric of the Cosmos.* New York: Vintage Books. 2004.

_____ *The Hidden Reality.* New York: Alfred A. Knopf. 2011.

LaViolette, Paul A, PhD. *Secrets of Antigravity Propulsion.* VT: Bear & Co., 2008.

_____ *Genesis of the Cosmos.* Rochester, VT: Bear & Co., 2004.

Lipton, Bruce, PhD. *The Biology of Belief.* CA: Mtn of Love/Elite Books, 2005.

Lloyd, Seth. *Programming the Universe.* New York: Random House, 2007.

Martinez, Susan, PhD. *The Mysterious Origins of Hybrid Man.* VT: Bear & Co., 2013.

McTaggart, Lynn. *The Field.* New York: HarperCollins/Quill, 2002.

Meyer, Stephen C. *Signature in the Cell.* New York: HarperCollins, 2009.

Modi MD, Shakuntala. *Remarkable Healings.* VA: Hampton Rds, 1997.

Monroe, Robert.           *Journeys Out of the Body.* NY: Broadway Books, 1977.
_____                *Far Journeys.* NY: Broadway Books, 1985.
_____                *Ultimate Journey.* NY: Broadway Books, 1994.
Pert PhD, Candace.        *Molecules of Emotion.* New York: Scribner, 1997.
Peterson, Dennis R.       *Unlocking the Mysteries of Creation.* 6th edition. El Dorado, CA:
                            Creation Resource Foundation, 1990.
Smith, Dr. Kyl.          *Brighter Mind.* Corinth, TX: Brighter Mind Media Group,
                            2011.
Stout, Dr. Martha,        *The Sociopath Next Door.* NY: Broadway Books, 2005.
Talbot, Michael.          *The Holographic Universe.* New York: HarperCollins, 1991.
Watson, James D.          *DNA.* New York: Alfred A. Knopf, 2003.
Wilcox, David.            *The Source Field Investigations.* NY: Dutton/Penguin, 2011.
Wolf, Fred Alan, PhD.     *The Yoga of Time Travel.* Wheaton, IL: Quest Books, 2004.

# Internet Sources

## Christianity & Gnosticism

Acharya S, "The Origins of Christianity and the Quest for the Historical Jesus Christ" is a lengthy article examining non-Biblical sources and other documents in a search for the existence of a man called Jesus. Comparisons to the same stories about Christ are found in the stories about the Buddha, Horus, Mithra, and Krishna. Website: http://truthbeknown.com/origins.htm

Acharya S, "The Origins of Good and Evil" is an article that outlines the sources and evolution of evil, as well as how religions take each other over. Website: http://truthbeknown.com/evil.htm

Acharya S./D.M. Murdock, "Apollonius, Jesus and Paul: Men or Myths?" takes an educated look at Apollonius as the source for the Jesus/Paul myth. http://truthbeknown.com/apollonius.html

Dr. R.W. Bernard, "Apollonius the Nazarene" is an ebook which covers as much of Apollonius's life as is extant, in nine chapters. It is based on the work of Philostratus in his *Life of Apollonius.* Website: http://www.apollonius.net/bernardbook.html

Tony Bushby, "The Forged Origins of the New Testament" is an article extracted from *Nexus Magazine,* vol. 14, no. 4 (June-July 2007). The author also wrote a related book called *The Bible Fraud,* via Joshua Books (Australia), 2001. Website: http://www.nexusmagazine.com/articles/NewTestament.html

Wikipedia, "Apollonius of Tyana" article on Wikipedia that is rather negatively biased but relates the generally-agreed on facts surrounding the sage's life. Website: http://en.wikipedia.org/wiki/Apollonius_of_Tyana

# Transformation of Man

"Ghandi on Christianity" set of his quotes in a section called AMOIRA; website:
http://koti.mbnet.fi/amoira/religion/gandhicr1.htm
see also: **http://whoisthisjesus.googlepages.com/westernchristianity**

Laura Knight-Jadczyk, "Schwaller de Lubicz and the Fourth Reich" is an article that deals with STO and STS elements of spiritual growth, including the relationship with Shamanism and the 4D STS entities. Website:
http://www.cassiopaea.org/cass/schwaller_de_lubicz_3.htm

John Lash, "Kundalini and the Alien Force" article that examines the Gnostic and Tantric practices of sacred sexuality, but also examines the Archons and Jehovah. Website: http://www.metahistory.org/KundaliniForce.php

Joseph Macchio, "The Orthodox Suppression of Original Christianity" is an electronic book of 15 chapters that explores the historical suppression of original Christian truths by the orthodox Church of Rome. It is a treasure-trove of Gnostic teaching, early Christian leaders Mani, Origen and Valentinus, as well as the actions and teachings of Constantine, Augustine and Iraneus. It also reinforces Mouravieff (see OPs/Mouravieff this Appendix). Websites: http://essenes.net/conspireindex.html
http://essenes.net/new/subteachings.html

**Also worth a look:**
"Apollonius of Tyana – Paul of Tarsus?" is an in-depth article on the unique parallels between Apollonius who existed and the putative Apostle Paul. Under 'Christian Origins' section, click on 'The True Identity of St. Paul.'
http://nephiliman.com/apollonius_of_tyanna.htm

# DNA and Genetics

Baerbel, "The Living Internet Inside of Us" is another translation of some of the Fosar-Bludorf work which can be found at Website: www.crawford2000.com

Baerbel, "Russian DNA Discoveries Explain Human 'Paranormal' Events" is another article edited and translated on various DNA aspects. Website: http://www.fosar-bludorf.com/index_eng.htm

"DNA study deals blow to Neanderthal breeding theory" is an article dealing with the possible interbreeding and non-interbreeding of Cro-Magnon and Neanderthals. Website: http://www.cbc.ca/health/story/2003/05/13/cro_magnnon030513.html

Dr. Barry Starr of Stanford Univ., "Whatever happened to those Neanderthals?" is a great article on possible interbreeding between Cro-Magnons and Neanderthals based on mtDNA, and speculates on the Neanderthal's mysterious disappearance. Also documents recent attempts to see just what was in Neanderthal nuclear DNA. Website: http://www.thetech.org/genetics/news.php?id=37

Grazyna Fosar and Franz Bludorf, "The Biological Chip in Our Cells: Revolutionary results of modern genetics" is an article written in the 95% perfect English of the German genetics researchers who also wrote the book Vernetzte Intelligenz (which is not available in English). The authors have an index with articles in English on
Website: http://www.fosar-bludorf.com/archiv/biochip_eng.htm

Related Websites worth visiting for further depth of the Fosar-Bludorf discoveries:
http://noosphere.princeton.edu/fristwall2.html
http://www.ryze.com/view.php?who=vitaeb
http://www.fossar-bludorf.com/index_eng.htm

Grazyna Fosar and Franz Bludorf, "The Cosmic Internet", article on group consciousness, how DNA acts as an antenna and communication device. Website:
http://www.fosar-bludorf.com/vernetz_eng.htm

Grazyna Fosar and Franz Bludorf, "UFO Experiences and Hypercommunication" is another article seeking to explain the UFO abductee experience as one of hypercommunication (via DNA) between alternate realities, or parallel dimensions, as Jacques Vallee suggested years ago. Website:
http://www.bibliotecapleyades.net/ciencia/ciencia_hypercommunication01.htm

Rick Groleau, "Tracing Ancestry with MtDNA" article on NOVA Online website that explains how the father's and mother's DNA propagates, and how ancestry can be reliably determined, and what they discovered about the Neanderthals. Website:
http://www.pbs.org/wgbh/nova/neanderthals/mtdna.html

Tory Hagen, "Mitochondria and Aging" article explains how oxidants affect the mitochondria's ability to accurately reproduce and resist aging. Website:
http://lpi.oregonstate.edu/sp-su98/aging.html

Kean, Sam, "Who's the Fittest Now?" article in Mental Floss magazine for March-April 2009, p. 55-57, presenting the subject of Epigenetics.

"UltraViolet Light" article describes how UV is used to purify/sterilize, and how it can also negatively affect DNA. Website: http://www.Frequencyrising.com

Carl Zimmer, "The Search for Intelligence." Article in *Scientific American* magazine for October 2008, vol. 299, no. 4, pp 68-75. Effect of genetics vs environment on IQ.

Resistance to AIDS/HIV – Sample Report "About Resistance to HIV/AIDS" on the genetic testing website **23and Me**: https://www.23andme.com/health/Resistance-to-HIV-AIDS/ See also: Randy Dotinga article: "Genetic HIV Resistance Deciphered" , website:
http://www.wired.com/medtech/health/news/2005/01/66198?currentPage=2

# Extraterrestrial Exposure Law
Michael Salla, PhD., "Extraterrestrials Among Us" (vol.1:4, originally from Exopolitics Journal website), is an interesting article on how ETs are among us who

look so much like us that we don't suspect, and secondly the article explores the Extraterrestrial Exposure Law of 1969. Website: http://www.bibliotecapleyades.net/exopolitica/esp_exopolitics_ZZZN.htm also see: http://exopolitics.com for author's general website.

## Extraterrestial Genes in Human DNA

"Scientists Find Extraterrestrial Genes in Human DNA" is another article seeking to explain "junk DNA" and its probable origin and significance. Website: http://www.bibliotecapleyades.net/vida_alien/esp_vida_alien_18n.htm

## Hidden Hand and The Insider

The Elite have revealed their part in the on-going catalyst that they have been charged with doing to/for Man, as part of the Prime Directive for the Earth School: "interfere for their benefit, but do not show yourselves." So, yes this is real, and not froo-froo (someone has to administer Man's corporate lessons, and it fell to them, for almost the same reason Man is here – to learn and grow). Note: an individual souls' Script is administered by the Beings of Light, but Man as a whole is to wake up and become aware of himself as a 'corporate' entity – so things are also done to Man as a whole. This is similar to attending a University: there are the Core Courses that all students have to take, and then there are the individual student lessons and courses (Elite catalyst vs one's Script).

### Hidden Hand:
Wes Penre at www.illuminati-news.com...
see also: Wes Penre, "Dialog with Hidden Hand" at Exopolitics website and Hidden Hand Dialogue at
http://www.bibliotecapleyades.net/sociopolitica/esp_sociopol_illuminati_55.htm

### The Insider:
"The Revelations of the Insider" is an article containing the blog during a 5-day visit by someone calling themselves an "insider" who had knowledge on most aspects of Earth history, science and religion. This was done anonymously via a proxy link to the GLP (Godlike Productions) forum in the Fall of 2005. The material is not copyrighted and can be reproduced as long as none of the original text is changed. Website: http://www.scribd.com/doc/403303/The-Revelations-of-an-Elite-Family-Insider-2005

## Music

### Country Western Music
Clive Thompson, **"Does country music cause suicide?"** article discusses effect of **negative music on one's lifestyle. Statistics show it encourages divorce and suicide. Website:** http://www.collisiondetection.net/mt/archives/000996.html

## Heavy Metal

Henry Makow, "Destroy! Rock Music's Satanic Message" article on extremely negative effect on our youth by Satanic messages imprinting people.
http://www.rense.com/general74/rrock.htm

# Organic Portals/Mouravieff

"Matrix Agents: Profiles and Analysis (Parts I & II)" is an article that summarizes and clarifies information on Organic Portals, also called pre-Adamic beings. Much of this data is footnoted back to its original sources, including Mouravieff, Gurdjieff, Ouspensky, and the Cassiopaean Transcripts. Website:
http://montalk.net/matrix/62/matrix-agents-profiles-and-analysis-part-i

"Organic Portals Theory: Sources" is a compendium of different writers' insights on the Organic Portal phenomenon. Particularly relevant are the significant Mouravieff quotes from Books II & III of Gnosis. Website:
http://www.montalk.net/opsources.pdf

**Bibliotecapleyades** website product of Jose Ingenieros, has a link to 3 volumes of original text of Gnosis work by Mouravieff. Book text is in English. Website:
http://www.bibliotecapleyades.net/esp_autor_mouravieff.htm

**Laura Knight-Jadczyk**, "Commentary on Boris Mouravieff's Gnosis." Extensive article from her website that interweaves her analysis of Mouravieff's Gnosis book and its meaning for Man's spiritual development. Also included are relevant quotes from her Cassiopaean material. Website:
http://www.cassiopaea.org/cass/mouravieff1.htm

## Soul Weight

**Wikipedia**, "Duncan MacDougall (doctor)" is the article examining Dr. Duncan's attempts to measure the weight of the soul at death, found on Website:
http://en.wikipedia.org/wiki/Duncan_MacDougall_(doctor)
There is further text on what MacDougall did, and some of his notes, on Website:
http://www.snopes.com/religion/soulweight.asp

Dr. Becker Mertens, from an article in German science journal *Horizon*, which corroborated MacDougall's finding that the soul has weight. Quoted on Website:
http://www.ilstu.edu/~kfmachin/FOIFall03/Weight%20of%20human%20soul.htm

# Videos of Interest

To stretch the imagination and stimulate thinking:

Groundhog Day.  Dir. Harold Ramis, Columbia Tristar.  1993.
Men In Black. I & II  Dir. Barry Sonnenfeld, Columbia Pictures.  2000.
The Matrix.  Dir./Written by The Wachowski Bros., Warner Bros. 1999.
The Mothman Prophecies.  Dir. Mark Pellington,  Screen Gems/LakeShore
    Entertainment. 2001.

Taken.  (TV miniseries) Stephen Spielberg,  Dreamworks.  2002.
The Truman Show.  Peter Weir, Paramount Pictures. 1998.
The Young Age of the Earth.  Aufderhar, Glenn. Earth Science Associates / Alpha
    Productions. 1996.  (Scientific DVD)
They Live.  Dir./Written by John Carpenter,  Universal Studios.  2003.
Prometheus I.  Ridley Scott, 2oth Century Fox. 2012.
The Thirteenth Floor. Columbia Pictures, Roland Emmerich. 1999.
The Day the Earth Stood Still.  Twentieth Century Fox, Erwin Stoff et al. 2009.

Iron Sky.  Timo Vuorensola, Ger/Fin release via Paramount Pictures, 2012.
Paul.  Universal Studios, Greg Motola. 2010.
2012.  Sony Pictures, Roland Emmerich. 2010.
The Adjustment Bureau.  Universal Pictures, George Nolfi. 2010.
Knowing.  Summit Entertainment, Alex Proyas. 2009.
Dark City.  New Line Cinema, Alex Proyas. 1998.
The Fourth Kind.  Universal Pictures, Olatunde Osunsanmi. 2010.
Source Code.  Summit Entertainment, Duncan Jones. 2011.
eXistenZ. Canadian Television Fund, David Cronenburg, 1999.

***

# Endnotes

## Chapter 1 Endnotes

[1] Dr Harold Bloom, *Jesus and Yahweh: the Names Divine.* 2, 91, 153.

[2] Baigent & Leigh, *Dead Sea Scrolls Deception.*
and Bart Ehrman, *Misquoting Jesus.*

## Chapter 2  Endnotes

[3] See Matt 11:14,  John the Baptist is Elijah reborn,  and  Jn 3:3 "born again"
                and  Matt 17:12  Jesus say John was Elijah.
See Jn 9:1-2, "man born blind from birth": if you only have one life, then how could the man
        have sinned before he was born?  The disciple asking the question was aware of
        reincarnation.  *Apologetics* cannot deal with this, and it doesn't help that the Bible
        is so generic and vague in key places (esp Genesis).
Also see  Father Origen and  his teachings ca. 100 AD.

[4] Wikipedia:  https://en.wikipedia.org/wiki/Hell#Judaism

[5]  Hogue, John. *NOSTRADAMUS: The Complete Prophecies.* (Rockport, ME:  Element Books
Ltd., 1997), 798; Cent X, Quatr. 72.

[6]  The Nexus Seven, "From the 33 Arks…" 1.12-13.  (code means: Ark/section 1, points 12-13.)
Eprint at:  http://soulresonance.8m.com/arks.html
[7] Ibid., 4.7.
[8] Ibid., 4.15-16.
[9] Ibid., 21.7-9.
[10] Ibid., 9.20.

[11] Wolf, Fred Alan, PhD.  *The Yoga of Time Travel.*  (Wheaton, IL: Quest Books, 2004), 103.
[12]  Ibid., 105.
[13]  Ibid., 122.
[14] Ibid.

[15] Morton, Chris and Ceri Louise Thomas. *The Mystery of the Crystal Skulls.* (Rochester, VT: Bear
& Co.,  2002), 268.

[16]  The Nexus Seven, "From the 33 Arks…"  19.3-19.7.
[17] Ibid., 9.9.
[18] Ibid., 22.25-26.

[19] "The Revelations of the Insider".  Eprint at:
http://www.scribd.com/doc/403303/The-Revelations-of-an-Elite-Family-Insider-2005

[20] "Timeline Dynamics" article.  Eprint at:
http://www.montalk.net/matrix/122/timeline-dynamics

[21] Robert Monroe, *Far Journeys*, 106.

[22] Laura Knight-Jadczyk, "Commentary on Boris Mouravieff's Gnosis." Eprint at: http://www.cassiopaea.org/cass/mouravieff1.htm
also see:
http://cassiopaea.org/forum/index.php/board,48.0.html?PHPSESSID=8f85678030cc993d4c2a0a26 52fa16a5

[23] Ibid.

[24] Ibid.

[25] The Nexus Seven, "From the 33 Arks…" 10.1-15.

[26] Ibid., 24.5.

[27] Icke, David. *Tales from the Time Loop*. (Wildwood, MO: Bridge of Love, 2003), 325-328.

[28] Ibid., 338.

[29] Ibid., 338.

[30] Ibid., 338-339.

[31] The Nexus Seven, "From the 33 Arks…" 18.4-6.

[32] Ibid., Sections 6-7-8.

[33] Ibid., 20.10-12.

[34] Ibid., 8.4.

[35] Ibid., 8.11.

[36] Ibid., 8.10.

[37] Ibid., 31.4, 8.9.

[38] Ibid., 10.20-22.

[39] Ibid., 23.3-6.

[40] Ibid., 23.10-11.

[41] Ibid., 23.16-18.

[42] Ibid., 23.17.

[43] Ibid., 23.20-22.

[44] Ibid., 15.20-30.

[45] Ibid., 24.7-8.

[46] Robert Monroe, *Journeys Out of the Body*, 74-75, 121.

[47] 1938 Cellphone: http://www.huffingtonpost.com/2013/04/04/time-traveler-cell-phone-1938-video-woman-factory_n_3013996.html

[48] https://www.youtube.com/watch?feature=player_embedded&v=gC2FKNIJiCA

[49] Op Cit, Nexus 7., 29.7-11.

[50] Lewels, Joe, Ph.D. *The God Hypothesis*. (Columbus, NC: Wild Flower Press, 2005), 160.

[51] Ibid., 160-161.

## Chapter 3  Endnotes

[52] Frejer, B. Ernest. *The Edgar Cayce Companion.* (New York: Barnes & Noble Press, 1995), 130: reading 440-5.
[53] Ibid.,443-445.

[54] Wikipedia, "Jane Roberts" article. Eprint at:
http://en.wikipedia.org/wiki/Jane_Roberts
[55] Ibid., 368.

[56] Roberts, Jane. *Seth Speaks. The Eternal Validity of the Soul.* (San Rafael CA: Amber-Allen Publishing/New World Library, 1994), 177.

[57] Elkins, Don and Carla Rueckert. *The RA Material, Book I.* Atglen, PA: Schiffer Publishing/Whitford Press, 1984.

[58] Picknett, Lynn & Clive Prince. *The Stargate Conspiracy.* (New York: Berkley Books, 1999), 190-198.
[59] Ibid., 196.
[60] Ibid., 217.

[61] Alejandro Rojas in *ETs and Religion* article in Open Minds magazine, Dec. 2011, pp 38-44.
[62] Ibid., p 40
[63] Ibid., p 40

[64] http://en.wikipedia.org/wiki/Potential_cultural_impact_of_extraterrestrial_contact

[65] Op Cit Rojas, p41-42.
[66] Ibid., p. 42

# Chapter 4 Endnotes

[67] Gittleman, Ann Louise. Guess What Came to Dinner? NY: Avery Books, 2001, 5-10..
[68] Ibid. 59-63

[69] Bloomberg article, by Adam Minter Sept 3, 2013.
http://finance.yahoo.com/news/dont-trust-chicken-nugget-thats-160339774.html

[70] see Wikipedia: http://en.wikipedia.org/wiki/Fluoride_controversy

[71] Batmanghelidj.MD, *Your Body's Many Cries For Water.* VA: Global Health Solutions, p 129.

[72] Mindell, Earl. The Vitamin Bible. NY: Warner Books, p. 142.

[73] Wikipedia: http://en.wikipedia.org/wiki/Excitotoxicity

[74] Op Cit, Mindell, p 113.

[75] Op Cit, Batmanghelidj, pp 123-32.

# Chapter 6  Endnotes

[76] Ring PhD, Kenneth. *Lessons from the Light*. NH: Moment Point Press, 1998. 173-184.
[77] Ibid., pp173-175.

[78] Moody, Raymond A., Jr., MD. *Life After Life*. New York: HarperCollins, 2001. p. 131.

[73] "Organic Portals Theory: Sources" is a compendium of different writers' insights on the Organic Portal phenomenon. Particularly relevant are the significant Mouravieff quotes from Books II & III of Gnosis. Website:
http://www.montalk.net/opsources.pdf

**Bibliotecapleyades** website product of Jose Ingenieros, has link to 3 volumes of original text of Gnosis work by Mouravieff. Book text is in English. Website:
http://www.bibliotecapleyades.net/esp_autor_mouravieff.htm
[80] Ibid.
[81] Ibid.
[82] Ibid.

## Chapter 7 Endnotes

[83] http://en.wikipedia.org/wiki/CCR5delta32#CCR5-.CE.9432 Be sure to check out some of the References at the end of the Wikipedia article – the CCR5delta 32 gene is predominantly found in Northern Europe among 5% of the world's population. It is rare. If one gets the gene from both parents, s/he has **complete immunity**; if one gets the gene from just one parent, s/he has **functional resistance** and will go thru a Flu-like phase while the virus is being killed.

[84] Bender, Albert K. *Flying Saucers and the Three Men*. 247-248.

[85] Keel, John, *Our Haunted Planet*, p. 282
[86] Ibid., pp 283-284

[87] Missler, Chuck and Mark Eastman. *Alien Encounters*. 34
[88] Ibid., 213, 240.
[89] Ibid., 241.
[90] Ibid., 244-246.
[91] Ibid., 247.
[92] Ibid., 247-248.

## Chapter 8 Endnotes

[93] Kerner, Nigel. *Grey Aliens and the Harvesting of Souls*. VT: Bear & Co., 2010. P.299.

[94] Dr. Jacobs, David. *The Threat*. NY: Simon & Schuster, 1998. p 84.
[95] Ibid., p.84.
[96] Ibid., p 87.

[97] Pye, Lloyd. *Everything You Know is Wrong*. NE: iUniverse, 2000. P. 71.

[98] Ibid., pp. 69-71.
[99] Ibid., pp73-74.
[100] Ibid., p. 99, 137.

[101] Wikipedia, http://en.wikipedia.org/wiki/Almas_(cryptozoology)

[102] Op Cit, Pye, pp 142-144.

[103] Op Cit., Wikipedia. Almas.

[104] Martinez, *Mysterious Origins of Hybrid Man*, 207.
[105] Ibid., 148-149.
[106] Ibid., 273-274, 293.
[107] Ibid., 334
[108] Ibid., 354.
[109] Ibid., 357.
[110] Ibid., 273-74.
[111] Ibid., 143-44.
[112] Ibid., 12.

[113] Sitchin, Zechariah. *There Were Giants Upon the Earth*. pp. 162-163.

[114] Op Cit., Jacobs. p. 251.
[115] Ibid., pp. 130-133.
[116] Ibid., pp. 168-169.
[117] Ibid. p. 175.
[118] Ibid., p. 177, 197-207.
[119] Ibid., pp. 206-207.
[120] Ibid., p 253.

# Chapter 9  Endnotes

[121] Ring, Dr. Kenneth. *Lessons From the Light*. (Portsmouth, NH: Moment Point Press, 2000), 19-26.
[122] Ibid., p26
[123] Ibid., pp 31-32.

[124] Becker MD, Robert O. *The Body Electric*. NY: Harper, 1985. Pp 86-94.

[125] Mack MD, John E. *Passport to the Cosmos*. NY: Three Rivers Press, 1999. Pp. 17-19.
[126] Ibid., p. 129.
[127] Ibid., p. 232.
[128] Ibid., p. 233
[129] Ibid. p. 233.
[130] Ibid. p. 255.

[131] Op Cit., Ring, 124-130.

[132] Mack MD, John E. *Abduction*. NY: Scribner. 1994. P. 186.
[133] Ibid., p. 186
[134] Ibid., p. 184-190.

[135] Monroe, Robert. *Ultimate Journey*. (New York: Random House/Broadway, 2000), 24.

[136] The Nexus Seven, "From the 33 Arks…"., 15.20-30.
[137] Ibid., 24.7-8.

[138] Monroe, Robert, *Far Journeys*. (New York: Random House/Broadway, 2001), 248.

## Chapter 10 Endnotes

[139] http://en.wikipedia.org/wiki/Maharishi_Mahesh_Yogi#Legacy

[140] Rasha, *Oneness*. 125, 171
[141] Ibid., 254
[142] Ibid., 254-255.

## Chapter 11 Endnotes

[143] http://en.wikipedia.org/wiki/Brown_rice

[144] http://en.wikipedia.org/wiki/Yin_and_yang_symbol

[145] Myss, Dr. Carolyn. *Why People Don't Heal and How They Can*. (NY: Three Rivers Press, 1997), 16-27.

[146] http://arnoldexposed.com/quotes.html
Also see:
http://www.democraticunderground.com/discuss/duboard.php?az=view_all&address=385x539879

[147] See Music Notes following:
**Country Western Music**
Clive Thompson, "Does country music cause suicide?" article discusses effect of negative music on one's lifestyle. Statistics show it encourages divorce and suicide.
**Website:** http://www.collisiondetection.net/mt/archives/000996.html

**Heavy Metal**
Henry Makow, "Destroy! Rock Music's Satanic Message" article on extremely negative effect on our youth by Satanic messages imprinting people.
http://www.rense.com/general74/rrock.htm

[148] http://www.youtube.com/watch?feature=player_detailpage&v=gPOfurmrjxo
(George Carlin on God and Religion)

## Chapter 12 Endnotes

[149] http://en.wikipedia.org/wiki/Kundalini:_The_Evolutionary_Energy_in_Man#Overview
The book is: Krishna, Gopi. *Kundalini: The Evolutionary Energy in Man*. Boston: Shambhala, 1970.

[150] Ibid.
[151] Ibid.

[152] http://en.wikipedia.org/wiki/Nikola_Tesla

[153] LaViolette, *Genesis of the Cosmos*, 268.

[154] http://en.wikipedia.org/wiki/Michelson-Morley_experiment

[155] Op Cit, LaViolette, 269.
[156] Ibid., 269-270.
[157] Ibid. 270.
[158] Ibid., 272.

[159] http://www.divinecosmos.com/start-here/articles/334-kozyrev-aether-time-and-torsion

[160] Ibid.
[161] Ibid.
[162] Ibid.
[162] Ibid.
[162] Ibid.

[163] Brendan B. Murphy, in
http://blog.world-mysteries.com/science/torsion-the-key-to-theory-of-everything/

[164] Op Cit, . in

http://www.divinecosmos.com/start-here/articles/334-kozyrev-aether-time-and-torsion

[165] Ibid.

[166] Op Cit., Brendan Murphy.
[167] Ibid.
[168] Ibid.

[169] Op Cit, LaViolette, 273-283.

[170] Carter & Weber, *Body Reflexology*, p. 38.

[171] J.C. Pearce, *The Biology of Transcendence*, 55-62.

[172] Braden, The Divine Matrix, 50-51.

[173] Op Cit, Pearce, 60.
[174] Ibid, 63

[175] Op Cit, Braden, 53.

[176] Gerber, *Vibrational Medicine*, 527-528.
[177] Ibid, 528.

[178] Richard Bartlett, *Matrix Energetics*, x, xv.
[179] Ibid., 45, 66.

[180] Karl Dawson, *Matrix Reimprinting*, 8-10.
[181] Ibid., 4-5.

[182] Energy Medicine Researchers, http://www.energetic-medicine.net/energy-medicine-researchers.html   Article on Richard Flook

[183] Dr. Modi, *Remarkable Healings*, 326, 328.
[184] Ibid., 383.

[185] Op Cit, Dawson, 78.

[186]  http://www.peace.ca/basicpsych-k.htm  This is from  " References: What is Psych-K" on http://psychology.wikia.com/wiki/PSYCH-K

[187] http://www.energybalancingservices.com/aboutpsychk.html

[188] Deepak Chopra, in http://en.wikipedia.org/wiki/Deepak_Chopra
[189] Ibid.

# Chapter 13 Endnotes

[190] Wikipedia: http://en.wikipedia.org/wiki/Blood_brain_barrier#Alzheimer.27s_Disease

[191] www.meganutritionorganicsuperfood.com

[192] Smith, Dr. Kyl,  *Brighter Mind*, xxxiii.

[193] Amen MD, Daniel G.  *Change Your Brain Change Your Body*,  18.
[194] Ibid., 24-27.

[195] Two recent reports: **both June 2014** and not related to each other:
http://www.nytimes.com/2014/06/13/nyregion/concerns-on-mad-cow-lead-to-recall.html?_r=0
and
http://www.cnn.com/2014/06/05/health/mad-cow-disease-texas/index.html

[196] Op Cit, Smith, 356.

[197] http://en.wikipedia.org/wiki/Huperzine_A

[198] http://en.wikipedia.org/wiki/Glutathione#Biosynthesis

[199] http://www.worldlifeexpectancy.com/cause-of-death/alzheimers-dementia/by-country/
and
 Inst Psychogeriatr. 2001;13,439-50.

[200] http://www.quibblo.com/quiz/fAL_Wkj/C4N-Y0U-R34D-7H15

---

[201] Thanks to : http://www.howtoimproveyourmemoryfast.com/blog/can-you-read-this/

[202] Dawson, Karl. *Matrix Reimprinting*, 26.
[203] Ibid., 27-28
[204] Ibid., 28.

[205] Myss, Carolyn. *Why People Don't Heal...*, 111.

[206] Francis, Richard. *Epigenetics*, xi.

[207] J.C. Pearce, *The Biology of Transcendence*, 41.
[208] Ibid., 27.
[209] Ibid., 36, 41.
[210] Ibid., p 46
[211] Ibid., 50.
[212] Ibid., 51-52.

# Appendix A -- Endnotes

[213] Marion, Jim. *Putting on the Mind of Christ.* p. 117.
[214] Ibid., p. 90.
[215] Ibid., p. 92
[216] Ibid., p. 112.
[217] Ibid., p. 133.

# Appendix B -- Endnotes

[218] http://en.wikipedia.org/wiki/George_carlin
[219] Ibid.
[220] Ibid.
[221] YouTube: http://www.youtube.com/watch?v=ls8RXqyZDsk
   ("I gave up on my species.")
[222] Ibid.

# Appendix C -- Endnotes

[223] The significance of this event is that it was Flight17, shot down on the 17th of July, and was exactly to the day when TWA flight 800 was shot down (July 17, 1996). And not counting the year 1996, counting forward there were exactly 17 years between MH 17 and TWA 800. Freaky coincidence or... symbology?

# Appendix D -- Endnotes

[224] "Matrix Agents: Profiles and Analysis (Parts I & II)" I. eprint at: http://montalk.net/matrix/62/matrix-agents-profiles-and-analysis-part-i

[225] Joseph Macchio, "The Orthodox Suppression of Original Christianity", Ch VII, Great Schools, Valentinus.

[226] Ibid., Ch. VII, Great Schools, Doc. of 3 Natures.

[227] Bramley, William. *The Gods of Eden.* (New York: HarperCollins/Avon, 1993), 176-177.

[228] Sitchin, Zechariah, *The Cosmic Code.* (New York: HarperCollins, 2007), 44, 58.

[229] Bramley, William. *The Gods of Eden.* 177.

[230] Ibid., 178.

[231] Bibliotecapleyades website product of Jose Ingenieros, Book III, p. 108. reprint at: http://www.bibliotecapleyades.net/esp_autor_mouravieff.htm

[232] "Organic Portals Theory: Sources", compendium: Book II of Gnosis. eprint at: http://www.montalk.net/opsources.pdf

[233] Ibid., II, 7.

[234] Ibid., II, 49.

[235] Ibid., (II, 8)

[236] Ibid., III, 8.

[237] Ibid., III, 109.

[238] Cannon, Convoluted Universe Book V, pp257-269 (Chapter 18).

[239] Ibid., p. 268.

[240] Ibid., 133.

[241] Ibid., 129-134.

[242] Ibid., 136.

[243] Bibliotecapleyades website product of Jose Ingenieros, Book III, p. 112-115. reprint at: http://www.bibliotecapleyades.net/esp_autor_mouravieff.htm

[244] W.H. Church, *Edgar Cayce's Story of the Soul*, pp. 137-39.

[245] Op Cit.., Bibliotecapleyades, 443-445.

[246] Hogue, John. *NOSTRADAMUS: The Complete Prophecies.* (Rockport, ME: Element Books Ltd., 1997), 798; Cent X, Quatr. 72.

[247] Lewels, Joe, Ph.D. *The God Hypothesis.* (Columbus, NC: Wild Flower Press, 2005), 160.

[248] Ibid., 160-161.

# Micro Index

# Micro Index

## NOTES

Books 1-5 are identified at the bottom of the Copyright page.  They are often abbreviated:   VEG is *Virtual Earth Graduate.*
This book is Book 2, or TOM.

Due to late-developing meetings and information from my readers, a much more clear look at Souls, Karma and Scripts, OPs and Timelines was developed in this Appendix D.  Additional key information came about as Book 5 (TSiM) was being written.

## Also by the same Author:

# The Science in Metaphysics

**by TJ Hegland**

**Proof from Science that the Principles of Metaphysics
Are Real and Why They Work.**

# NOTES

Made in the USA
San Bernardino, CA
08 August 2019